Working Women
in America

Working Women in America

Split Dreams

Second Edition

Sharlene Nagy Hesse-Biber
Gregg Lee Carter

New York   Oxford
OXFORD UNIVERSITY PRESS
2005

Oxford University Press

Oxford   New York
Auckland   Bangkok   Buenos Aires   Cape Town   Chennai
Dar es Salaam   Delhi   Hong Kong   Istanbul   Karachi   Kolkata
Kuala Lumpar   Madrid   Melbourne   Mexico City   Mumbai   Nairobi
São Paulo   Shanghai   Taipei   Tokyo   Toronto

Copyright © 2005 by Oxford University Press, Inc.

Published by Oxford University Press, Inc.
198 Madison Avenue, New York, New York 10016
www.oup.com

Oxford is a registered trademark of Oxford University Press

Library of Congress Cataloging-in-Publication Data
Hesse-Biber, Sharlene Nagy.
     Working women in America : split dreams / Sharlene Nagy Hesse-Biber, Gregg Lee
Carter.—2nd ed.
       p.   cm.
     Includes bibliographical references and index.
     ISBN 978-0-19-515047-6
     1. Women—Employment—United States. I. Carter, Gregg Lee, 1951–II. Title.
HD6095.H474 2005
331.4'-0973—dc22   2004046523

Printed in the United States of America
on acid-free paper

Contents

Chapter 3. Gender Inequality: Economic and Legal Explanations 72

Chapter 4. Gender Inequality and Socialization: The Influences of Family, School, Peers, and the Media 111

Chapter 5. Women in Everyday Jobs: Clerical, Sales, Service, and Blue-Collar Work   141

Chapter 6. Professional and Managerial Women   192

Chapter 7. Working Women and Their Families 221

Chapter 8. Changing the Lives of Working Women 247

Tables and Figures

Preface

In *Working Women in America: Split Dreams*, we highlight current research on the critical issues affecting women in the workplace. We also examine the historical legacy of working women, as well as the social, political, and economic forces that have shaped the contemporary situation of women workers.

We examine the diversity of women's work experiences, ranging from those who work in "top jobs" in management and within the professions to the majority of women who labor for low pay in jobs that carry little prestige. Whether toward the top or toward the bottom, the jobs of working women contribute diverse and essential services to our economy, from managing our businesses to serving our food to teaching our children to providing our health care.

The developed world is linked in a web of production and consumption to working women around the globe. Examining a clothing label, one almost always finds that the manufacturer is located in a developing country, where tens of millions of women toil in factories—factories that can only be considered "sweatshops" when compared to the working conditions, wages, and benefits found in the manufactories of the first world. We examine the social and economic impact of the global factory on workers in both developing and developed societies; globalization is increasingly creating jobs that are deskilled, contract oriented, and insecure.

While we primarily explore the situation of women in America, we compare and contrast their working lives with those of women workers in the developing world. We ground our discussion in a wide range of historical, quantitative, and qualitative data. Quantitative data sources include the U.S. Bureau of the Census, the U.S. Department of Labor, the United Nations, the Gallup Poll, and the General Social Survey. We give life to the numbers by offering many first-person accounts of the experiences of working women, from their successes, to the many faces of discrimination that are particular to women, to the special difficulties facing those women trying to combine their work and family aspirations. We believe it is through listening to the life experiences of women that we can uncover and record the subjugated knowledge of their lives that so often remains invisible within the dominant society.

In this new edition, we extend our discussion of the role of women's activism, both within and outside their places of work. We examine women's efforts in demanding equal pay and adequate childcare, as well as their efforts in combating the ill effects of the glass ceiling, the "old boys' network," and sexual harassment. We describe the roles women have played in the creation of the American labor movement and the problems women have encountered in trying to unionize their workplaces.

It has been over forty years since Betty Friedan's *The Feminine Mystique* (1963) launched a profound revolution in our culture and our consciousness, helping to set in motion the second wave of feminism. Friedan's book documented how many white middle-class women's lives were tightly bound by traditional roles exemplified in the 1950s by the famous *Leave it to Beaver* television series. Upon marriage, and especially with the birth of a first child, these women stayed home to raise their children; they were full-time housewives. The assumption was that the father would provide the economic means to support this traditional lifestyle, which was held up as the model of family life that young girls aspired to achieve. It was a definitive model of a happy, stable family. The dreams of many young women were to have a house in the suburbs with a two-car garage and a white picket fence, and to be caring for the family on a full-time basis.

Friedan identified the stirrings of discontent among many white middle-class women of the 1950s—their lives just didn't seem fulfilling. Was this all there was? Was this really their appropriate destiny? In fact, it was so taken for granted that being a housewife was the natural option for married women that such dissatisfaction seemed to be "a problem with no name":

> The problem lay buried, unspoken, for many years in the minds of American women. It was a strange stirring, a sense of dissatisfaction, a yearning that women suffered in the middle of the twentieth century in the United States. Each suburban wife struggled with it alone. As she made the beds, shopped for groceries, matched slipcover material, ate peanut butter sandwiches with her children, chauffeured Cub Scouts and Brownies, lay beside her husband at night—she was afraid to ask even of herself the silent question—"is this all?" (p. 15)

Often women blamed themselves. Often they themselves attempted to deny that there really was a problem:

> If a woman had a problem in the 1950s and 1960s, she knew that something must be wrong with her marriage, or with herself. Other women were satisfied with their lives, she thought. What kind of a woman was she if she did not feel this mysterious fulfillment waxing the kitchen floor? She was so ashamed to admit her dissatisfaction that she never knew how many other women shared it. If she tried to tell her husband, he didn't understand what she was talking about. She did not really understand it herself. For over fifteen years women in America found it harder to talk about this problem than about sex. Even the psychoanalysts had no name for it. When a woman went to a psychiatrist for help, as many women did, she would say, "I'm so ashamed," or "I must be hopelessly neurotic." . . . Most women with this problem did not go to see a psychoanalyst, however. "There's nothing wrong really," they kept telling themselves. "There isn't any problem." (p. 19)

Today the daughters and granddaughters of the feminine mystique era do not feel bound by the traditional role of housewife. For many, if not most women there is a sense that they can "have it all." For example, we asked our female students from an undergraduate course titled "women and work" to envision their life at age forty. They had no trouble telling us how they would "combine it all." One young woman said, "At age forty, I can see myself as a wife and mother and as a successful corporate lawyer working in a well-established firm. I see myself as happily able to integrate the career-marriage-family triad. I am making [$175,000] a year." Another student noted:

> As most people, by the age of forty, I hope to be settled in a satisfying and happy way of life. I plan to have at least a master's degree by then, and to have established myself in a rewarding and stimulating career. Perhaps I will be self-employed, thus being my own boss. I can do what I want and on my own schedule. This, too, will enable me to spend time with my children. At forty, I also wish to have a successful, equal, loving, and supportive marriage, with three children. It is very important to me to have a sound marriage in which I share the same attitudes and values with my husband. He must be able to understand and practice feminism for the relationship to work. We must share equally all the daily chores and financial burdens. He must do as much child caring as I do. Ideally, we will be great parents and have great kids. In addition, hopefully we will be comfortable financially so we can live in a nice house, have nice things, be able to travel, and send our children to college. My life at forty will be fruitful and happy.

Female students around the country report that they expect to have careers in the professions and management, and that they look forward to good pay, high status, and rapid advancement. Few students report that they expect at age forty to be working as a secretary or clerk with a low ceiling on pay and no chances for promotion. They expect to earn an advanced degree. They intend to work hard and assume that, in doing so, they will be rewarded with rank and earnings commensurate with their education, training, and ability. In short, female students accept the American creed about equal opportunity, advancement, and reward for performance. They believe that they can also fulfill equally well their roles as wife and mother. For the most part, they expect to combine easily their work and family lives.

However, not all is well in Camelot. As Sylvia Hewlett (2002) warns us, many of our young women may be left childless if they chose to develop a career during their twenties and thirties instead of having children. Women, she argues, are biologically most ready to give birth at the same time in which they are ready to be intensely devoted to their careers. If women choose to invest in a career, then they are inevitability faced with issues of infertility. Those women who continue along the current path of combining getting ahead in the work world with having children, will find the going, by and large, more than tough. Indeed, social science research indicates that to combine work and family life during the course of just one year, women must work the equivalent of an extra month of twenty-four-hour work days compared with men. Arlie Hochschild (Hochschild and Machung, 1989) calls this the "second shift" of work that women must do in addition to their occupational role. As one working mother put it, "You're on duty at work. You come home, and you're on duty. Then you go back to work and you're on duty" (p. 7). That extra duty amounts, roughly, to about fifteen hours more work for women each week than men.

The "perfect" family

Hochschild notes: "When I telephoned one husband to arrange an interview with him, explaining that I wanted to ask him about how he managed work and family life, he replied genially, 'Oh, this will really interest my wife'" (p. 6).

We subtitled this book *Split Dreams* to highlight the fact that most women who work are constantly juggling their work and family dreams—feeling torn in many different directions. The following excerpts from interviews with working women articulate the gap between women's dreams and the realities of their work and family lives (U.S. Department of Labor, Women's Bureau, 1994):

> Being a working woman is like having two full-time jobs. We're expected to be perfect in both career and taking care of the home, but without adequate compensation for either.
>
> —thirty-four-year-old manager from Georgia

> It's a never-ending workload. Most women have "jobs" not careers, because of family needs. More flextime and job-sharing is needed. Women are to be recognized for their contributions (not taken for granted).
>
> —forty-two-year-old mother of three from Pennsylvania

> You have to be better than any males in your job. You have to juggle family and work and still do better just to prove you are a career person and a mother. It puts a lot of stress into your life.
>
> —thirty-one-year-old sales worker, married, with one child

Between balancing home and work and job, you always feel like you are doing four things at one time. You're doing your job, but you're thinking about what you are going to cook for supper and who is going to pick up the kids.

— working mother from Milwaukee

It's like trying to put on a shoe two sizes too small. There are not enough hours in a day to do anything outside of working.

— mother of two from Texas

Women need understanding from their employers for children's sickness and doctor's appointments. I was terminated due to my son's knee surgery. I only missed one day of work in four months, but I had to leave work for doctor's visits at 3:00 or 4:00 p.m.

— forty-six-year-old mother, a clerical worker in Florida

When a woman stays home with a child it's viewed as another day out (nonproductive). When a man does it, he's viewed as a "great" father and a responsible parent.

— forty-three-year-old professional from New York

We need more time to take care of our children (paid time). Having a baby deserves much more than just six to eight weeks of recovery.

— thirty-six-year-old clerical worker with two children

There are a lot of women out there who work hard. I worked so much that my children would ask me on the phone, "Mom, are you coming home so we can see you?" That really hits home.

— mother of two from North Carolina

Childcare is a disgrace in this country. On the one hand, it's too expensive for many women considering their salaries, on the other, it does not provide the childcare provider a decent wage. Locating good childcare is a nightmare.

— woman from Oregon with two grown children, two foster teenagers, and one grandchild

Working moms already have a limited time on their hands, but when they feel like they're searching for a needle in a haystack when it comes to childcare it can be a real hassle. The way things are set up, you either make too much for state programs or private day care is well out of reach.

— single mother, clerical worker from Illinois

If you've got a big ball game to play tonight and the team needs you, it's "Oh, don't bother to come in, we'll get somebody to come in for you." But you come in and tell them you've got babysitting problems, that your mother's in a home and you need to be there to authorize some special treatment. Well, they can't do that! "We're supposed to upset the whole store because of your problems?"

— working mother, retail worker in St. Louis, Missouri

Other evidence suggests that reality may fly in the face of the rosy expectations of work and family that so many of our female students possess. The General Social Survey reveals that most adults agree with the proposition that "employers tend to give men better paying jobs than they give women," as well as that "women's family responsibilities keep them from putting as much time and effort into their jobs as men do." The combination of these factors, Americans believe, can account for the persistence of the earnings inequality between men and women in the full-time workforce. As we show in this book, sociological reality coheres with these beliefs.

Do we go back to the *Leave it To Beaver* lifestyle? Economically, that is not an option for most women, at least for any length of time. Women who are the sole providers for their families cannot even consider it.

As a society we need to rethink our ideas concerning work, family, and gender roles, and this book provides us with the opportunity to begin this process. Using a variety of theoretical and empirical lenses, we trace the dramatic changes in the lives of working women. We examine the societal stereotype of the woman worker and provide an in-depth look at those historical factors that have propelled women into the workforce. We examine the diversity of women's experiences, taking into account how women's lives differ by factors such as race, class, ethnicity, and sexual preference. The women's movement of the 1960s tended to ignore such differences among women. Little recognition was paid to the fact that, although women of color and white working-class women have always had high labor-force participation rates, they were struggling on a daily basis—then as now—with the issue of combining their work and family lives. We stress the importance of taking a structural approach to solving women's work and family life dilemmas. A structural perspective emphasizes the need for institutions, like the economy, to adapt the demands of the workplace to the labor force, which is increasingly made up of men and women with children. The structural perspective leads us to reject the notion that occupations must follow the traditional model of full-time worker and full-time homemaker, and proposes instead alternative scheduling and career patterns that provide greater flexibility in lifestyles of work and family. The structuralist approach makes it obvious that basic changes in the current structure of work and family are required.

We have made a commitment in this volume to discuss the diversity of women's working lives, paying particular attention to issues of race, ethnicity, class, and sexual preference. To do this, we use a range of imperfect socially constructed terms such as "minority women" and "nonwhite women," which, regrettably, can seem to marginalize the experiences of these women. We acknowledge that these terms are fraught with issues of hierarchy and often assume a universal "white" experience against which other racial/ethnic groups are to be viewed. Also, the use of such terms as white, Latina, Asian American, Native American, and women of color often masks distinct historical differences within these categories. All of these terms are problematic. We address this issue up front in the hope that our readers will be aware of the limitations of these terms and the importance of language in shaping our reality.

We would like to acknowledge the contributions of many people to the substance of this book. Annalaura D'Errico co-authored Chapter 7, while Deb Natsitka is a contributor to Chapter 5. A few sections of Chapters 1, 2, and 4 are fully revised versions of chapters that appeared in *Women at Work* (Fox and Hesse-Biber, 1984).

We are indebted to Professors Ashley W. Doane, Jr. (University of Hartford), Ronnie Elwell (Lesley College), Michael Fraleigh (Bryant College), Margot B. Kempers (Fitchburg State College), Judith McDonnell (Bryant College), Helen Raisz (Trinity College), and Frances Marx Stehle (Portland State University), who were gracious enough to review all eight chapters of the first edition.

Our research benefited greatly from the information technology and library divisions at Bryant College. The entire staffs of these two divisions have been helpful, but the following individuals deserve special recognition: in information technology, Raymond Lombardi, David Louton, Karen Renaud, and Michael Thompson; in library services, Holly Albanese, Colleen Anderson, Connie Cameron, Patricia Crawford, Tom Magill, Gretchen McLaughlin, and Patricia Sinman. The secretarial staffs at Bryant College and Boston College were always helpful. Elaine Goodwin, Joanne Socci, Steve Vedeer, and Patricia Giraldo performed many valued services, as did our student research assistants Stacey Baron, Erin Caulfield, Sadie Fischesser, Clay Howard, Christine Hughes, Faith Kirkpatrick, Olga Makovetskaya, Jennifer Mathieu, Kristen McMahon, Yu Meng, Katie Morganti, Greg Tumolo, Michael Vieira, Ingrid Wulczyn, and Michelle Yaiser.

We want to thank South End Press for permission to use portions of the data published in *Race, Gender, and Work* (Amott and Matthaei, 1996), and we are grateful to Janet Lee Mills for granting permission to use her photos that are reproduced in Chapter 4. The administrations of Boston College and the Bryant College were very cooperative and supportive of our research, and we especially thank Earl Briden, David Karp, David Lux, Ronald Machtley, and V. K. Unni. Our Oxford University Press editors for the first edition, Layla Voll and Gioia Stevens, were encouraging and enthusiastic from the moment each joined our project, as was our editor for the second edition, Peter Labellea. In a word, our copy editor, Rachel Davis, is peerless.

On a personal note, Gregg Carter wants to thank his children, Travis, Kurtis, and Alexis, and his wife, Lisa, for their love and forbearance. Sharlene Nagy Hesse-Biber thanks her family for their support and encouragement, especially her exceptional and energetic daughters, Sarah Alexandra Biber and Julia Ariel Biber. She is grateful to the students in her Women and Work course at Boston College for all their insightful comments on the first edition. She also extends a heartfelt thanks to Jodi Wigren for her wisdom and guidance. She dedicates her work on this book to her loving and dynamic sisters, Janet Nagy Green Fischer, and Georgia Nagy Geraghty.

Of course, none of the individuals acknowledged here shoulders responsibility for any factual or analytic errors we commit herein.

Sharlene Nagy Hesse-Biber   Gregg Lee Carter
Chestnut Hill, Massachusetts   Smithfield, Rhode Island

October, 1998
December, 2003

1 Models of Women and Work

Dramatic structural changes have been taking place in the U.S. economy in recent years, among them the downsizing of American corporations, the globalization of the economy, and the decline of selected manufacturing industries.
Within the labor market there has been a subtle revolution—the dramatic
growth in the labor-force participation of women. Between 1890 and the first
years of the twenty-first century, women's rate of participation grew from 18
percent to just over 60 percent. In the last decade of the nineteenth century, 19
percent of all mothers with small children younger than one year were in the
labor force (Apter, 1993, p. 26); by 1975, this number rose to 31 percent; by
1985, to 49 percent; and by 2000, to 58 percent (U.S. Bureau of the Census,
2002a, Table 578, p. 373). The traditional *Leave it to Beaver* family—a male
breadwinner, a housewife, and one or more children—is no longer the norm.
On the contrary, by the early 1990s it represented only about 10 percent of all
American families (Bureau of Labor Statistics, 1994b).

The dramatic growth in the labor-force participation of women in the
United States has matched similar change in most industrialized nations. For
example, between 1960 and 2000, women's participation rates grew from 33.8
to 64.8 percent in Australia, from 30.1 to 69.5 percent in Canada, from 46.1 to
74.6 percent in Sweden, and from 40.1 to 67.5 percent in the United Kingdom
(Bureau of Labor Statistics, 1994c; U.S. Bureau of the Census, 2002a, Table
1354, p. 848). Overall, women's labor-force participation averaged nearly 55
percent in developed nations by the early 1990s (United Nations, 1995a, p. 110)
and has grown steadily since then: by 2000, Italy had the smallest participation
rate at 46.0 percent, while Denmark (75.8 percent) and Norway (76.3 percent)
had the highest rates (U.S. Bureau of the Census, 2002a, Table 1354, p. 848).

Many developing countries have also witnessed extraordinary growth in
women's labor-force participation. The rate is strongest in those areas characterized by export manufacturing: Mexico, Brazil, and the Caribbean, as well as
East and Southeast Asia (Stichter and Parpart, 1990). The overall labor-force
participation rate for women in developing countries in the mid-1990s was 48
percent (Sivard, 1995).

In the past twenty-five years, the total paid labor force in many regions of
the world has become nearly equally divided between men in women. More
specifically, women comprise more than 40 percent of the labor forces in sub-
Saharan Africa, the Caribbean, most of Asia, all of Europe, and in virtually all
economically developed nations throughout the world. Women's total economic
contribution in the remaining regions of the world is on par with that of men,
but they are less likely to be in the *paid* labor force in Northern Africa (where
26 percent of the total labor force comprises women), Central (33 percent) and

1

South (38 percent) America, and Southern (33 percent) and Western (27 percent) Asia (see United Nations, 2000).

Women's labor-force participation affects many aspects of our lives, including child-rearing patterns, trends in fertility rates, and the division of labor at home. We are told by "experts" that our houses are getting dirtier as a result of women's working outside the home. We are also told that men are having to share more in household chores. Indeed, many men have moved from the category of reluctant helpers to willing participants, supporting the concept of sharing such responsibilities fifty-fifty, although in actuality women most often still end up doing more (see Costello and Krimgold, 1996, pp. 92–94; Gershuny and Robinson, 1988; Robinson, 1988; Shelton, 1992; and Spain and Bianchi, 1996, pp. 169–171). Women's working is said also to be responsible for many of the social ills of our society, from the breakup of marriages to the unhappy lives of some professional women who early on invested themselves primarily in their careers, only later to find they were caught in a "marriage squeeze," with their biological clocks ticking and no marriageable mate in sight.

The purpose of this book is to study the dramatic growth in women's labor-force participation and to understand what the actual experience of working women is today. There are many issues we need to examine as we go about this task. How is work defined? (We will look at both paid employment and unpaid domestic work, and the relationships between the two.) What are the features of women's work that make it distinctive? How do women's work experiences differ by class and by race? What is the relative status of males and females in the labor force, as regards rank, pay, prestige, power, and opportunity? What accounts for the discrepancies? Do women's work choices simply reflect their interests and abilities, or are there external factors such as education, the economy, polity, and culture that play a role in their experiences? What is the impact of the globalization of work on women's employment? How do women's work experiences compare in a global context? By analyzing these issues, we will develop a more complex understanding of the experiences of all working women and, as a result, develop more effective strategies for addressing the exploitation of women in the labor force.

The Politics of Knowledge Building

In formulating our questions about women's working conditions and in pondering solutions to such pressing issues as the gender gap in earnings, the continued pervasiveness of sex segregation at work, the lack of adequate childcare for working parents, and the growing feminization of poverty across the globe, we need to be vigilant with respect to the assumptions or models we hold up as windows through which we view women and work. It is important not to lose sight of the fact that the study of women and work has a *political* dimension.

In *The Structure of Scientific Revolutions*, Thomas Kuhn (1962) argues that science at any one time is characterized by a particular paradigm, or way of thinking. Knowledge is filtered through the particular model or paradigm or set of paradigms currently dominant within a particular field. These paradigms are theoretically derived world views that provide the categories and concepts through and by which we construct and understand the world. A paradigm tells us what is there and what is not, what is to be taken seriously and what is not, what are data and what are not. Kuhn argues there are no facts that are paradigm-free or theory-independent, because those that we regard as "fact" differ according to the world view or paradigm we live and work within.

During a period of "normal science" (see Figure 1.1), scientists work within the reigning paradigm, accumulating knowledge. Work within this paradigm inevitably spawns anomalies, or factors that cannot be explained. If there are many of these aberrations, a crisis stage occurs, which inevitably ends in a revolution. The reigning paradigm is discredited, and a new paradigm takes its place. Then this process or cycle repeats itself. One of Kuhn's key points is that the reasons one paradigm wins out over another are primarily political in nature. Often it is irrational and subjective phenomena that affect the development of science. The paradigm that emerges victorious is the one that has the most converts—it need not have the greater explanatory power (Ritzer, 1975, p. 10).

Kuhn's basic idea of the structure of science and his view of the political process involved in the building of knowledge provide a good starting point in our attempt to (1) understand the study of work in American society and (2) understand the concepts or models of knowledge building in the area of women and work. Such understanding will help point us toward new models/paradigms in our exploration of women and work.

Historically, it has been men who have had the power to define knowledge, formulate questions, construct models or paradigms, and formulate explanations of reality in relation to themselves. As Dale Spender (1981, pp. 1–2) observes:

> . . . they have usually generated the explanations and the schemata and have then checked with each other and vouched for the accuracy and adequacy of their view of the world. They have created men's studies (the academic curriculum), for, by not acknowledging that they are presenting only the explanations of men, they have "passed off" this knowledge as human knowledge. Women have been excluded as the producers of knowledge and as the subjects of knowledge, for men have often made their own knowledge, and their own sex, representative of humanity.

Sociology developed as a male enterprise, defined by males and overwhelmingly concerned with questions about the aspects of sociology that were almost entirely populated by males (Acker, 1978, pp. 135–136).

Figure 1.1. The Development of Science. *Source:* Adpted from Ritzer, 1975, p. 3.

Dorothy Smith (1978, p. 281) has described how the process of exclusion operates, noting that men tend to listen and consider "significant only that which men treat as significant." Women, she says, have been "largely excluded from the work of producing the forms of thought and the images and symbols in which thought is expressed and ordered." Further, there is a *circle effect*: "The circle of men whose writing and talk was significant to each other extends backwards in time as far as our records reach. What men were doing was relevant to men, was written by men about men for men. Men listened to what one another said." Smith argues that over time a tradition (or in Thomas Kuhn's terms, a paradigm) is formed—one that has its own questions, situations, explanations, and solutions. Because women have not been present within this "circle" of knowledge, their particular concerns and questions have not been addressed.

The Functionalist Paradigm

A dominant paradigm within the field of sociology is *functionalism*. With regard to gender, this paradigm's basic assumption reflects the separation of men and women into a public and a private sphere. Functionalism was developed in the 1940s and 1950s, but remains a theoretical force in sociology today—though it is rarely called by this name.

To the functionalist, society is a social system composed of interrelated parts, each of which contributes to the maintenance of the others. Men and women play specific roles and hold specific statuses within the social system. Women's roles are defined in terms of the family, as wife and mother; men's roles are defined in terms of work in the outside world, the key role being that of breadwinner. Men perform task-oriented, public, and visible roles, while women perform socioemotional, private, and invisible roles. Women's status is determined by the social and economic position of the male "head of household." This theoretical perspective, which has both biosocial (see Wilson, 1975) and cultural (see Hartmann, 1976; Laws, 1976) origins, is made explicit by sociologist Talcott Parsons (1942, p. 611) in his classic formulation:

> The most fundamental basis of the family's status is the occupational status of the husband and father. The woman's fundamental status is that of her husband's wife, the mother of his children, and traditionally the person responsible for a complex of activities in the management of household, care of children, etc.

Parsons and other functionalist theorists condone the notion that women and men should focus on different activities because such a division is efficient and also increases the cohesiveness of the family, in particular, and of society, in general. When men and women both focus on economic roles, there is too much competition and the role each family member should play becomes too indistinctive (Parsons et al., 1955). Parsons—and most of his contemporaries— believed that the classic formulation was not only the best description of the division of labor within the family, but the best prescription for it too.

In spite of a growing body of data and theory that mitigates against continued acceptance of functionalist assumptions concerning social roles, research on women has historically reflected and frequently continues to reflect these assumptions. A number of models of the woman worker that reflect functionalist assumptions have not only become popular images, but also serve to constrain what is studied in the area of work and occupations, what questions are asked and what explanations researchers provide. These assumptions also frame social policies regarding women and work.

The functionalist paradigm has spawned five major models of the woman worker, as follow.

Model 1—The Employed Woman as Invisible

Methodological frameworks used to record and measure economic activity reflect a functionalist view of women's place at home and men's at work. Key terms such as "work" (usually meaning only paid work) and "head of household" make certain assumptions concerning the roles of men and women. Until the 1970s, the study of work was primarily the study of *men* at work (Acker, 1978, Bernard, 1974; Brown, 1976; Feldberg and Glenn, 1979; Huber, 1976; and Laws, 1979). Sociologist Christine Bose (1987, p. 98) argues, in fact, that

> . . . the increase in women's employment in the twentieth century is due, in large part, to shifts in the definitional ability of that work to be counted. At the turn of the century . . . women's part-time remunerative work caring for boarders, selling eggs, and the like was not counted as work by the census unless it provided the bulk of their economic support. Such tasks were culturally viewed as a natural extension of women's service work for their families.

Bose (1987:98) notes that as a consequence "the amount of recorded home-based work was very low, comprising in 1900 only 14.1 percent of all working females, including seamstresses, laundresses, and boarding housekeepers. In actuality, Bose et al. (1987, p. 4) notes that rarely was the work of women easily separated into "paid" and unpaid work. Instead, "women have been required to do both." (Bose et al., 1987, p. 4). Taking into account married women's household work, employment in their husband's or father's farm or business, caring for boarders, as well as more public factory work would, she argues, yields an actual labor-force participation rate of between 48.5 and 56.7 for women in 1900. This rate is comparable to the 56.6 percent of women counted as employed in 1988!

Traditional economic measures, however, start out by having their focus restricted to *paid* employment. Work done outside the market economy is not measured or recorded as work. Occupational data collected refer only to individuals who work inside the market economy. Work that is nonpaid, including the majority of work done by women (especially in developing societies where women are much of the time engaged in subsistence activities such as collecting firewood and water, planting the family garden, and so on), is not counted as part of the Gross National Product (GNP, defined as the total market value of all goods and services produced by a nation during a specified period). As a result, women's work remains invisible; it is not measured and it therefore is of no economic value (see Acker, 1978; Bell, 1978; United Nations, 1995a, pp. 113–114; 2000, p. 113). This invisibility is the case even though, as noted economist John Kenneth Galbraith (1973) has estimated, if it *were* measured, the work of housewives in America alone would amount to approximately one-fourth of the U.S. GNP.

There is a strong economic motive for not recognizing the invisible work of women. This economic motive comes to light when we look at the relationship of paid work to unpaid work. The capitalist depends on women's unpaid labor—both productive and reproductive. Women's labor in the household helps maintain the current workforce, of which husbands or significant others are typically a part, and also, through child-rearing, provides the next generation of workers (see Lewenhak, 1992, especially ch. 2). Being left out of economic indicators presents problems for women, especially those living in poverty in both developed and developing societies. They and their work activities are consequently also left out of the minds of policymakers, especially in the areas of employment and development policies—and thus women's particular problems and concerns are not addressed. Or, if women are not completely left out, they are "subordinated and exploited" as part of national development strategies (Stichter and Parpart, 1990, p. 9).

Many researchers have begun to address the invisible aspects of women's work (see Acker, 1988; Aguiar, 1986; Beneria and Roldan, 1987; Fernandez-Kelly and Garcia, 1988; Mies, 1986; Mies, Bennholdt-Thomsen, and von Werlhof, 1988; Sokoloff, 1980; United Nations, 1995a, 2000; and Ward, 1990). They are redefining our traditional conceptions of work as paid employment to include all aspects of women's work roles. Maria Mies (1986), for example, has redefined production to encompass women's "production of life, or subsistence production" (p. 48). Women's work is thus contrasted with men's and capitalists' productive activities, which too often involve the exploitation of women's "unwaged" or low-paid work.

Noted black feminist theorist bell hooks (1984, p. 9) suggests that white middle-class feminists have been too quick to dismiss household work as demeaning and unliberating:

> Work outside the home, feminist activists declared, was the key to liberation. Work, they argued, would allow women to break the bonds of economic dependency on men, which would in turn enable them to resist sexist domination. When these women talked about work they were equating it with high-paying careers; they were not referring to low-paying jobs or so called "menial" labor. They were so blinded by their own experiences that they ignored the fact that a vast majority of women were (even at the time the *Feminine Mystique* was published) already working outside the home, working in jobs that neither liberated them from dependence on men nor made them economically self-sufficient.

Upholding work outside the home as the ultimate in liberation of women—and thus disparaging work inside the home—is, in hooks's opinion, a very white and a very middle-class mode of thinking.

In sum, recent writings on working women are casting aside functionalist assumptions concerning the traditional roles of men and women. These writings now acknowledge that women have always "worked," and that by their traditional neglect of women's nonpaid work, functionalists have perpetuated the artificial divisions between so-called public (male) and private (female) spheres.

Model 2—The Employed Woman as a Social Problem Model

Much of the literature on women at work is characterized by a social problems model. Researchers ask: Why do women work? Asking this question implies tacit acceptance of women's traditional place "at home." It also implies the contrasting cultural norm for men: that men ordinarily work throughout their lives (analogous studies of men focus on their absence—unemployment). Studies generally focus on "unusual" factors that influence women's participation in the workforce—such as being single, child-free, divorced, having a low income—for why else would women want to work?

The social problems' orientation toward the study of women's paid work results in a focus on those facets of women's work that seem to create problems for the family (see Brown, 1976; Kanter, 1977; Kreps, 1971; and Laws, 1979). Researchers ask: What effect will work activities have on her family? Will her children become delinquent? How will work affect her relationship with her husband? Will divorce be prevalent among working women? How will a woman's working outside her home affect her community—will she devote less time to important community affairs? How will working affect women's mental and physical health? (See Etaugh, 1974; Ferber and Birnbaum, 1982; Hoffman, 1974, 1979; Hoffman and Nye, 1974; and Siegal and Haas, 1963). Other sociologists and demographers focus on the adverse effects of employment on fertility levels.

Two or three decades ago, it was widely believed that maternal employment had only adverse effects on child development, with the seriousness of these effects increasing in proportion to the youthfulness of the children when their mothers began to work (Lamb, 1982, pp. 62–63). A 1982 extensive review of empirical studies of the effects of maternal employment on child development failed to substantiate these pessimistic conclusions (see Lamb, 1982, p. 63). While it is not the case that maternal employment has no effect on child development, a variety of other factors must be taken into account. A woman's employment status "has little explanatory value unless attempts are made to view [this] in the context of her social and family circumstances as well as her values and goals" (Lamb, 1982, p. 63). Harvey (1999), using data from the 1994 National Longitudinal Survey of Youth, studied the effects of early parental employment during the first three years of a child's life. Her findings revealed no relationship between early parental working and children's behavioral problems, self-esteem, and compliance issues in later childhood. There were only slightly lower ratings on cognitive development before the age of seven and slightly lower scores on academic achievement before age nine. These differences become nonexistent after these ages. In fact, some of Harvey's findings suggest that early parental working can have an overall positive effect on children's development, perhaps through increasing a family's earnings.

An intensive empirical analysis of the effects women's working has on the development of their children concludes that "there is no simple answer to questions concerning the benefits or dangers of maternal employment. Much depends on the quality of that employment, the demands of partners' occupations, and the demands of other children. It is clear that both mothers' and fathers' work may be more or less helpful to children, depending on other resources on which partners may draw and other responsibilities they must shoulder" (Parcel and Menaghan, 1994, p. 159).

Employment has been considered so problematic for women that only a few researchers have actually bothered to inquire into a woman's *positive* feelings about her work (for exceptions, see Bailyn, 1970; Hoffman, 1961). In this regard, Kanter (1977, pp. 60–61) has noted: "As one reads the literature, women would seem rather unconnected to their work and unaffected by it (certainly this view has been taken by employers for many years to the detriment of women)."

We are, however, beginning to learn that women enjoy their work. Even though many women work out of economic necessity, many state they would want to work even if they didn't need to (see Komarovsky, 1962; Walshok, 1981). A national survey conducted in 1976 found, for instance, that 75 percent of women who were employed said they would remain employed even if it were not economically necessary (Dubnoff, Veroff, and Kulka, 1978). Similar findings were found more than a decade later: 79 percent of working mothers reported that they would not leave their current jobs to stay at home with the children; moreover, 56 percent of full-time housewives reported that they would choose to have a career if they had it to do all over again (DeChick, 1988). Today, the decision to work appears to be only slightly related to economic necessity; indeed, the greatest relative increase in female labor-force participation during the 1960s and 1970s took place among wives who had high-earning husbands (Ryscavage, 1979). More recent national survey data* reveal that married women across the economic spectrum overwhelmingly approve of a married woman's earning money in business or industry even if she has a husband capable of supporting her (see Figure 1.2).

---

*The national survey to which we refer most often throughout this volume is the General Social Survey (GSS). Except for the years 1979, 1981, and 1992, the GSS was conducted annually between 1972 and 1994 by the National Opinion Research Center at the University of Chicago. For each of the survey years, approximately 1,600 adult Americans were asked about their family backgrounds, personal histories, behaviors, and attitudes toward a variety of issues. Beginning in 1996, the survey became biennial and expanded to a sample size of approximately 3,000. Because the National Opinion Research Center uses rigorous scientific sampling strategies and has a high response rate, it is safe to assume that the data are of a very high quality. For more information on the GSS, see http://www.icpsr.umich.edu/gss/.

Family Income

	<$25,000	$25,000–$60,000	>$60,000
Approve	79.5%	83.5%	87.3%
	(58)	(172)	(137)
Disapprove	20.5%	16.5%	12.7%
	(15)	(34)	(20)
	100.0%	100.0%	100.0%

Figure 1.2. Attitude of Married Women Toward the General Social Survey Item "Fework" by Annual Family Income. *Source:* NORC (1998); General Social Survey Question: "Do you approve or disapprove of a married woman earning money in business or industry if she has a husband capable of supporting her?" ("Fework"). *Source:* NORC, 1998–2000. Statistics usually calculated for crosstabulations for these kinds of data reveal that there is no significant relationship between Family Income and Fework (χ^2 = 2.4, p > .25; gamma = .17, p > .10)

There is evidence that working increases a woman's sense of well-being. Work can have a rehabilitative effect on mental health, measured in terms of psychological distress (see Baruch, Barnett, and Rivers, 1983). Women who work display fewer psychological distress symptoms—and greater feelings of competence and self-fulfillment—than housewives (Bernard, 1971, 1972). The feeling of competence spills over into family life: working women are more assertive with respect to family decision making (for instance, they are involved in more of the family's financial planning) and also demand greater respect from their children and husbands (Barnett and Baruch, 1979). Recent national survey data support the notion that working wives are as happy with their marriages as their counterparts who stay home and keep house (see Figure 1.3). Moreover, the Gallup Poll consistently reveals that in the United States working women are

Work Situation

	Keeping House	Part Time	Full Time	Other
Very Happy	58.7%	53.3%	60.5%	60.7%
	(135)	(80)	(262)	(85)
Pretty Happy	39.1%	41.3%	36.5%	33.6%
	(90)	(62)	(158)	(47)
Not too Happy	2.2%	5.3%	3.0%	5.7%
	(5)	(8)	(13)	(8)
	100.0%	100.0%	100.0%	

Figure 1.3. Attitude of Married Women Toward the General Social Survey Item "HapMar" by Work Situation ("WrkStat"). *Source:* NORC (2000–2002); General Social Survey question: "Taking things all together, how would you describe your marriage?" ("HapMar"). The statistic usually calculated for crosstabulations for these kinds of data reveals that there is no significant relationship between Work Situation and HapMar (χ^2 = 7.3, p > .25). Note that the "Other" category includes those on leave, unemployed, in school, or retired.

as satisfied with their jobs as working men; for example, in 2003, 54 percent of working women responded that they were "very satisfied" with their jobs, while 55 percent of working men so responded (Saad, 2003).

Concentrating on the problematic aspects of women's employment has ironically had the effect of neglecting some important problems that women *at home* experience. In the 1960s, Friedan (1963) identified this "problem that had no name" as the *feminine mystique*. Research into the world of the housewife revealed an underside to this role: Many housewives succumbed to depression. They were more impaired in their functioning than women who worked outside their homes, suggesting that there was something protective in the work situation (Kanter, 1977, p. 61, citing research from Weissman and Paykel, 1974).

The functionalist paradigm also ironically prevented researchers from seeing the other real problems of women—primary among these is the problem of poverty. Within a functionalist framework, men are the providers and women are the nurturers. Thus few researchers recognized the growing problem of women's poverty until the late 1970s—when it acquired the label "the feminization of poverty" (Pearce, 1978)—even though high poverty rates among women had existed for decades prior. "The latest estimates are that . . . almost one-fourth of the world's population, now live in absolute poverty, that even more do not have access to the most rudimentary health care. Most—an estimated 70 percent—of the world's poorest are women" (Sivard, 1995, p. 17).

Yet economic development programs, including the $450 billion in official foreign assistance provided during the 1990s, have tended to see development as primarily a male function requiring more technology and training for greater productivity (e.g., see Sivard, 1995, p. 17). More recently, there is growing recognition by "public and private development agencies that women do not automatically benefit from aid targeted to poverty in broad terms and that women's poverty must be addressed more directly" (Sivard, 1995, p. 7).

Model 3—Male Work Experience Is the Norm

Another prevalent model in the study of women at work is the tendency to generalize findings from male experience. When men's and women's experiences at work are studied, research often treats men's as the norm. If women's experience is different, it is treated as "deviant." Eichler (1991, p. 49) notes that "men's experience tends to be seen as an appropriate basis for making general statements about practically anything but . . . women's experience tends to be seen as an appropriate basis for overgeneralization only about some aspects of family life or reproduction."

A good example of this is the concept of career. It has been decades since researchers first examined the work issues facing dual-career families (e.g., see Holmstrom, 1972), yet in many career textbooks there is the assumption that all family patterns are traditional. Career development literature assumes a particular monistic career model based on an idealized male life cycle. We are told that, especially in the "early years," successful careers depend on a challenging first assignment, and that investment in career during these years is critical to an individual's future development. Identification and encouragement of "fast-trackers" is based on the assumption that the employee has a family support system (see Finch, 1983; Hochschild, 1976; and Papanek, 1973). Many businesses and other organizations definitely use these "early years" to set career paths. The corporation appears locked into a particular view of success in terms of a sprint model of early and intense career devotion. If women's careers differ from this model (and most do) and they don't succeed like men, blame is placed on women themselves. Their failure is a product of their being "less serious" or "less committed" (see Strober, 1975).

Yet monistic models of "work" and "career" based on an idealized "male life cycle" are inadequate in describing (much less predicting) women's life and work (Laws, 1980, p. 2). Ginsberg's (1966) research illustrates this point. He and his associates wanted to study the career development of a group of male and female graduate students at Columbia University. Ginsberg's original questionnaire had assumed a monistic model—querying men and women about career plans alone—ignoring important contingencies such as marital/family life:

> A scanning of the completed questionnaires showed us that something was awry. While some women filled in all the requested information and returned the questionnaire without special comment, many others did not. Some said the questionnaire did not fit their situation, some said they had not pursued a career. Others pointed out that the questions were much better suited to elicit information about the work and life experiences of men than women. (Ginsberg, 1966, p. 2)

By focusing only on the narrow concern of preparation for work and on experiences at work, the questionnaire ignored important contingencies that women contend with "off the job." Ginsberg observed that, while the men followed an uncomplicated, straightforward pattern of career development, a much more complex career and life pattern characterized the majority of women in his sample:

> When she marries and particularly after she has children, her life will be conditioned by a host of circumstances and conditions over which she will have a little maneuverability, but little control. Since they realize this, many young women are loath to make long-range educational and occupational plans. In fact, many move in the opposite direction and select their fields and careers with the expectation that they will shift after they marry. They therefore plan for this by seeking to acquire occupational flexibility. This search can mean, for example, that an able woman prepares for elementary or secondary teaching on the assumption that she will be able to get a teaching job in almost any community. (Ginsberg, 1966, p. 174)

To allow for such complications, some have argued for a *mommy track* especially for employed mothers. In 1989, Felice Schwartz, founder and president of Catalyst, a nonprofit research organization that works with corporations to advance women's careers and leadership potential, wrote a controversial article in the *Harvard Business Review* (Schwartz, 1989) in which she argued that corporations should recognize two types of women: *career-primary* and *career-*

family women. Career-family women ("mommy trackers") are those who need flexible hours for childcare and/or time to care for their aging parents. Career-primary women, on the other hand, should be treated like any male. Schwartz assumed that mothers should and would accept the *mommy track* with open arms. However, this has not been the case. And, indeed, research shows that women interrupting their careers to care for young children—or for other family reasons—never catch up to the income and promotion levels of their female counterparts who do not take time off (see Jacobsen and Levin, 1992).

Clearly there are other options that would make it possible to move family values to the center of corporate values and credos. For example, the Johnson and Johnson Corporation has implemented what it calls its "family plan" (see Lauer, 1992, p. 336). The plan includes a nationwide referral service for childcare and elder care; a year of leave given to any employee having to care for a child, spouse, or parent; and the training of supervisors to sensitize them to the problems of balancing work and family demands. But as of the early 2000s, only a tiny fraction of women employees have access to a Johnson and Johnson kind of program.

Model 4—Socialization and "Ladies Choice"

When problematic issues regarding women's employment—such as income inequality and sex segregation—are discussed, explanations are usually phrased in terms of women's preferences for "supportive," nurturing occupations such as nursing and elementary school teaching. The more intellectually demanding, task-oriented jobs—such as lawyer, doctor, or executive—are thought to belong primarily to men. Furthermore, women are said to seek employment that allows them the flexibility to spend time with their families. This preference may prevent them from obtaining the training and other credentials they would need to compete with men in the labor market. Women choose to invest less, therefore they earn less. Sometimes the key reason given for this choice is socialization; that is, almost since birth, females are taught that one of their key roles in life will be that of mother and, further, that this role will preclude their working full time, especially when their children are young. For example, Doob (1995, pp. 165, 166) contends that "socialization plays a significant part in packing women into relatively low-paying, low-status jobs. . . . A host of studies have indicated that many families have discouraged their female children from pursuing careers that would adversely affect performance of domestic duties, require a change in physical location, or produce greater income and prestige for wives than for husbands." Other times, innate psychological reasons are given to underscore or explain women's choices (see Horner, 1972). One popular book with the title *Wising Up* offers the following explanation for the "mistakes" women make:

> Why don't more of these underpaid, undervalued women move on to better things? Ann Hyde, President of Management Woman, an executive recruitment firm specializing in placement of women ($30,000 a year minimum), says it can be summed up in one bleak, bad word. "Fear." Asked for more words,

Hyde explains: "Time and time again, I've seen very superior women walk away from spectacular opportunity when all systems were 'Go.' They've come to us brimming with confidence and determination, ready to move up the executive ladder to the positions their backgrounds have prepared them to command. We have matched their credentials up with corporations actively seeking gifted women for their executive staffs—only to have the whole thing come a cropper at the last minute! At the moment of truth, she panics. Panics! The confidence and determination collapse. She says she's sorry but she's afraid she wouldn't be right for the job." (Foxworth, 1980, pp. 92–93)

To suggest that women's inferior economic position results from choices they make is to identify them as "victims by choice." This perspective reflects the conservative bias of functionalist theory: locating causes within individuals, in their characteristics and deficiencies, while overlooking the structural factors influencing women's disadvantaged economic situation. Explanations such as discrimination in hiring and wages, for example, are seldom discussed. In actuality, such discrimination accounts for much of the earnings gap between men and women. Evidence suggests that even career women who are employed full time earn less than men in similar positions (Bureau of Labor Statistics, 1996a; Dingell and Maloney, 2002; Robertson, Carter, and Hesse-Biber, 2004; U.S. Bureau of the Census, 2002a, Table 621, p. 403). Overlooking these and other structural factors precludes consideration of structural changes that are necessary to improve women's labor market position. We will further explore the implications of a structural viewpoint in our discussion of alternative paradigms.

Model 5—Superwoman

This model of employed women is in part the creation of the mass media. The Superwoman is the woman who can make a full, nourishing breakfast for her wonderful and well-dressed children, then go to work and chair a meeting of the board of trustees in the morning, and meet with ten new clients during the course of the afternoon. After work, she comes home to cook and serve a gourmet dinner for her family. She is the woman who entertains in her spotless house, and who has a warm, nonproblematic relationship with her husband.

The Superwoman reached her zenith in the 1980s and early 1990s, though as a media image, she is still very much with us. While, for example, Linda Stoker's 1991 book entitled *Having It All: A Guide for Women Who Are Going Back to Work* cautions against expecting to have it all 1980s-style, it still suggests that having it all is within reach (Stoker, 1991). What such books and articles suggest, a little oversimplified, is that having it all is not having all of everything, but instead is finding out what is and is not important and learning to accent the former (cf. Apter, 1993, p. 115; Nicols, 2002).

The mass media's glamorizing of the employed Superwoman has done a disservice, for we don't see women's working life portrayed in realistic terms. This type of image can intimidate women, suggesting as it does that to combine work and family, a woman must be "super." By implying that only exceptional women can integrate work and family life, the image is perpetuating a functionalist framework that says work and family don't mix. Furthermore, by suggesting that women can or should somehow be able to "do it all," the Superwoman myth also perpetuates the traditional notion that household labor is women's work.

Research on the actual division of labor within the household shows "that men whose wives are employed do little if any additional housework and take on no significantly greater share of the more arduous or unpleasant tasks of child care" (Ferree, 1987, p. 162; also see Berk, 1985; Goldscheider and Waite, 1991; Marini and Shelton, 1993; Michelson, 1985; and Shelton, 1992). "A man's work ends at sun, while a woman's work is never done" is a cliché most women do not fully appreciate until they try to combine career and family. The Superwoman myth, some have argued, gets men "off the hook": "By defining the successful woman as one who is happily carrying this multiple burden, and in addition suggesting that it was women who sought this change, the superwoman ideal de-legitimates discontent. While it defines women's paid employment as perfectly acceptable and appropriate, it continues to put household labor in first place as a morally prior responsibility for women" (Ferree, 1987, p. 163).

Summing Up

These, then, are models that appear frequently in the study of work and of women at work. All these models or perspectives—the questions they raise and the explanations they provide—are within a functionalist paradigm. Most research in this area has not broken out of this paradigm. There have been, however, some promising anomalies and some movements toward a crisis, perhaps in Kuhn's terms, even a movement toward a "revolution" in the study of women at work. One such alternative approach is structural.

An Alternative Perspective: The Structural Approach

An analysis of women's poor economic position from the functionalist perspective focuses on the choices women make and their lack of qualifications for better jobs that bring higher salaries. This approach emphasizes the different functional roles, norms, and values for men and women. Women's position in the labor market is said to reflect this broader division. The occupations held by women—secretarial, childcare, waitressing, nursing, elementary school teaching—reflect traditional female nurturing and supportive roles. The "productive" jobs belong to men. The essence of the functionalist analysis of women's position is that women's preferences for traditionally female-typed jobs and the priority they place on family are the primary determinants of women's labor-force position. Such an analysis assumes women's freedom of choice in selecting occupations.

The *structuralist* perspective, on the other hand, questions the assumption that the choice is free and points instead to the constraints imposed by society. Such an approach focuses on basic societal institutions—that is, the organization and practices of the economy, the law, religion, and the family—that operate in a connected fashion to confine the majority of women to jobs characterized by low wages, little mobility, and limited prestige. This approach passes judgment on the structure instead of the victim, and it suggests a different strategy for improving women's labor-force status.

To understand women's positions at work, this perspective emphasizes that we must first take into account the structure of work. For Western countries, this means the system of capitalism, with its social arrangements and processes; for developing countries, the structure of multinational corporations, which tend to treat women as a cheap source of labor, while still viewing them as primarily wives and mothers. We must also consider how work organizations (many of which continue to operate as if workers have no families, and many of whose hiring and promotion policies and practices serve to discriminate against women) interface or connect with other basic societal institutions: the family system (which assumes there is a full-time wife/mother who will take care of the children), the educational system (which often tracks women out of math and science pursuits), and religious and legal institutions (which often convey the patriarchal message that women's role is primarily that of wife and mother).

While individual characteristics of women—their motivations, aspirations, credentials, qualifications, and abilities—are important, individual-level alterations will have little effect on women's labor-force position unless the external structural barriers that have restricted women's opportunities are eradicated. This realization has motivated us to adopt the structuralist perspective in this book.

Our use of this perspective fits well with our concerns—both professional and personal—with issues of discrimination and oppression of women in work and society. In particular, we explore how patriarchal arrangements within societal institutions perpetuate women's disadvantaged position in the work setting.

We also recognize the diversity of women's experiences. There has been a strong tendency for those studying women and work to generalize from the perspective of the white, middle-class, heterosexual woman worker. However, women's experiences are shaped not only by their gender, but also by their racial, ethnic, cultural, sexual preference, age-cohort, and economic backgrounds. We must guard against creating a model of women at work that unwittingly assumes too much homogeneity. Women of color, for example, typically work in occupations that are low paying and of lower prestige than white women (Bureau of Labor Statistics, 1997a, 2003a). The work history and experiences of working-class women also differ significantly from those of middle-class women (Walshok, 1981). Ethnic background is another critical determinant of women's participation and mobility within the labor market. Historically, for example, there has been a tendency for certain ethnic groups (e.g., Italian, Irish) to do paid work out of their homes (see Cantor and Laurie, 1977). Latino women from Mexico, Central America, and South America tend to have work experiences that diverge greatly from those of white women of European heritage. Also significant are differences in women's stage in the life cycle and the particular historical period in which they grew up (see, for example, Spain and Bianchi, 1996, pp. 86–90).

A structural approach must look, further, at the *interconnections* among the categories of race, class, and gender. As Evelyn Glenn, among others, observes:

> It may be tempting to conclude that racial ethnic women differ from white women simply by the addition of a second axis of oppression, race. It would be a mistake though, not to recognize the dialectical relations between white and racial ethnic women. Race and gender [and I would add class, sexual preference] interact in such a way that the histories of white and racial ethnic women are intertwined. (1987, p. 72)

For example, many white women have relied on the labor of women of color. A high-profile example of this drew attention in 1993 when President Clinton nominated Zoe Baird to be the first female attorney general of the United States. Her appointment was thwarted when it came to light that she had hired an undocumented woman of color to care for her young family and had failed to pay the woman's Social Security taxes. The scandal, which came to be known as "Nannygate," revealed how one group of working women resolves its work and family issues through the exploitation of another group of women.

In fact, if we go back to the central argument of functionalism that assumes a "natural gender division of labor" between the sexes, we should note that maintaining the fiction of a protected private sphere for women—the "lady-of-leisure" household—has historically been dependent on the availability of cheap female domestic labor. In this way the racial division of labor (different races have different jobs) reinforces the gender division of labor (different jobs for men and women) and the class division of labor (different classes hold different jobs). As long as the gender division of labor remains intact, it will be in the short-term interest of many white women to support or at least overlook the racial division of labor because it ensures that the very worst labor is performed by someone else. Yet as long as white women are in support of the racial division of labor, they will have less impetus to struggle to change the gender division of labor.

In studying the diversity of women at work, we must pay close attention to racial, class, and other inequities (sexuality, age, and so on). The adequacy and justice of any solutions we arrive at concerning how to deal with the problems women encounter in the workplace will depend on our sensitivity to these issues.

For example, while expanding childcare and elder care services will assist many white women workers, it raises problematic issues regarding who is going to deliver these services and who exactly will benefit from them. Glenn (1992) notes that historically women of color and new immigrants provide such labor, often at exploitative wages, while white middle-class women receive the benefits. For another example: a comparable-worth policy—which calls for the equalizing of wages between men and women's jobs with similar levels of skill and responsibility—seems like a good idea. However, as Glenn notes, while such a policy may promote wage equity between nurses and pharmacists, it maintains and justifies inequities between skill levels ("skilled" and "unskilled"), and it is in just this distinction that the racial division of labor resides. A diversity approach to understanding women at work would argue that it is the very hierarchy of worth of jobs that must be attacked—the division between skilled (jobs held by white workers) and unskilled (jobs held by persons of color). Such an approach would argue for a "flattening of wage differentials between the highest and lowest ranks" (Glenn, 1992).

Last, the structuralist perspective also recognizes that one cannot ignore the place of our own economy in the context of the world economy. The increasing globalization of markets and economies affects the overall situation of working women. Between 70 and 90 percent of the total workforce employed in export industries are women workers, the majority of whom are in their late teens and early twenties (Kirk and Okazawa-Rey, 2001, p. 265; Wichterich, 2000, p. 1).

For the past three decades, multinational shoe corporations such as Reebok and Adidas; electronic, computer, and microchip industries such as IBM and NEC; clothing manufacturers like The Gap and Levi's; and automobile corporations such as General Motors have been able to extend their manufacturing operations across national borders to countries where workers are paid at a much lower wage and receive very few protections from unfair and hostile working conditions. These multinational corporations receive lucrative tax and investment incentives and liberal protection from organized labor. They often operate outside the government regulations of their home country (see Enloe, 1985; Fernandez-Kelly, 1983; Fuentes and Ehrenreich, 1983; Greider, 1997; Lim, 1983; and Wichterich, 2000).

The increasing globalization of markets and economies affects the overall situation of millions of women workers, from poor and working-class women employed in sweatshops in New York City, Los Angeles, Mexico City, and Southeast Asia, to the many thousands of U.S. working-class and poor women workers in the manufacturing sector who have lost their jobs through "runaway" shops and corporations (Bonacich and Appelbaum, 2000; Dickinson, 1997). Women workers around the globe are feeling the effects of global-scale markets. The effect on the U.S. economy has been a growing separation of the U.S. labor market into "professional" and "low-skilled" service workers. As many American factories exit to less developed countries, jobs everywhere are continually being deskilled as technological advances influence the industrial and service sectors (Kirk and Okazawa-Rey, 2001, p. 266). The information technology (or IT) revolution has also contributed to a "dumbing-down" of the global workforce, often replacing women workers with computer-operated machines or else placing them in jobs that require few if any labor skills (Hacker, 1987; Webster, 1996). This massive deskilling of the labor force has concurrently "feminized" the global workplace, placing many women workers in low-income jobs that threaten basic worker rights of safe conditions, living wages, and fundamental human treatment.

Examining women workers' need in the context of this global economy helps to uncover the broader link between women workers everywhere. Through the processes of production and consumption, more well-to-do first world women workers are connected to third world women workers. As a consumer in U.S. society, you may shop at The Gap, Wal-Mart, or Ralph Lauren, and you are participating in the globalization of female wage labor. Understanding where all women fit in this growing market economy better enables us to find common and certainly some uncommon threads between those women who live worlds apart. Yet, through the recognition of such difference, a common identity as women workers can be championed. Professional and immigrant workers alike are a part of the global future, and they all will make a significant difference in the state and structure of women's work.

Exploring the nature and structure of women's work in the context of our growing world economy therefore becomes important to an overall study of women's work. As more and more women everywhere enter the labor force, women working both in the United States and abroad are contributing to the feminization of labor conditions and processes that define their work experiences. Whether women are corporate executives, waitresses, or sweatshop workers, women are becoming a part of the globalized workforce. The political, economic, and social impact of this trend will affect the future conditions of working women.

A few questions come to mind when thinking about women's work at the global level. What does globalization mean for their daily work experiences and is it good or bad for these women? What does it mean to say that globalization affects women workers? What do their experiences tell us about the state of gender inequality both in the United States and abroad? In sum, where possible, we will compare and contrast the situation of working women in the United States with those of women in other developed and developing societies.

To understand the position of working women today, we need to understand how their present-day experiences have been shaped by historical factors. The next chapter provides a brief history of women at work. This historical perspective is intended to provide a solid foundation for understanding the working situation of women today.

World Wide Web Resources

At the end of each chapter, we present a list of Web resources intended to assist readers in exploring in more detail some of the topics that have been discussed. All URLs were functional as of July 2003.

For the art of doing feminist research, see the syllabus for this San Diego State University graduate seminar on Methods of Inquiry in Women Studies: http://www.mith2.umd.edu/WomensStudies/Syllabi/Methods/research-methods3.

Women and Workplace Stress provides a discussion of how job stress affects women in their working lives: www.ed.gov/databases/ERIC_Digests/ed401496.html.

Mount Holyoke College has published a data-filled introduction to working women based on information assembled by the Women's College Coalition:

www.academic.org. This Web site also offers suggestions, possible resources, and profiles of role models that can help parents raise their daughters to aspire to enter the workforce.

The Canadian Labour Congress offers an explanation of how the women's labor movement can be strengthened: www.clc-ctc.ca/woman/femorg3.html.

WomensWork.Org has developed a "role model registry" that allows working women to offer their experiences to young girls thinking about joining the workforce: www.womenswork.org/girls/.

The research of Elisabeth Hayes and Wendy Way—both of the University of Wisconsin—reveals how African American women view work and what kind of impact their adult education has on this view: http://www.edst.educ.ubc.ca/aerc/2000/hayesewayw1-web.htm.

Women.Ink is a project of the International Women's Tribune Centre and offers hundreds of publications that are written from the perspectives of women from the Global South: www.womenink.org.

Catalyst is an organization dedicated to advancing women in business and the professions. Its Web site offers many suggestions for bringing about improvements in the lives of working women: www.catalystwomen.org.

2 A Brief History of Working Women

The number of women in the paid workforce has steadily increased throughout the twentieth century, from around 20 percent in 1900 to around 45 percent in 1975 and just under 60 percent in 2002 (see Figure 2.1).

Even so, for much of the twentieth century women were "invisible" workers, whose labor and skills were considered insignificant compared to those of men. Traditional studies perpetuated this illusion by treating the topic of labor-force participation as though it involved only men, as we discussed in Chapter 1.

Until the 1970s, there was little historical research on women workers, or on women in general. Studies of women's history tended to be limited to (1) institutional histories of women's organizations and movements; (2) biographies of important suffragists and "token women," such as first ladies or isolated nineteenth-century professional women; and (3) "prescriptive history," or discussions of class or societal ideals rather than actual cultural practices; for example, analyses of recommended child-rearing methods. There were few studies on women's work either inside or outside the home. Little attention was paid to the diversity of women workers, to contemporary or historical effects of race, class, or ethnicity.

Over the past three decades, however, women have become the subject of wider historical interest. The contributions over the decades of a diversity of women workers have begun to be identified. We have a better understanding of who they were, why they worked, in which occupations and industries, and what problems they encountered. A historical overview enriches our understanding of the interplay of social, economic, and political factors that have influenced and shaped women's relationship to the paid labor force. Knowing more about "where women have been" helps us understand "where women are" now and "where they are going" in the future.

Women Workers in Preindustrial America

Between 1600 and 1700, 750,000 Europeans came to America. The bulk of them were from Britain, but the colonies also saw significant numbers from Holland, France, and Germany. Many came as indentured servants, exchanging their labor for the cost of passage to the American colonies. Indentured servants often worked from five to ten years to pay back their creditors. As early as the 1600s, prior to the slave trade, some Africans also came to the colonies as indentured servants; they often worked side by side with white indentured servants.

Figure 2.1. Percentage of U.S. Women in the Paid Labor Force, 1890–2002. Note: pre-1945 data are for ages 14 and older; 1945–2001 are for ages 16 and older. *Sources:* Bureau of Labor Statistics, 1979, 1980, 1997b; U.S. Bureau of the Census, 2002a (Table 576, p. 372).

Women's lives in this country differed drastically, depending on their race, class, and marital status.

White Women

European women usually arrived in the New World with their families, as daughters and wives under the auspices of fathers or husbands. In the preindustrial economy of the American colonial period (from the seventeenth century to the early eighteenth century), work was closely identified with home and family life. The family was the primary economic unit, and family members were dependent on one another for basic sustenance. Men performed the agricultural work, while women's work was done chiefly in the home, which was a center of production in colonial America. In addition to cooking, cleaning, and caring for children, women did spinning and weaving, and made lace, soap, candles, and shoes (Flexner, 1959). Indeed, they manufactured nearly all articles used in daily life. This work was highly valued, and the colonies relied on the production of these "cottage industries."

Single women remained within the domestic sphere, living with relatives, often as "assistant homemakers" (Matthaei, 1982, p. 51). For married women, the nature of their work depended on the economic circumstances of their husbands:

> In cash-poor homes and among frontier families, women bore the burden of filling most of the family's basic needs. They worked to reduce cash expenditures by growing vegetables in the kitchen garden and making the family's clothes, candles, soap, and household furnishings. If a husband were a craftsman or the proprietor of a shop or tavern, his wife and children might also work in the business, in addition to all the other tasks. In contrast, the wife of

a successful farmer, plantation owner, or merchant did little actual work; instead, she supervised household servants and slaves who purchased or made the goods the family needed, cooked the meals, and maintained the house. (Amott and Matthaei, 1996, p. 99)

The social codes of colonial America did not exclude a woman from working outside the home, and many did so. Colonial women engaged in a great range of occupations and, as old documents are discovered and new histories of women's work are written, that range appears greater still. Women were innkeepers, shopkeepers, crafts workers, nurses, printers, teachers, and landholders (Dexter, 1924). In the city of Boston during 1690, for example, women ran approximately 40 percent of all taverns. During that year, city officials also granted more than thirty women the right to saw lumber and manufacture potash (Chafe, 1977, p. 19). Women acted as physicians and midwives in all the early settlements, producing medicines, salves, and ointments. Many of the women who worked outside their homes were widows with dependent children, who took their husbands' places in family enterprises. It seems that at one time or another, colonial women engaged in many of the occupations practiced by men (Leonard, Drinker, and Holden, 1962). Indeed, most models of the "patriarchal family economy" ill fit the historical evidence; for example, eighteenth-century diaries describe "a world in which wives as well as husbands traded with their neighbors" and "young women felt themselves responsible for their own support" (Ulrich, 1987, p. 33). Not surprisingly, however, women's wages in this period were significantly lower than those of men.

For poor women, there were special incentives to work outside the home. Local poor laws encouraged single poor women to work rather than become recipients of relief. The choice of jobs was much more limited, and many poor women became laundresses, house servants, or cooks. Again, however, female laborers were paid approximately 30 percent less than the lowest-paid unskilled, free, white male workers and 20 percent less than hired-out male slaves.

The fact that some women worked in so-called masculine fields—that they were merchants, tavern owners, shopkeepers, and so on—has sometimes been interpreted to mean that the colonial period was a "golden age of equality" for women. Contemporary historians argue instead, however, that these jobs were exceptions to the rule, and that in fact "colonial times were characterized by a strict and simple division of labor between men and women, which assigned them to fields and house, or to the public and private spheres, respectively" (Matthaei, 1982, p. 29; see also Abbot, 1910; Smuts, 1971). The dominant ideology was still that a woman's place was at home, raising children. Although the daily activities of most women's lives may appear to indicate otherwise, people also held idealized beliefs about the appropriate social roles for the sexes (Chafe, 1977, p. 20). Research on 450 eighteenth-century families indicates that people held "very definite ideas of which tasks were properly 'feminine' and which were not, and of what functions 'the sex' was expected to perform. Moreover, both men and women continually indicated by subtle forms that they believed women to be inferior to men" (Norton, 1980, p. xiv).

Some indications of women's "inferior" position were anything but subtle. The law during the early colonial period was based on English common law tradition, characterized by rigid notions about the role of women (Lee, 1980). Under the law, when a woman married, she lost all control over her property, she lost the right to contract or sue, and she was legally obligated to perform domestic services for her husband. Wife-beating was a fairly common and socially sanctioned husband's right, a way to maintain discipline and assert male authority. Early colonial records often reveal the underlying gender differences in power. For example:

> When Daniel Ela was found beating his wife, he defended his actions to his neighbors by appealing to the fundamental power relationships of patriarchy. His wife, he argued, "was his servant and his slave." Likewise, when John Tillison chained his wife by the leg to a plow in order to keep her from leaving the house, or when a Maine husband kicked his wife and hit her with a club because she refused to feed his pig, they were considered to be exercising their right to discipline subordinates disrespectful of legitimate authority. (Berkin, 1996, p. 31)

The married woman's (*feme couverte*) legal status was lower than that of a single woman (*feme sole*). But in commercial areas of the colonies, some married women were declared "*feme-sole* traders," giving them the right to sue, to enter into contracts, to sell property, and to have the power of attorney in the absence of their husbands, rights that unmarried women enjoyed. In many cases, a widow inherited her husband's trade, often keeping it going under her own name, even if she remarried. Thus, while colonial America believed in patriarchal authority, in practice women sometimes came into positions of power: "The patriarchs simply did not live long enough. . . . Virginia daughters stood a good chance of inheriting land, and Virginia wives were very often given larger legacies than the law required. What is more, the Virginia wife was usually named her husband's executrix—the pivotal person who controlled the property until it was finally handed over to the heirs" (Lebsock 1990, p. 15). Similarly, while in theory women were not to participate in the public affairs of colonial life—they were forbidden to serve on juries, vote, and hold office—in actuality they often did. One Margaret Brent, for example, "had served as the executrix of Maryland's governor, she had headed off a mutiny of hungry soldiers, and she had asked for the vote—the first woman in America to do so. In fact, she asked for two votes in the Maryland assembly, one as executrix and one in her own right. When she was denied, she lodged a protest against all the assembly's further actions" (Lebsock, 1996, p. 18).

The traditional norms might not have precluded the day-to-day sharing of labor between the sexes, but they did dictate the forms that official recognition would take on ritual occasions. Ann Catherine Green, an eighteenth-century citizen of Maryland,

> married and bore fourteen children, eight of whom died before maturity. When her husband died also, she took over his printing business, assuming responsibility as editor of the *Maryland Gazette* and official printer of the colony. For

eight years she carried on the business, performing the same work and receiving the same payment from the government, as had her husband. Yet upon her death, the obituary read: "she was of a mild and benevolent disposition, and for conjugal affection and parental tenderness, an example of her sex." (Chafe, 1977, p. 21)

Women of Color

Historically, the experiences of women of color have differed dramatically from those of white women. If we consider only the present time period, it may appear that women of color and white women have certain experiences in common: relatively low economic position, being the target of discriminatory practices in education and in work, and overall marginality in the power structure. But women of color and white women have reached their present circumstances through very different histories. Although white women's status was clearly inferior to that of white men, they were treated with deference, and they shared in the status privileges of their husbands. African American women almost never had the option of choosing between work and leisure, as did some white women. They were not included in the image of the "colonial housewife." African American women were not considered "weak" females, but were treated more like beasts of burden (King, 1975, p. 121). Thus these women of color suffered a double oppression of sexism and racism.

Nowhere is this double oppression more clearly demonstrated than within the institution of slavery, which became established in late seventeenth- and early eighteenth-century colonial society, largely as a result of the demand for

Five generations of a family on Smith's Plantation, Beaufort, South Carolina.

cheap agricultural labor, especially within the southern plantation economy. Historians estimate that the slave population in the United States, Caribbean, and Brazil consisted of 9.5 million blacks. More than double that number are estimated to have died in transit to the New World (Anderson, 1996, p. 101). Slave women in the Southern colonies were without doubt the most exploited of all women. They were exploited not only as workers but as breeders of slaves. The following advertisement was typical of the time:

> **Negroes for Sale:** A girl about twenty years of age (raised in Virginia) and her two female children, four and the other two years old—remarkably strong and healthy. Never having had a day's sickness with the exception of the smallpox in her life. She is prolific in her generating qualities and affords a rare opportunity to any person who wished to raise a family of strong and healthy servants for their own use. (Flexner, 1959, p. 21)

Slave women were also sometimes exploited as sex objects for white men. Like male slaves, they were considered intrinsically inferior. Slaves were property, not people. They faced severe cultural and legal restrictions: Their family lives were controlled by their owners, their children were not their own, and their educational opportunities were almost nonexistent (Almquist, 1979, p. 46).

Sojourner Truth, formerly a slave and an activist in the abolitionist and women's rights movements, eloquently expressed the differences in treatment, under slavery, of black and white women: "That man over there says that women need to be helped into carriages and lifted over ditches, and to have the best place everywhere. Nobody ever helped me into carriages, or over mud puddles, or gives me any best place . . . and ain't I a woman?" (Truth, 1851, quoted in Almquist, 1979, p. 61).

Before the Civil War, a black woman in one of the "cotton states," working on one of the larger plantations, would have been either a house servant or one of several million field hands who produced major cash crops. In the Southern plantation economy, we thus find a "bifurcated" concept of woman. The European woman became "the guardian of civilization," while the African American woman was "spared neither harsh labor nor harsh punishment" (Liu, 1994), although the experience of slaves differed depending on the economic status and individual personality of the slave owner. Even pregnancy did not deter some slave masters from cruel treatment: "One particular method of whipping pregnant slaves was used throughout the South; they were made to lie face down in a specially dug depression in the ground, a practice that provided simultaneously for the protection of the fetus and the abuse of its mother" (Jones, 1985, p. 21).

Some white women benefited from such slave labor and shared with their husbands the role of oppressor, although the slave-mistress relationship was psychologically complex: "In their role as labor managers, mistresses lashed out at slave women not only to punish them, but also to vent their anger on victims even more wronged than themselves. We may speculate that, in the female slave, the white woman saw the source of her own misery, but she also saw herself— a woman without rights or recourse, subject to the whims of an egotistical man"

(Jones, 1985, p. 25). Conflict between white and African American women often resulted in violence, in which "mistresses were likely to attack with any weapon available—knitting needles, tongs, a fork, butcher knife, ironing board, or pan of boiling water" (Jones, 1985, pp. 25–26). Yet, while the relationship was often filled with strife, white and African American women "also shared a world of physical and emotional intimacy that is uncommon among women of antagonistic classes and different races" (Fox-Genovese, 1988. p. 25).

Slavery was justified by notions of race involving the "biological superiority" of the colonists. It was assumed that Europeans in the colonies made up an easily identifiable and discrete biological and social entity; a "natural" community of class interests, racial attributes, political and social affinities, and superior culture. This was, of course, not exactly true, but given that the differences between white skin and black skin were more noticeable than many of the differences among Europeans themselves, and given that whites were in dominant positions politically and socially, it could easily *seem* to be true.

Slave families often resisted the oppressive workloads by banding together to help one another in the fields and to lessen the workloads of older, weaker, or sicker workers. The extended family was of vital importance under the slave system. African American mothers labored most of the day, some of them caring for white women's families, while their own children were left under the care of grandmothers and old or disabled slaves. While the two-parent, nuclear family may have been the most typical form of slave cohabitation (Gutman, 1974; Jones, 1985, p. 32), close relatives were often very much involved in family life. Stevenson's (1996) study suggests that in colonial and antebellum Virginia the slave family was a "malleable extended family that, when possible, provided its members with nurture, education, socialization, material support, and recreation in the face of the potential social chaos that the slaveholder imposed" (p. 160).

Even though African American men were unable to own property, to provide protection and support for their children, or to work within the public sphere, there was a sexual division within the slave household. Men collected the firewood and made furniture—beds, tables, chairs—and other articles of wood, such as animal traps, butter paddles, and ax handles. They also wove baskets and made shoes. African American women grew, prepared, and preserved foods; spun thread, wove and dyed cloth, and sewed clothes; and made soap and candles (Jones, 1985, pp. 30, 36).

In the North, while slavery was an accepted practice, it was not nearly as widespread. Many African American women worked as free laborers as domestic servants; others worked as spinners, weavers, and printers (Wertheimer, 1977). Historian Carol Berkin (1996, p. 125) gives us a sense of what life was like for women slaves in the Northern colonies:

> A slave woman in these Northern cities spent her days engaged in housework—cooking, cleaning, washing and ironing, tending the fields and the gardens, and looking after her master's children. She passed her nights sleeping in the garret or the kitchen. She might be hired out to nurse the sick, to put in a neighbor's garden, to preserve food or wait on tables for a special occasion, but few

urban slave women were ever hired our to learn a craft. Colonial artisans considered their shops a male domain.

Some enslaved women both in the middle colonies and in New England "resisted, ran away, and rebelled" (Berkin, 1996, p. 127). Slave rebellions were rare during this time, but in the 1712 Slave Revolt of New York City, several women slaves actively participated and were sent to prison. It was also a woman slave who was the first to ask for a "petition for freedom" to the then newly constituted state legislature of Massachusetts in 1782. Berkin (1996, p. 127) notes that the "woman, Belinda, pressed these Revolutionaries to make good on their state constitution's pledge to discontinue slavery, stating her case with eloquence: 'I have not yet enjoyed the benefits of creation. . . . I beg freedom.'"

Emancipation had important implications for black women's family and work roles. The economic hardship experienced by both men and women after being freed from slavery served to create problems concerning the division of power and authority within the family. Prior to emancipation, married slaves often lived on different plantations, which made it difficult to come to joint decisions regarding family life, and often decisions regarding family life were made for them by slave owners. As a result, one historian observes, "the sources and degree of male authority in black households were both unclear and contested in the postwar period. One freeman, angry over his wife's infidelity, wrote to the Freedman's bureau and asked: 'Can I not by moderate chatisement compel her to obey me? If she insists on leaving me can I not keep the children?'" (Anderson, 1996, p. 163).

The severe economic oppression black men confronted after slavery sometimes resulted in the abandonment of their breadwinner role altogether. Some women did not want to continue their marriages while others could not find their husbands or found that their husband had died or were already married someone else. All these factors often left black women as the sole economic and emotional supporters of their children and dependents. Thus, it was of little surprise that by 1940, more than three times as many married black women than married white women reported that their husbands were "absent" (14 percent vs. 4 percent). The problem was even more common in urban areas, where "5 percent of white and 19 percent of black married women did not live with their husbands" (Anderson, 1996, p. 168).

Black women's work roles after slavery continued to remain within the agricultural or domestic service occupations, with 90 percent working within these occupations. It was not until post–World World II period that black women experienced significant occupational change (Anderson, 1996, pp. 184; also, see Figure 2.2 later in this chapter).

Native American Women

The work and family life experience of Native American women prior to European colonization differed depending on the region of the country and the type of tribal society. But in every Native American nation, women played very important roles in the economic life of their communities:

They had to be resourceful in utilizing every aspect of the environment to sustain life and engaging in cultural exchanges to incorporate new productive techniques. They gathered wild plants for food, herbs for medicines and dyes, clay for pottery, bark and reeds for weaving cloth. In many nations, they also tilled the soil and sowed the seeds, cultivated and harvested, made cloth and clothing, dried vegetables, and ground grains for breads. In hunting societies, they cured the meats and dried the skins. They also assisted in the hunt in some cultures. (Anderson, 1996, p. 21)

As a general rule, men hunted and women engaged in agricultural work. The more important hunting was to a community's survival, the more extensive the male power within the community; the greater the dependence on agriculture, the greater the power and independence of women (Berkin, 1996, p. 58). Women had the responsibility for raising children and maintaining hearth and home. Men engaged in hunting, fishing, and warfare.

In the East especially, many Indian communities were predominantly agricultural. Women constituted the agricultural labor force within these communities. An English woman who was held captive by a Seneca tribe observed that

Household duties were simple and Seneca women, unlike English wives and daughters, were not slaves to the spinning wheel or the needle. In the summer, the women went out each morning to the fields, accompanied by their children, to work cooperatively and in the company of friends and relatives, planting and tending the corn, beans, and squash at a pace geared to their individual rhythms and skills rather than to the demands of an overseer. They moved from field to field, completing the same tasks in each before returning to the first. (Berkin, 1996, pp. 61–62)

Apsaroke woman scraping hide.

Women within agricultural communities would often maintain control over tools and land—as well as any surplus foods they gathered from the land. This often enabled them (especially elderly women who were heads of households) to garner some political clout within their tribal communities. For instance, if Iroquois women opposed war on certain occasions, they might refuse to let the men have the cornmeal they would have needed to feed their raiding parties or armies (Berkin, 1996, p. 62). These communities often had a matrilineal family structure (inheritance and family name were through the female line, with family connections through the mother) and matrilocal residence (upon marriage a man lived with his mother-in-law's relatives).

Through the lens of the white colonist, the work roles and family structure of Native American society appeared deviant and, in some cases, perverse. After all, English society was characterized by a patriarchal family structure with patrilocal residence:

> To Europeans, Indian family patterns raised the specter of promiscuous women, freed from accountability to their fathers and husbands for the offspring they produced. . . . Equally incomprehensible—and thus perverse—to many Europeans were the work roles accepted by Indian men and women. In the world the English knew, farming was labor and farmers were male. Masculinity was linked, inexorably, to agriculture: household production and family reproduction defined femininity. That Indian men hunted was not a sufficient counter-

Arikara woman gathering rush.

poise, for, in the England of the seventeenth century, hunting was a sport, not an occupation. Many concluded that Indian men were effeminate, lazy; Indian women were beasts of burden, slaves to unmanly men. (Berkin, 1996, pp. 59–60)

European colonization and conquest pushed Native Americans off their land, depriving them of food and livelihood, culture and traditions. Disease or warfare demolished whole societies. Others were radically transformed, especially with regard to the traditional gender and work roles. Having used military force to remove Native Americans from their lands onto reservations, the U.S. government "began a systematic effort to destroy their cultures and replace them with the values and practices of middle-class whites" (Anderson, 1996, p. 27).

Confined to relatively small reservations, Native American men could no longer hunt as extensively as before (nor, defeated by U.S. forces, could they any longer carry on warfare). They therefore needed to redefine their social roles and to find new economic activities. In many a Native American tribe, the men took over agriculture, traditionally the women's work. Family structure also changed, at the prompting of missionaries and others, including government officials, to become more like that of the Europeans, with less emphasis on the matrilineal extended family and more on the nuclear family and the husband-wife relationship.

The Arrival of Industrialization

The transformation from an agrarian rural economy to an urban industrial society ushered in a new era in women's work. With the advent of industrialization, many of the products women made at home—clothes, shoes, candles—gradually came to be made instead in factories. For a while, women still performed the work at home, using the new machines. Merchants would contract for work to be done, supplying women with the machines and the raw materials to be made into finished articles. The most common of these manufacturing trades for women was sewing for the newly emerging clothing industry. Since women had always sewn for their families, this work was considered an extension of women's traditional role, and therefore a respectable activity. As the demand for goods increased, however, home production declined and gave way to the factory system, which was more efficient in meeting emerging needs.

The rise of factory production truly separated the home from the workplace. With the decline of the household unit as the center of industrial and economic activity, the importance of women's economic role also declined. Male and female spheres of activity became more separated, as did the definitions of men's and women's roles. Man's role continued to be primarily that of worker and provider; woman's role became primarily supportive. She was to maintain a smooth and orderly household, to be cheerful and warm, and thus to provide the husband with the support and services he needed to continue his work life (Kessler-Harris, 1981, p. 35). The industrial revolution created a set of social and economic conditions in which the basic lifestyle of white middle-class women more nearly approached society's expectations concerning woman's role. More and more middle-class women could now aspire to the status formerly reserved for the upper classes—that of "lady" (Chafe, 1977). The nineteenth-century concept of a lady was that of a fragile, idle, pure creature, submissive and subservient to her husband and to domestic needs. Her worth was based on her decorative value, a quality that embraced her beauty, her virtuous character, and her temperament. She was certainly not a paid employee. This ideal was later referred to as the "cult of true womanhood" because of its rigid, almost religious standards (Gordon, Buhle, and Schrom, 1971, p. 28).

Biological and social arguments were also often used to justify women's exclusion from the labor force. Women were seen as too weak and delicate to participate in the rough work world of men. It was believed they lacked strength and stamina, that their brains were small, that the feminine perspective and sensitivity were liabilities in the marketplace. Such arguments rationalized women's accepting the roles of homemaker and mother almost exclusively, as the industrial revolution spread across the country (Kessler-Harris, 1981, p. 14).

During the early years of industrialization, however, because many men were still primarily occupied with agricultural work and were unavailable or unwilling to enter the early factories, male laborers were in short supply. American industry depended, then, on a steady supply of women workers. Yet how could society tolerate women's working in the factories, given the dominant ideology of the times, which dictated that a woman's place was at home? Single white women provided one answer. Their employment was viewed as a fulfillment of their family responsibilities, during an interlude before marriage.

The employment of young, single women in the early Lowell (Massachusetts) mills is a prime example of the reconciliation of ideology with the needs of industry. Francis Cabot Lowell devised a respectable route into employment for such women. Recruiting the daughters of farm families to work in his mill, which opened in 1821 in Lowell, he provided supervised boardinghouses, salaries sufficient to allow the young women to offer financial aid to their families or to save for their own trousseaux, and assurances to their families that the hard work and discipline of the mill would help prepare them for marriage and motherhood (Kessler-Harris, 1975). The boardinghouse was the center of social life for young factory workers, integrating them into an urban life style and factory life. The average boardinghouse erected in the mid-1830s consisted of series of apartments arranged in a long housing block. Twenty-five residents usually comprised each house, with up to six living in each room. The women had little privacy and, as historian Thomas Dublin (1979, p. 80) observes, " . . . pressure to conform to group standards must have been strong."

Work life in the mills was arduous and the hours were long. Hannah Borden, noted to be the "best weaver of her day," learned how to weave when she was eight and became one of the first weavers to work at the mills in Fall River, Massachusetts, in 1817 (Wertheimer, 1977, p. 66). Historian Barbara Mayer Wertheimer (1977, p. 65) gives us a sense of the typical daily routine for mill girls like Hannah Borden:

The factory bell woke her at 4:00 in the morning. Taking her breakfast along, she readied her looms by 5:00, when the bell signaled the start of work. At 7:30 it announced the breakfast break, and called workers back afterward. At noon it rang the half-hour lunch period, and at 12:30 summoned them back. It dismissed them at 7:30 each evening, unless they worked overtime. When they got back to their boardinghouses at night, they were often too tired to eat. At 10:00 the bell rang for bed and lights out. Sundays it called them to church.

Even though their work day was long, many women still found the time and strength "to organize and attend lectures, forums, and language classes, sewing groups, and literary improvement circles" (Wertheimer, 1977, p. 65). The literary journal *The Lowell Offering* was written "by and for" mill women. "The women who wrote for the *Offering* . . . found an outlet for their talents and a vindication of their role as millworkers; they portrayed themselves in a dignified light, and this gave status to their work" (Wertheimer, 1977, p. 66).

While employment in the mills gave many young women a sense of independence and filled an important economic need for their families, working life in the mills began to deteriorate in the 1830s. Absentee owners allowed the factory supervisors to have complete control over their workforce. They initiated work rules that provided little time for women to have their meals and strict punishments if they did not comply with company policy: "So little time was allowed for meals—one half-hour at noon for dinner—that the women raced from the hot humid weaving rooms several blocks to their boardinghouses, gulped down their main meal of the day, and ran back to the mill in terror of being fined if they were late" (Wertheimer, 1977, p. 66).

As the power and authority of mill management continued to become more oppressive, women's resentment toward mill owners erupted into several strikes. In February 1834 and October 1836, the women of Lowell Mill went out on strike to protest a reduction in their wages and an increase in the board rate charged for their company housing. The solidarity women gained through their years of community living, and the formation of the Factory Girls' Association in 1834, assisted them in their ability to organize. Eight hundred women took part in the in the 1834 strike, and this number nearly doubled for the 1836 strike (Dublin, 1979, pp. 86–88; Wertheimer, 1977, pp. 68, 70). The testimony of Harriet Hanson, who was only eleven years old at the time, provides a gripping account of happened during the 1836 strike:

> I worked in a lower room where I had heard the proposed strike fully, if not vehemently, discussed; I had been an ardent listener to what was said against this attempt at "oppression" on the part of the corporation, and naturally I took sides with the strikers. When the day came on which the girls were to turn out, those in the upper rooms started first, and so many of them left that our mill was at once shut down. Then, when the girls in my room stood irresolute, uncertain what to do. . . . I, who began to think they would not go out after all their talk, became impatient, and started on ahead, saying with childish bravado, "I don't care what you do, I am going to turn out, whether anyone else does or not"; and I marched out, and was followed by the others. . . . I was more proud that I have ever been since at any success I may have achieved and more

proud than I shall ever be again until my own beloved State gives to its women citizens the right of suffrage." (Wertheimer 1977, p. 70)

While few labor organizations arose among women textile workers in the 1830s, these early protests eventually paved the way for future strikes and the eventual movement of women into organized labor (see Dublin, 1979, pp. 88–89).

In the early industrial era, working conditions were arduous and hours were long. By the late 1830s, immigration began to supply a strongly competitive, permanent workforce willing to be employed for low wages in the factories, under increasingly mechanized and hazardous conditions. By the late 1850s, most of the better-educated, single, native-born women had left the mills, leaving newly immigrated women (both single and married) and men to fill these positions.

While women thus played a crucial role in the development of the textile industry, the first important manufacturing industry in America, women also found employment in many other occupations during the process of industrialization. As railroads and other business enterprises expanded and consolidated,

Young working women in the mills of Lowell, Massachusetts (circa 1860).

women went to work in these areas as well. In fact, the U.S. Labor Commissioner reported that by 1890 only 9 out of 360 general groups to which the country's industries had been assigned did not employ women (Baker, 1964).

By 1900, more than five million women or girls, or about one in every five of those ten years old and over, had become a paid employee (Baker, 1964). The largest proportion (40 percent) remained close to home in domestic and personal service, but domestic service was on the decline for white working-class women at the turn of the century. About 25 percent (1.3 million) of employed women worked in the manufacturing industries: in cotton mills, in the manufacture of woolen and worsted goods, silk goods, hosiery, and knitwear. The third largest group of employed women (over 18 percent) were working on farms. Women in the trade and transportation industries (about 10 percent) worked as saleswomen, telegraph and telephone operators, stenographers, clerks, copyists, accountants, and bookkeepers. Women in the professions (about 9 percent, and typically young, educated, single, and of native-born parentage) were employed primarily in elementary and secondary teaching or nursing. Other professions—law, medicine, business, college teaching—tended to exclude women. The fastest growing of these occupational groups were manufacturing, trade, and transportation. In the last thirty years of the nineteenth century, the number of women working in trade and transportation rose from 19,000 to over half a million (Baker, 1964). These women also tended to be young, single, native-born Americans; immigrants and minority women were excluded from these white-collar positions (Smuts, 1971).

Only a small minority of married, working-class women, with the exception of African American women, worked away from their homes during this time. Most continued to be heavily involved in childbearing and child-rearing and in the heavy responsibility for the domestic work within the family unit. Even fewer middle-class wives worked outside of the home; those who did work tended to be divorced, widowed, or supporting disabled or unemployed husbands (Pleck, 1979, p. 367). Among many immigrant groups, cultural traditions of male authority effectively discouraged married women from working, even when the husband was unemployed and the family's economic situation was precarious. Immigrant wives with jobs not infrequently withdrew from the marketplace when family finances permitted, "to pursue the goal, often elusive, of equipping their children to join the middle class" (Brownlee and Brownlee, 1976, p. 31).

Although at least some working-class men were becoming successful in large enterprises and in the professions, working-class women were limited to low-paying jobs and unskilled jobs that carried little if any promise of advancement. The single, white woman workers were never fully integrated into the workforce, either. The young ones were assumed to be working only temporarily—until they married. Women who complained of low wages were often asked "but haven't you a male friend that helps support you?" (Baker, 1964). The older ones were considered "spinsters"—women who had been unsuccessful in getting a husband and who had substituted work for family life (Grossman, 1975).

In addition, sexual harassment was a growing occupational hazard affecting women in almost every occupation. In 1908, *Harper's Bazaar* printed a series of letters in which working women wrote of these difficulties. The following letter, from a woman seeking a job as a stenographer, describes such an experience:

> I purchased several papers, and plodded faithfully through their multitude of "ads." I took the addresses of some I intended to call upon. . . . The first "ad" I answered the second day was that of a doctor who desired a stenographer at once, good wages paid. It sounded rather well, I thought, and felt that this time I would meet a gentleman. The doctor was very kind and seemed to like my appearance and references; as to salary, he offered me $15 a week, with a speedy prospect of more. As I was leaving his office, feeling that at last I was launched safely upon the road to a good living, he said casually, "I have an auto; and as my wife doesn't care for that sort of thing, I shall expect you to accompany me frequently on pleasure trips." That settled the doctor; I never appeared. After that experience I was ill for two weeks. (*Harper's Bazaar*, 1908, quoted in Bularzik, 1978, p. 25)

Women's working conditions were also aggravated by women's exclusion from the organized labor movements of the day, which were steadily improving conditions for men. For the first half of the nineteenth century, unions—which were primarily for craft and skilled workers—did not accept female members (Wertheimer, 1977, p. 341). By 1920, only 7 percent of women workers belonged to trade unions, compared with 25 percent of male workers (Baxandall, Gordon, and Reverby, 1976, p. 255). In a number of industries, women formed their own unions, but these affected only a small minority of those employed. The Working Girl's Societies, the Women's Trade Union League, and other such groups tried to little avail to change the widely held beliefs that women were temporary workers whose motivation was to earn pocket money, or who, if they had other goals, were selfish creatures ignoring family responsibilities. Such attitudes persisted well into the twentieth century (Gordon et al., 1971, p. 43).

While women's labor organizations were not initially successful in directly achieving their goals, they did develop a sense of unity among working women. This was an important step in the future formation of a women's movement. The industrial revolution pushed women from the domestic sphere into the factory, where they worked alongside one another. The result was an interchange of ideas, values, and attitudes, and the subsequent ability to share common concerns and dreams—a phenomenon that would not have been possible if they remained agrarian homemakers. Economic historian Ivy Pinchbeck (1930; 1969, p. 307) observes that the movement of women into the industrial workforce benefited women by the "wider experience and more varied interests they gained by working together in a community." Pinchbeck's observation is echoed by another contemporary chronicler of the industrial revolution, Caroline Foley. Writing in 1894, Foley noted that "the factory and workshop take the girl out of 'the home,' cribbed, cabined, and confined as to space, light, air, ideas and companionship, mould her in habits of punctuality, promptness, handiness, gumption, and sustained attention and effort, spur her on to work well, bring our her capacities for comradeship and social action, and train her in self-respect, self-reliance and courage" (Foley, 1894, p. 187, as cited in Pinchbeck, 1969, p. 308).

By the turn of the century, the labor market had become clearly divided according to gender, race, and class. Fewer manufacturing jobs were being defined as suitable for white women, especially with the rising dominance of heavy industry employment for which female workers were considered too delicate. Working-class women were increasingly devalued by their continued participation in activities men had primarily taken over (such as factory work), because these activities were regarded as lacking in the Victorian virtue and purity called for by the "cult of true womanhood." As the economy expanded and prosperity came to more and more white middle-class families, middle-class women could "become ladies." A "woman's place" was still defined as at home. If these women did work outside the home, the appropriate occupation was a white-collar job (sales, clerical, and professional occupations). White women's occupations shifted from primarily domestic service—which became increasingly identified as "black women's work"—and from light manufacturing to the rapidly growing opportunities in office and sales work. These jobs were also considered more appropriate for feminine roles as defined by the cult of true womanhood. Women of color did not share in this occupational transformation. In 1910, for example, nine out of ten African American women worked as agricultural laborers or domestics, compared with three out of ten white women (Aldridge, 1975, p. 53).

The Legacy of Slavery

African American women were not part of the "cult of true womanhood." They were not sheltered or protected from the harsh realities and, "while many white daughters were raised in genteel refined circumstances, most black daughters were forced to deal with poverty, violence and a hostile outside world from childhood on" (Chafe, 1977, p. 53). After emancipation, their employment and economic opportunities were limited, in part because the skills they had learned on the plantation transferred to relatively few jobs, and those only of low pay and status.

African American women's concentration in service work—especially domestic work—was largely a result of limited opportunities available to them following the Civil War. The only factory employment open to them was in the Southern tobacco and textile industries, and until World War I most African American working women were farm laborers, domestics, or laundresses. Life as a domestic worker in 1912 sounds remarkably like life as a slave:

> I am a Negro woman, and I was born and reared in the South. I am now past forty years of age and am the mother of three children. My husband died nearly fifteen years ago. . . . For more than thirty years—or since I was ten years old—I have been a servant . . . in white families. . . . During the last ten years I have been a nurse. . . . I frequently work from fourteen to sixteen hours a day. . . . I am allowed to go home to my children, the oldest of whom is a girl of eighteen years, only once in two weeks, every other Sunday afternoon—even then I am not permitted to stay all night. I not only have to nurse a little white child, now eleven months old, but I have to act as playmate . . . to three other chil-

dren in the home, the oldest of whom is only nine years of age. . . . I see my own children only when they happen to see me on the streets when I am out with the children, or when my children come to the "yard" to see me, which isn't often. . . . You might as well say that I'm on duty all the time—from sunrise to sunrise, every day of the week. I am the slave, body and soul, of this family, and what do I get for this work? . . . Ten dollars a month. (Anonymous, 1912, quoted in Lerner, 1972, pp. 227–228)

Following the abolition of slavery, African American women faced a great deal of opposition as they entered the labor force. As observed by historian Rosalyn Terborg-Penn (1985), to ensure the survival of their communities African Americans had to traverse the harsh realities of racism and sexism left by the legacy of slavery. African American women developed unique organizational forms of assistance based upon mutual aid and support that did not follow the contours of the typical labor unions that were developing among the working classes. These organizational forms were rooted in traditional African culture, "where women had a long tradition of self-organization for mutual support in relation to most life activities, including work. Labor was an essential role and responsibility in traditional Africa, and indeed, women's labor output generally far surpassed that of men" (Terborg-Penn, 1985, p. 140).

Despite the limited range of job opportunities, a relatively large proportion of African American women were employed. The legacy of slavery may partly account for the relatively high labor-force participation rate of African American women. Although women's labor-force participation rate is generally lower than men's, African American women's participation rate was historically much higher than that of white women. Thus, for example, white women's labor-force participation in 1890 was 16.3 percent, while African American women's rate was 39.7 percent (Goldin, 1977, p. 87). Even today, African American women have a higher rate of participation than their white counterparts: 62.9 percent versus 59.7 percent (Bureau of Labor Statistics, 2003b).

World War I and the Depression

World War I accelerated the entry of white women into new fields of industry. The pressure of war production and the shortage of male industrial workers necessitated the hiring of women for what had been male-dominated occupations. Women replaced men at jobs in factories and business offices, and, in general, they kept the nation going, fed, and clothed. The mechanization and routinization of industry during this period enabled women to quickly master the various new skills. For the most part, this wartime pattern involved a reshuffling of the existing female workforce, rather than an increase in the numbers of women employed. Although the popular myth is that homemakers abandoned their kitchens for machine shops or airplane hangars, only about 5 percent of women workers were new to the labor force during the war years. Figure 2.2 shows that there was a significant decrease in the number of white women employed in domestic occupations (cleaners, laundresses, dressmakers, seamstresses, and servants) and a sharp increase in the number of female office workers, laborers in manufacturing, saleswomen in stores, schoolteachers, telephone operators, and trained nurses.

Thus the wartime labor shortage temporarily created new job opportunities for women workers, and at higher wages than they had previously earned. This was not necessarily the case for African American women, however. Although World War I opened up some factory jobs to them, these were typically limited to the most menial, least desirable, and often the most dangerous jobs—jobs already rejected by white women. These jobs included some of the most dangerous tasks in industry, such as carrying glass to hot ovens in glass factories and dyeing furs in the furrier industry (Greenwald, 1980, p. 26).

World War I produced no substantial or lasting change in women's participation in the labor force. The employment rate of women in 1920 was actually a bit lower (20.4 percent) than in 1910 (20.9 percent). The labor unions, the government, and the society at large were not ready to accept a permanent shift in women's economic role. Instead, women filled an urgent need during the wartime years and were relegated to their former positions as soon as peace returned. As the reformer Mary Von Kleeck wrote, "When the immediate dangers . . . were passed, the prejudices came to life once more" (quoted in Chafe, 1972, p. 54).

Factory Worker, circa 1920.

Figure 2.2. Increase and Decrease in the Number of Women Employed in the Principal Nonagricultural Occupations, 1910–1920. *Source:* U.S. Bureau of the Census, 1929).

When the men returned from the war, they were given priority in hiring and, although a number of women left the labor force voluntarily, many were forced out by layoffs. Those remaining were employed in the low-paying, low-prestige positions women had always occupied and in those occupations that had become accepted as women's domain. For example, although during the war some women had worked in nontraditional occupations (such as machinists) in the railroads, after the war the railroads employed women only as typists, card punchers, accountants, receptionists, file clerks, janitresses, laundresses, and railroad matrons (Greenwald, 1980). Many women resented having been encouraged to enter a nontraditional occupation only to be fired at the war's end. One who had been employed as a laborer in a machine shop during the war wrote to the director general of the railroad administration in hopes of restoring such jobs:

> We are women that needed the work very much. [O]ne woman gave her only support to the army [;] one has her aged Father[;] another has a small son [;] and I support my disabled Sister . . . We never took a soldier's place, a soldier would not do the work we did . . . such as sweeping, picking up waste and paper and hauling steel shavings . . . We are . . . respectable but poor women and were liked and respected by all who knew us . . . Women's work is so very hard to find that time of year and expenses are so high with Liberty bonds and insurance to pay and home expenses it is hard to get by. We like our job very much and I hope you will do for us whatever you can and place us back at the shop. (quoted in Greenwald, 1980, p. 135)

The common image of women workers, even in business and the professions, was still that they were "temporary" employees (Chafe, 1972, p. 65).

The Great Depression of the 1930s threw millions out of work. In 1933, a quarter of the American labor force was unemployed, compared to about 3 percent in 1929. Business failures devastated both owners and workers. Total personal income plummeted from eighty-four billion in 1929 to forty-seven billion in 1933. Due to the shortage of employment opportunities, efforts to "maintain the family's claim on women appeared almost immediately on many fronts" (Kwolek-Folland, 1998, p. 145). To secure employment opportunities for men, married women were urged to stay out of the workplace. A 1936 Gallup Poll asked if women should work if their husbands were employed; 82 percent of those polled answered "no." Business leaders were bombarded with letters from the media, politicians, and others to terminate married women workers (Kwolek-Folland, 1998, p. 145). The attitude that emerged among Americans is clear in a letter from a private citizen named Earl Leiby to President Roosevelt in 1933. It read, in part, that "homes are being wrecked daily due to the fact that married women are permitted to work in factories and offices. . . . You and we all know that the place for a wife and mother is at home. . . . These women's husbands would naturally be paid a higher salary, inasmuch as male employees demand a higher salary than females" (as quoted in Kessler-Harris, 1990, p. 57).

This national sentiment resulted in people turning to both the state and federal governments for a response. For example, in 1933 the National Economy Act only allowed one federal salary per married couple. What inevitably followed was that many women were forced to resign out of practicality, due to the fact that their husbands almost always earned higher wages (Kwolek-Folland, 1998, p. 145).

As this Depression-era situation unfolded, however, efforts to keep women—especially those who were married—out of the workforce were not very successful. In fact, during the 1930s, an increasing number of women went to work for the first time. The increase was most marked among younger, married women, who worked at least until they had their first child, and among older, married women, who re-entered the marketplace because of dire economic need or in response to changing patterns of consumer demand (Scharf, 1980, p. 158). The disappearance of "male jobs" in manufacturing and heavy industry—combined with the rising prominence of "female jobs" in white-collar, light industry, and service arenas—allowed women to increase their numbers in the workforce during the Depression (Kwolek-Folland, 1998, p. 145). Even though these "female jobs" usually had pay scales that were significantly lower than "male jobs," the income women earned was enough to clothe and feed the children of many families that suffered from this devastating economic downturn (Kwolek-Folland, 1998, p. 145). Still, many of the jobs held by women were often parttime, seasonal, and considered marginal. In sum, women's labor-force participation increased slowly throughout this period and into the early 1940s (see Figure 2.1), except in the professions (including feminized professions such as elementary teaching, nursing, librarianship, and social work). The proportion of women in all professions declined from 14.2 percent to 12.3 percent during the Depression decade (Scharf, 1980, p. 86).

World War II

The ordeal of World War II brought about tremendous change in the numbers and occupational distribution of working women. As during World War I, the shortage of male workers, who had gone off to fight, coupled with the mounting pressures of war production brought huge numbers of women into the workforce. A corresponding shift in attitudes about women's aptitudes and proper roles resulted (Trey, 1972, p. 40). Indeed, for women the "liberative potential of wartime changes is undeniable because the dislocations of a nation at war have always created important challenges to traditional assumptions and practices" (Anderson, 1981, p. 4). Women entered the munitions factories and other heavy industries to support the war effort. The War Manpower Commission instituted a massive advertising campaign to attract women to the war industries. Patriotic appeals were common:

> Women, let it be understood, have a double stake in the winning of this war. Citizens of the United States of America, and partners in the United Nations, they are in and a part of the common struggle to crush Fascism—the acknowledged Number One foe of the progress of women. No women are supernumerary. All must fight with their fathers, their husbands, their brothers, their sweethearts, to make certain that never again will dictators and aggressors such as Hitler, Mussolini, and Hirohito, have the freedom to rise and persecute and enslave and murder first their own people, and then peoples of other nations. The essence of Fascism is bullying individuals and whole races of people—and women and men alike must destroy this monstrous organism of fear and cruelty once and for all. (quoted in Anthony, 1943, p. 3)

During the war years, white women had access to skilled, higher-paying industrial jobs. Many women in industrial positions had worked before, but only at lower paying unskilled service jobs. Women now became switchmen, precision-tool makers, overhead-crane operators, lumberjacks, drill-press operators, and stevedores (Baxandall et al., 1976). Women in these jobs had to "toughen up." Polly Ann Stinnett Workman describes her experience as a welder at the Stockton-Pollock Navy Yard in California:

I was the only woman welder on the graveyard shift. I was welding fifty-foot walls in the hull of the ship. The working conditions were wonderful. As far as I'm concerned, it was the best job I've ever had. It gave me a sense of accomplishment. When I went in, they were working on a cost-plus job, and the first night I was there the supervisor took me around to get me on a crew, and nobody wanted me because I was a woman. They'd say, "We have all we need." Finally, the supervisor said to the leadman, "This is your welder."

They tried every way in the world to show me up. They put me on a cost-plus job, working out in the rain, on a big tunnel they had contracted . . . The tunnel was part of a ship. This was in January, which is the worst. We had to wear those heavy leather pants and jackets, and it was so cold you just darn near froze to death. When he put me on that job, I was terrified. There was all this loud noise, the shipwrights, the chippers, people dropping hammers and dropping metal; this was really terrifying to me but I didn't let them know it. (quoted in Wise and Wise, 1994, p. 135)

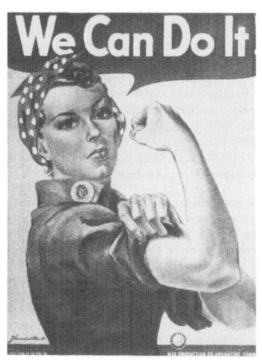

"We Can Do It" poster, circa 1943.

Airplane factory workers, circa 1944.

Equal work did not mean equal pay for the women in these varied wartime occupations. Although the National War Labor Board issued a directive to industries that stipulated equal pay for equal work, most employers continued to pay women at a lower rate. Furthermore, women had little opportunity to advance in their new occupations.

World War II marked an important turning point in women's participation in the paid labor force. The social prohibition concerning married women working gave way under wartime pressure, and women wartime workers demonstrated that it was possible for women to maintain their households while also assuming the role of breadwinner with outside employment. More women than ever before learned to accommodate the simultaneous demands of family and work. The experience "pointed the way to a greater degree of choice for American women" (Anderson, 1981, p. 174).

However, at the war's end, with the return of men to civilian life, there was tremendous public pressure on women to abandon their work roles; thus, for many it meant a return to the domestic sphere they had left behind before the war. Yet for some women, especially the poor and those in the working class, this return was not an option.

The post–World War II work environment for women was less than hospitable. It included a range of discriminatory employment and union practices— key among them was the preferential hiring of veterans. Women often found that the male-dominated jobs they held during the war were now out of reach; what were left were "female jobs," most of which were well below their skill levels and pay expectations (Anderson, 1981, p. 7). Thus, the late 1940s and 1950s marked the reestablishment of the sex-segregated labor market.

During this time, a new social ideology began to emerge; Betty Friedan (1963) later called it "the feminine mystique." This ideology drew in social workers, educators, journalists, and psychologists, all of whom tried to convince women that their place was again in the home. It was not unlike the "cult of true womanhood" advanced in the late 1800s to differentiate middle-class women from working-class women. As Friedan notes, in the fifteen years following World War II, the image of "women at home" rather than "at work" became a cherished and self-perpetuating core of contemporary American culture. A generation of young people were brought up to extol the values of home and family, and woman's role was defined as the domestic center around which all else revolved. Women were supposed to live like those in Norman Rockwell *Saturday Evening Post* illustrations. The idealized image was of smiling mothers baking cookies for their wholesome children, driving their station wagons loaded with freckled youngsters to an endless round of lessons and activities, returning with groceries and other consumer goods to the ranch houses they cared for with such pride. Women were supposed to revel in these roles and gladly leave the running of the world to men (Friedan, 1963, p. 14).

This image was nourished by the new psychological and child-development theories of the time. Psychoanalytic theory held that "biology is destiny" and that "a woman's personality was completely defined by her sex" (Anderson, 1981, p. 176). Meeting the needs of her family best fulfills a woman's needs, it was argued. These new "experts" maintained that women's employment during the war years had fostered certain individual neuroses and social maladjustments, which could be corrected only by women's return to a domestic (and subordinate and dependent) status. In this way, " 'Rosie the Riveter' was transformed with dizzying speed from a wartime heroine to a neurotic, castrating victim of penis envy" (Anderson, 1981, p. 176; also see Honey, 1984).

Along with these ideological arguments to bring women back to the home were important economic considerations. The traditional notion of women's place in the home became, after the war, integrally linked with the housewife's function as primary consumer of goods. The war had wound up the economy with massive production, inflation, growth, and low rates of unemployment. With the reduction in military spending, the country could not support full employment or continued industrial profits without an increase in a major market such as household goods. Both Federal Housing Administration-guaranteed loans and government-subsidized construction of commuter highways encouraged a general migration to the suburbs, where families would buy more household goods. Women were the key to this market, and homemaking was encouraged as a necessary stimulant to the postwar industrial economy (Baxandall et al., 1976, pp. 282–283).

Yet, unlike the post–World War I period, after World War II women did not go back to the kitchens. Instead, women's labor-force participation continued to increase throughout the post–World War II decades, so that by the late 1960s, 40 percent of American women were in the labor force, and by the beginning of the twenty-first century, 60 percent were. Who were the women most likely to be part of this "new majority" of women at work?

After World War II: The Rise of the Married Woman Worker

Between 1890 and the beginning of World War II, single women comprised at least half the female labor force. The others were mostly married African American, immigrant, or working-class women.

The decade of the 1940s saw a change in the type of woman worker, as increasing numbers of married women left their homes to enter the world of paid work (see Figure 2.3). Although single women continued to have the highest labor-force participation rates among women, during the 1940s the percentage of married women in the workforce grew more rapidly than any other category. Between 1940 and 1950, single women workers were in short supply because of low birthrates in the 1930s. Furthermore, those single women available for work were marrying at younger ages and leaving the labor market to raise their families. On the other hand, ample numbers of older, married women were available, and these women (who had married younger, had had fewer children, and were living longer) were eager for paid employment.

In 1940, about 15 percent of married women were employed; by 1950, 24 percent. This increase has continued: by 1960, 32 percent of married women; in 1970, over 41 percent; in 1980, 50 percent; and by 1995, 61 percent (U.S. Bureau of the Census, 1996a, p. 399); it continues to inch up slowly, and was 61.3 percent by the end of 2000 (U.S. Bureau of the Census, 2002a, Table 576, p. 372). Indeed, as the twenty-first century proceeds, we can see that labor-force

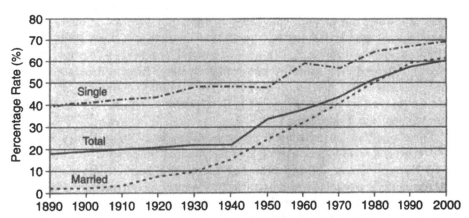

Figure 2.3. Women's Labor-Force Participation Rates by Marital Status, 1890–2000. *Sources:* Goldin (1977); U.S. Bureau of the Census (1996a, p. 399; 2002a, Table 576, p. 372).

participation rates of single and married women will become almost identical (Figure 2.3).

During the 1940s, 1950s, and 1960s, it was mainly older, married women entering the workforce. In 1957, for example, the labor-force participation rate among women aged forty-five to forty-nine years exceeded the rate for twenty to twenty-four-year-old women (Oppenheimer, 1970, p. 15). During the early 1960s, young married mothers with preschool- or school-age children began to enter the workforce. This trend continued for the next four decades; by the early 2000s, more than three-quarters of married women with children between six and seventeen years of age were employed, and, most significantly, almost two-thirds of those women with children under the age of six were in the labor force (see Table 2.1). In short, whereas before 1970 the overwhelming majority of married women stopped working after they had children, today the overwhelming majority of married women do not.

Organizing Women Laborers: The Role of Unions

Women have participated in the labor movement both as leaders and rank-and-file members. Indeed, women factory workers in the United States were among the first labor activists.

Historian Ruth Milkman (1985, p. xi) observes that feminist scholars do not agree on how the development of the labor movement in the United States affected women. In the view of some feminists, organized labor has been an "enemy" of women workers; for example, many unions prevented women from obtaining union cards, and discriminated against those women who did. From this vantage point, unions have reinforced and promoted gender inequality in the labor force. Other feminists, however, view unions more positively—observing, for example, that women in unions have historically fared better (higher wages, more benefits, healthier working conditions) than their nonunionized counterparts.

Indeed, unionization has helped women to increase their pay and to diminish the historical income gap between men and women. In 2002, union women earned about 30.8 percent more than nonunion women ($667 versus $510 per week; see Table 2.2). Women, in general, and women of color, in particular, are helped even more by union membership: African American union members earned 32.1 percent more than their nonunion counterparts, and for Latino workers the union advantage is 46.5 percent (versus 33.4 percent for white women; see Table 2.2).

The women's labor movement began in the early 1920s as factory workers in Pawtucket, Rhode Island, participated for the first time in a strike. Historian Philip Foner (1979, p. 29) observes that "about one hundred female weavers joined with male workers to protest a wage reduction and an attempt to increase working hours." The strikes at the Lowell mills in 1834 and 1836 continued women's large-scale efforts to demand fair treatment in the workplace regarding wages. Over the next several decades, this protest would grow into a series of more permanent labor organizations for women.

Table 2.1
WOMEN'S LABOR-FORCE PARTICIPATION RATES BY MARITAL STATUS AND PRESENCE AND AGE OF CHILDREN, 1960–2000

Year	Total			With Children Under 18			With Children 6–17			With Children Under 6		
	Single	Married	Other	Single	Married	Other	Single	Married	Other	Single	Married	Other
1960	44.1	30.5	40.0	n/a	27.6	56.0	n/a	39.0	65.9	n/a	18.6	40.5
1970	53.0	40.8	39.1	n/a	39.7	60.7	n/a	49.2	66.9	n/a	30.3	52.2
1980	61.5	50.1	44.0	52.0	54.1	69.4	67.6	61.7	74.6	44.1	45.1	60.3
1990	66.4	58.2	46.8	55.2	66.3	74.2	69.7	73.6	79.7	48.7	58.9	63.6
2000	68.6	62.0	50.2	73.9	70.6	82.7	79.7	77.2	85.0	70.5	62.8	76.6

Source: U.S. Bureau of the Census (1996a, p. 400; 2002a, Table 577, p. 373).

Table 2.2
UNION AFFILIATION AND MEDIAN WEEKLY EARNINGS OF FULL-TIME WAGE AND
SALARY WORKERS BY SEX, RACE, AND LATINO ORIGINS, 2002

	Percent Unionized	Median Weekly Wages Union Workers	Nonunion Workers	Ratio of Union to Nonunion Wages (%)
Men	14.7	780	652	119.6
White	12.8	804	674	119.3
African American	18.2	651	502	129.7
Latino	11.1	666	422	157.8
Women	12.8	667	510	130.8
White	10.9	695	521	133.4
African American	15.7	588	445	132.1
Latina	9.8	558	381	146.5

Source: U.S. Department of Labor (2002a, 2002b).

The Ten-Hour Movement in the 1840s, which pressed for ten hours as the legal limit to the work day in factories, helped to forge a new labor movement emerging in the Lowell mills (Dublin, 1979, p. 108). This movement was instrumental in reforming working conditions for women laborers. By January of 1845, the Lowell Female Labor Reform Association had established—due in no small part to the efforts of a new class of female labor activists, such as Sarah Bagley and Huldah J. Stone. Within six months, almost five hundred women were members. Bagley was elected to the position of president, while Stone was voted in as secretary (Wertheimer, 1977, p. 73).

In their struggle to gain fair wages and better working conditions, women activists also came to a new understanding of their own identity concerning what it meant to be a woman worker. "In the course of the labor struggles of the 1840s, women activists came to a new sense of the 'sisterhood' of working women and developed a critique of the 'cult of true womanhood,' that ideology of women's sphere that evolved in the period and was expressed in popular women's magazines and domestic advice books" (Dublin, 1979, pp. 125–126).

Sarah Bagley was aware of the crossing of traditional gender boundaries in women's attempts at union organizing. She spoke to these concerns in a speech before the first convention of the workingmen's association in 1845: "For the last half a century, it has been deemed a violation of women's sphere to appear before the public as a speaker, but when our rights are trampled upon and we appeal in vain to legislators, what shall we do but appeal to the voice of the people?" (from *The Voice of Industry*, June 5, 1845, as quoted in Wertheimer, 1977, p. 73).

Women's participation in reform movements had to upend some central perspectives on women's traditional role within society, and this permeated down to the rank-and-file. As one female factory worker bemoaned society's traditional view of women's roles and the narrowness of this view:

Woman is never thought to be out of her sphere, at home; in the nursery, in the kitchen, over a hot stove cooking from morning till evening—over a wash-tub, or toiling in a cotton factory fourteen hours per day. But let her once step out, plead the cause of right and humanity, plead the wrongs of her slave sis-ter of the South or of the operative of the North, or even attempt to teach the science of Physiology, and a cry is raised against her, "of out of her sphere." (Dublin, 1979, p. 127)

By the 1850s workers were successful in seeing the ten-hour work week garner state legislative approval in some states, as Wertheimer (1977, p. 83) observes, this success was, at best, only partial:

Workers did succeed in achieving laws in some states to limit the hours of work for children and guaranteed them several months of school a year, although these laws were seldom enforced. When New Hampshire (in 1847), Pennsyl-vania, Massachusetts, and other states passed ten-hour laws, each legislature in-cluded "contracting out" clauses providing that, when necessary, employers could sign contracts with individual employees to work more than the ten hours permitted under the law. Mill owners insisted from the start on workers sign-ing these individual contracts as a condition of employment. Workers signed . . . but not without a fight.

Labor unions sometimes supported women's organizing efforts. In 1863, for example, seamstresses working throughout the North lived in dire poverty. In New York City, seamstresses were among the most impoverished of workers. Few earned more than 17 to 24 cents per day—even though the work day was often fifteen hours long. "Moreover, they often were unable to collect from their employers even the little that was owed them" (Wertheimer, 1977, p. 152). Some New York trade unions helped to lay the foundations for women to unionize. For example, they organized a meeting of women workers in November of 1863 to strategize on how to boost their earnings and recoup unpaid wages. Wertheimer (1977, p. 152) notes that "it is likely that a suc-cessful strike of women shirtmakers that month was a direct outgrowth of this meeting."

The Era of the Craft Union

The organized labor movement in the early twentieth century all but shut out working women. The American Federation of Labor (AFL), which set the norms for union practices in this period, sought to mobilize skilled workers, the vast majority of whom were white, native-born men. Working women, on the other hand, tended to be unskilled and were quite often recent immigrants from Eu-rope. Unions that did accept women stipulated that they should start their own locals. For many factory women, union dues were often high, which precluded may of them from joining. Women were prevented from learning certain trades through establish apprenticeship programs and this tended to confine them to low status, low-paying, unskilled jobs (Foner, 1979; Wertheimer, 1977, pp. 200–201). The attitude of the AFL and other unions at the time echoed specific views of women's traditional roles, which was captured by the rubric the "cult of true womanhood" (Triece, 2001, pp. 186–187). For the most part, women were viewed as "temporary workers," even though they dominated the textile and garment trades (Milkman, 1985, p. 307).

For African Americans, acceptance into labor unions like the AFL was virtually impossible. Institutionalized racism and sexism served to define African Americans as fit only to carry the burden of hard labor, and women as inferior workers not worthy of the monetary compensation given to men's work. Thus, this double oppression of black women workers made it almost impossible for them to attain membership into any type of labor union (Foner, 1979, p. 267).

In response to this discrimination, both white and black women laborers sometimes tried to form their own organizatons. For example, in Chicago, white women formed the Women's Trade Union League. In 1897, affluent black women in New York City founded the White Rose Industrial Association to aid black women domestics whose working conditions in "the Bronx slave market" were deplorable (Terborg-Penn, 1985, p. 142).

Black women's organizations developed remedies to unfair treatment that embodied traditional African survival strategies. For example, older women in Africa were responsible for socializing, training, and providing emotional support to younger women. This tradition carried over to America and served as a means for victims of racial discrimination in the labor force to unite for purposes of teaching one another valuable skills to obtain employment as well as for mutual support against that very discrimination (Terborg-Penn, 1985, pp. 142–143).

Middle- and upper-middle class women came to the aid of immigrant and working-class women workers' plight. Such was the case with the genesis of the Working Women's Protective Union; while not a labor union, it was directed and staffed by middle- and upper-class women "concerned particularly about the powerlessness of working women, who had neither knowledge of the law nor money to hire lawyers to collect the wages due them" (Wertheimer, 1977, p. 155). The Protective Union in New York City provided women workers with free legal advice. Many prominent New York City attorneys represented these women in civil disputes against their employers. In the first decade-and-a-half of its existence, the Protective Union handled over twenty-seven thousand cases, and it managed to settle the majority of them out of court, recovering almost twenty-five thousand dollars in unpaid wages. It also lobbied successfully for the passage of a law establishing criminal penalties for business owners who failed to fully compensate their workers (Wertheimer, 1977, p. 156).

The Rise of "New Unionism"

While many of the early women's labor organizations did not survive, craft unions became the dominant model for organizing women workers. The turn of the twentieth century began to see women's unionism grow dramatically, beginning within the clothing industry. A series of tragedies and militant strikes forged a coming together of a diversity of women workers from different ethnic and racial backgrounds that led to the fortification of unions such as the International Ladies' Garment Workers Union (ILGWU), which was founded in 1900. Another organization of garment workers, the Amalgamated Clothing Workers of America, was founded in 1914 under the leadership of Bessie Abramowitz Hillman and Dorothy Jacobs Bellanca (see Wertheimer, 1977, pp. 321–330). These two organizations, observes historian Barbara Mayer Wertheimer (1977, p. 335), were "the first unions of substance, power, and durability to include large numbers of women and to effect changes in a low-wage, traditionally female sweatshop industry, although differentials between men's and women's wages would remain for a long time."

It was through garment workers strikes, such as the 1909 uprising of the 20,000 garment workers in New York City, that served to change the ILGWU into a modern industrial union. The New York City strike demonstrated the "previously untapped potential for militancy among young female Jewish and Italian immigrant workers, and dramatically challenged the conventional stereotypes of the era, which constructed women workers as passive and uninterested in unionism" (Milkman, 1993, p. 281). The first president of the AFL, Samuel Gompers, had this to say of the great impact of this strike:

[it] brought to the consciousness of the nation a recognition of the extent to which women are taking up with industrial life, their consequent tendency to stand together in the struggle to protect their common interests as wage earners, the readiness of people in all classes to approve of trade-union methods in behalf of working women, and the capacity of women as strikers to suffer, to do, and to dare in support of their rights. (as quoted in Milkman, 1993, p. 281)

The tragedy of the 1911 Triangle Shirtwaist Fire—which claimed the lives of 146 factory workers—was another critical turning point in organizing women garment workers. Wertheimer (1977, p. 310) describes how crowding and violation of the fire codes of the time, including the locking of factory doors and a nonexistent sprinkling system, cost women their lives:

... of the 500 workers crowded into the top three floors of the Asch Building, 146, most of them women and girls, jumped to their death, were burned, or suffocated that afternoon in a building where no fire drills had been held, where doors opened inward rather than out, where factory doors were locked each working day to keep the women in and the union organizers out, where there was no sprinkler system, and where the city's fire-fighting equipment proved totally unequal to the rescue task required.

Eye-witnesses to the fire relate the following details of the tragedy:

... a "bale of dark dress goods" being thrown out of a window. Another who saw it thought the factory owner was trying to save his cloth from the fire. But then the screams began. It had not been a bundle of cloth, but a human being leaping from the windows. Then came another, and then another. (Wertheimer, 1977, p. 310)

Industrial Unionism

Women entered the mass production industries in large numbers during World War I, joining male-dominated trade and industrial unions, especially the Congress of Industrial Organizations (CIO). Union membership resulted in both positive and negative experiences for women industrial workers:

> They gained the strength of membership in permanent organizations. But there was a price. Once women had led unions of their own, ephemeral though these were. Women leaders had defied tradition to speak out on behalf of women workers. Now they would be absorbed into unions led entirely by men. This process was accelerated when the National Labor Relations Act, passed during the Great Depression of the 1930s, at last gave workers the legal right to organize and bargain collectively. Breaking from the AFL, a Committee for Industrial Organization . . . reached out to industiral workers, to blacks and other minorities, and to women. (Wertheimer, 1977, pp. 371–372)

Public Sector and Service Workers and the Influence of the Women's Movement

Women working in the public sector of society were, for the most part, not adequately represented by unions. This began to change in the 1970s, when an increasing number of unions began representing state and local government workers—many of whom were women. The most notable of these unions were the American Federation of State, County and Municipal Employees (AFSME) and the Service Employees International Union (SEIU). The unionization of government workers, in contrast to workers in the private sector, held steady during the 1980s and 1990s; and by the early 2000s, workers in the public sector had a union membership rate over four times that of the private sector: 37.5 percent versus 8.5 percent. The most unionized are locale government workers, especially teachers, police officers, and fire fighters (see U.S. Department of Labor, 2002c).

Historian Ruth Milkman (1985, p. 307) observes that during the 1950s and early 1960s, before the second wave of feminism, the American labor movement held a very traditional attitude toward women workers. They were seen as a group that needed special treatment and protection. Few women held any positions of power within the union hierarchy. However, all of this changed in the 1970s. Unionized women began meeting in caucuses and committees, taking over leadership roles, and becoming more active in general. As a consequence, union leadership improved its attitudes regarding women's issues. For example, in the early 1970s, the AFL-CIO approved the Equal Rights Amendment, and the Coalition of Labor Union Women (CLUW) held its first conference. Unions took up those issues most pressing to women, including daycare, affirmative action, and pay inequities.

Women of Color

Denied entrance to the factories during the rise of industrialization and, for much of the twentieth century, facing discriminatory hiring practices that closed off opportunities in the newly expanded office and sales jobs, many women of color entered domestic service. From 1910 to 1940, the proportion of white women employed in clerical and sales positions almost doubled, and there was a decline in the numbers of white women in domestic work. Private household work then became the province of African American women: The percentage of African American household workers increased from 38.5 percent in 1910 to 59.9 percent in 1940, as shown in Table 2.3. For the next three decades, African American women remained the single largest group in domestic service.

African American women's economic status improved dramatically from 1940 through the 1960s, as a result of an increase in light manufacturing jobs, as well as changes in technology. African American women moved from private household work into manufacturing and clerical work, and made significant gains in the professions. Whereas in 1940, nearly six in ten of employed African American females worked in private households, by the late 1970s only two in ten did. Their job prospects continued to improve, and by the 1980s, almost half of all working African American women were employed in "white collar" jobs: clerical and sales positions as well as professional jobs in business, health care, and education. Through the 1990s and into the 2000s, the historic job-prestige gap between African American and white working women continued to close. Almost two-thirds of working African American women had jobs in the white-collar world by 2001, compared with nearly three-quarters of working white women. Moreover, as evident in Figure 2.4, the gap has never been narrower, and the overall trend is unmistakable; that is, we can expect this narrowing to continue.

Other Women of Color at Work

Each minority group has had a different experience in American society and has faced different opportunities and obstacles. Women in each group share with African American women the concerns of all minority women; they share with the men of their ethnic groups the problems of discrimination against that particular ethnic minority.

Native American Women. As we noted earlier, gender roles in Native American communities were disrupted during the conquest and oppression by whites. For example, Navajo society was traditionally matrilineal, with extended families the norm; Navajo women owned property and played an important role in family decisions. But, beginning in the 1930s, government policy disrupted this system by giving land only to males. As they could no longer make a sufficient living off the land, more and more Navajo men had to seek employment off the reservations. Nuclear families became the norm. Navajo women became dependent on male providers. With the men away much of the time, these women

Table 2.3
PERCENTAGE DISTRIBUTION OF EMPLOYED WOMEN BY OCCUPATION, RACE, AND ETHNIC ORIGINS, 1910–2001

	Professional	Managerial & Administrative	Technical, Sales, & Clerical	Craft	Operatives & Nonfarm Laborers	Private Household Workers	Other Service Workers	Farm Laborers
1910								
White	11.6	1.5	17.5	8.2	23.7	17.2	9.2	12.1
Afr. Amer.	1.5	0.2	0.3	2.0	2.3	38.5	3.2	52.0
1940								
White	17.7	4.3	32.8	1.1	21.2	10.9	12.7	2.3
Afr. Amer.	4.3	0.7	1.3	0.2	7.0	59.9	11.1	15.9
1950								
White	13.3	4.7	39.3	1.7	22.2	4.3	11.6	2.9
Afr. Amer.	5.3	1.3	5.4	0.7	16.8	42.0	19.1	9.4
1960								
White	14.1	4.2	43.2	1.4	18.1	4.4	13.1	1.5
Afr. Amer.	7.7	1.1	9.8	0.7	15.5	38.1	23.0	4.1
Native Amer.	9.1	2.0	17.8	n/a	18.1	16.8	25.8	10.5

1970								
White	15.6	4.8	43.4	1.1	14.9	3.7	15.1	1.5
Afr. Amer.	10.0	1.4	21.4	0.7	17.6	19.4	29.0	0.5
Native Amer.	10.3	2.5	30.2	n/a	22.3	6.6	25.9	2.1
Latina	8.1	2.1	33.9	2.3	28.9	4.6	18.3	2.1
1980								
White	16.9	6.7	43.5	1.8	11.8	2.1	16.2	1.0
Afr. Amer.	12.7	3.0	31.6	1.3	16.1	8.0	26.8	0.5
Native Amer.	14.5	6.6	35.4	n/a	17.0	1.4	23.9	1.2
Latina	7.5	3.7	37.0	2.1	26.3	2.6	19.2	1.5
1990								
White	16.6	11.8	46.3	2.1	8.8	1.2	15.2	1.1
Afr. Amer.	11.2	7.5	39.1	2.3	12.2	3.1	30.2	0.3
Native Amer.	15.7	9.4	36.2	n/a	14.2	1.0	22.4	1.1
Latina	7.3	6.7	38.5	3.1	20.9	4.2	20.8	1.9
2001								
White	15.4	19.0	39.9	2.0	6.1	1.1	15.3	1.2
Afr. Amer.	11.4	14.6	38.3	1.8	9.0	1.0	23.7	0.2
Native Amer.	n/a	n/a	n/a	n/a	n/a	n/a	n/a	n/a
Latina	9.4	9.3	37.0	3.0	13.0	3.7	23.3	1.6

Note: 1910 data for ages ten and older; 1940–1960 for ages fourteen and over; 1970–2001 for ages sixteen and over. For a discussion of this and other problems associated with comparing decennial censuses, see Amott and Matthaei (1996, pp. 414–415).

Sources: Aldridge (1975, p. 53), Amott and Matthaei (1996, p. 48), Bureau of Labor Statistics (1980, p. 74; 1997c; 1997d; 2003b).

Figure 2.4. Percentage of "White-Collar" Women by Race and Ethnic Origins, 1950–2001. *Note:* "White-Collar" = sum of (a) Professionals, (b) Executives, Administrators, and Managers, and (c) Technical, Sales, and Administrative Support Workers. *Sources:* Aldridge (1975, p. 53); Amott and Matthaei (1996, p. 48); Bureau of Labor Statistics (1980, p. 74); 1997c, 1997d, 2003b); U.S. Equal Employment Opportunity Commission (2002; this source used for Native American estimate for 2001).

are often isolated and powerless. They often face divorce or desertion and thus economic difficulties because the community frowns on women seeking work off the reservation.

Such disruption of the traditional Native American society left Native American women in very grim economic circumstances. But, in recent decades, more and more of them have gotten jobs. Native American women's labor-force participation rate in 1970 was 35 percent (compared to 43 percent for all women). This rate rose sharply to 55 percent by the early 1990s and is now within a few percentage points of the rate for all women (56.8 percent in 2000, see U.S. Bureau of the Census, 2002b, Table P150C).

Like their African American counterparts over the past half century, Native American women have gradually moved out of low-skill farm and nonfarm work and domestic jobs into clerical, sales, professional, technical, and other "white-collar" jobs. In 1960, one in six working Native American women was employed as domestic household worker; by the early 1990s only one in a hundred was. During the same period, the proportion of Native American women involved in agricultural work also went from ten to one in a hundred. Manufacturing work was increasingly replaced by white-collar work, reflecting the overall trends in the occupational structure; more specifically, while the percentage involved in factory work (much of it in textiles and traditional crafts) fell from 18.1 to 14.2, the percentage employed in white-collar work soared from 28.9 to 61.3. Although many of these white-collar jobs are classified as "professional" (15.7 percent of all working Native American women) or "managerial" (9.4 percent), two-thirds of Native American women are still concentrated in the "secondary" sector of the labor market,* which is characterized by low wages, few or no benefits, low mobility, and high instability. They are kept there because of the "stagnation of the reservation economy," discrimination, and their relatively low level of educational attainment (Amott and Matthaei, 1996, p. 51). A significant number of Native American women do not even have a high school diploma—in 2000, more than one-quarter (28.3 percent) of all those over the age of twenty-five, compared to one-sixth (16.3 percent) of white women (see U.S. Bureau of the Census, 2002b, Tables P148A and P148C).

Latina Women. The term "Latina" is used to denote populations of women with Mexican American (Chicana), Puerto Rican, Cuban, and other Central and South American origins (including, most notably, the Dominican Republic, Colombia, El Salvador, and Nicaragua). Mexican Americans (58.5 percent) and Puerto Ricans (9.6 percent) constitute the largest segments of the Latina population (see Guzmán, 2001, Table 1), and we will focus on these two groups.

Large numbers of Chicanas migrated, usually with husband and children, from Mexico to the United States during the 1916–1920 labor shortage created by World War I. They found work in the sprawling "factory farms" of the Southwest, harvesting fruits, vegetables, and cotton in the Imperial and San Joaquin valleys of California, the Salt River valley of Arizona, and the Rio Grande valley of Texas (Amott and Matthaei, 1996, p. 75). They also went to the Midwest, for instance to Michigan and Minnesota, to harvest sugar beets. Such migrant workers typically were exploited, spending long, tedious, and physically demanding hours in the fields for very low pay. Some became tenant farmers, which might seem a step up, except too often this system "created debt peonage; unable to pay the rent, tenants were unable to leave the land and remained virtually permanently indebted to their landlords" (Amott and Matthaei, 1996, p. 75).

During the 1920s, with a shortage of European immigration, new job opportunities opened up for Mexican Americans, and they began to migrate from rural farm country to the urban industrial centers, where they found work as domestics and factory workers. By 1930, a third of working Chicanas were domestics and a quarter worked in manufacturing; at the time, the share employed in agriculture, forestry, and mining had fallen to 21 percent (Amott and Matthaei, 1996, pp. 75–76). Wage scales varied according to ethnicity, however. It was not uncommon to pay Chicana workers lower wages than "Anglo" (whites of European descent) women for doing the same job, whether as domestics, laundresses, or workers in the food-processing industries of the West and Southwest (Zavella, 1987, p. 8). The Depression years of the 1930s, with the general shortage of jobs, brought a backlash against Mexican American labor, and thousands of Mexicans were deported or pressured to leave.

---

*The "secondary" job market comprises most of those jobs falling under the following Bureau of the Census occupational classifications: sales, clerical, operatives, nonfarm labor, household work, low-level ("other") service work, and farm labor. The "primary" job market comprises most of those jobs that are labeled as technical, executive, administrative, professional, and (skilled) craft.

World War II once again opened up the American labor market for Mexican migrants, as their labor was needed to offset wartime labor shortages. However, their treatment was deplorable by modern standards. In short, Mexican workers comprised a "reserve army" of exploited labor. Through the government-sponsored Bracero or "Manual Workers" program, Mexican workers were granted temporary work visas so that they could be employed on large corporate farms and elsewhere, but too often they were treated like slaves or prisoners.

World War II and the years following saw a massive shift in the occupational and geographical distribution of Chicana workers:

> Many left Texas for California, and the population became increasingly more urban. Women continued their move from the fields into garment factories throughout the Southwest. . . . [A] comparison of the 1930 and 1950 [census] data shows the magnitude of these shifts. For instance, the share of employed southwestern Chicanas working on farms dropped from 21 percent in 1930 to 6 percent in 1950, while the percentage in white-collar work doubled. (Amott and Matthaei, 1996, p. 80)

By the 1960s, the largest occupational category for Chicana workers was operatives, followed by clerical and service work. Chicanas became concentrated in particular industries: food processing, electronics (including telecommunications), and garments. Like their Native American counterparts, Chicana women have made some progress in entering professional and managerial occupations (primarily noncollege teaching, nursing, librarianship, and social work). In 1960, 8.6 percent were in these occupations; by 1980, 12.6 percent, and by the early 2000s, 18.7 percent. However, like Native American women, Chicana women are still overwhelmingly found in the secondary labor market (75.5 percent); much more so than women (59.9 percent) and men (49.2 percent) of white European heritage (see Bureau of Labor Statistics, 2003b).

The dominant reasons behind the low occupational prestige of all minority groups are the same: discrimination and low educational attainment. In the case of Chicana women, over 15 percent "are illiterate by the standard measure (completion of less than five years of schooling)," but studies of functional illiteracy during the 1970s and 1980s suggest "much higher rates—perhaps as high as 56 percent" (Amott and Matthaei, 1996, p. 86). At the other end of the educational attainment spectrum, only 10.7 percent of Latina women have completed four or more years of college—compared with 15.2 percent of African American women and 24.1 percent of white women (U.S. Bureau of the Census, 2002b, Tables P148A, P148C, and P148H). However, education is only part of the formula for success in the U.S. occupational system: Even when education is held constant and we compare only workers having a college-level education, Latina women only make 90.8 percent of what non-Latina white women do (see Bureau of Labor Statistics, 2003c; pp. 64, 84).

Beyond lack of education, Chicana women face other important obstacles in the labor market. They have high rates of unemployment and underemployment. Many of the jobs they hold are seasonal and often nonunionized. This lack of advancement translates into higher poverty rates and lower incomes compared to most other U.S. racial and ethnic groups. For Latina women (in general) with children under eighteen and no husband present, the poverty rate is 44.5 percent compared to 27.8 percent for non-Latina white women in this situation (U.S. Bureau of the Census, 2002b, Tables P150A and P150H).

Increasingly, Chicana women, like many female workers of color around the globe, are doing service or assembly work for multinational corporations, especially in the apparel, food-processing, and electronics industries. These women have often displaced men in assembly work because they can be paid less and many do not receive job benefits. The work hours are long, and women are often assigned monotonous tasks that are dangerous to their health.

In recent years, the labor-force participation of U.S. Puerto Rican women has averaged about 55 percent, somewhat less than the overall rate for women of 60 percent (U.S. Department of Labor, Women's Bureau, 2000). The employment of U.S. Puerto Rican women is complicated by frequent migration between the island and the mainland, which often leads to instability both in work and in family life. It is not unusual to find women working in the United States whose children are cared for by grandmothers or other relatives in Puerto Rico, or to find wives and children living in Puerto Rico while their husbands find work on the mainland.

Like African American women, Latina women may find that their social, cultural, and historic bonds with white women of European descent are somewhat tenuous. Latin cultures tend to be even more male dominated than in U.S. culture, with women assigned an almost exclusively familial role. In addition, the discrimination that both Latin men and women have faced tends to draw them together in the struggle against racism, making sexism almost a peripheral issue for many of these women. As Lorenzana (1979, p. 336) observes regarding Mexican American women: "When a people are undernourished, ill, socially alienated, and powerless members of a society, male chauvinism is of trivial concern." Thus, gender-based affirmative action programs are looked on skeptically because they are perceived as pitting Latin women against Latin men in the search for jobs.

Some Summary Comparisons. As Table 2.3 reveals, African American and Latina women are less likely than white women to be managers or professionals and more likely to hold low-level service and factory jobs. Moreover, as shown in Table 2.4, African American and Latina women earn substantially less within occupations (and white women earn less than their male counterparts—see the discussion in Chapter 3 on the female/male earnings gap). African American women heading households with children under eighteen and no husband present are also about one-and-a-half times more likely to be living in poverty, while Latina women in the same situation are approaching a one-and-two-thirds times greater likelihood; and both African American and Latina women are twice as likely as their white counterparts to be unemployed (Table 2.5). These occupational differences reflect educational differences among the three groups. As is evident in Table 2.5, African American and Latina women are much less likely to have college degrees and much more likely to have never finished high

Table 2.4
USUAL (MEDIAN) WEEKLY EARNINGS OF FULL-TIME FEMALE WORKERS (AGE 16
AND OVER) BY SELECTED OCCUPATION, RACE, AND LATINA ORIGINS, 2001

Selected Occupation	Non-Latina White	African American	Latina	Ratio Afr. Am./ Non-Latina White (%)	Ratio Latina/ Non-Latina White (%)
All	521	451	385	86.6	73.9
Professional Specialty	754	679	670	90.1	88.9
Executive, Administrative, Management	711	630	636	88.6	89.5
Teachers (Primary & Secondary)	720	632	638	87.8	88.6
Administrative Support (Including Clerical)	469	461	424	98.3	90.4
Operators, Fabricators, Laborers	374	352	308	94.1	82.4
Sales Workers (Retail) & Personal Services	316	295	289	93.4	91.5
Private Household	251	264	247	105.2	98.4

Source: Bureau of Labor Statistics (2003d).

school. However, educational differences are only part of the picture, because—as displayed in Table 2.6—holding education constant, we still see small but significant earnings gaps among the three groups, with non-Latina white women at the top, Latina women at the bottom, and African American women falling between the two. In short, as of the early 2000s many minority women still suffer a "double-whammy"—they suffer economically from both their gender and their racial/ethnic backgrounds.

During the 1960s and 1970s, the earnings differences between African American and white women narrowed considerably, with equality peaking in 1980. However, since the late 1980s, the earnings differences between these two groups—as well as between Latina women and white women—have fluctuated from year to year but with an overall trend revealing greater inequality (Table 2.7). The 1965–1980 narrowing of African American/white incomes reflected, in part, the growing effects of equal opportunity laws and affirmative action programs—and the consequent opening to black women of occupational choices that were closed to them before the mid-1960s. Back then, the occupational segregation of African American women was enormous, and their being relegated to low-prestige jobs was responsible for much of the income differences between themselves and their white counterparts. In addition to the lingering

Table 2.5
POVERTY, UNEMPLOYMENT, AND EDUCATIONAL ATTAINMENT OF WOMEN BY RACE AND ETHNICITY (2000 CENSUS SF-3 FILE)

	White (%)	Afr. Amer. (%)	Ratio Afr. Amer./ White (%)	Latina (%)	Ratio Latina/ White (%)	Native Amer. (%)	Ratio Nat. Am./ White (%)	Asian (%)	Ratio Asian White (%)
Below Poverty Line (Female Householder with Children Under 18 and No Husband Present)	27.8	41.2	148.2	44.5	160.1	45.7	164.5	27.9	100.2
Unemployment (Age 16 and Over)	4.6	10.9	237.1	10.7	231.6	11.7	253.3	5.3	114.8
Education (Age 25 and Over) Percent with 4 or more years of college	24.1	15.2	63.1	10.7	44.4	11.6	48.1	40.4	167.6
Percent with no high school diploma	16.3	26.6	163.4	35.0	214.5	28.3	173.6	22.2	136.2

Source: U.S. Bureau of the Census (2002b, Table Series 148, 150, and 160).

Table 2.6
USUAL WEEKLY EARNINGS OF FULL-TIME FEMALE WORKERS BY EDUCATION,
RACE, AND LATINA ORIGINS, 2001

	No High School Diploma	Percent- age of White	High School Diploma Only	Percent- age of Non-Latina White	B.A. Degree or Higher	Percent- age of Non-Latina White
Non-Latina White	319	100.0	439	100.0	774	100.0
African American	300	94.0	382	87.0	717	92.6
Latina	293	91.8	386	87.9	703	90.8

Source: Bureau of Labor Statistics (2003c).

effects of historical discrimination and current institutional discrimination, the lack of decline in African American/white and Latina/white female wage in-equality in recent years reflects the educational differences between the three groups of women and the higher educational attainment of white women (24.1 percent of whom are college educated versus 15.2 percent for African Ameri-can women and 10.7 percent for Latina women), which allows them to take greater advantage of increasing opportunities for women in managerial and pro-fessional occupations. The decline in Latina/white female wage equality, more-over, reflects the heavy immigration of Latina women into the United States

Table 2.7
MEDIAN ANNUAL EARNINGS OF FULL-TIME FEMALE WORKERS
(AGE 15 AND OVER) BY YEAR, RACE, AND LATINA ORIGINS, 1988–2001
(IN CONSTANT 2001 DOLLARS)

Year	Non- Latina White	African American	Latina	Asian	Ratio Afr. Am./ Non-Latina White (%)	Ratio Latina/ Non-Latina White (%)	Ratio Asian/ Non-Latina White (%)
1988	26,045	23,779	21,344	27,819	88.5	74.9	108.8
1989	26,526	23,973	21,592	29,450	85.8	75.7	105.4
1990	26,735	23,692	20,582	28,005	87.3	72.6	105.1
1991	26,736	23,727	20,589	26,837	86.3	75.0	102.7
1992	27,071	24,437	21,126	28,192	85.0	73.2	107.2
1993	27,002	23,905	20,216	29,369	84.3	71.5	100.7
1994	27,406	23,523	20,758	28,890	88.4	70.8	104.6
1995	27,293	23,836	19,814	28,695	84.8	69.3	105.3
1996	27,959	24,121	20,967	28,706	86.3	69.8	99.6
1997	28,502	24,235	20,867	30,554	88.5	74.9	108.8
1998	29,152	24,563	20,846	29,358	85.8	75.7	105.4
1999	29,125	25,736	20,619	30,454	87.3	72.6	105.1
2000	30,430	25,808	21,098	32,031	86.3	75.0	102.7
2001	30,801	26,595	21,493	30,685	85.0	73.2	107.2

Source: U.S. Bureau of the Census (2003a).

since 1980. Immigrants typically begin their work careers at lower wages in less prestigious fields, but as they live in the United States longer, their economic prospects improve.

Asian American Women.   The term Asian American subsumes many different ethnic groups (Japanese, Chinese, Filipino, Korean, Asian-Indian, Pakistani, Sri Lankan, Bangladeshi, Vietnamese, Lao, Hmong, Cambodian, Iu Mien, and several other groups), with their unique histories, languages, and cultures. We focus here on the three largest contemporary groups of Asian American women: those of Chinese, Japanese, and Filipino descent.

Asian American women have had and continue to exhibit high labor-force participation rates and relatively high economic status compared to women of other racial and ethnic groups. In recent years, the overall Asian American women's labor-force participation rates have been on par with that of white women: 56.4 percent in 1999, for example, compared with 57.5 percent (U.S. Bureau of the Census, 2002b). However, rates among Asian groups varied considerably, ranging from more than 70 percent for native-born Japanese, Chinese, and Filipinos to less than 50 percent for Japanese immigrants (Yamanaka and McClelland, 1994, p. 94). As Table 2.8 reveals, Asian women working full time are less likely to be poor or of very modest income (36.2 percent being in the lowest income category of under $25,000 per year—the lowest of all race/ethnic groups) and more likely to be prosperous (with 7.8 percent in the over-$75,000 category) than their white, African American, Latina, and Native American counterparts.

Asian Americans are considered to be the "model minority" and, on the face of it, the data in Tables 2.5, 2.7, and 2.8 contribute to such a view. However, this characterization is an overstatement. While many Asian Americans among both the native-born and the recent arrivals have high levels of education and professional skills and can readily fit into the labor market, others lack such advantages, often finding work only as undocumented laborers in low-paying jobs with long work days, little or no job mobility, and no benefits; these facts are partly revealed in Table 2.5, where it is shown that Asian women are

Table 2.8
INCOME DISTRIBUTIONS (PERCENTAGES) FOR WOMEN EMPLOYED FULL-TIME BY RACE AND ETHNICITY (2000 CENSUS SF-3 FILE)

Income Level	White	African American	Latina	Native American	Asian
Up to $24,999	41.1	47.9	59.1	55.9	36.2
$25,000 to $49,999	43.6	41.5	33.1	36.1	40.6
$50,000 to $74,999	10.4	8.0	5.6	6.0	15.5
$75,000 and Over	4.8	2.6	2.2	1.9	7.8

Source: U.S. Bureau of the Census (2002b, Table Series PCT73).

significantly more likely to be college educated compared to white women, but also significantly more likely never to have finished high school.

> We are told we have overcome our oppression, and that therefore we are the model minority. Model refers to the cherished dictum of capitalism that "pulling hard on your bootstraps" brings due rewards. . . . Asian American success stories . . . do little to illuminate the actual conditions of the majority of Asian Americans. Such examples conceal the more typical Asian American experience of unemployment, underemployment and struggle to survive. The model minority myth thus classically scapegoats Asian Americans. It labels us in a way that dismisses the real problems that many do face, while at the same time pitting Asians against other oppressed people of color. (Lai 1998, p. 209)

In 1999, 40.4 percent of Asian women who were twenty-five years and over had at least a bachelor's degree, compared with 24.1 percent of whites (U.S. Bureau of the Census, 2002b, Tables 148A and 148D). Filipina American women secured the highest college graduation rate of all women, a rate 50 percent greater than that of white males. Following closely behind are Chinese American and Japanese American women, who exceed both the white male and female college graduation rates (see Woo, 1998, p. 253). The statistics explain, in part, the greater likelihood of Asian women to have higher levels of income compared to whites and other racial and ethnic groups (see, for example, the last two rows in Table 2.8).

However, it would be incorrect to equate "Asian" with being "well educated" and "well off" because the majority of Asian women immigrating to the United States since 1980 have low levels of education. Even though, as just noted, Asian women are much more likely to be college educated than white women, they are also much more likely—two-and-a-quarter times more likely— to be grade-school dropouts: In 1999, 12.9 percent of Asian women had not gone beyond the eighth grade, compared to only 5.8 percent of their white counterparts. This fact is linked to a key difference between Asian and non-Latina white women revealed in Table 2.9: the proportions working as "operators, fabricators, and laborers," where we find significantly more Asian women (one in twelve employed in these kinds of jobs versus one in twenty for non-

Table 2.9

PERCENTAGE DISTRIBUTIONS OF EMPLOYED WOMEN BY RACE (ASIAN VERSUS NON-LATINA WHITE), 2000

Occupation	Asian	Non-Latina White
Managerial and Professional Specialty	38.7	34.6
Technical, Sales, and Administrative Support	32.4	41.3
Service	17.7	15.4
Precision Production, Craft, and Repair	2.7	2.1
Operators, Fabricators, and Laborers	8.1	5.4
Farming, Forestry, and Fishing	0.4	0.8
	100.0%	100.0%
Total Employed (in thousands)	2,450	46,423

Source: U.S. Bureau of the Census (2001a).

Latina white workers). It is also linked to the slight declining of Asian/white female wage equality over the past two decades (see the last column in Table 2.7).
Finally, recent census data reveal that even though a third of all Asian families
have annual incomes over $75,000—which is considerably higher than the na-
tional median about $50,000 in the early 2000s (U.S. Bureau of the Census,
2002c)—a fifth have incomes under $25,000 (see Foo, 2002, Introduction).

These women at the bottom of the job-prestige and income scales are most
commonly employed as sewing machine operators at home or in small sweatshops in the Chinatowns of New York and San Francisco. Asian immigrant
women are also heavily employed in the microelectronics industry. Women in
general comprise 80 to 90 percent of assembly workers in this industry, and approximately "half of these assembly workers are recent immigrants from the
Philippines, Vietnam, Korea, and South Asia" (Espiritu, 1997, p. 73). Within
the microelectronics industry jobs are often "structured along racial and gender lines, with men and white workers earning higher wages and being much
more likely to be promoted than women and workers of color" (Espiritu, 1997,
p. 73; also see Villones, 1989).

As presented in Foo (2002, ch. 4), one white male manager in the Silicon
Valley area of northern California stated that he has a very simple formula
for hiring: "Just three things I look for in hiring entry-level manufacturing
operatives—small, foreign, and female. These little foreign gals are grateful to
be hired—very, very grateful—no matter what." Silicon Valley managers are
white men; and they hire immigrant women for their low-tech work. They prefer Asian women because, as offered up by one manager, "Asian women are more
subservient that American females; if I refer to them as 'girls' it is because to
me, they act like girls: they only speak when spoken to, do exactly as they're
told, and so forth. So I play into it—I treat them firmly like a father figure."
Such stereotyping of poor Asian women lays the foundation for paying them
less and being quick to lay them off when factory orders are down. Foo (2002,
ch. 4) quotes one factory owner as admitting: "Let's face it, when you have to
expand and contract all the time, you need people who are more expendable.
When I lay off immigrant housewives, people don't get as upset as if you were
laying off regular workers." By regular workers, the owner was implying white
workers. According to Foo (2002, ch. 4), most managers don't hire Africans
Americans because of the stereotype that they are troublemakers and are not de-
pendable. Indeed, African American workers have been "frozen out of Silicon
Valley almost entirely"—as a "conscious decision on the part of manufacturers."

Karen Hossfeld's (1990) research on relationships between poor Asian and
Latina immigrant women production workers and their white male managers
in Silicon Valley reveals how immigrant women of color negotiate and often
employ resistance to primarily white, middle-class management demands. One
Filipina circuit board assembler put it this way:

> The bosses here have this type of reasoning like a seesaw. One day it's "you're
> paid less because women are different than men," or "immigrants need less to
> get by." The next day it's "you're all just workers here—no special treatment
> just because you're female or foreigners."

> Well, they think they're pretty clever with their doubletalk and that we're just a bunch of dumb aliens. But it takes two to use a seesaw. What we are gradually figuring out here is how to use their own logic against them. (Hossfeld, 1990, p. 149)

As clerical or administrative support workers, Asian American women are disproportionately represented as cashiers, file clerks, office machine operators, and typists. They are less likely to obtain employment as secretaries or receptionists (Woo, 1998, p. 254). Noting that there is an "overrepresentation of college-educated women in clerical work," Woo (1985, pp. 331–332) suggests that education functions less as a path toward mobility into higher occupational categories and more as "a hedge against jobs as service workers and as machine operatives or assembly workers."

Asian American women with a college education who obtain professional employment are often restricted to the less prestigious jobs within this category. Asian American women "are more likely to remain marginalized in their work organization, to encounter a 'glass ceiling,' and to earn less than white men, Asian American men, and white women with comparable educational backgrounds" (Espiritu, 1997, p. 68). They are least represented in those male-dominated positions of physician, lawyer, and judge, and are heavily concentrated in the more female-dominated occupations of nursing and teaching (Woo, 1998, p. 252).

Asian women have been subjected to a range of stereotypes. The Lotus Blossom stereotype depicts them as submissive and demure sex objects: "good, faithful, uncomplaining, totally compliant, self-effacing, gracious servants who will do anything and everything to please, entertain, and make them feel comfortable and carefree" (Wong, as cited in Amott and Matthaei, 1996, p. 254). At the opposite extreme, the Dragon Lady stereotype portrays Asian women as "promiscuous and untrustworthy,"

> as the castrating Dragon Lady who, while puffing on her foot-long cigarette holder, could poison a man as easily as she could seduce him. "With her talon-like six-inch fingernails, her skin-tight satin dress slit to the thigh," the Dragon Lady is desirable, deceitful and dangerous. (Espiritu, 1997, p. 94)

Asian American feminist Germaine Wong notes how stereotypes concerning Asian women operate in the workplace, serving to deter their advancement into leadership roles and to increase their vulnerability to sexual harassment. Additionally, these stereotypes have fostered a demand for "X-rated films and pornographic materials featuring Asian women in bondage, for 'Oriental' bathhouse workers in U.S. cities, and for Asian mail-order brides" (Espiritu, 1997, p. 95).

In sum, the notion of Asian Americans as the "model minority" deviates considerably from sociological reality. While many Asian American women have achieved considerable success in terms of education, occupational prestige, and income, many others have not "escaped the stigmatization of being minority and recent immigrants in a discriminatory job market" (Yamanaka and McClelland, 1994, p. 108; cf. Foo, 2002).

The Globalized Woman at Work

After World War II, the U.S. economy steadily became more and more connected to the economies of other nations. The "globalized economy" wrought new changes in the nature of women's work. Multinational corporations based in the United States—such as Nike and The Gap—were able to have the bulk of their manufacturing work performed by the citizens of developing nations like Indonesia, Mexico, and Taiwan, and even by those living in some developed European and North American enclaves (especially by immigrants working in garment sweatshops in major cities). These changes in the production of goods in mass assembly lines have often taken the form of free trade zones, (FTZs), sweatshops, and subcontracting establishments. Thomas Friedman (1999, p. 8), a global studies expert, observes that "culturally speaking, globalization is largely, though not entirely, Americanization—from Big Macs to iMacs to Mickey Mouse—on a global scale."

The number of firms qualifying as multinational, or transnational enterprises has risen considerably. As noted by Clegg (1996, p. 104),

> multinationals originating in the fourteen leading industrialized countries of the world numbered just 7,000 in 1969, but in the early 1990s they reached a figure of around 24,000. The world as a whole is estimated to hold a total of 37,000 multinational firms, which control in total (that is, within their home plus host economies) around one-third of all private sector capital. These capital assets generate a sales value of approximately $U.S 5.5 trillion.

Globalization cannot be ignored. It is the extension of free market capitalism to all regions of the world; it represents the widening and deepening of the international flows of trade, capital, technology, and information within a unitary, worldwide market (Petras and Veltmeyer, 2001, p. 11). Wherever cheap labor can be found, the profit motive tends to drive corporations to engage in a "race to the bottom," in which they compete to obtain the cheapest possible labor and raw materials from the developing world. Capital is now so fluid that companies "drop anchor wherever wage costs are lowest" (Wichterich, 2000, p. 3; see also Safa, 1981). The majority of workers in the global assembly lines are women, most of whom are paid below the standard minimum wage:

> The typical employee of a world market factory is a woman between the ages of sixteen and twenty-six years. In general, MNEs [multinational enterprises] prefer women as they are more compliant than men in accepting working conditions that are significantly inferior in terms of security of employment, safety, shift work, wages, and fringe benefits. In general, these women work between 20 percent and 30 percent more hours per year than their counterparts in the labor force of developed countries—as much as 50 percent in some cases. On the other hand, wages tend to be only between 10 percent and 20 percent of those paid in core economies. For example, experienced female labor can be paid as little as $U.S. 0.15 per hour in Indonesia; this figure rises to $U.S. 0.36 in Thailand, $U.S. 0.57 in El Salvador, and $U.S. 0.80 in Mexico. In some instances, these wages barely provide for the necessities of life. (Coffey, 1996, pp. 54–55)

In one form or another, globalized economies have existed since antiquity. From the sixteenth century onward, for example, the nations of Western Europe colonized much of Africa, Asia, and the Americas. Colonial nations of Western Europe plundered these regions of their raw materials and exploited indigenous populations for immense profit (Brettell and Sargent, 2001). Indeed, there are similarities between the Lowell mill girls during the early industrialization of the United States and today's factory women in developing nations: In both situations we have young women working long hours at subsistence wage levels. However, the globalized economy of today is qualitatively different from that of previous time periods in that "nearly every corner of the world is rapidly becoming an integral part of a global economic system that is increasingly dominated by large transnational corporations" (Harris and Seid, 2000, p. 5).

The present globalization process is, in part, a product of neoliberal policies that promote the ideology of free markets and free trade. These policies were promoted heavily in the 1980s and 1990s during the Ronald Reagan and George Bush administrations in the United States and the Margaret Thatcher and John Major governments in the United Kingdom. The policies prompted the United States to seek out developing nations as fertile grounds for corporate production. Companies moved to offshore sites outside the United States because labor laws did not strictly regulate production as they did back home. For example, a 1993 Commerce Department report noted that multinational corporations with foreign investments "avoided paying one-half of their U.S. taxes; collectively, this saved companies $30 billion dollars a year" (Dickinson, 1997, p. 126; Greider, 1997, p. 96).

Globalization was built on the belief that women workers—especially young and unmarried women—would be "docile" and "malleable," with "nimble fingers" to do the tedious labor of assembling a range of manufactured goods (Elson and Pearson, 1981). Traditional views of women as "secondary earners" helped to justify paying these young women wages that were far below the standard minimum wage, as well as denying them basic benefits.

Christa Wichterich, in her book *The Globalized Woman*, points out that, odd as it seems, Le Thi, a young Vietnamese woman, and basketball great Michael Jordan shared a common employer—the Nike Corporation. While Jordan made upward of $20 million each year to promote Nike products, Le Thi made less than $500 to create that Air Jordan logo that sold millions of products during the height of his fame. In 1997, an investigation of factories doing contract work for Nike in Vietnam exposed the extremely harsh working conditions under which the workers were forced to perform. Women were forced to work months of overtime with no extra compensation, and they were allowed only one bathroom break per eight-hour shift. Some observers commented that "Nike treated its shoes better than its workers" (Wichterich, 2000, p. 13).

Do Women Workers Benefit from Globalization?

There are opposing voices on the issue of the extent to which women across the world do or do not benefit from globalization. On the one hand, the liberalization of markets offers new opportunities for women everywhere, not just in the economically established first world countries, to challenge patriarchal authority and tradition. It begins opening up possibilities for women to become independent wage earners. These women now have jobs outside of the home where they are able to forge identities outside of the family sphere. This phenomenon represents a doubled-edge sword, however. With their families becoming dependent on the secondary wages, these women feel pressure to accept less than desirable working conditions brought on by greedy institutions. In short, as women's secondary income has grown indispensable to their family's livelihood, the earning of money, regardless of the conditions under which it is done, sometimes seem to take precedent over anything else (Wichterich, 2000, p. 32).

In sum, globalization has had both negative and positive impacts on women's lives in the developing world. On the one hand, the policies associated with globalization have served to increase the number of women living in poverty and ill health. The United Nations, in its investigation of the "feminization of employment," concludes that the global woman worker earns between 16 and 60 U.S. cents per hour, and very often does not receive any form of social security or health coverage (United Nations, 1995b, p. 48; Wichterich, 2000, p. 2). At the same time, they continue to pick up the brunt of the nonwage work, ensuring that a certain level of life quality can be met for their families. On the other hand, employment increases the degree to which women feel empowered within their family unit and their communities as a whole—for even having a low income is highly valued by women, "not only for what it buys, but for the greater dignity it brings" (Elson, 1992, p. 52). Working for wages takes women out of households and thus out of the direct control of their husbands—encouraging women to think more about themselves and their aspirations as individuals (Gadio and Rakowski 1998; Korzeniewicz, 1997; Rakowski, 2000, p. 126).

Women of the developed world, as consumers of globally produced goods, are economically tied to women of the developing world who generate these products and services. Maria Mies (1986, pp. 134–135) provides a specific example of the nature of this linkage via women's making of lace goods—for meager wages—in households of India. These goods are sold to large export houses and then resold on the world market. Women in the developed world are the major consumers of these luxury products. Even working-class women can afford the lace goods—because of the very low wages paid to Indian women.

Mies suggests that an awareness of this linkage is a first important step in challenging the negative effects of the international division of labor on women workers of the developing world. Indeed, these global women have begun making such a challenge. This challenge would not be predicted by the stereotype of global women workers as "passive pawns of men, their families, religion, underdevelopment, modernization, and global restructuring" (Ward, 1990, p. 14). Recent studies have shown, however, that many acts of resistance have gone unnoticed because scholars have been blinded by this stereotype and because resistance has usually been recognized only when it takes the form of unionization (see Kandiyoti, 1988; Mintz, 1971; and Ward, 1990, p. 14). Indeed, the seeds of change are in the air and, in recent years, in a number of developing countries women workers have begun voicing opposition to harsh workplace practices, including long hours, low pay, unhealthy work environments, lack of benefits, and the employment of children.

Marianne Marchand's (1994) research on women's protests in Latin America provides an example of such opposition. Marchand found that women use oral testimony as a powerful form of resistance. By telling their stories to a third party (e.g., a journalist or a social scientist), who then publishes their words, women in the developing world are able to initiate public discourse on the need for change. Such discourse often leads to the creation of coalitions to resist and challenge government policies (e.g., on childcare and the minimum wage) and government repression. For example, in 1998, working-class women in Bogotá, Columbia, "organized a week-long strike against the government's austerity program" (Dickenson and Schaeffer, 2001, p. 218). At about the same time, workers in Tijuana, Mexico, successfully fought to organize an independent union to bargain with a Korean-owned *maquila* assembly plant. When management and the government disregarded the union, workers went on a twenty-two-day hunger strike. As Dickenson and Schaeffer (2001, p. 217) observe, "this was the first time an independent union had managed to represent workers at one of the 2,700 *maquila* plants along Mexico's border."

Working women in developing nations have also forged alliances with women's groups and political organizations across national borders. For example, STITCH (Support Team International for Textileras) consists of female organizers in the United States and Guatemala who work with the American Friends Service Committee to promote social justice for women workers. STITCH has won a variety of lawsuits against multinational corporations regarding wage disputes as well as poor and unhealthy working conditions (see Kirk and Okazawa-Rey, 2001, p. 276).

The Status Quo: No Shangri-La

We have traced the historical upswing of women in the labor force—more women moving from the domestic sphere into paid employment—and we have observed the growing heterogeneity of women workers. But, while the number and types of women who work have changed dramatically, numerous other aspects of women's work have remained impervious to change: the clustering of women into sex-typed jobs, the disproportionate number of women in low-ranking positions and their comparatively low earnings relative to men, as well as the overall underutilization (unemployment and underemployment) of women workers. Although the women's movement and recent legislation have produced pressure for changes, such changes often run counter to deeply held attitudes and institutionalized practices concerning the differential treatment of the sexes.

In general, the problems of occupational restrictions and discrimination are more severe for women of color than for white women. Social scientists speculate that as the labor-market position of women of color becomes more like that of white women, their lot will improve. The underlying assumption is that racial discrimination is the major problem, and that to the extent that racist attitudes and practices diminish, women of color will be treated like white women and can expect to enjoy the same labor-market opportunities and earnings. Asian American women and some African American women now experience such "success." And that certainly is an improvement, especially when we compare the present situation of these women and white women with that of Latina and Native American women. But women of color will find, if and when racial discrimination vanishes, that they face gender discrimination as well. And, as one African American woman has observed, it isn't always easy to tell what one is fighting: "Although it's difficult to distinguish between the two, most days I think it's sexual because I see white women experiencing the same things I am. . . . In the matter of salaries, you can't tell whether it is racist or sexist" (Leggon, 1980, p. 195). Certainly women of color need to have education and training, but, as many well-qualified women can attest, credentials are not necessarily enough. And while certainly there has been progress, real progress will come only when sexism and racism are confronted simultaneously and when educational and employment opportunities now available to white men become equally available to everyone.

World Wide Web Resources

For the history of working women across a broad range of topics, see the "Learning Page–Links" Web link of the National Women's History Project: http://www.nwhp.org/tlp/links/links.html; also see http://womenshistory.about.com/cs/work.

For current statistics on working women, see the various related links at the Bureau of Labor Statistics main Web site: http://www.bls.gov/.

3 Gender Inequality: Economic and Legal Explanations

The economy is structured such that some jobs bring greater rewards than other jobs. Certain occupations and activities are considered more important than others in responsibilities, degree of power, and the range of social and economic areas affected by the decisions of those who hold such positions. These jobs require high levels of ability, training, and expertise; their rewards, in terms of prestige and compensation, are correspondingly high. Society rewards its chiefs of state, its business executives, and its physicians well. Positions of less responsibility—requiring less experience, expertise, and training—have correspondingly lower levels of status and compensation. Housekeepers earn less than lawyers, waitresses less than scientists, and nurses less than doctors.

This overview is part of the "functionalist" paradigm that we described in Chapter 1. It assumes that inequalities such as unequal rewards are necessary for society because they motivate individuals to work hard and to aspire to difficult work that requires talents and skills not everyone possesses. The functionalist perspective assumes that some positions in society are "more important" than others and should therefore be more highly rewarded. This perspective differs from the "conflict perspective," which argues that inequalities result not from the fact that some jobs are more important than others (a claim it disallows) but from the ability of those in control—of the political and economic structures of society—to maintain their privileged positions.

The conflict perspective directs our attention to another pervasive characteristic of the American occupational structure, one that runs counter to its achievement ideology: The higher-level, better-paying jobs tend to be held by the members of one dominant group (white males) and the lower-level, poorer-paying jobs tend to be held by all others (women and minority-group members). Some believe that this reflects differences in abilities and qualifications, differences in interests, talents, and preferences. Others argue that it results from exclusionary practices that reflect discriminatory attitudes. Most observers would likely agree that the situation results from a combination of these and other, related factors.

In this chapter, we will detail the pervasiveness of sex segregation and inequity in our society's workforce, and we will then focus on the major explanations and rationales that have been offered to account for them.

Sex Segregation of Occupations

Women today are still clustered in traditionally "female" occupations. Although women are represented in all occupational groups, they remain concentrated in the clerical and service occupations—a situation that has not changed over the most recent decades. Women are much more likely to become bank tellers, data-entry clerks, secretaries, schoolteachers, and nurses. Indeed, scanning the vast list of occupational titles that currently exist in the U.S. economy, we find men and women segregated into different kinds of jobs ("men's jobs," "women's jobs"), and we also find men holding down many more types of jobs—indeed, more than four in ten of all women (43 percent) who work full time do so in just twenty occupations, and each of these occupations is 60 percent or more female (U.S. Department of Labor Women's Bureau, 2003). This phenomenon alone would be of little concern if it were not for the fact that across the gamut of the occupational prestige scale—that is, at every level (low, middle, high)—we find "men's jobs" paying more. Indeed, there is a strong statistical relationship between the concentration of women in given occupations and the wage levels therein (Dill, Cannon, and Vanneman, 1987, as cited in Scarpitti, Andersen, and O'Toole, 1997, p. 226).

Table 3.1 summarizes the strong degree to which the occupational world is still sex segregated and the repercussions for gender inequality thereof. Not evident in this table, however, is another phenomenon that tends to depress the wages of women compared to men; that is, women tend to be toward the lower end of the wage/prestige scales of those predominantly male fields that they do enter. For example, females entering medicine are much more likely to go into family practice or pediatrics, which average about 80 percent of the annual salary of surgery—which is male-dominated (Bureau of Labor Statistics, 2001a). Women now represent about a third of the nation's physicians; female doctors are, however, only about half as likely as their male counterparts to be earning more than $2,000 a week (19.9 percent of women versus 36.3 percent of men; see Bureau of Labor Statistics, 2003e). Women represent only about 12 percent of the board of directors in the nation's five hundred largest companies, and women of color only about 1 percent (Catalyst, 2003a). Similarly, women comprise only about 16 percent of the senior executives (corporate officers) of these companies (Catalyst, 2003a); moreover, these women earn only about two-thirds of their male counterparts (Brooks, 1993). Women now constitute 34 percent of all lawyers, but only 15 percent of the partners in major law firms (Bureau of Labor Statistics, 2003e; Williams, 2001). And, as with physicians, female lawyers are only about half as likely as their male counterparts to be earning more than $2,000 a week (16.9 percent of women versus 32.1 percent of men; see Bureau of Labor Statistics, 2003e).

On the positive side, however, it should be noted that each year women slightly increase their presence in the boardrooms of corporate America and by 2027 it is predicted that a fourth of all Fortune 500 corporate board seats will be held by women, a substantial minority of which will be Asian, Latina, and

Table 3.1
SEX SEGREGATION IN U.S. OCCUPATIONS, 2001

Rank	Top 10 Male Full-Time Occupations	#Men	%Men	Median Weekly ($) Earnings
1	Operator, Fabricator, or Laborer	11,310,000	77.6	501
2	Executive, Administrative, or Managerial Occupation	8,349,000	52.9	1,060
3	Construction Worker	4,407,000	97.9	613
4	Mechanic	3,951,000	95.1	670
5	Precision Production, Craft, or Repair Occupation	2,537,000	78.0	680
6	Truck Driver	2,421,000	95.7	593
7	Sales Supervisor/Proprietor	1,957,000	57.9	712
8	Engineer	1,787,000	90.3	1,149
9	Police, Fire, or Protective Worker	1,783,000	82.3	658
10	Food Preparation and Service	1,648,000	50.1	343
	Selected Other Heavily Male Occupations			
	Mover	1,001,000	95.2	540
	Miner	123,000	98.4	789
	Logger	41,000	91.1	615
	All Full-Time Male Workers	55,928,000		672

Rank	Top 10 Female Full-Time Occupations	#Female	%Female	
1	Administrative Support, including Clerical	10,954,000	77.0	469
2	Executive, Administrative, or Managerial Occupation	7,446,000	47.1	706
3	Operator, Fabricator, or Laborer	3,258,000	22.4	368
4	Sales Rep.–Retail and Personal Services	1,971,000	56.7	313
5	Food Preparation and Service	1,638,000	49.9	309
6	Elementary School Teacher	1,596,000	81.5	731
7	Registered Nurse	1,459,000	91.0	820
8	Sales Supervisor/Proprietor	1,423,000	42.1	502
9	Nursing Aide, Orderly, or Attendant	1,309,000	88.2	356
10	Cashier	1,075,000	77.7	292
	Selected Other Heavily Female Occupations			
	Bookkeeper	975,000	92.2	474
	Personal Service (e.g., Hairdresser, Daycare, Attendant)	919,000	74.0	355
	Receptionist	697,000	97.9	401
	Preschool Teacher	487,000	98.2	476
	Teacher's Aide	384,000	92.5	356
	Private Household Worker (e.g., Cleaning, Childcare)	340,000	96.0	255
	Legal Assistant	289,000	84.0	637
	Licensed Practical Nurse	271,000	94.4	562
	Textile Sewing Machine Operator	231,000	72.9	311
	Dental Hygienist	46,000	95.8	725
	All Full-Time Female Workers	43,671,000		511

Source: Bureau of Labor Statistics (2003e).

African American (Catalyst, 2003b). Women are making similar—that is to say small but steady—gains in the high-prestige specialties within medicine, law, and the other professions.

More generally, as we will document in later chapters, there have been many improvements in female opportunity in many careers that have been traditionally male-dominated. Among the more prominent examples are medicine, dentistry, law, college teaching, and various managerial specialties in business. Yet, in the high-paying professions, we still find men predominating: The ratio of men to women physicians is 2.1 to 1; for dentists also 2.1 to 1; architects, 3.2 to 1; engineers, 9.4 to 1; computer scientists, 1.8 to 1; natural scientists (e.g., chemists, geologists, biologists), 2.7 to 1; and for lawyers, 1.9 to 1 (Bureau of Labor Statistics, 2003e). Furthermore, in many traditional "men's" fields, especially those in the high-paying areas of blue-collar work and the highly technical professions such as aerospace, chemical, and mechanical engineering, women are finding entry tough. This is partly because of socialization during childhood and partly because of the different educational tracks taken by males and females. To these factors can be added organizational policies that encourage sex segregation (e.g., the policy of only hiring women as telephone operators) and the resistance put forth by men. This resistance can take the form of open opposition (women don't belong "in squad cars," "on construction sites," "in the military," and so on), sexual harassment, and reduced opportunities for advancement.

The Glass Ceiling

In the mid-1970s, fewer than one in five working women in the United States (17.6 percent) held a managerial or professional job, but by the early 2000s more than one in three (36.5 percent) held such jobs; moreover, by 2001, women had become *more likely* than men to hold these jobs (36.5 percent of women working full time versus 29.1 percent of men working full time; see Bureau of Labor Statistics, 2003e). On the face of it, it appears that American women have reached parity with—and even exceeded—men in acquiring the most prestigious jobs in the occupational structure. However, these gross figures mask much detail. Most importantly, they do not reveal that men hold the best paying and most influential managerial and professional jobs. As already noted, women hold only 16 percent of the top executive positions in the nation's largest corporations (the Fortune 500) and only 12 percent of the boards of directors of these companies.

The gross figures also mask the significant income inequality between men and women—even when we take into account similarities in education and type of occupation. As revealed in Table 3.2, women's weekly earnings for every occupational category except "private household" average only about three-fourths of what men earn (from a low of 62 percent to a high of 89 percent, with a weighted average of 76 percent). And, as demonstrated in Figure 3.1, when education is held constant, we still see women, on average, making only between two-thirds and three-quarters of what men are making. Finally, college-

Table 3.2
PERCENTAGE DISTRIBUTION AND MEDIAN WEEKLY EARNINGS OF FULL-TIME WORKERS BY OCCUPATION AND SEX, 2001

Occupation	MEN			WOMEN			Earnings Ratio (W/M) (%)
	Number	Percent	Weekly Earnings	Number	Percent	Weekly Earnings	
Managerial & Professional Specialty	**16,265,000**	**29.1**	**1,038**	**15,956,000**	**36.5**	**732**	**70.5**
Executive, Administrative, and Managerial	8,349,000	14.9	1,060	7,446,000	17.0	706	66.6
Professional Specialty	7,916,000	14.2	1,021	8,510,000	19.5	749	73.4
Technical, Sales, & Administrative Support	**10,733,000**	**19.2**	**667**	**17,411,000**	**39.9**	**473**	**70.9**
Technicians and Related Support	1,870,000	3.3	783	1,883,000	4.3	580	74.1
Sales Occupations	5,599,000	10.0	692	4,574,000	10.5	429	62.0
Administrative Support, Including Clerical	3,264,000	5.8	576	10,954,000	25.1	469	81.4
Service Occupations	**5,330,000**	**9.5**	**438**	**5,812,000**	**13.3**	**335**	**76.5**
Private Household	15,000	<0.1	255	340,000	0.8	255	100.0
Protective Service	1,783,000	3.2	658	383,000	0.9	509	77.4
Other Service	3,532,000	6.3	374	5,089,000	11.7	332	88.8
Precision Production, Craft, & Repair	**11,018,000**	**19.7**	**648**	**1,102,000**	**2.5**	**479**	**73.9**
Operators, Fabricators, & Laborers	**11,310,000**	**20.2**	**501**	**3,258,000**	**7.5**	**368**	**73.5**
Machine Operators, Assemblers, & Inspectors	3,954,000	7.1	512	2,119,000	4.9	369	72.1
Transportation & Material Moving	4,149,000	7.4	587	356,000	0.8	439	74.8
Handlers, Equipment Cleaners, Helpers, & Laborers	3,207,000	5.7	401	783,000	1.8	342	85.3
Farming, Forestry, & Fishing	**1,271,000**	**2.3**	**366**	**222,000**	**0.5**	**308**	**84.2**
All	**55,928,000**	**100**	**672**	**43,671,000**	**100**	**511**	**76.0**

Sources: Bureau of Labor Statistics (2003d, 2003e).

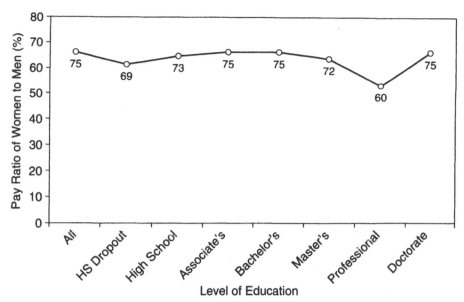

Figure 3.1. Pay Ratios of Women to Men by Level of Education, 2001 (Full-Time Workers, Age Twenty-five and Older). *Sources:* U.S. Bureau of the Census (2003h, 2003c).

educated men are one-and-a-half to three times more likely to be "top" income earners (making more than $75,000 per year) in the contemporary United States (see Figure 3.2). Cross-national trends parallel those in the United States. As is evident in Figure 3.3, women abroad have made significant inroads in acquiring managerial and administrative positions; for example, they hold down more than a third of these positions in Eastern European nations and a quarter of such positions in Western Europe, Southern Africa, Latin American, and Southeast Asia. However, as in the United States, very few women can be found at the top of the organizational chart. A mid-1990s survey reports no women as chief executive officers in large corporations outside of the United States, only 1 percent at the senior vice president level, and only 2 percent at the junior or assistant vice president tier (United Nations, 1995a, p. 152). In Nordic countries, famous for their recent advances in gender equality, almost no women are managing directors in the one hundred largest private enterprises and there are very few women at other levels of management and on corporate boards (United Nations, 1995a, p. 152; see also, Nordic Council of Ministers, 1994). The United Nations (2000, p. 31) reports that only 3 percent of board members in large corporations in the United Kingdom are women and that the situation is no different in Germany.

The barrier that prevents many women from attaining the most powerful, the most prestigious, and the highest-paying jobs in work organizations has been labeled the *glass ceiling* (Federal Glass Ceiling Commission, 1995). The metaphor of "glass" implies that the barrier is invisible; there are no obvious obstacles barring women from these jobs—no advertisements saying "women

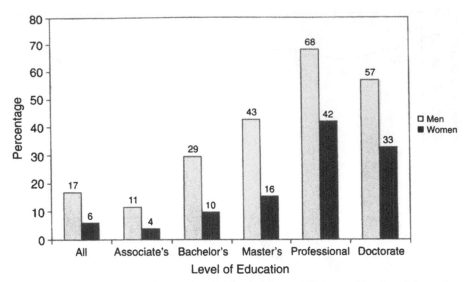

Figure 3.2. Percentage of Men versus Percentage of Women Earning More than $75,000 per Year by Level of Education, 2001 (Full-Time Workers, Age Twenty-five and Older). *Sources:* U.S. Bureau of the Census (2003b, 2003c).

need not apply," nor any formal mandates that dictate that "women are not el-igible" for the company's highest-level positions. Rather, women face organi-zational cultures that favor men. As we shall explore in Chapter 6, these cul-tures often serve to exclude women from the necessary "networking" and "mentoring" that it is required for promotion to the top positions in the cor-poration; they also fail to recognize—and make adjustments for—women's greater caregiving responsibilities.

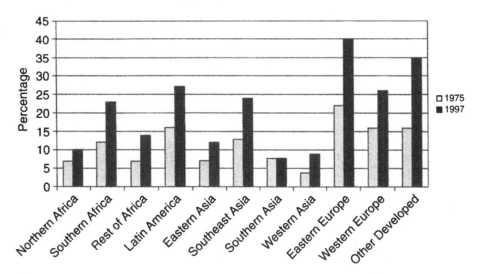

Figure 3.3. Percentage of Managerial and Administration Positions Held by Women in Selected Regions of the World, 1975, 1997. *Source:* United Nations, 2000, p. 130.

In recent decades, women have entered the world of white-collar work en masse, though they still must contend with the "glass ceiling."

The Growing Importance of the Female/Male Earnings Gap

Set the value of a male between the ages of twenty and sixty at fifty shekels of silver, according to the sanctuary shekel, and if it is a female, set her value at thirty shekels.

Leviticus 27:3–4

So spoke the Lord to Moses in the Old Testament. Fortunately, the prevailing earnings gap between men and women has narrowed, but it is still very large, and increasingly significant.

Labor-force participation of U.S. women has increased steadily since the end of World War II: In 1948, approximately 33 percent of women and 87 percent of men were in the paid labor force; by 2003, the percentage of working women had risen to just over 60, while the percentage of working men had dropped to just under 75. Moreover, the United States Bureau of the Census predicts these trends—an increasing female rate and decreasing male rate of labor-force participation—to continue for the coming decade (U.S. Bureau of the Census, 2002a, Table 568, p. 367). More of these women in the past three decades work full time: up from 41 percent in 1970 to 69 percent in 2000 (Bureau of Labor Statistics, 1971; U.S. Bureau of the Census, 2002a, Tables 572 and 621). Meanwhile, the percentage of all households headed by women, which includes families with children as well as living alone, during this period doubled—from 21.1 to 42.1 (U.S. Bureau of the Census, 2001b).

The growing labor-force participation of women brings into the limelight the problem of economic inequality between the sexes. Among full-time workers, women currently earn only about three-quarters (76 percent) of what men earn (Bureau of Labor Statistics, 2003d, 2003e; see also the last row in Table 3.2). In days gone by, when a woman's income was seen as a mere supplement to her husband's or to the overall family income, one might have used a twisted model of fairness to justify men being paid more than women for the same work or job. However, such a model is clearly inappropriate today, when it is common for women to be heads of families (that is, raising children with no husband present), or to live alone, or, if married, to be contributing heavily to family income and significantly defining the standard of living. All of these issues are magnified when we consider that the same phenomena exist throughout the world: In both developed and developing regions, women are increasingly joining the paid labor force (Figure 3.4). And everywhere, even though they are contributing significantly to—if not providing all of—their families' incomes, women's incomes tend to fall far short of men's. Controlling for the type of job being held, women in developed nations earn only about 77 percent of what men do; and this percentage is about the same, and often even less, in developing nations (for manufacturing jobs, see Figure 3.5). And, as in the United States, women in both developed (Figure 3.6) and developing nations are much more likely now than in the past to have children out of wedlock and to be the major or sole supporters of their families (as recognized by their being designated "head of household" by census-takers; see Figure 3.7). For example, the

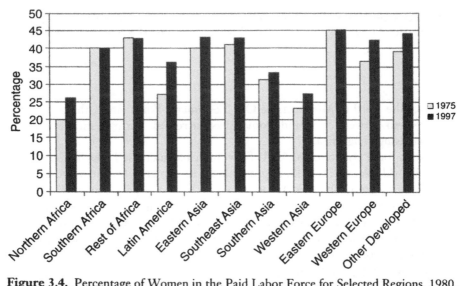

Figure 3.4. Percentage of Women in the Paid Labor Force for Selected Regions, 1980, 1997. Note: The steadily rising rate of economic participation of women does not reveal the full extent of their contribution to economic development because these "official" rates do not fully recognize work done at home and outside the formal economy (see United Nations, 1996a, p. 625). Also note that the participation rates for men dropped slightly in every region. *Source:* United Nations (2000, p. 110).

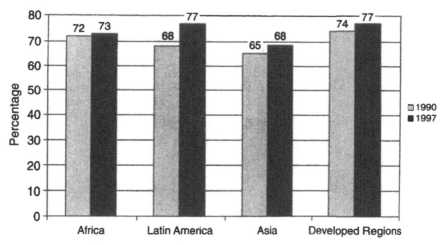

Figure 3.5. Women's Wages as a Percentage of Men's Wages for Selected Regions (Manufacturing Jobs), 1990, 1997 *Source:* United Nations (2000, p. 132).

percentage of births to unmarried women in Austria leaped from 13 to 30 between 1970 and 1998; during this period the percentage also leaped in Denmark from 11 to 45, in France from 7 to 40, and in the United Kingdom from 8 to 38. Among developing regions, by the early 1990s, 45 percent of all births in Latin America were to unmarried women, while these rates in central (8 percent) and western (9 percent) Asia had risen to levels previously unheard of in these strongly family-oriented areas (United Nations, 1995a, p. 19; 2000, p. 36). Furthermore, by the late 1990s, almost a third of the households in developed nations were headed by women, with the percentage in most developing countries not far behind (Southern Africa's percentage, 42, was even greater).

Figure 3.6. Out-of-Wedlock Births for Developed Regions, 1970–1998. *Sources:* United Nations (1995a, p. 19; 2000, p. 36).

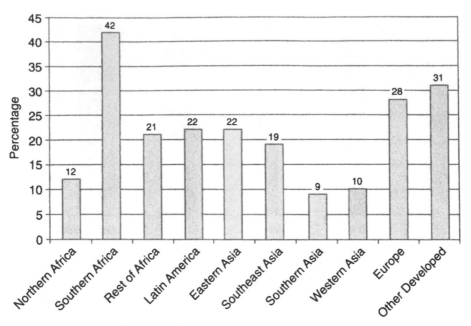

Figure 3.7. "Head of Household" Designation for Women, Selected Regions, 1997. *Source:* United Nations (2000, p. 42).

Explaining Occupational Segregation and Inequality

How is occupational segregation by sex to be explained? How can we account for the differences between men and women's earnings? To what extent are discriminatory practices to blame? To what extent does the disparity reflect differences in individual characteristics, such as women's training, credentials, and their particular interests, innate abilities, preferences, and socialization? To what extent, on the other hand, does the disparity reflect structural features of the society—in particular, its economic and legal institutions?

The Economic Context—The Individual Approach

The underlying assumption of the individual approach is that inequalities in the labor force reflect differences in individual workers—differences in ability, training, and the like. Women workers are viewed as lacking the essential qualities to "make it" in an economic setting. Their deficiencies range from a lack of specific job-related credentials (such as education, training, relevant work experience) to a variety of presumed personality traits (such as women's "fear of success" or characteristic submissiveness). The typical suggested solution lies in changing the woman—with appropriate career counseling and education and perhaps through assertiveness training or the like.

Such individual-level explanations suggest that the woman worker does not have the motivation, qualifications, or personal attributes necessary for the pursuit of higher-prestige and higher-paid employment. These reasons imply that women's poor economic position stems from choices they make and from their personal capacities. But such observed differences between male and female workers are not surprising, because the socialization process emphasizes different roles, norms, and values for men and women.

Sex-Role Socialization and Women's "Choices"

Men and women are brought up to behave in particular, culturally prescribed ways. Their respective social responsibilities involve a division of labor whereby women assume the role of wife and mother and men the role of provider. The sex segregation of the labor market reflects this broader division of labor. The occupations held predominantly by women (such as waitressing, childcare, secretarial work, nursing, elementary school teaching) are those that reflect the traditional female nurturing and supportive roles. The more task-oriented and intellectually demanding jobs (such as doctor, lawyer, executive, crafts worker) have traditionally belonged to men. Even when women enter male-dominated occupations such as medicine, gender roles and family responsibilities may influence the specialty areas they select. For example, women physicians tend to go into fields most compatible with traditional female roles: pediatrics and family practice.

Furthermore, women often seek employment that allows them the flexibility to spend time with their families. Putting family first frequently prevents women from obtaining the training and other credentials needed to compete more effectively in the job market. Thus it is possible to say that women end up concentrated in "women's jobs" *partly* because they choose to do so. Surveys over the past two decades lend some support to this belief. For example, a 1979 survey of 5,000 young women between the ages of twenty-one and thirty-one found that the majority aspired to "traditionally" female occupations, even though they rejected the role of full-time homemaker (Barrett, 1979, p. 53). Surveys of women's choices of college majors have consistently revealed that they tend to pick the humanities, education, library science, or foreign languages; and when women do go into science, they overwhelmingly concentrate in the social sciences and psychology (Eisenhart, 1996; also see Chapter 4). A large-scale national survey of teenagers conducted in the 2002 revealed that significantly more girls than boys say it is most important to have a career in which they can help others and improve society (73 percent of girls versus 55 percent of boys ranked "helping others" as extremely or very important in a career). This survey also revealed that the priorities of girls and boys differed regarding career and family: While 80 percent of the girls reported that they expect to work full time as adults, almost 60 percent believe they will take time off from their jobs when they have children; in contrast, only 11 percent of boys expect to take a career break for family (see Committee of 200, 2002).

The essence of the individual model is that women's preferences—for traditionally female-typed jobs, and thus the types of training they receive, the types of work for which they apply, and the occupations they wind up in—are the *primary* determinants of women's labor-force position. This model assumes women's freedom of choice in the selection of a given occupation.

But many observers question whether a woman's choice is so free. They point to the constraints imposed by society that serve to limit a woman's ability to choose freely. Critics also note that explanations emphasizing female choice rely on "an elusive factor termed tastes to explain why women 'chose' to enter a given occupation or to have a given preference for non-market work, without providing an underlying theory that explains the choice. Moreover, it is not clear why *only* women should have such tastes, nor is it clear why a large proportion of women should exhibit the same set of tastes—as demonstrated by their occupational distribution" (Blau and Jusenius, 1976, p. 188).

Human-Capital Theory

A related argument, one that shifts the focus only slightly, comes from "human-capital theory." As a result of socialized attitudes and values, women are said to invest less in their own "human capital." That is, they do not invest in those qualities—education, training, or job-related experience—that lead to a "return on investment" in the labor market. Men do invest in their own human capital; they are therefore able to make a greater economic contribution to society. Their occupational opportunities and their rewards are correspondingly greater. Men's and women's positions in the labor market are said to reflect these differences in human-capital investment.

Human-capital theory derives from a neoclassical view of economics, which suggests that workers are in an ideal competitive labor market in which the economic rewards received by workers and the occupations they obtain are determined entirely by their investments in human capital (see Becker, 1964, 1975; Cohn, 1996; Mincer, 1962; and Polachek, 1976, 1978, 1979). These human investments are similar to investments an employer makes in physical capital—a factory or machinery—because they help to ensure high productivity and earnings. The term *human capital* refers to those dimensions that affect one's ability to produce on the job—such things as educational level attained, number of years worked, job training, absenteeism, and turnover. Because men and women make unequal investments in human capital, they have unequal productive skills; the result is unequal occupational attainments and differences in wages. For example, "women are more likely than men to quit their jobs prematurely. Because of this, firms are reluctant to hire them for high-status positions because such positions customarily involve extensive training" (Cohn, 1996, p. 108).

Human-capital theory has both conceptual and empirical problems. The conceptual problems result largely from the theory's attempt to focus exclusively on individual factors, when in truth there is an unavoidable tangle of individual and structural factors. This tangle produces difficulties when human-capital researchers attempt to translate the theory into empirical terms for research.

To measure wage inequities that result from differences in qualifications, human-capital theorists have compared wage differences with differences in economic contributions or productivity. Any remaining wage differences are attributed to discrimination. Treiman and Hartmann's (1981) review of human-capital studies indicates, however, that only two of the seven studies examined—Corcoran and Duncan (1979) and Mincer and Polachek (1974)—explain a fair percentage of the gap in wages between men and women.

Corcoran and Duncan's study is the more detailed of the two. They obtained a thorough history of the educational attainment, on-the-job training, work experience, and degree of labor-force commitment for a national sample of husbands and their spouses in the labor force in 1975. These factors accounted for only about 44 percent of the differences in men's and women's wages. The largest single factor was differences in work history. Women had less work experience in terms of general on-the-job training. (On-the-job training cannot properly be considered part of a worker's "investment" in his or her human capital, as it is typically under the employer's [rather than the employee's] control.) Treiman and Hartmann (1981) argue that women's lesser job experience needs a fuller explanation than the conventional interpretation that women voluntarily limit their labor-force experience because of family demands. The difference may also reflect discriminatory restriction of occupational opportunities, including employers' reluctance to hire or train women based on an assumption that they may leave to have children.

Human-capital studies have other shortcomings. It is difficul to measure differences in productivity among jobs. Such things as education, training, and work experience are taken as indirect measures; but these variables do not easily translate into measures of productivity.

Other research indicates that, even if women equaled men in human-capital investment and achievement, their earnings would still be markedly lower. For example, Suter and Miller (1973) reported that, even when male and female differences in education, year-round full-time employment, occupational status, and lifetime work experience are accounted for, a wage gap of 38 percent remains unexplained.

In one of the most important tests of human-capital theory, England (1982) analyzed data from the 1967 National Longitudinal Survey (NLS) of a sample of women between the ages of thirty and forty-four. She concluded that human-capital theory fails to explain occupational sex segregation. Among England's specific observations: Women whose employment is more continuous are not more apt to choose male occupations. And women are not penalized less for time spent out of the labor force if they choose a female occupation. On the contrary, women have higher wages if they are employed in occupations containing more males (holding schooling, home time, and experience constant).

Human-capital theory does not adequately explain the wage differences between men and women; the sizable earnings gap cannot be explained simply by differences in the characteristics of the workers, such as their educational level and their job experience. The theory fails to provide an adequate account of the underlying mechanisms of discrimination because it relies solely on characteristics of individuals to explain women's inferior economic position. This exclusive focus on individual factors limits the theory's usefulness.

Limitations of the Individual Approach

The individual approach to explaining women's inferior economic position implies that the individual is the locus of the problem and that therefore the solution to the problem lies within the individual. The Foxworth quotation in Chapter 1 (p. 12–13) is typical of this approach. Clearly, efforts to provide women with better information, increased access to job training, and help for their various "personality deficits" would be useful in improving their labor-force status. However, by concentrating solely on individual deficits and by focusing on changing the individual—that is, locating causes within individuals, perceiving their characteristics and deficiencies as causes—the structural factors influencing women's disadvantaged economic situation are overlooked. Overlooking the structural factors precludes consideration of structural changes that are necessary to improve women's labor-market position.

The individual approach amounts to "blaming the victim"—not unlike attempts to blame the homeless for being homeless, the poor for being poor, and so on. Those who blame the victim typically claim that this sort of person is somehow different from the norm.

> [Victim blamers] must learn how to demonstrate that the poor, the black, the ill, the jobless, the slum tenants, are different and strange. They must learn to conduct or interpret the research that shows how "these people" think in different forms, act in different patterns, cling to different values, seek different goals, and learn different truths. Which is to say that they are strangers, barbarians, savages. This is how the distressed and disinherited are redefined in order to make it possible for us to look at society's problems and to attribute their causation to the individuals affected. (Ryan, 1971, p. 10)

Such views all fail to consider the problem within the wider social-structural context.

To suggest that women's inferior economic situation results from their choices is to make women into "victims by choice." The following account is typical of individual-level explanations for women's lower economic standing:

> If women were to press for admission to medical schools and law schools and academic disciplines . . . they would crash the gates. They do not. . . . This is because they accept the cultural mandate in defining their own priorities as belonging to the family. The reason for this lies in the most familiar of all facts: that almost every woman is married or hopes to be married to a man. The family is the locus of consensus regarding the cultural mandate. (Coser and Rokoff, 1971, p. 540)

Human-capital theory assumes that women freely choose to obtain only certain "female" jobs, to acquire less formal education than men, to enter into lower-paying work, and to be underemployed. As one critic has pointed out,

> Neoclassical theory abstracts economics from power by assuming that individuals exercise freedom of choice. This is not an unreasonable assumption in a world populated by atomistic individuals with roughly equal endowments of material and human capital. But in a world in which men and women, and workers and capitalists, have unequal wealth and power, their abilities to exercise freedom of choice differ. In such a world, all women may be subject to discrimination. All may be saddled with child-rearing responsibilities. Working-class wives may have little choice about whether or not to work. The working class as a whole has no choice at all. If this is the kind of world which one believes to exist, then the neoclassical assumption of freedom of choice yields no insights into the realities of women's problems. It mystifies them. (Amsden, 1980, p. 32)

Of course, many in any society have vested interests in making the status quo appear chosen—especially those who are presently in a privileged position. And indeed the individual perspective is inherently conservative. But we need to look further, beyond the individual, to fully comprehend—and grapple with—the complexities of the problem of gender inequality.

The Economic Context—Structural Approach

Many observers argue that structural rather than individual factors are most critical in determining women's labor-force position (see Benokraitis and Feagin, 1995; Headlee and Elfin, 1996). The structural approach focuses on the policies and practices of basic societal institutions—the economy, the legal system, the family, the educational system, religion—that tend to confine women to particular jobs characterized by low wages, little mobility, and limited prestige. This approach blames the structure instead of the victim and suggests a different strategy for improving women's labor-force status. Even at the level of specific jobs, for example, we may find that the characteristics of the job are more blameworthy than the characteristics of the individual who occupies the job:

> It is often said that women "have higher turnover rates," as though this were a property of women and not of the jobs which they occupy. Of course, it may be true to say that women, as a group, are more likely to want to leave jobs more frequently than men, but this should not be confused with the existence of higher *involuntary* turnover rates for women (a property of the job), nor should we ignore the possibility that higher *voluntary* turnover rates can also reflect properties of the job—like low pay and poor work conditions. A failure to unravel the different strands of "individual" and "structural" causation can lead to a crude reification of individual characteristics and an unwanted emphasis upon these characteristics as causes. (Barron and Norris, 1976, p. 50)

From a structural perspective, it appears that even if women were to increase their "human capital" they would meet with resistance—due not to the nature of their qualifications, but instead to their structural position in the labor market. Individuals work within a setting that determines educational and occupational attainment. The structure of the labor market (its hierarchy, its hiring and firing practices) largely determines women's status in the labor force.

Dual Labor Markets

In contrast to the assumptions of human-capital theory, Piore (1975) argues that there is no single competitive labor market in the economy. He contends that the labor market consists of two distinct sectors. The primary sector comprises, most notably, professional and managerial-administrative and technical jobs with relatively high wages and status, good working conditions, opportunity for advancement, equity, due process in the administration of work rules, and employment stability. In the secondary sector, in contrast, jobs are characterized by low wages, poor working conditions, little chance for advancement, lack of stability, and highly personalized employer/employee relations, which are conducive to arbitrary and capricious work discipline. Secondary-sector jobs include semiskilled, operative, nonfarm labor, and service work. Generally, these two labor market sectors are mutually exclusive; workers rarely move from one to the other (Doeringer and Piore, 1971; Piore, 1975).

The sectors are further divided into tiers. In the primary sector, the upper tier consists of the already mentioned professional, managerial-administrative, and technical jobs with high pay and status. Formal education is an absolute prerequisite for entry into the upper tier, where the jobs allow for individual creativity and initiative and provide greater economic security. The jobs in the lower tier are primarily white-collar and clerical positions, sales jobs, and positions for skilled workers. In many ways, the difference between the upper and lower tiers is as great as the difference between the primary and secondary sector. In this dual labor market, women are concentrated in certain occupations, primarily in the lower tier of primary-sector jobs (for example, white-collar clerical jobs).

The dual labor market reinforces the differences in earnings between men and women through what is called the "crowding" effect (Bergmann, 1971; Stevenson, 1975). Women's crowding in lower-tier primary sector (and in some secondary-sector) jobs inflates the supply of labor in those areas, thus reducing women's level of earnings (for these jobs) below what one might anticipate in a truly competitive market (Bergmann, 1971). Men (especially white men) are concentrated, on the other hand, in upper-tier primary-sector occupations, where there is not a great deal of competition from women. This situation operates to men's advantage, because the labor supply in the upper-tier primary sector is "artificially reduced and male earnings are thereby inflated" (Stevenson, 1975, p. 175).

In keeping with assumptions of the dual labor-market theory, Blau's (1977) research on pay differentials and the occupational distribution of male and female office workers found that differences in earnings of men and women within occupations are largely attributed to pay differences *among* firms rather than *within* a given firm. For example, a male clerk and female clerk will earn more nearly the same wage if they work in the same firm than if they work in different firms (even in the same industrial sector). Blau also found that the higher the wages a firm pays across occupations, the smaller the proportion of women employed in the firm—a finding consistent with dual labor-market theories. Because women are concentrated in lower-wage firms, they earn less than men (even in the same occupations—clerk, bookkeeper, janitor) in the higher-wage firms in which men are concentrated.

Despite the fact that dual labor-market theory has consistently received empirical confirmation (Blau, 1977; Dickens and Lang, 1985; Sakamoto and Chen, 1991), it—like human-capital theory—is only descriptive. Both theories describe the results (that is, women's inferior economic position), but neither addresses the issue of how these patterns emerge. In general, however, it is assumed that discriminatory practices of one sort or another are involved.

Discriminatory Practices

Exclusionary practices by employees are one mechanism that can help explain the presence of a dual labor market. Male employees, especially those employed in primary-sector jobs, wish to protect their current economic advantages (see Bergmann, 1971; Bonacich, 1972) by reducing competition and increasing wages in male-dominated occupations. There are some grounds for the fear that if women enter a particular occupation, wages will fall (see Hodge and Hodge, 1965): Men employed in industries and occupations that exclude women are reported to have higher earnings than men in less sex-segregated industries and occupations (see Blau, 1977; Cotter et al., 1997, p. 723; Dill, Cannon, and Vanneman, 1987; and Fuchs, 1971, p. 14).

Male workers have traditionally used various means to control the sex composition of their occupations. Craft unions, for example, have frequently excluded female workers (Hartmann, 1976; Milkman, 1980). Although it may be argued that such practices are not directed toward women in particular but toward unskilled workers in general (Beechey, 1977, p. 55), it must be acknowledged that craft-union policies have contributed to the underrepresentation of women in the skilled trades. Similarly, professional associations until the 1970s commonly restricted female entry into medicine, law, and the other higher professions, while male-dominated "chambers of commerce" tended to keep women out of executive positions (Burris and Wharton, 1981, pp. 9–10; Walsh, 1977).

Another important factor in explaining the dual labor market lies in employers' "tastes." Just as women choose certain jobs that fit the traditional image of appropriate work for women, employers also are influenced by such cultural images. Thus, they may choose male or female workers because they seek traits believed to be masculine or feminine, regardless of whether specific women or men possess such traits. To this extent, women's labor-market situation is a result of employers' "irrational preferences" (Becker, 1957).

An illustration of the attitudes that produce irrational preferences is given in a hallmark study of women in management:

> In our professional work, we have often spent many hours convincing a man in management that it was important for him to try to understand the differ-

ences which women were bringing to the organizational setting. He would respond to our argument by repeating again and again that he agreed that men
and women are different but that he thanked God that they are. He would
agree that women are less successful in management careers but say thank God
that is so. . . . (Finally) we would say to him. . . . "If you had known on the day
your daughter was born that starting at the age of twenty she would have to
work continuously to survive, would you have . . . done anything differently
with her than you have done up until now?" . . . One corporate senior vice-
president . . . said, "I feel sick to my stomach. If she has to work, then I have
done it all wrong." (Hennig and Jardim, 1977, pp. 203–204)

A variation on "irrational preferences" is "statistical discrimination" (Phelps,
1972; Treiman and Hartmann, 1981). This form of discrimination operates in
the following way: Employers screen potential workers according to certain statistical guidelines. To minimize training and turnover costs, employers try to
select those workers who have the best cost/benefit potential. Believing that
women and minorities have higher turnover rates, employers prefer not to hire
them. This practice is intended as good (cost-effective) business procedure, but
it produces sexual and racial discrimination. On the basis of statistical information of group characteristics, employers can eliminate those candidates they assume least likely to be productive workers. Employers acknowledge that the system is not foolproof, but they assume that it is fairly reliable. Workers excluded
from such jobs will be hired in occupations for which turnover rates are less important or for which wages are sufficiently low that employers are compensated
for their expected higher costs (Treiman and Hartmann, 1981, p. 64). Note that
despite the strong expectation that women will have higher turnover rates because of their childbearing/rearing responsibilities, only about a third of the empirical studies to date show this; about a third indicate that men have higher
turnover than women, and about a third find no differences between the sexes
(Cohn, 1996).

Whether these practices are considered to be unfair sexual discrimination
or whether they are viewed as standard "sound" business practice, the effect is
the same: Women remain concentrated in lower-tier primary-sector jobs and
in secondary-sector jobs. It may be that these practices actually hurt employers; for example, if the costs of screening statistically undesirable workers are
greater than the costs of hiring the excluded workers (see Treiman and Hartmann, 1981, p. 64). Opinions vary along conservative/radical lines. Conservative economists argue that in the long run employers lose financially because
female labor is cheaper (Becker, 1957) and that therefore discrimination is not
in the interests of employers. More radical economists argue that employers do
benefit from discrimination (Edwards, Reich, and Gordon, 1975) because it pro-
tects their economic interests by dividing the interests of workers and prevents
workers from gaining firmer control of their economic situation (Edwards, 1979;
Gordon, 1972). Employers may also benefit by the segregation of women in
lower-tier primary-sector or secondary-sector jobs, because this concentration
permits employers to pay women less and thereby to maximize profits.

Given the formidable structural limits on women's access to better labor opportunities, one may ask whether women should even bother to try to change the personal characteristics that the individual approach identifies as problematic, such as lack of aggressiveness. Such improvements are probably worthwhile, nevertheless, in that they could help solve those work problems that result from factors within the individual's control. And ideally, of course, if women were to solve all such individual problems, the remaining constraints on women's economic advancement would be unequivocally identifiable as structural.

Structural problems, or problems considered from a structural perspective, require a different course of action, however. Just as the individual approach implies individual change, the structural approach implies structural change. Structural change is often effected through legal means, but legal institutions and practices also *reflect* the prevailing social and economic structure. Though we might assume that we can have reliable recourse to the law to make amends, we may find instead that the law more often supports the status quo.

The Legal Context

When Susan B. Anthony stood on trial in June 1873 for having voted the previous November, she accused the judge of having convicted her using "forms of law all made by men, interpreted by men, administered by men, in favor of men, and against women" (quoted in Sachs and Wilson, 1978, p. 92). Unfortunately, Anthony's words describe, to a large extent, the legal history of women in America until the last three decades. While Anthony was struggling with the legal question of whether she was a person, and therefore a citizen entitled to vote, still other women were seeing their property and contractual rights narrowed and their status in the workplace constricted by paternalistic protective legislation. Even with the achievement of the right to vote in 1920, the legal status of women was little improved, with most of the crucial issues lying dormant until the women's movement in the 1960s. Up until this movement, U.S. law had done little more than sanction discriminatory practices that had served to perpetuate occupational segregation and earnings differentials between men and women.

A Short History: The Colonial Period

The law during our early colonial period was based on English common-law tradition, characterized by rigid notions about the role of women (Lee, 1980). Under the law, when a woman married, she lost all control over her property, she lost the right to contract or sue, and she was legally obligated to perform domestic services for her husband. However, colonial times may in fact have been more liberal for the status of women than were later periods, as local customs often took precedence over established law (Sachs and Wilson, 1978). As noted in Chapter 2, the married woman's (*feme couverte*) legal status was lower than that of a single woman (*feme sole*), as it was in English common law. But in commercial areas of the colonies, some married women were declared "*feme-sole* traders*," giving them the right to sue, to enter into contracts, to sell property, and to have the power of attorney in the absence of their husbands, rights that unmarried women enjoyed.

Similarly, because of a general labor shortage, common-law restrictions on female activities were often ignored. Because of the wide range of occupations in which females participated, it seems that the job market was not as sex segregated during the colonial period as it was to become later (see Chapter 2). For example, in Philadelphia, women were employed as silversmiths, barbers, bakers, brewers, tanners, lumberjacks, gunsmiths, butchers, harness makers, printers, morticians, woodworkers, tailors, and in many other crafts. In other areas of the colonies as well, women worked as artisans, merchants, blacksmiths, teachers, nurses, and midwives, and in taverns and coffeehouses (Foner, 1978). In many cases, a widow inherited her husband's trade, often keeping it going under her own name, even if she remarried. In short, at that stage in American history, social mores favoring women's participation in the labor force superseded the existing common-law restrictions. Not surprisingly, however, women's wages in this period were significantly lower than those of men (Foner, 1978).

Things began to change at the end of the eighteenth century and in the early nineteenth century, "as increased mercantile specialization demanded greater economic stability and hence a closer application of the more conservative aspects of English common law" (Sachs and Wilson, 1978, p. 71). Widows had previously been granted "dower rights" by the court, which in fact overruled the common-law provision prohibiting them from inheriting property, and had often been named executrices of their husbands' estates. However, by 1800 dower rights had been renounced, and 85 percent of wills named sons as executors. Further codification of law throughout the nineteenth century contributed to the regression in the legal status of women. The Married Women Property Acts, passed by nine states before the Civil War, were designed to protect (rather than liberate) women. In fact, they ended up protecting the common-law property rights of fathers who were afraid their sons-in-law would squander their daughters' dowries. These acts also "strictly adhered to the traditional ideas of patriarchy by denying women the right to sell, sue, or contract without their husbands' or other male relatives' approval" (Sachs and Wilson, 1978, p. 78). Obviously, such legislation served to exclude women from the many businesses and trades to which they had had access in the pre-Revolutionary times, and led the way to the "cult of true womanhood" that characterized the nineteenth century (see Chapter 2).

Women, the Factory System, and Protective Legislation

With the coming of the industrial revolution, women's place in the workforce underwent major changes. By the 1820s and 1830s, the New England textile mills had recruited thousands of young women. As described in Chapter 2, the "Boston system" of factories, pioneered by Francis Cabot Lowell, consisted of young women (rather than whole families) working in the mills and living in company-owned boardinghouses with house mothers and strict rules and regulations. Within the factories, men held the supervisory and the skilled-labor positions, while women tended spinning machines and looms. Men's wages were established by negotiations; women were paid on a piecework basis. "Wages were set at a level that was high enough to induce young women to leave the farms and stay away from competing employment such as household manufacture and domestic service, but low enough to offer the owners an advantage in employing women rather than men" (Foner, 1978, p. 25).

As a result of the long tedious hours, the work speedups, and the low wages, strikes broke out in the 1830s and 1840s, and women formed organizations such as the Female Labor Reform Association in 1844. The association's founder, Sarah Bagley, the first woman labor leader in American history, spoke out against the falsely glamorous image of factory life fostered by the owners and joined with other factory girls to work for a ten-hour workday and for improvements in sanitary and lighting conditions in the textile factories. (The typical workday was fourteen hours, from 5 a.m. to 7 p.m., with two half-hour breaks, for breakfast and dinner.)

As we saw in Chapter 2, the battle for the ten-hour day was a key issue for women workers in the nineteenth century. Foner (1978) speaks of this issue as uniting working men and women of the 1840s. However, while it is true that mill workers, male and female, struggled for reduced hours, other (male) occupations had long since achieved these hours. "Male workers had frequently won by the 1840s, 50s, and 60s the hours limitations which legislation began to win for women in the 70s, 80s, and 90s" (Baer, 1978, p. 16). For example, in the 1840s the building trades, dominated by men, had achieved a sixty-hour, six-day work week. Improvements in women's industries lagged behind men's "partly because of their [women's] particular suitability for such work, and partly because usually only the least fortunate women were permanent workers" (Baer, 1978, p. 23). In addition, women lacked strong labor organizations.

Clearly, legislation was needed to regulate women's hours and working conditions, which were considerably worse than those of men. This need for special legislation pertaining to women in the workforce became all the more emphatic in the mid- to late nineteenth century as recently immigrated women, destined to spend a lifetime in the mills, replaced the New England farm girls, who usually spent only a few years there. However, the vast body of "protective legislation" that grew out of these conditions did more than remedy the real problems; these laws often went on to place unnecessary constraints on women who sought a better and larger role in the labor force.

Protective Legislation.   Baer (1978) explores the physical, social, economic, and political factors that have been used to promote and justify protective legislation. Most arguments for such legislation are based on women's lesser physical strength and their childbearing responsibilities. Needless to say, such arguments are simplistic, since some women may be stronger than some men and not all women bear children; even those who do are not doing so constantly. More importantly, it seems that the real differences between men and women are the social expectations that surround their roles. The greater responsibility of women for housework and childcare has been used by "reformers" as a rationalization for special legislation. A more insidious factor contributing to protective legislation is economic. Florence Kelley (cited in Baer, 1978, p. 25), a reformer in women's legislation, claimed that men whose own occupations were threatened by competition from women workers demanded restrictions on women's hours of work, thus making women less desirable as employees. Alternatively, some men managed to obtain reduced hours for themselves by getting restrictions on the work hours of the women and children whose work schedules interlocked with their own.

Thus, protective legislation had a dual advantage for men: It drove women out of certain occupations, while it gained reduced hours for men in those occupations in which women remained. Political factors facilitated these developments. The idea of women participating in unions (or in strikes) challenged the core assumptions that women's place was in the home and that women were to be passive, not assertive (Groneman and Norton, 1987, p. 13). Indeed, women had so little power in unions that legislation was viewed as the only remedy to their deplorable job conditions. But the fight became a vicious circle: because of male-dominated unions, working women had to turn to male legislators, who exploited the situation to their own advantage. Baer (1978, p. 26) points out that discriminatory legislation was not necessarily the best remedy, because "if most of the workers subjected to bad conditions were women, legislation which applied to all workers, regardless of sex, would have achieved the desired results."

For the most part, protective legislation began with maximum-hour laws and then branched out to other areas. The earliest maximum-hour laws provided for a ten-hour day, in the absence of a contract to the contrary. This provision often rendered the laws useless, because employees who would not agree to a contract providing for longer hours were often dismissed. By the late nineteenth century, such laws were passed for eight-hour days. Some of these laws were designed specifically for women, as were laws prohibiting them from working certain hours, usually at night. Although one can argue that these laws were progressive in that they improved the working conditions of some women, they were quite difficult to enforce. "Out of the twenty-six maximum-hour and night-work laws in twenty-five states, then, only four—the Massachusetts ten-hour and night-work laws, the Maine ten-hour law, and the New Jersey eleven-hour law—could be enforced with any regularity or predictability" (Baer, 1978, p. 32).

Other types of protective legislation entirely barred women from entering certain occupations. Mining, smelting, working in taverns, cleaning, and moving machinery were forbidden for women by laws in fourteen states. Unions also found ways to keep women out of the trades by enforcing apprenticeship rules (that allowed those licensed in a trade to apprentice whomever they desired—which was tantamount to older men apprenticing younger men) and, ironically, by demanding equal pay for women—so that employers would not hire women just because they could be paid lower wages.

Clearly, so-called protective legislation placed undesirable constraints on women. However, in the fight for suffrage in the early twentieth century, even women's groups tended to ignore the other constraints of the law. Questions of personhood, divorce settlements, and child custody (Sachs and Wilson, 1978, p. 111), which had far-reaching implications for working women, were virtually ignored, while protective legislation was viewed by many women's groups as a boon rather than a burden.

Numerous court cases upheld these protective practices, while invalidating some others. Perhaps the most important of these was the *Muller v. Oregon* (208 U.S. 412, 1908) decision. This court ruling upheld an Oregon statute that placed limits on the number of hours a woman could work, on the theory that the court has a right to protect the "procreative functions" of all working women. The court decided to grant special treatment to women because, it reasoned, a woman was at a disadvantage in the "struggle for subsistence" because of her "physical structure and the performance of maternal functions" and that this was "especially true when the burdens of motherhood are upon her." Furthermore, it argued that

> By abundant testimony of the medical fraternity continuance for a long time, on her feet at work, repeating this from day to day, tends to injurious effects upon the body, and as healthy mothers are essential to vigorous offspring, the physical well-being of women becomes an object of public interest and care in order to preserve the strength and vigor of the race.
>
> Still again, history discloses the fact that woman has always been dependent upon man. He established his control at the outset by superior physical strength, and this control in various forms, with diminishing intensity, has continued to the present. As minors, though not to the same extent, she has been looked upon in the courts as needing especial care that her rights may be preserved . . . even with the consequent increase of capacity for business affairs it is still true that in the struggle for subsistence she is not an equal competitor with her brother. Though limitations upon personal and contractual rights may be removed by legislation, there is that in her disposition and habits of life which will operate against a full assertion of those rights. . . . Differentiated by these matters from the other sex, she is properly placed in a class by herself, and legislation designed for her protection may be sustained, even when like legislation is not necessary for men and could not be sustained. (*Muller v. Oregon*, 208 U.S. 412 [1908], quoted in Sachs and Wilson, 1978, pp. 113–114)

This decision had an important impact on the history of protective legislation. Some states that had previously taken a stand against protective legislation reversed their positions, and others instituted protective and restrictive laws covering women's work hours (Sachs and Wilson, 1978, p. 114). Although the intention of these laws was originally to protect women's interests, they limited women's job opportunities (Lloyd and Niemi, 1979). Protective legislation after the Muller decision served less to protect women and more to protect men's jobs and to reinforce occupational sex segregation. It has served as an excuse for refusing to hire women. For example, the American Telephone and Telegraph Company (AT&T), which was investigated in the 1970s for its almost total segregation of jobs, relied for its defense on state protective laws. The company asserted that this legislation prevented them from employing women in the craft jobs that led to managerial positions (Gates, 1976).

Protective legislation (especially those laws prohibiting women's employment in jobs requiring long hours, night work, heavy lifting, and so on) not only contributed to sex segregation of occupations, but also served to reduce women's wages compared to men's. The "crowding" of women into a limited number of occupations creates an oversupply of employees for a small number of opportunities, and this in turn reduces wages in these female-typed jobs.

Domestic-Relations Laws and Other Legislation

Beyond protective labor-legislation laws, domestic-relations laws also reinforce women's traditional role and perpetuate sex segregation in employment. Perhaps the most fundamental of these domestic-relations laws is the marriage contract, whose origins go back to common law.

In 1853, Elizabeth Cady Stanton wrote to Susan B. Anthony, "I feel, as never before, that this whole question of women's rights turns on the pivot of the marriage relation, and mark my word, sooner or later it will be the topic for discussion" (quoted in Sachs and Wilson, 1978, p. 148). Stanton foresaw the subtle ways in which the marriage contract could undermine women's rights by perpetuating and reinforcing the existing inequalities between men and women. The marriage contract, as interpreted by the courts, clearly gives higher status to men. As late as 1970, an Ohio Supreme Court held that a wife was "at most a superior servant to her husband . . . only chattel personality, no property, and no legally recognized feelings or rights."

> As recently as 1974, the Georgia legislature approved a statute that defined the husband as "head of the family" with the wife . . . "subject to him; her legal existence . . . merged in the husband, except so far as the law recognizes her separately, either for her own protection, or for her benefit, or for the preservation of the public order." (*The Spokeswoman*, January 15, 1977, p. 11; quoted in Sachs and Wilson, 1978, p. 149)

Until the last three decades, the marriage contract and other domestic-relations laws (for example, those concerning property and credit rights, Social Security and other pension benefits, pregnancy and other disability insurance, as well as maternity-leave policies and benefits) have reinforced and perpetuated "women's place at home" and "men's place at work." This legislation also made it more difficult to counteract employers' attitudes concerning the ability of women workers:

> Because a man is the legally appointed breadwinner, he is considered to be serious about his work, ambitious, and responsible. Jobs with a future must be reserved for him so that he can meet the financial needs of his growing family. . . . A woman, on the other hand, makes a poor foreman or sergeant if she is not even boss in her own home.

> If marriage were legally a partnership, a real contractual relationship, employers might be less inclined to channel young men and women into jobs believed to be appropriate for them as stereotypical husbands and wives. (Gates, 1976, p. 68)

Still other legislation penalized women more directly. Among these were laws that specifically pertained to working mothers, such as those regarding maternity leave. For example, in *General Electric Co.* v. *Gilbert* (321 U.S. 125, 1976), the court ruled that employers did not need to compensate women for maternity-related disabilities as they compensate employees for other disabilities. This type of legislation penalized a woman directly by placing a financial penalty on her for being pregnant. It reinforced society's message that a woman, especially a mother, belongs at home rather than at a paying job. Partly in response to this ruling, legislation has been passed over the past two decades that secures the rights of pregnant workers. Most importantly Public Law 95-555 was approved in 1978, amending Title VII to ban discrimination based on pregnancy. Fifteen years later, the spirit of this law was extended by the 1993 Family and Medical Leave Act, which requires employers of more than fifty persons to grant unpaid leaves of twelve weeks a year to any employee to meet family obligations (such as the birth of a child). Although the leave act was symbolically important, its objective effects have been minimal because 95 percent of all American businesses employ fewer than fifty employees and because few working families can afford to take *unpaid* leaves.

Other Significant Legislation:
Sex Discrimination and Equal Opportunity

It was not until the early 1960s that protective legislation was overridden by the Equal Pay Act (1963) and the equal employment-opportunity provisions of Title VII of the Civil Rights Act of 1964. These new laws and regulations nullified the protective labor laws of the states and provided a different legal environment, one that legally prohibited overt sex discrimination. They were unexpectedly invigorated by the passage of Title IX of the Education Amendments Act of 1972.

The Equal Pay Act. The Equal Pay Act of 1963 is the oldest federal legislation that deals with sex discrimination. It stipulates that men and women must receive equal pay on jobs for which performance requires equal skill, effort, and responsibility, and which are performed under similar working conditions. Differences in pay rates are allowed only in relation to a nondiscriminatory seniority system, a merit system, or a system that measures earnings by quality or quantity of production, as well as a differential based on any factor other than sex (Task Force on Working Women, 1975, p. 57). Thus, for example, airline companies cannot—as was once common—pay stewards more than they pay stewardesses. Both stewards and stewardesses perform the same work, and both must put forth the same amount of skill and effort. The Equal Pay Act encouraged these companies to create the title "flight attendant" and a uniform pay scale (Conrad and Maddux, 1988, p. 7). Many companies had justified differential-pay policies by observing that men were the "breadwinners" in American families and that women's income was merely "supplemental"; and many of these companies further acknowledged that such differential-pay scales lowered their costs and, therefore, the costs incurred by consumers.

The Act's major objective was to help women who were doing work substantially equal to that done by men but who were being paid less for it—and in this it has been a success. Indeed, it produced tens of millions of dollars in back-pay settlements, both in and out of court (Gelb and Palley, 1982). However, the Act did not address the more pervasive discrimination affecting women whose work, though different from work performed by men, is perceived to be of equal value—the issue of "comparable worth."

Comparable Worth. As we have already seen, the U.S. occupational structure is highly segregated by sex, and those jobs women are most likely to hold generally pay less than those jobs men are most likely to hold. Pay differences between the sexes for the same job have been illegal since the Equal Pay Act. Although such differential-pay policies no longer exist with regard to specific jobs, they still exist with regard to broad categories of jobs, and proponents of gender equality have long fought for the enactment of "comparable worth" laws that would grant equal pay for broad categories of jobs when it can be shown that the skill, responsibilities, effort, risk, and economic contribution levels to the company are essentially the same. For example, is being an appliance sales worker any more demanding or more important than being an apparel sales worker? One would be hard-pressed to show that it is, yet appliance sales workers, 71 percent of whom are men, average $26,312 per year while apparel sales workers, 77 percent of whom are women, average $17,472 (Bureau of Labor Statistics, 2003e; note that male appliance sales workers average $509 per week, while their female counterparts average $465; and that male apparel sales workers average $372 per week, while their female counterparts average $329!). In short, the doctrine of comparable worth challenges the dual occupational and wage structure of "male" and "female" jobs.

Civil service jobs in twenty states are being studied in detail to determine the skills and responsibilities involved, with the ultimate aim of ensuring comparable worth and thereby mitigating the effects of the gender segmentation of work. The aim is to make sure that job categories dominated by women are not given less pay than job categories dominated by men when the two sets of categories are approximately equal in levels of responsibility and required skills. The comparable worth programs of Iowa, Minnesota, New York, Oregon, Washington, and Wisconsin are particularly strong. Although the jury is still out on their overall effect, an assessment of Minnesota's comparable worth laws revealed that they significantly narrowed the wage gap between comparable women-dominated and men-dominated jobs, improved women government workers' wages by 15 percent, resulted in no loss of jobs for either men or women, and involved no penalizing of male wages (Benokraitis and Feagin, 1995,

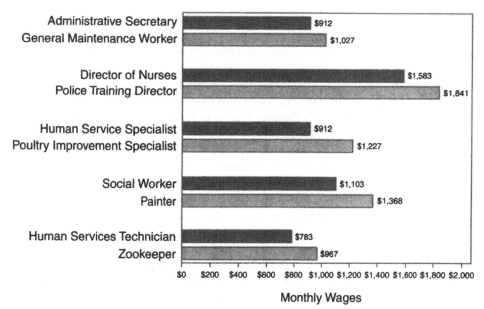

Monthly Wages

Figure 3.8. Comparison of Monthly Salaries for Equally Valued Public-Sector Jobs in Minnesota Prior to the Implementation of Comparable Worth Laws. Note: Black bars represent jobs held predominantly by women; gray bars indicate jobs held predominantly by men. *Source:* Evans and Nelson, 1989, p. 174).

pp. 68, 295). Figure 3.8 illustrates the kinds of disparities at which state comparable worth laws are aimed. At all levels of the occupational prestige hierarchy, the wage differences between comparable jobs for Minnesota's public employees were (prior to its implementation of a strong comparable worth program for state workers) a function of the predominance of males versus females.

Despite the success of some state and local governments in reducing gender inequality for their civil servants, legislative attempts to ensure comparable worth in the private sector have failed—ultimately because businesses resist, realizing the economic costs that would be incurred from assessing the worth of the work that women do and then increasing their pay (Andersen, 1997, p. 141). As a consequence, federal law does not require equal pay for work that is comparable but not exactly equal. Indeed, in some cases the federal government itself has actively resisted the notion. For example, in the early 1980s, the American Federation of State, County and Municipal Employees, a union with a large female presence, successfully sued the state of Washington in a federal district court for paying lower wages for female-dominated jobs than for comparable male-dominated jobs. However, the U.S. Department of Justice joined in the state of Washington's appeal to Ninth Circuit Court, which eventually decided against the notion of comparable worth (Benokraitis and Feagin, 1995, pp. 196–197). This decision illustrates the overall point that "governments and the courts have not been overly energetic in their support of comparable worth proposals" (Soroka and Bryjak, 1994, p. 239).

Title VII. Title VII of the Civil Rights Act of 1964 is perhaps the most important legislation dealing with discriminatory practices, making it unlawful to "discriminate because of race, color, religion, or national origin, in hiring or firing; wages; fringe benefits; classifying, referring, assigning, or promoting employees; extending or assigning facilities; training or retraining or apprenticeship; or any other terms, conditions, or privileges in employment" (U.S. Department of Labor, Women's Bureau, 1980a, p. 9). Sex was added to this list in 1967 by Executive Order 11375.

Title VII has been the motivation behind 150 gender-related affirmative-action programs within the federal government and tens of thousands of such programs in state and local governments and in private industry.

Affirmative Action. Beginning in the mid-1970s, the legal context began a gradual shift from prohibition of discrimination to affirmative-action laws. Employers were required to seek out and give preference to women and minorities for those occupations in which they were underrepresented, even if male candidates appeared to have better credentials (Barrett, 1979a: 57). This practice, of course, invites charges of "reverse discrimination."

Many critics of affirmative action feel that women and minorities ought not to be hired under affirmative-action policies because they would thus end up in positions for which they are not qualified. These critics, in accordance with their assumption that the causes of inequality lie within the individual, suggest that women and minorities instead need to become better prepared for jobs. Benokraitis and Feagin (1995, pp. 205–206) note that what is "particularly strange" about this argument is that the evidence is to the contrary. They note that "when the population is canvassed, there is hardly a scarcity of qualified women and minorities for many, if not most, jobs," and that many companies had reportedly found significant numbers of qualified women and minorities.

Other critics, both male and female, feel that men are being hurt by affirmative-action programs geared toward the hiring of more women or the offering of government contracts to more female-owned businesses. Certainly there are many isolated cases in which particular men have not gotten a job or a contract because of affirmative action. For example, a white male in Pittsburgh scored very high on the firefighters' application test, but was passed over because one-third of the hiring slots had been reserved for women—even though only 15 percent of the applicant pool was female. In *Quirin v. Pittsburgh* (1992), the man sued and won. Two or three cases of this sort are heard each year in federal court (Blumrosen, 1995). The rarity of such cases would seem to indicate that men do not find affirmative action harmful to themselves. However, Louis Harris's systematic random sampling of the American public found that more than a quarter of the adult population knows "personally someone whose job chances have been negatively affected by affirmative action programs" (Institute for Research in Social Sciences, 1991). Moreover, half of U.S. adults agree with the statement that "once affirmative action programs for women and minorities are started, the result is bound to be reverse discrimination against white men and the imposition of a quota system" (Institute for Research in Social Sciences, 1991). Public opinion polls in general reveal a strong undercurrent of anti–affirmative action feeling. For example, a 2001 Gallup Poll revealed that 61 percent of whites, as well as 27 percent of African Americans, are against affirmative action based on race or ethnicity (as indicated by their agreeing with the statement that "the government should not make any special effort to help minorities because they should help themselves"; Gallup Organization, 2001). A 1995 *Los Angeles Times* poll indicated that 73 percent of adults (including 58 percent of African Americans) favor a national law to "make it unlawful for any employer to grant preferential treatment in hiring" based on race or gender (*Daily Labor Report*, 1995). However, when asked whether they support affirmative action as it is currently practiced, only 39 percent responded that it "goes too far" (46 percent of whites, 8 percent of African Americans). And when the National Opinion Research Center at the University of Chicago asked a national probability sample of U.S. adults whether "employers should make special efforts to hire and promote qualified women . . . because of past discrimination," 56 percent agreed (see NORC, 2000).

Although the wording of questions concerning affirmative action obviously significantly affects the answers, no matter how they are phrased a significant portion of the overall public (40 to 60 percent) seems to be against it. At the national level, the sentiments of this portion are not strong enough to support the dismantling of affirmative action (even though in the Republican-controlled Congresses of the early 2000s, several bills have been introduced to do exactly this), but in some states and many municipalities the dismantling has already begun (with confidence, in part, because recent Supreme Court and other federal court decisions have begun applying "strict scrutiny" tests to affirmative-action programs; difficult to meet, strict scrutiny requires that any affirmative-action program must "serve a compelling governmental interest and is narrowly tailored to further that interest"; see Jung, Wadia, and Haberman, 1996). Most notably, in California, Proposition 209, intended to dismantle affirmative-action programs in public education, public employment, and public contracts, passed by a 54.6 percent—46.4 percent margin, in November 1996. Although it was immediately challenged by the American Civil Liberties Union in court and other groups, all court decisions let the vote stand; indeed, it is now Article I, Section 31, of the California Constitution. In 1998, Washington state voters passed Initiative 200, a measure modeled on Proposition 209 and that similarly banned affirmative action in state and local government hiring, contracting, and education.

All of this said, when we look at the most important social scientific study to date on the effects of affirmative action, we find very little evidence that men have suffered from reverse discrimination. Blumrosen's (1995) intensive analysis of 3,000 federal affirmative-action-related court cases reveals that only thirty-nine involved claims of reverse discrimination, and of these only twelve have been found to be justified. And of these twelve, only three involve men claiming gender discrimination. Blumrosen's (1995, pp. 13–14) overall conclusions are unequivocal: "no widespread abuse of affirmative action programs in employment is reflected in the decisions; [indeed,] many of the cases were the result of a disappointed applicant failing to examine his . . . own qualifications, and erroneously assuming that when a woman or minority got the job, it was because of race or sex, not qualifications; [in short,] nothing in these cases would justify dismantling the existing structure of equal employment opportunity programs." Further, Blumrosen's analysis of employment data between 1960 and 1992 led him to the conclusion that "the influence of all EEO [Equal Economic Opportunity] programs has produced significant improvement in the occupational position of women . . . six million women are in higher occupational categories today than they would be if we still distributed people through the labor force the way we did in the sixties" (p. 2).

These findings have been either ignored or dismissed by the anti–women's movement groups that have arisen in the past decade. The sentiments of those who have dismissed them are captured in Fumento's (1996) assessment that

> the reason there are so few official complaints about reverse discrimination is that the practice is legal. It's the law of the land. A person denied a job or promotion in 1994 because he's a white male is no more likely to file a complaint than would a black man denied a job or promotion back in 1954. Blumrosen is like a 1950s southern sheriff saying, "Yup, our Negroes here are happy as pigs in slop. They almost never complain. And when they do, they're always wrong." . . .
>
> Reverse discrimination is the inherent flip side of affirmative action. For every person given a position who would not have gotten it on individual merit, someone else who did merit it has been denied. Blumrosen himself says 12 million Americans [half of them women] have benefited from affirmative action. If so, then that's the number of Americans who have suffered reverse discrimination: 12 million.

EEOC. The Equal Employment Opportunity Commission (EEOC) was created specifically to enforce Title VII. However, the EEOC not only initially resisted enforcing the provisions concerning sexual discrimination, but even encouraged such discrimination by publishing guidelines that expressly allowed employers to publish employment ads in classified columns labeled by sex (Eastwood, 1978, p. 114). The EEOC's limited budget and administrative problems further hampered Title VII's enforcement, and efforts to force compliance were "still left primarily to the private individuals who had been discriminated against, through private lawsuits in the courts" (Cahn, 1977, p. 76).

It was only when women's action groups such as the National Organization for Women (NOW) began to bring political and legal pressure at the local, state, and federal levels in the late 1960s and 1970s that the EEOC was compelled to enforce these laws (Eastwood, 1978; Sachs and Wilson, 1978). And, since 1972, the EEOC has been empowered to bring civil-action suits against private firms engaged in discriminatory practices (Barrett, 1979).

The EEOC's guidelines have clarified important issues. One such guideline, for example, makes it illegal for firms to assign characteristics to individuals on the basis of the attributes of a group. Thus the guideline addresses the "statistical discrimination" practices described earlier in this chapter. This said, the EEOC still lacks effective enforcement power and is overloaded with cases: In 2001 it had a backlog of 32,481 complaints—with more than 80,000 new charges filed with it each year (31 percent of which involve sex discrimination; see EEOC, 2002). In the words of former EEOC chair Eleanor Holmes Norton, "these cases will bury the agency" (as quoted in Leonard, 1996, p. 8).

Title IX.   By mandating equal opportunity for boys and girls to participate in sports, Title IX of the Educational Amendments Acts of 1972 caused female participation in team sports to grow enormously (the surprising-but-real impact of playing team sports on gender inequality is discussed in the next chapter). Title IX's impact also extended into admissions policies of professional schools and a host of affirmative-action programs on college campuses, expanding opportunities for women in all areas of education. For example, by the mid-1990s, nearly half of admissions to professional schools (e.g., law, medicine, dentistry) were granted to women. These educational opportunities are reflected in the growing proportions of management, executive, and professional positions held by women.

The Women's Movement

The women's movement has always recognized that the *idea* of gender equality must be actively promoted, both at the institutional (in the media and in ed-

Girls' rates of participation in school sports are now nearly equal to boys' rates. Interpersonal skills learned playing team sports contribute to success in the business world.

ucation) and personal levels, and that ideas promoting gender inequality must be actively resisted. And the movement has always recognized the need for women to have more *power* within the institutions that control their lives. In women's quest for more power, they have made very significant strides in political, health care, and legal institutions.

For example, the number of women holding high-level political positions has grown steadily—from 11 women in the U.S. Congress in 1969 to 73 by 2003 (14 senators; 59 out of 435 seats in the House of Representatives; 73 represents 13.6 percent of the 535 members of the 108th U.S. Congress). Women in Congress both reflect and encourage the rising power of women in politics and in society in general. The Congressional Caucus for Women's Issues has been strongly involved in virtually every important piece of national legislation promoting women's rights since the mid-1970s. At the state level, women now hold 6 governorships, 17 lieutenant governorships, 5 attorney general offices, 10 secretaries of state, 9 treasurerships, and 80 (26.3 percent) of the 316 major, statewide elective executive offices (up from 10 percent in 1977); in 1969, 4 percent of state legislative positions were held by women, but by 2003 this figure had risen to 22.3 percent (with a third or more of the state legislatures in Washington, Colorado, and Maryland comprising women). At the municipal level, fewer than 5 percent of the mayorships in cities of over 30,000 were held by women in the mid-1970s; by 2002, nearly 20 percent were—including Dallas, Portland, Cleveland, and Atlanta (all data on women in elective offices were taken from CAWP, 1997b, 1997c, 2003; Women Mayors of American Cities, 2003).

The women's movement has also been crucial in getting women to register and to vote; until 1980, men were more likely to register and to vote, but since then women have been edging ahead of men in both registration and voting. In 1964, 71.9 percent of voting-age men voted in presidential elections, compared with 67.0 percent of voting-age women; by 1992, 60.2 percent of men voted compared with 62.3 percent of women. In the presidential election of 2000, 56.2 percent of voting-age women versus 53.1 percent of their male counterparts voted (51.5 million men versus 59.3 million women; see CAWP, 1997d, 2002). Moreover, women are significantly more likely to vote democratic, which the majority of women view as representing their interests better than the Republican Party (see CAWP, 1997e; Feminist Majority Foundation, 2001a, 2001b); for example, in the 1996 presidential election, 11 percent more women voted for the democratic candidate William Clinton than for the republican Robert Dole (CAWP, 1997f). Similarly, in 2000, 12 percent more women voted for democratic candidate Al Gore than for the republican George W. Bush (Feminist Majority Foundation, 2001b).

The authors of one of the most in-depth studies on the impact of women in Congress observe that, regardless of their political party affiliation, "women members . . . ha[ve] an impact in every area of legislation . . . [notably,] Democrats and Republicans alike fe[el] a special responsibility to represent the concerns and interests of women." The same authors report that "the congresswomen t[ell] us that because they br[ing] to Washington different life experiences from their male colleagues, they [a]re more likely to look at legislation with the needs of women, children, and families in mind." The authors' overall conclusion is that women "translate their distinctive perspectives into action at points in the legislative process from introduction of a bill to the final vote" (see Dodson, Carroll, and Mandel, 1995; quotes taken from CAWP, 1995).

In the legal/criminal justice system, the women's movement has fought for and achieved great success not only in assuring women's rights for equal opportunity (e.g., via Title VII of the 1964 Civil Rights Act, especially the creation of the EEOC, Title IX of the 1972 Education Amendments Act, the 1975 Equal Credit Opportunity Act), but also in areas of abortion rights, sexual assault (virtually inventing the term "date rape" and sensitizing the general public to the phenomenon), sexual harassment, and family violence. Women in recent years have made real inroads into acquiring power in the legal system, from the top to the bottom of occupational prestige hierarchy. In the early 1980s, Sandra Day O'Connor became the first woman appointed to the U.S. Supreme Court, and she was joined in the early 1990s by Ruth Bader Ginsburg. In 1993, President William Clinton appointed the first woman U.S. attorney general, Janet Reno—who proclaimed her first day in office that she would "work to end . . . gender discrimination and disharmony in America by enforcing the laws to ensure equal opportunity for all Americans" (United States Information Agency, 1997). Women judges and police officers (save for "meter maids") were virtually unheard of in the early 1960s, but by the early 2000s more than 1 in 8 police officers were female (73,000 of the 545,000 police and detectives, or 13.4 percent) and there were over 11,000 female judges in municipal, district, state, and federal courts (29 percent of the 38,000 total judgeships; data taken from Bureau of Labor Statistics, 2003e). In the 1960s, Presidents John F. Kennedy, Lyndon B. Johnson, and Richard M. Nixon had no women in their presidential cabinets, but by the early 1990s, one in five of William Clinton's cabinet was a woman (3 of 14 positions), and this proportion was maintained by his successor George W. Bush (3 of 15 positions; the Department of Homeland Security increased the number of executive departments from 14 to 15 in 2002; for the historical and current data on the appointment of women to presidential cabinets, see CAWP, 2001; Whitehouse.gov, 2003).

Among Clinton's cabinet women was Donna E. Shalala, who headed the U.S. Department of Health and Human Services. Her leadership—which focused heavily on issues of gender equity in the areas of childcare, welfare, and health care—is symbolic of the growing presence of women in medicine and in the health care system in general. In 1960, fewer than 5 percent of all physicians were female; by 2001, nearly a third were women (Bureau of Labor Statistics, 2003d). Women's activists in health care and research pointed out and were able to partially ameliorate the male bias in health research. For example, prior to the early 1990s, most studies on the nation's number-one killer, car-

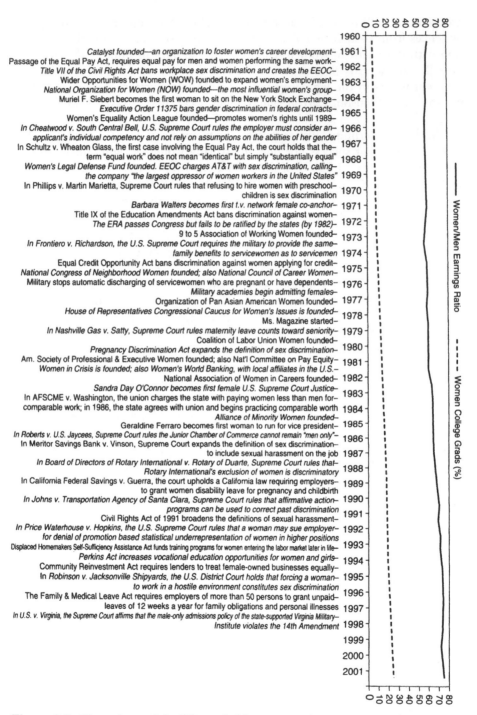

Figure 3.9. Chronology of the Women's Movement and Accompanying Decreases in Gender Inequality, 1960–2001. *Sources:* Schneider and Schneider (1993); U.S. Bureau of the Census (2003d, 2003e).

diovascular disease, focused exclusively on men. Even though men are more likely to suffer from heart disease, women suffering from it are much more likely to die. One reason is that women's physical complaints are taken less seriously then men's, and treatments are less aggressive (Glazer, 1994).

Identifying such bias has been important in redirecting recent research to give equal study to heart disease in women, as well as breast cancer and a host of other diseases. Pushed forward by women in Congress, the National Institutes of Health (NIH, the federal government's umbrella organization for the bulk of the research it sponsors in health) created the Office of Research on Women in September of 1990. The office's mandate is to develop and codify research on women's health and to ensure that women are represented in NIH-supported studies. All evidence indicates that the office is fulfilling its mandate: By 2003, it had sponsored hundreds of scientific inquiries into women-specific health problems (including depression, endometriosis, eating disorders, and incontinence in older women). Its flagship study (the Women's Health Initiative) is a $625 million investigation of the effects of diet, hormones, and vitamin/mineral supplements on the health of older women, due to be completed in 2007 (see U.S. Department of Health and Human Services, 1999). Soon after the Office of Research on Women's Health was established, and with the proddings of women activists both within and outside of the federal government, the Federal Drug Administration (FDA) began urging drug companies to include women—who had heretofore generally been excluded—in their studies of drug effectiveness and safety. The arm of the women's movement involved with gender inequities in health care is the Campaign for Women's Health, a coalition of ninety women's groups, all of which lobby for reform legislation. The campaign sees its primary goal of redressing the inequities women have incurred in the health care system as being attained by increasing the presence of women professionals and women health activists, to the point where "we won't need a movement pushing or watch-dogging," according to the National Women's Health Network, one of the campaign's largest members (as quoted in Glazer, 1994, p. 428).

The impacts of laws and court decisions aimed at increasing gender equality are difficult to assess directly, separately from other factors that have influenced the situations. However, Figure 3.9 provides a timeline revealing that wage and educational inequalities between the sexes have steadily declined as the number of equal-rights victories have steadily increased. All of these victories in legislation, court decisions, and executive orders were pushed for and won via the efforts of one or more women's groups (e.g., Catalyst, NOW, WOW—Wider Opportunities for Women, and WEAL—Women's Equality Action League). The sum total of the victories to date has been to promote gender neutrality, yet to recognize that women must (or should) be given benefactions with regard to pregnancy and early infant care. (For a comprehensive history of the women's movement and its affects, see Ferree and Hess, 1994. As of 2003, there are approximately 2,500 women's groups involved in the quest for gender equality, five dozen of which donate money predominantly to women candidates in state and federal elections).

Summary

Although women's gains have been steady and cumulatively very large over the past three decades, significant economic inequality currently exists between men and women in the United States and throughout the world. Women earn less than men, even controlling for full-time work status and education; women at the upper ends of the occupational prestige scale are much less likely to find themselves in high-level management positions (due to the glass ceiling), while women toward the bottom end are much more likely to slip repeatedly in and out of poverty. Women have been increasingly more likely to be heads of households, single mothers, living on their own, and major contributors to their families' incomes and overall standard of living. The combination of women increasingly becoming monetary providers and a social system that restrains women economically has made the problem of gender inequality one of the most serious of the contemporary era.

In this chapter we have examined the economic and legal factors that help explain women's position in the labor force. Economic explanations may be categorized as individual or structural, in terms of their focus on the individual woman workers versus a focus on structural features of the economy.

The individual approach assumes that women themselves are responsible for the fact that they wind up in low-paying, dead-end jobs. Human-capital theory is an example of the individual approach. It argues that women are concentrated in such jobs because they do not have the qualifications for better-paying positions with higher responsibility, commitment, and prestige. Women are less well qualified than men, it is assumed, because women have invested less in their human-capital assets, such as education and on-the-job training—assets that lead to the better jobs. Women's prior socialization fosters their choice of jobs requiring little training or expertise; such jobs allow more flexibility, which permits women to spend more time with their families. This approach in effect blames the victims for their own predicament and ignores the influence of the wider context—the structural features of the labor market and the economy.

A structural approach focuses on the structural aspects of the economy and labor market that constrain women's work situation. Even if women were better qualified for the higher-paying jobs typically held by men, they would meet with resistance related to their position within the structure of the labor force. A prime example of a structuralist approach is dual labor-market theory. According to this view, the labor market is stratified into a primary sector (jobs with high wages and status, good working conditions, and opportunity for advancement) and a secondary sector (low wages and status, poor working conditions, little chance for advancement); moreover, the primary sector has two tiers, with upper-tier positions having the greatest earnings, power, and prestige. Women are more likely than men to be found in the lower tier of the primary sector (for example, white-collar clerical jobs) because of the discriminatory attitudes and policies (such as statistical discrimination) of both employers and employees.

Structural change is often effected through legal means. Until the 1960s, however, laws more often supported the status quo and thus were an additional source of structural resistance. These laws sanctioned discriminatory practices that perpetuated the occupational segregation and earnings differentials between men and women. Protective legislation is a case in point. With the coming of the industrial revolution and women's entrance into the workforce, protective laws and regulations governed the hours women were permitted to work and the type of work they could perform. These laws originally arose out of the efforts of feminists, labor unions, and social reformers to protect women and children from sweatshop conditions. The legislation soon became an excuse that employers used to discriminate against women when they chose to do so.

Protective legislation was overridden by the Equal Pay Act in 1963, Title VII of the Civil Rights Act of 1964, and Title IX of the 1972 Education Amendments Act. These laws helped overcome some of the more blatant forms of discrimination, but their effectiveness has been limited, in part because they did not address the problem of "comparable worth," and in part because of the underfunding, understaffing, and underenforcement capacities of the EEOC. In the 1970s, the legal climate shifted from antidiscrimination legislation to affirmative-action laws that require employers to seek out and give preference to women and minorities in hiring for those occupations in which they have been underrepresented. Affirmative action brought much success to women, but is being dismantled in many municipalities and one state (California) and is under attack in many others.

Successes that have been won via the legal system over the past three decades have come from pressure applied by the women's movement. The movement has been responsible for the significant strides women have made in acquiring power in political, health care, and legal institutions. The number of women holding high-level political positions has grown steadily. There are significantly more women in the U.S. Congress and in the presidential cabinet. Many more women serve as judges in municipal, district, state, and federal courts. The women's movement has also been crucial in getting women to register and to vote. However, although changes have been enormous over the past three decades, women are still only a slim minority of those having power in the legal and political institutions of the contemporary United States.

The economic and legal contexts are but two of the important structural influences on gender inequality. In the next chapter, we will see how the institutions of the family, education, and the media have also contributed to women's inferior labor-market position.

World Wide Web Resources

For voluminous census and survey data on women, go to the U.S. Census Bureau's home page and click on "W" to find "Women Data" in the *Subjects A–Z* list: http://www.census.gov/.

For a host of links on women's issues and how they are linked with the women's movement, visit the Feminist Majority Foundation Online home page: http://www.feminist.org/default.asp.

For historical and current data on women in politics (at the local, state, and national levels), see the Center for American Women and Politics home page: http://www.rci.rutgers.edu/~cawp/.

For a comprehensive list of women's organizations, see Women's Information Services Project at the University of Wisconsin: http://www.library.wisc.edu/libraries/WomensStudies/orgs.htm.

The leading organization in the women's movement is the National Organization for Women; see its home page for information on a broad range of women's issues: http://www.now.org/.

The AFL-CIO has a number links on comparable worth and equal pay: http://www.aflcio.org/.

The National Women's Law Center is dedicating to protecting and advancing the progress of women and girls at work through legal means. This Web site outlines the current and future actions that this organization has taken on, and provides information for getting involved: http://www.nwlc.org.

The Equal Rights Advocates law center aims to protect and secure equal rights and economic opportunities for women and girls through litigation and advocacy: http://www.equalrights.org/.

4 Gender Inequality and Socialization: The Influences of Family, School, Peers, and the Media

Sex is biologically determined at conception by the type of sperm that fertilizes the egg. A "Y" sperm produces a male, an "X" sperm yields a female. In contrast, *gender* is determined socially; it is the societal meaning assigned to male and female. Each society emphasizes particular roles that each sex should play, although there is wide latitude in acceptable behaviors for each gender. These gender roles are powerful and coercive. Consider, for example, the necessity most young men feel either to work or go to school: This is a product of their having been socialized into believing that these are really the only two life choices open to them. That most young men do not wear makeup, put on lipstick, or shave their armpits is also a product of gender socialization (these aren't things "real men" do). On the other hand, although many young women feel the motivation to enter the work world or attend school, many of them also feel that marriage and devotion to children and home are acceptable choices; moreover, many women see little problem with adorning themselves with makeup and lipstick, as well as shaving their axillas. These attitudes are also a product of gender socialization. In this chapter, we will explore the ways in which socialization for gender roles ultimately generates inequalities between the sexes in income, prestige, power, and life chances in general. Our focus is on U.S. society, but the basic arguments are applicable to most societies (see Soroka and Bryjak, 1994, ch. 8, for international examples).

Gender Roles—Products of Biology or Socialization?

In the long view of history, there were powerful biology-related reasons why women were restrained to household duties or other work taking place within or near the home. Until the last few hundred years in economically developed societies, as still today in many developing nations, infant mortality rates were extremely high. For a society to survive, birth rates had to be very high, and cultural norms arose that encouraged women to marry young and to "be fruitful and multiply." And this is exactly what occurred: women married soon after puberty and were much of the time either pregnant or nursing, until menopause or death, whichever came first. However, with the advent of public sanitation—especially preventing sewage from contaminating drinking water—and other public health measures, such as childhood immunization and fortifying food staples with micronutrients (e.g., adding vitamins A and D to milk products), infant and childhood mortality rates have dropped dramatically, and so too birth rates. Now the typical American woman can expect to have only one or two children during her lifetime.

Low birth rates have freed women from having to concentrate so heavily on the roles of mother and keeper of the house. However, some students of society, coming from the perspectives of evolutionary psychology and sociobiology, contend that tens of thousands (if not hundreds of thousands) of years of enacting such roles have left their genetic, hormonal, and related biologic impacts on women. In short, they contend that women are inherently better suited than men to raise children and are inherently less fit for the worlds of politics and work (see, for example, Allen and Gorski, 1992; Goldberg, 1974; Gorman, 1992; LeVay, 1993; Parsons et al., 1955, and Rossi, 1977). Evolution thus not only partly explains the way social arrangements (including gender inequality) are, in this view, but also the way they should be.

Scientific studies on the relationship between female-versus-male genes, hormones, and other biologic traits, on the one hand, and of behavioral differences between men and women, on the other hand, show these two sets of variables correlate only weakly, at best (for reviews see, for example, Deaux, 1992; Fausto-Sterling, 1992; Jacklin, 1989; Kelly, 1991, ch. 4; McCoy, 1985; Shapiro, 1990; Tavris, 1992; and Tavris and Wade, 1984). Females tend to score better on tests of verbal ability, while males tend to test better in mathematical and visual-spatial ability; furthermore, females are much less likely to act out their feelings of aggression. But such differences are often small, and, in many studies, statistically insignificant. "Collectively, research findings presently do not support the conclusion that women and men are significantly different in temperament or in intellectual abilities" (Soroka and Bryjak, 1994, p. 228).

Among the most convincing studies showing that biologic differences in the sexes do not provide a blueprint for gender roles—and consequently for gender inequality—are those having to do with the behaviors of individuals whose gender socialization does not match their genetic sex (XX females raised as "boys"; XY males raised as "girls"). For example, Money and Ehrhardt's (1996) study of infant boys whose penises were either accidentally ablated (cut off) or intentionally removed because they suffered from severe microphallia (had minuscule penises) and who were subsequently raised as "girls" reveals that the children enjoyed imitating their mothers doing dishes, cooking, and other household roles; in short, what made them act "feminine" was the way in which they had been reared by their parents. Similarly, children with ambiguous genitalia at birth (some aspects indicative of being a male, other aspects of being a female) who were later discovered through genetic testing to have been assigned the "incorrect" gender (e.g., an XX female having been raised a "boy") acted in accordance with their socially encouraged gender roles and not according to their genetics. Thus, for example, when a thirteen-year-old boy was discovered to have an XX chromosomal pattern (he had been referred to a sex specialist after it was discovered he was experiencing menstrual bleeding), the proposition that he should undergo sex reassignment was completely nixed by both the teenager and his family:

> The decision was against a reassignment [for] the same reason as it would be for the vast majority of thirteen-year-old American boys. His mother said: "He has a sister, and they are completely different. He does not think like a girl, and he does not have the same interests. Right now, the one thing that made me very sure, is that he has a girlfriend. And that to me was a relief, because that was just the clincher that he wasn't a girl." . . . For the father, the boy was very much a son, and they shared many evenings, weekends, and vacations with rifle and rod. The boy's other recreational interest, shared with a boy friend, was motorbike racing in the dry riverbed. He gave an authentic biographical account of the early phase of teen-aged romantic attraction, and had a particular girlfriend. He experienced erotic arousal . . . from being with her, and also from girl watching. (Money and Ehrhardt, 1994, p. 483)

(This particular boy eventually had all of the female sex organs surgically removed and was given testosterone therapy to masculinize his appearance.)

John Money's writings on David Reimer, an infant who accidentally lost his penis during circumcision at eight months old and who was subsequently raised as a "girl" under Money's guidance, received extreme criticism in the media during the early part of 2000 (the media having been ignited by John Colapinto's book, *As Nature Made Him*). During the 1970s, Money reported that Reimer was being successfully raised as a girl, when in fact he was not; indeed, Reimer eventually opted to become a "boy" during adolescence. This failed experiment was used to raise the petard of "biology/genes" as the key determinant of gender identity. However, Money's research on hermaphrodites (individuals born with ambiguous genitalia), as noted earlier, negates this stance. Moreover, according to many scholars, the Reimer case should not be overemphasized—mainly because it represents a sample of one. Furthermore, as observed by sociologist Lisa Jones (2000), the causes of the trauma and Reimer's "boyish" personality are not at all necessarily a result of his "true male psyche" as implied. Many girls are not comfortable with the feminine gender role either. Furthermore, David Reimer wasn't raised like most girls are raised:

> "He went through a traumatic relationship with a researcher that broke many dominant cultural norms. . . . People attempted to raise David as a girl, but it seems to me that he was treated uniquely from day one and there was so much emphasis put on how his genitals differed from both males and females that it is no surprise that he chose to identify with the more empowered gender role of boy/man. I think his unusual treatment as a patient, the power relations involved vis-à-vis both gender and the doctor/researcher vs. patient/subject, and the focus put on his physiology are all too confounded with being raised as a girl to claim that we know anything about which was influential in making David "boyish." Certainly physiology and the cultural meanings we attach have important interactive effects. But to say so is quite different from saying there is a natural male psyche." (Jones, 2000)

Studies of isolated cultures, such as those in the islands of the South Pacific, provide further evidence that biologic differences in the sexes do not provide a blueprint for gender roles. Indeed, such studies reveal that many of the "masculine" behaviors associated with the male sex in Western society (e.g., aggressiveness, emotional coolness, and being oriented more toward the worlds of politics and work outside the home than toward childcare and work within the home) do not characterize these other men. Similarly, many traits that are "feminine" by Western standards (e.g., nonaggressiveness, emotionality, the desire to nurture, and being child and home oriented) do not characterize these women. For example, Margaret Mead found in New Guinea that

> Mundugumor women actively dislike childbearing, and they dislike children. Children are carried in harsh opaque baskets that scratch their skins, later on their mother's shoulders, well away from the breast. Mothers nurse their children standing up, pushing them away as soon as they are the least bit satisfied. ... Women are masculinized to a point where every feminine feature is a drawback. (1994, pp. 468–469)*

Mead's study of such isolated tribes led her to the fundamental conclusion that "male and female personality are socially produced" (1994, p. 471).

Taken together, biologic and cross-cultural anthropological research demonstrate that gender roles are malleable and that there are no inherent or universal reasons why current social and economic arrangements should involve so much gender inequality. Indeed, such research makes it clear that the fountainhead of gender role expectations is *socialization*. This is the process of learning how to think about and act in particular situations and particular social roles. By way of gender socialization, individuals learn what men are supposed to do and what women are supposed to do. Such socialization is entwined with almost every aspect of society, but four domains in which it occurs are especially important: the family, the educational system, peer groups, and the media.

The Family

An individual's first gender socialization experiences happen at home. Parents transmit gender information both directly (e.g., "big boys don't cry") and indirectly by way of the toys they buy (e.g., dolls for girls, road racers for boys) and

---

*In the early 1980s, Mead's research came under heavy attack from the respected anthropologist Derek Freeman (1983), who questioned her methods and findings. Anthropologists and sociologists debated and assessed Freeman's accusations for several years. The outcome was a realization that Mead had made some errors, but that many of her findings and conclusions, included those presented here, were solid. Anthropologist Nancy McDowell (1984, pp. 138–139) studied the Mundugumor during three extended field trips between 1972 and 1981, and she found the women there were just as "harsh and aggressive" as Mead had reported.

the activities they encourage their children to pursue (e.g., many more girls take ballet than play youth football). Such transmission may sometimes be unintentional (e.g., encouraging nurturance in girls to a far greater degree than in boys, as was observed by Frisch, 1977, and Smith and Lloyd, 1978, who found this to be the case even for mothers who espoused egalitarianism between the sexes and other liberal ideals).

Parents typically begin gender socialization as soon as the child's sex is known. A study of the home environments of infants between five and twenty-five months found that the number and variety of toys were similar between the sexes, but that boys were provided with more sports equipment, tools, and large and small vehicles, while girls had more dolls, fictional characters, and child furniture (Pomerleau et al., 1990). These differences appear critical to later child development and ultimately to gender inequality. Infants who are encouraged to play with dolls and child furniture, or sports equipment and tools, will be more likely to choose these objects as they grow older:

> They are familiar with these objects, and they know what can be done with them. They have also learned that these objects are appropriate for them, and for children of their own gender. Also, repetitive play with some types of objects is likely to promote the development of specific skills, abilities, and behaviors in male and female children, and in parent-child interaction. Tools, cars, and sports equipment elicit more active play than dolls, dollhouses, and domestic objects. . . . The times are changing. However, the changes do not seem to occur quickly enough to provide equal opportunities for girls and boys during their early development. (Pomerleau et al., p. 366).

Hundreds of studies conducted over the past three decades have repeatedly demonstrated that children have developed gender stereotypes and gender-role expectations well before the age of five, and further, that many of these stereotypes have changed only marginally during the "gender aware" 1970s, 1980s, and 1990s (see Albert and Porter, 1988, and Pomerleau et al., 1990, for reviews of some of this literature). By age three, almost all children have developed a gender identity ("I'm a boy" or "I'm a girl"), and many—if not most—prefer playing in sex-segregated groups. By age five, girls prefer dolls, doll accessories, soft toys, drawing, painting, cutting, and pasting—while boys prefer blocks, small vehicles, tools, and rough-house play. When pictures of children of their age group whom they do not know are presented to them, four- to ten-year-olds predict that girls will prefer "feminine" toys (dolls, etc.) and boys "masculine" toys (toy race cars, etc.) (Martin, 1989). During middle childhood and early teens, parents are much more likely to sign their daughters up for dance classes, and even though female participation in team sports has grown enormously since the Educational Amendments Acts of 1972 (its Title IX provisions mandate equal opportunity for boys and girls to participate in sports), boys are still more likely to be encouraged to play sports, especially team sports (Malec, 1997), and to have their gender identities more powerfully shaped by sports (Messner, 1992).

Gender socialization is well underway even during infancy.

Sociologists have long recognized that much social learning occurs via role models. And despite the huge increase in women's labor-force participation, the role models in many families support traditional gender stereotypes. In particular, regardless of the work status of their mothers (not employed outside of house, employed part time, employed full time), many children see household chores still predominantly done by their mothers. Indeed, even though many men have come to support (at least in theory) the concept of sharing housework responsibilities equally, they often view their contribution as "helping out"

"Sugar and spice."

their wives; women are held responsible if essential tasks are not done (Abbot and Wallace, 1997, p. 153; Oakley, 1982). Moreover, regardless of the willingness of many modern men to share in housework, women still most often end up doing more. Children are also likely to witness power imbalances in the interactions between their fathers and mothers. For example, Fishman's (1983) intensive analysis of conversational patterns between husbands and wives revealed that women try harder to communicate but succeed less. Both men and women regard topics introduced by women as tentative, and more often than not they are dropped. In contrast, topics introduced by men are almost always pursued. Fishman's overall conclusion is that husbands "control what will be produced as reality by the interaction. They already have, and they continually establish and enforce, their rights to define what the interaction, and reality, will be about" (p. 405).

The effects of gender socialization in the family are cumulative. Gender-role expectations and stereotypes increase with age, and within the home many—if not most—children learn that boys and girls, men and women, differ in the levels of independence, aggression, activity, strength, fearlessness, dominance, obedience, expressiveness, concern with physical appearance, nurturance, intellectual ability, and mechanical competence. Moreover, even though race, ethnicity, and social class can influence gender socialization (as we will discuss later), such influence is often relatively minor. In other words, children from a wide variety of social and economic backgrounds develop many of the same gender stereotypes.

The family is also the locus for decisions as to where and how children will be educated, and schooling has enormous consequences for gender socialization.

Dance class.

The Educational System

School has traditionally been one of the strongest arenas in which gender so-cialization has occurred. Prior to the mid-1970s, virtually all aspects of the cur-riculum and of extracurricular activities reinforced traditional gender roles. Textbooks and readers showed males in many occupations and females mainly as housewives and mothers. Sentences referring to both sexes used the male pronoun almost exclusively. Both fiction and nonfiction tended to focus on male characters and their exploits; females were usually depicted in supportive and ancillary roles. Boys were encouraged (or required) to take metal- and wood-working shop; technical-vocational education prepared them to work as carpenters, plumbers, mechanics, auto-body repairmen, and in other skilled trades. Girls were encouraged (or required) to take courses in home econom-ics; those not headed for college were trained to take dictation, to write in shorthand, and to do filing and typing. Guidance counselors encouraged girls to pursue traditional female occupations (secretary, nurse, elementary school teacher) and boys to pursue traditional male occupations (mechanic, engineer, lawyer, white-collar office worker). Girls' sports were treated as much less im-portant than boys' sports. Only as cheerleaders were girls in the spotlight at sports events.

In response to the feminist movement of the 1960s and its manifold repercussions (from legislation attempting to ensure sexual equality in pay, to women entering the workforce, to changing cultural norms that transformed "career woman" from an epithet to a compliment, to scientific studies show-ing the pervasiveness of gender stereotypes in the educational process and the negative consequences thereof), schools began changing in the 1970s. The

Until the 1970s, girls were required to take "home economics" in junior or senior high school, while boys were required to take "shop."

changes were directed at promoting equal opportunities for the sexes in all areas of the curriculum and in extracurricular activities. And, to a large degree, this has occurred. For example, public schools that once required either home economics (for girls) or shop (for boys) now require that both sexes take both courses (Giele, 1988, p. 303). Differences in the scores of male and female high school students have narrowed for some tests of mathematical ability (e.g., on the National Assessment of Education Progress examinations; see National Center for Education Statistics, 2001, p. 24). Children's books now portray more women in nontraditional roles. Girls' participation in school sports programs has increased dramatically—in 1972, there were fewer than 300,000 girls participating in high school sports programs, compared to more than 3.6 million boys, a ratio of about 1:12; however, by 1995, there were 2.2 million girls involved in high school sports, compared to 3.5 million boys, a ratio of about 2:3 (Malec, 1997); and, by 2003, nearly 3 million girls were involved, versus nearly 4 million boys, the ratio now having narrowed to 3:4 (Wolff, 2002). Girls now have accessible to them more team sports than in years past: not only basketball, field hockey, softball, and volleyball, but even the most "macho" sports—including soccer, ice hockey, lacrosse, and rugby. Individual sports such as gymnastics, swimming, tennis, and track are now more widely available.

The change in girls' sports participation is more important than the average person might think. Social scientists have long contended that team sports provide boys with valuable learning environments that have an impact on future economic success. Team sports cultivate social skills: learning to deal with diversity in memberships in which each person is doing a special task; learning to coordinate actions and maintain cohesiveness among group members; learning to cope with impersonal rules; learning to work for collective as well as personal goals; developing one's strategic thinking; gaining experience in leadership positions; learning to deal with interpersonal competition in a forthright manner; experiencing face-to-face confrontations—often involving a close friend—and learning how to depersonalize the attack; learning self-control and keeping one's "cool" under fire (Lever, 1978, pp. 480–481).

Nevertheless, the changes in schooling aimed at equalizing opportunity and life chances between the sexes are far from complete. As just noted, girls are still only about three-fourths as likely as boys to participate in school sports programs. Although improved, many texts and readers still most commonly depict women in domestic roles and as more helpless, more emotional, and less adventuresome than men (Ferree and Hall, 1990; Peterson and Kroner, 1992; Peterson and Lach, 1990; Purcell and Stewart, 1990), thereby perpetuating "the cultural stereotype that men tend to be stronger, more active, and working in the world to solve problems, whereas women are more likely to be weaker, more passive, and focusing their interests around home and family" (Sullivan, 1997, p. 252). In two major reports during the 1990s, the American Association of University Women (1994, 1998) documented that schools are still a place where many girls are "shortchanged." In particular, these reports reveal that boys are much more likely than girls to say they are "pretty good at a lot

Recent federal court decisions have lent strong support to Title IX, ensuring that girls' and women's sports programs will continue to narrow the participation and funding gaps they traditionally suffered vis-á-vis boys' and men's programs.

of things" and to list their talents as the thing they like most about themselves, while girls, on the other hand, list aspects of their physical appearance. Moreover, boys are much less likely to say they are "not good enough" or "not smart enough" to achieve their career goals. The reports also make it clear that the sources of these disparities in feelings of competence are rooted in classroom experiences. Teachers give boys more attention and more encouragement to be assertive. Furthermore, as girls advance through school, their interest in mathematics and the hard sciences decreases, and those girls who take such courses are only half as likely as boys to feel competent in them. These latter findings are highly significant, for other studies have shown "that a loss of confidence in math usually *precedes* a drop in achievement, rather than vice versa," and indeed a difference in level of confidence, rather than ability, "may help explain why the number of female physical and computer scientists actually went down during the 1980s" (Orenstein, 1997, p. 44). A final factor related to the historical shortchanging of girls in the sciences and mathematics—but one that has almost been ameliorated—has been the lack of same-sex role models. Until the early 1980s, only 25 percent of the teachers in these fields were female (National Science Foundation, 1982); however, in recent years, the number of female teachers in these areas has grown dramatically, to about 42 percent of high school science teachers and 51 percent of high school math teachers (National Center for Education Statistics, 1996b, Table 2.10). Nevertheless, comparing the average mathematical scores of males and females on the Scholastic Assessment Test over the past three decades reveals little consistent change in the gap between boys and girls (see Figure 4.1); for example, the dif-

Figure 4.1. Scholastic Assessment Test (formerly known as the Scholastic Aptitude Test) Score Averages for College-Bound High School Seniors by Sex, 1967–2001. Note: Data for 1967 to 1986 were converted to the recentered scale by using a formula applied to the original mean and standard deviation. For 1987 to 1995, individual student scores were converted to the recentered scale and recomputed. For 1996 to 2001, most students received scores on the recentered scale score. Any score on the original scale was converted to the recentered scale prior to recomputing the mean. *Source:* National Center for Education Statistics (2002a, Table 135).

ference between the sexes was 35 points in 1971 (M = 529, F = 494), and 35 points in 2001 (M = 533, F = 498).

The Special Case of Single-Sex Schools.   Research on mixed-sex versus single-sex high schools reveals that girls prosper in the latter (Lockheed and Klein, 1985; Riordan, 1990, 1997). Female cognitive development is greater; female occupational aspirations and their ultimate attainment are increased; female self-confidence and self-esteem are magnified. Moreover, in such schools, females receive better treatment in the classroom; they are more likely to be encouraged to explore—and to have access to—wider curriculum opportunities; and teachers have greater respect for their work. Finally, females attending single-sex schools have "more egalitarian attitudes toward the role of women in society than do their counterparts in mixed-sex schools" (Riordan, 1997, p. 178). Single-sex schools accrue these benefits for girls for a variety of reasons, including the following: (1) a diminished emphasis on "youth culture," which centers on athletics, social life, physical attractiveness, heterosexual popularity, and negative attitudes toward academics; (2) the provision of more successful same-sex role models (the top students in all subjects and all extracurricular activities will be girls); (3) a reduction in sex bias in teacher-student interaction (there are not boys around that can be "favored"); and (4) elimination of sex stereotypes in peer interaction (generally, cross-sex peer interaction in school involves male dominance, male leadership, and, often, sexual harassment).

Peer Groups

Child and adolescent peer groups are powerful agents of socialization. Even though there are many cross-gender activities and many cross-gender groups, peers from the earliest ages (two or three) on through high school tend to congregate in same-sex groups and to engage in gender-appropriate behavior. "Both boys and girls who select gender-appropriate toys are more likely to have other children play with them" (Renzetti and Curran, 1995, p. 99).

As noted, studies of single-sex schools have revealed that one of the reasons for their success is their de-emphasizing youth cultures and the kinds of peer pressures involved therein. Such cultures are imbued with traditional gender stereotypes—boys are to be athletic, tough, and not overly expressive; girls are to be beauty oriented and demure. Good grades are OK, but they should not be flaunted, as such academic performance is associated with nerds, dweebs, and geeks. For both sexes, to be "cool" is to be physically attractive and heterosexually popular. Youth cultures generally yield more favorable results for males in the long run. With the greater emphasis on sports for males and "looks" for females, the message being sent is that a woman's status is determined by her appearance, a man's by his accomplishment.

Dating patterns during adolescence reinforce this depiction of reality. Girls often date older boys, who because of their age have acquired more knowledge and experience. One effect is that both sexes begin thinking that males are more sophisticated and worldly and are on firmer ground when they act aggressive. The idea that males should be more aggressive is bolstered by the fact that boys are supposed to "ask out" girls; that is, to be the initiators in the dating game. Further, boys are most often expected to supply the transportation, picking up the girl at her home and then driving to the movie theater or restaurant or party.

Studies of peer interactions reveal that females learn to act in ways that suggest they are less powerful and more vulnerable than males. Females learn that to get along with males they must be willing to accept interruptions and to defer to male decisions on the choice and character of conversations (see Fishman, 1983; and Thorne, Kramarae, and Henley, 1983). They also learn that to be successful in heterosexual interactions their body language must send out signals that they are demure: they should not sit with their legs wide apart; they should not recline with their hands behind their head and elbows thrusting outward; during conversation, they should smile often, tilt their heads, look attentive, avert their gazes, and nod their heads often. In the words of body language expert Janet Lee Mills (1985, pp. 8–9), to be successful in social interaction, a woman must learn "to be passive, accommodating, affiliative, subordinate, submissive, and vulnerable." Such traits win her "popularity, dates, and admiration in her social life." Mills notes that these traits are exactly opposite to those encouraged in males, those that produce success in the business world; that is, being active, dominant, aggressive, confident, competent, and tough. Figure 4.2 displays five photographs starkly illustrating Mills's observations on the differences in body language that we have learned to expect from males versus females.

Figure 4.2. Illustrations of "Proper" Male versus "Proper" Female Body Language. In which photograph does the man's posture seem appropriate? In which does the woman's? Note: Male nonverbal behavior typically includes very few affiliative displays, such as smiles and head cants, and many power cues, such as expanded limb positions and serious facial expressions. Female nonverbal behavior, however, is ordinarily just the opposite, containing many affiliative displays and few power cues. The overall impression males create is one of power, dominance, high status, and activity, particularly in contrast to the overall impression females create, which is one of submissiveness, subordination, low status, and passivity. *Source:* Mills, 1985, pp. 11–12; used by permission.

Finally, although the "double standard" regarding sex has diminished considerably, Lees (1986) has shown that adolescent males control adolescent females by threatening to label them as promiscuous. It is still all right for young men to "sow their oats," but young women who try to become sexually powerful are labeled "sluts" and "easy lays." This remnant of the double standard serves to maintain traditional gender stereotypes (Abbot and Wallace, 1997, p. 125).

The Media

Images of gender in the mass media—newspapers, magazines, television, and motion pictures—partly reflect the relationships and behavior of males and females in the dominant society. However, the media also act as an agent of gender socialization that can shape our expectations and perceptions. Very often the media reinforce traditional gender stereotypes (e.g., men as aggressive, active, problem solvers versus women as passive and more interested in relationships than in work, politics, and power) or overemphasize certain aspects of them to the point of distortion (e.g., promoting the notion that many men use their fists and guns on a daily basis to solve problems, which makes women love these men a lot more than they otherwise would).

Newspapers and news magazines are largely the province of men. Men are twice as likely as women to read these publications (*Media Report to Women*, 1993a), and stories about men and written by men predominate. Eighty-five percent of front-page news stories focus on men; men author two-thirds of front-page stories and three-quarters of opinion pieces; women predominate in the "non-news" (sometimes called "soft") sections of the daily paper (*Media Report to Women*, 1993b, 1993c, 2003). When women do appear in "hard" news stories, aspects of their gender that would be considered trivial for men are often highlighted. Stories involving women very often include descriptions of their physical appearance and family status. For example, the *Washington Post's* characterizations of the candidates in a Pennsylvania senatorial race

> described the democratic candidate Lynn Yeakel, as a "feisty and feminine 50-year-old with the unmistakable Dorothy Hamill wedge of gray hair and the dazzling silk suit of lime, tangerine, and blue." In addition, it was noted that she was a congressman's daughter, currently married to a stockbroker, and formerly a full-time mother. In contrast, her opponent, republican senator Arlen Specter, was described as a "crime-busting district attorney and mayoral hopeful." The profile of Specter did not mention his hair or wardrobe. (Renzetti and Curran, 1995, p. 156; also see *Media Report to Women*, 1992)

Non-news magazines are purchased and read by women much more than by men—in ratios that are estimated to be from 2:1 to 3:1 (Audits and Surveys, 1991). Analyses of the advertisements, editorials, and stories in the most popular women's magazines reveal that themes of getting and keeping a man and making oneself beautiful have been dominant since the 1940s (Cantor, 1987; Ferguson, 1983; Glazer, 1980; McCracken, 1993; Phillips, 1978; Synnott, 1991—as cited in Simon and Henderson, 1997); moreover, even though many articles about career and job concerns began appearing in the 1980s, achievement in the work world is "often presented as being dependent on physical attractiveness, e.g., 'dressing for success,' applying the right make-up, or fixing one's hair a particular way" (Renzetti and Curran, 1995, pp. 160–161).

Analyses of gender on television reveal that women play only a little more than one in every three roles and that this figure has not changed since the early 1950s; recent data reveal a percentage of thirty-seven, just about the same as in 1991 (Gerbner, 1993; *Media Report to Women*, 2003). Moreover, despite women being shown in recent years as working outside of the home and doing nontraditional jobs (e.g., police officer), in the media they are depicted much more often than men as submissive and unsuccessful (*Media Report to Women*, 2003;

Metzger, 1992). When they are successful (such as the character Murphy Brown), they become so at the risk of being failures with men and in their domestic lives (Japp, 1991). Further, compared to males, females are much more likely to be young, blond, thin, and scantily clad; and when depicted as older women they are much more likely to be shown as societal outcasts and social misfits (Fejes, 1992; Metzger, 1992; Silverstein, Peterson, and Kelly, 1986).

Television advertising perpetuates gender stereotyping to a greater degree than the programs being sponsored (Fejes, 1992; Lazier-Smith, 1989; McCracken, 1993; Strate, 1992). Men are shown in a wide variety of roles, and as in control (or if not in control, with the distinct possibility of being so if they would only buy the product at hand). Women are depicted as "sweet young things" (whether shown in the work world or not) or as housewives and mothers. Women demonstrate household products, while the voice-overs are overwhelmingly male; indeed, 96 percent of voice-overs are male (because the male voice is the voice of authority; see *Media Report to Women*, 2003; Renzetti and Curran, 1995, pp. 173–174).

Although it is difficult to tease out the direction of the causal arrow (which factor is causing which factor), the amount of time spent in front of the television set correlates with espousing gender stereotypes (Comstock and Paik, 1991). Social psychology experiments tend to support the television → stereotyping model as opposed to its reverse (that those with strong gender stereotypes tend to watch more television). For example, Geis et al. (1984) found that when female students were shown commercials in which gender stereotypes were prevalent, they were later much more likely to project images of themselves in traditional statuses (e.g., wife, mother) than other female students shown commercials that depicted women having nontraditional statuses and playing nontraditional roles (compare similar findings in Morgan, 1972).

Consequences of Gender Socialization for Career Choices

Gender socialization in each of these domains—the educational system, the family, the peer group, and the media—undoubtedly strongly influences choice of career. Here we focus on the effects of such socialization in the schools.

As we have already noted, one reason why schools have historically been so important in the creation and maintenance of gender roles is sex-based curriculum tracking. Boys not oriented toward college either were placed in or encouraged to take courses that would prepare them for blue-collar trades; girls either were placed in or encouraged to take courses that would prepare them to be secretaries, receptionists, file clerks, cashiers, or sales workers. Blue-collar occupations, which are and always have been predominantly male, traditionally and presently pay considerably better wages than low-level office and retail work. For example, among the blue-collar trades, we find the following median annual salaries for the early 2000s: automotive mechanic, $28,132; carpenter, $29,796; electrician, $37,128; plumber, $34,944; and sheet metal worker,

$35,048; while in fields non-college-oriented females typically enter, we find bank tellers averaging $19,552 per year, bookkeepers $24,804, cashiers $15,548, data entry operators $23,192, file clerks $20,904, secretaries $24,700, and word processors $25,324 (Bureau of Labor Statistics, 2003e). Moreover, despite the manifold changes in U.S. schools over the past two decades that were intended to equalize opportunities for the sexes, we still find males six times more likely than females to be taking "trade and industrial" vocational-education courses (National Center for Education Statistics, 2002a, Table 141).

During the past decade, about 12 percent of high school seniors, both males (11.9 percent) and females (11.6 percent), were in vocational-education programs, and another 43 percent were taking college preparatory curricula. Females (44.2 percent) were more likely than males (41.8 percent) to be in college preparatory programs (National Center for Education Statistics, 1996a, Table 132). Moreover, in recent years, females (82.0 percent) have been more likely than males (73.9 percent) to report that they plan to go to college after high school (National Center for Education Statistics, 2001, Table 19-1), p. 140; and, indeed, they actually do—of the nearly two million students entering college full time each year, more than half are females, and of the more than seven million full-time undergraduate students currently enrolled in U.S. colleges and universities, 56 percent are female (National Center for Education Statistics, 2002b, p. 99). Finally, as of the late 1990s, women were receiving more than half (56 percent) of the more than one million bachelor's degrees being granted each year (National Center for Education Statistics, 2001, p. 50). Such statistics are of great interest to students of gender inequality

Young women are more likely than young men to graduate from college, but tend to major in fields that lead to lower-paying jobs.

because, at the individual level of analysis, the strongest predictor of annual income is years of education. Now if females are more likely to be enrolled in college preparatory programs in high school, are more likely to go on to college, and are more likely to graduate from college, why then is there such a wide discrepancy between the incomes of men and women? Put differently, why do women appear to be getting less monetary return on their investments in education?

A large part of the answer rests in the types of education men and women pursue, both at the undergraduate and postgraduate levels. At the undergraduate level (see Table 4.1), women are significantly more likely than men to major in traditional "female" fields of study (elementary education, English, home economics, paralegal training, library science, and the performing arts), all of which lead to careers that pay substantially less than careers arising from those majors men are significantly more likely to choose (business, computer science, engineering, the physical sciences, medicine, dentistry, and law). The median annual salary for social workers is, for example, $33,488; for public elementary school teachers, $38,480 (considerably less for private schools); for public secondary school teachers, $40,248 (again, much less at private schools); for librarians, $41,700; and for registered nurses, $44,840; while in predominantly male careers, we find architects making $52,510; electrical engineers, $64,910; computer systems analysts, $67,670; lawyers, $88,280; dentists, $129,030; and physicians, $160,000 (Bureau of Labor Statistics, 2003e, 2003f; note: where these two sources conflict, the higher of the two estimated medians is given here).

There is, however, a strong and clear bright side to the bachelor's education data—a side that bodes well for near and distant future of increasing gender equality: Women have been steadily increasing their proportions of those degrees earned in almost all of the higher paying technical fields—a trend that has continued unabated for the past three decades. Figure 4.3 reveals steadily increasing biology, business, mathematics, physical sciences, computer science, and engineering degrees earned by women relative to men.

At the graduate level, just as at the undergraduate level, we find more female than male students: of the slightly more than 2.1 million postgraduate students studying full time and part time for master's degrees, PhDs, and professional degrees (dentistry, law, medicine), 56 percent are women (National Center for Education Statistics, 2002b, Table 6-1, p. 131). However, just as at the undergraduate level, women are more likely to be enrolled in graduate programs that will put them in careers that pay less. As noted, a social worker with a master's degree averages $43,222 a year, while the average attorney makes $88,280 a year; nurse practitioners with graduate degrees average $65,705 and physicians $160,000 (note: current salary figures for a wide variety of jobs are available at the Web site salary.com). Figure 4.4 compares the distribution of men and women receiving doctorates in the high-paying fields of engineering, computer science, mathematics, the physical sciences, and business, as well as in the lower-paying fields of English, foreign languages and literature, and ed-

Table 4.1

BACHELOR'S DEGREES BY SEX OF STUDENT AND FIELD OF STUDY, 1999–2000.

	Total	Men	Women	Percent Women
All Fields	1,237,875	530,367	707,508	57.2
Agricultural business and production	5,883	3,970	1,913	32.5
Agriculture and natural resources				
Agricultural sciences	8,656	4,250	4,406	50.9
Conservation and renewable natural resources	9,708	5,630	4,078	42.0
Architecture and related programs	8,462	5,193	3,269	38.6
Area, ethnic, and cultural studies	6,381	2,064	4,317	67.7
Biological sciences/life sciences	63,532	26,504	37,028	58.3
Business management, administrative services, and marketing operation/ marketing and distribution	253,162	127,783	125,379	49.5
Communications and communications technologies	56,910	22,063	34,847	61.2
Computer and information sciences	36,195	26,042	10,153	28.1
Education, total	108,168	26,124	82,044	75.8
Engineering and engineering-related technologies	72,299	58,911	13,388	18.5
English language and literature/ letters	50,920	16,341	34,579	67.9
Foreign languages and literatures	14,968	4,375	10,593	70.8
Health professions and related sciences, total	78,458	12,727	65,731	83.8
Home economics and vocational home economics	17,328	1,962	15,366	88.7
Law and legal studies, total	1,925	520	1,405	73.0
Liberal arts and sciences, general studies, and humanities	36,104	12,250	23,854	66.1
Library science	154	77	77	50.0
Marketing operations/marketing and distribution	4,178	1,652	2,526	60.5
Mathematics	12,070	6,382	5,688	47.1
Multi/interdisciplinary studies	27,460	9,136	18,324	66.7
Parks, recreation, leisure, and fitness studies	19,111	9,170	9,941	52.0
Personal and miscellaneous services	369	229	140	37.9
Philosophy and religion	8,366	5,228	3,138	37.5
Physical sciences and science technologies	18,213	10,871	7,342	40.3
Protective services	24,877	14,069	10,808	43.4
Psychology	74,060	17,430	56,630	76.5
Public administration and services	20,185	3,816	16,369	81.1
Social sciences and history	127,101	62,062	65,039	51.2
Theological studies/religious vocations	6,809	4,791	2,018	29.6
Transportational and material moving	3,395	2,985	410	12.1
Visual and performing arts	58,791	24,003	34,788	59.2
Other	3,677	1,757	1,920	52.2

Source: National Center for Education Statistics, 2002c (Table 19, pp. 33–35).

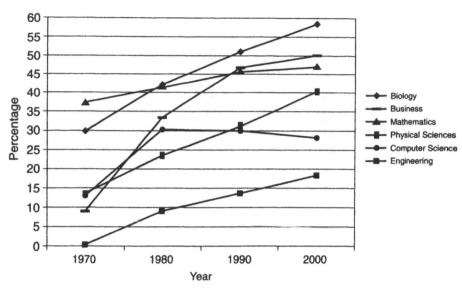

Figure 4.3. Percentage of Bachelor's Degrees Conferred to Women in Selected Technical Fields, 1970–2000. *Sources:* National Center for Education Statistics, 2000 (p. 66), 2002c (Table 19, pp. 33–35).

ucation. These data clearly show that women predominate in the fields of study that lead to lower-paying careers, while men predominate in the fields that lead to higher-paying careers. Moreover, when they do pursue degrees at the graduate level, women are more likely than men to be enrolled in master's programs (see Figure 4.5). Master's degrees yield smaller income returns than doctoral

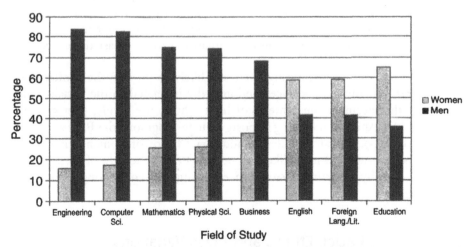

Figure 4.4. Percentage of Doctorates Awarded in 1999–2000 by Sex for Selected "Higher-Paying" (Engineering, Computer Science, Mathematics, Physical Sciences, Business) and "Lower-Paying" (Education, Foreign Language and Literature, Education) Fields of Study. *Source:* National Center for Education Statistics, 2002c (Table 21, pp. 39–41).

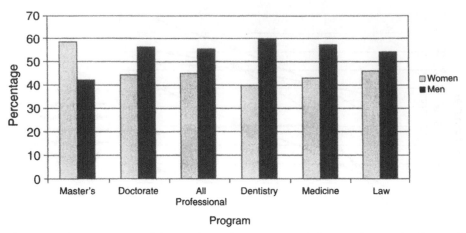

Figure 4.5. Percentage of Postgraduate Degrees Awarded in 1999–2000 by Type of Program and Sex. *Source:* National Center for Education Statistics, 2002c (Tables 20–22, pp. 36–42).

(e.g., PhD, DBA, EdD) and professional degrees—the postgraduate programs in which men predominate. Of the dozens of professional careers detailed in the Bureau of Labor Statistics (2003f) *Occupational Outlook Handbook*, in every instance it is noted that individuals with doctorates make more than their colleagues with only master's degrees.

As with the undergraduate degree data, the trends in graduate and professional degree data bode extremely well for a future of greater gender equality: Women have been steadily increasing their proportions of graduate degrees earned in all of the professions (including dentistry, law, and medicine), as well as their proportions of the doctorates earned in all of the higher paying technical fields (including biology, business, computer science, engineering, physical sciences)—a trend that has continued unabated for the past three decades (see Figure 4.6).

Why women have historically been less likely to go into the professions, engineering, and the hard sciences undoubtedly is related to the socialization influences that occur in the contexts of high school, the family, peer groups, and the media. And when looking at postgraduate programs (the PhD and professional degrees), we can include the additional factor of women being more likely to be married and more likely to be involved in the care of their young children—thereby deterring them from enrolling and completing degrees in these programs.

Racial, Ethnic, and Class Variations in Gender Socialization

Although we might suspect that the gender socialization processes described here vary by race, ethnicity, and class, there has been little research in the

Figure 4.6. Percentage of Professional Degrees and Doctorates in Selected Higher-Paying Technical Fields Conferred to Women, 1970–2000. *Sources:* National Center for Education Statistics, 2000 (p. 72), 2002c (Tables 21–22, pp. 39–42).

area—and the studies that have been done have produced contradictory findings. "Much more research is needed to elucidate the rich diversity of gender socialization practices and their outcomes among various races and classes" (Renzetti and Curran, 1995, pp. 99–100). We present here some tentative findings.

Women of Color

In the words of one student of gender socialization, "many of the characteristics associated with the feminine stereotype—dependence on men, weakness, and learned helplessness, for example—simply are not typical of women of color" (Anderson, 2003, p. 38). One difference between white and African American girls is the greater emphasis placed on female self-sufficiency in African American homes and the expectation that a woman's role includes material support of the family, whether she is a single parent or married. African American children in two-parent homes are also more likely to witness more egalitarianism in the division of household labor and in decision making. Research has shown that African American children, regardless of sex, "are expected to be assertive, independent, and emotionally expressive" (Figueira-McDonough, 1985, p. 124; also see Hale-Benson, 1986). One key exception occurs within black Muslim families, in which male dominance in both public and private life is an essential part of their credo. Another important variation: poor African American men face discrimination that may prevent them from fulfilling the traditional male role of provider; as a result, some "develop roles of exaggerated mas-

Two generations.

culinity—the 'tough guy' or the 'player of women'" (Scarpitti, Andersen, and O'Toole, 1997, p. 219; also see Oliver, 1984).

An expected empirical consequence of such differences in gender socialization would be the greater likelihood that African American women work, compared with white women. Indeed, this has always been the case. However, with gender-role expectations having changed for white girls and women over the past two decades such that the desire to combine work and family has become the norm, we would expect this difference to narrow or disappear.

At least one study (Isaaks, 1980) found the same differences for Latino children as just detailed for African American children: in short, that they are exposed to—and consequently subscribe to—fewer bipolar gender stereotypes (e.g., males as tough, females as demure). However, other researchers have found "at least as much, if not more, gender stereotyping among blacks and Hispanics as among whites" (Renzetti and Curran, 1995, p. 101). Indeed, Hale-Benson's (1986) study revealed that African American boys are encouraged—especially by their peers—to be athletic, sexually competent, street smart, and tough, while African American girls are socialized into "a very strong motherhood orientation" (as quoted in Renzetti and Curran, 1995, p. 100). General Social Survey data consistently show that African Americans are slightly more likely than whites to agree with the statement that "women should take care of running their homes and leave running the country up to men" (NORC, 1991–1994, 1994, 1996, 1998).

As for Asian American women, it has often been noted that they are socialized "in the context of a culture with devalued and subordinate roles for women" (Scarpitti, Andersen, and O'Toole, 1997, p. 218). However, the present gender socialization picture is surely much more complicated, considering the number of prominent female Asian American role models in various fields.

Consequences of Differential Gender Socialization for the Career Choices of Women of Color

To the degree that career choices are dictated by socialization and to the degree that there exists a strong pattern to this process that cuts across racial and ethnic origins, we would expect to find more similarities than differences among contemporary working women of different racial and ethnic origins—and indeed we do (for example, women of all racial/ethnic backgrounds are much more likely than their male counterparts to be secretaries and much less likely to be mechanics).

Nevertheless, given the less restrictive gender socialization of many women of color compared to their white counterparts, we would expect them to be less apprehensive in pursuing "male" careers. Indeed, as revealed in Table 4.2, this is the case for African American, Latina, Native American, and Asian women. Although there are some exceptions, the overall pattern of the data in this table reveals that, compared to non-Latina white women, women of color are more likely to pursue higher-paying technical degrees at the undergraduate level and are, likewise, more likely to pursue high-paying professional jobs compared to their male counterparts. This social fact is more sharply drawn in Figures 4.7–4.11, where we find it is graphically displayed for the bachelor's degree in business and in engineering and for the professional degree in law, medicine, and dentistry. Such data bode well for the future of gender equality, regardless of racial and ethnic background. And, even though women of color are less likely to pursue higher education, when they do they are studying fields that are in higher demand, and thus the data also bode well for reducing racial and ethnic inequality—as a high level of education in a high-demand field represents one of the strongest resources individuals of color have in combating racism.

Social Class

Most studies of the impact of race and ethnicity on gender socialization have used middle-class samples, so firm conclusions on the effects of social class on gender socialization are few. A number of studies have shown a modest negative relationship between education and gender stereotyping (Burns and Homel, 1989; Brooks-Gunn, 1986; Lackey, 1989), and, as evidenced in Figure 4.12, recent national survey data support this conclusion. However, one major study (Bardwell, Coebran, and Walker, 1986) found white children to be exposed to greater gender stereotyping as one moves up the social class scale; similarly, Figueira-McDonough (1985) found that African American girls raised in middle-class homes were more likely to express traditional gender views (e.g., girls should not be aggressive) than their counterparts raised in poor homes.

Table 4.2
BACHELOR, DOCTORATE, AND PROFESSIONAL DEGREES IN SELECTED FIELDS BY SEX, RACE, AND ETHNICITY, 1999–2000.

Field of Study	Wht* Men	Wht* Women	% Women	Blk* Men	Blk* Women	% Women	Latino Men	Latino Women	% Women	Asian Men	Asian Women	% Women	Nat.Am Men	Nat.Am Women	% Women
BS															
Biology	18,649	25,161	57.4	1,375	3,346	70.9	1,342	1,878	58.3	3,562	4,453	55.6	156	223	58.8
Business	93,123	83,780	47.4	8,561	13,917	61.9	6,519	7,562	53.7	7,665	9,064	54.2	619	782	55.8
Mathematics	4,524	4,089	47.5	466	501	51.8	328	283	46.3	489	461	48.5	33	37	52.9
Physical Sciences	8,422	5,210	38.2	472	668	58.6	373	254	40.5	836	723	46.4	55	53	49.1
Computer Science	16,325	4,879	23.0	1,762	1,615	47.8	1,183	567	32.4	3,562	1,703	32.3	108	58	34.9
Engineering	31,689	7,258	18.6	1,979	1,089	35.5	2,397	702	22.7	5,186	1,664	24.3	237	89	27.3
PhD															
Biology	1,534	1,246	44.8	40	64	61.5	75	64	46.0	222	197	47.0	5	3	37.5
Business	421	219	34.2	28	26	48.1	7	10	58.8	30	31	50.8	4	1	20.0
Mathematics	337	129	27.7	10	6	37.5	6	6	50.0	53	17	24.3	0	2	100.0
Physical Sciences	1,500	516	25.6	42	26	38.2	46	23	33.3	132	69	34.3	11	3	21.4
Computer Science	237	52	18.0	10	5	33.3	11	2	15.4	49	7	12.5	0	0	NA
Engineering	1,608	340	17.5	62	29	31.9	70	16	18.6	299	81	21.3	3	2	40.0
Professional															
Law	15,786	12,399	44.0	1,030	1,589	60.7	1,056	952	47.4	1,050	1,190	53.1	152	153	50.2
Dentistry	1,694	913	35.0	83	110	57.0	99	78	43.8	502	428	46.0	8	6	42.9
Medicine	6,042	4,119	40.5	418	655	61.0	456	344	43.0	1,456	1,103	43.1	62	58	48.3

*Non-Latino.
Source: National Center for Education Statistics (2002c, Tables 19, 20, and 22, pp. 34–42).

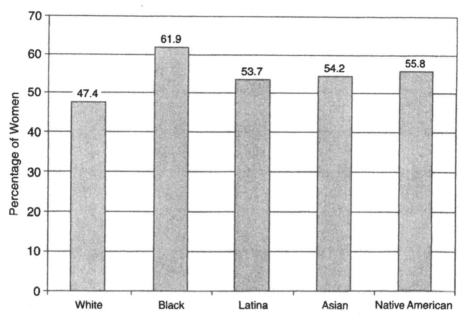

Figure 4.7. Percentage of Undergraduate Business Degrees Awarded to Women by Race and Ethnicity, 1999–2000 (e.g., of all business degrees awarded to non-Latino whites, 47.4% went to women). Note: White = Non-Latino White; Black = Non-Latino Black. *Source:* National Center for Education Statistics, 2002c (Table 19, p. 34).

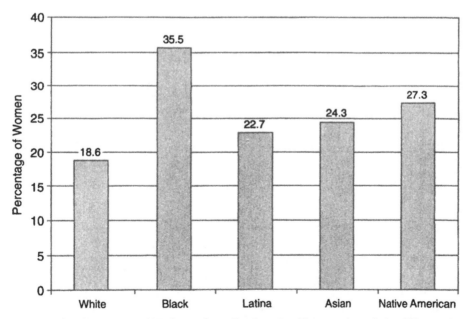

Figure 4.8. Percentage of Undergraduate Engineering Degrees Awarded to Women by Race and Ethnicity, 1999–2000 (e.g., of all engineering degrees awarded to non-Latino whites, 18.6% went to women). Note: White = Non-Latino White; Black = Non-Latino Black. *Source:* National Center for Education Statistics, 2002c (Table 19, p. 34).

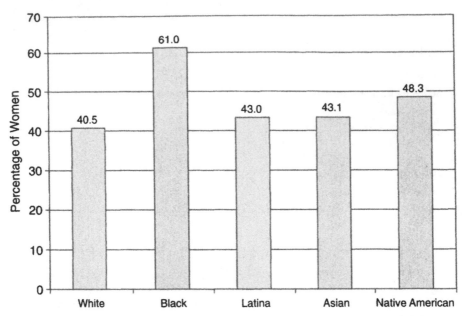

Figure 4.9. Percentage of MD Degrees Awarded to Women by Race and Ethnicity, 1999–2000 (e.g., of all medical degrees awarded to non-Latino whites, 40.5% went to women). Note: White = Non-Latino White; Black = Non-Latino Black. *Source:* National Center for Education Statistics, 2002c (Table 22, p. 42).

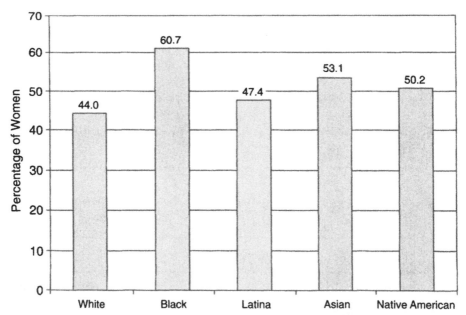

Figure 4.10. Percentage of Law Degrees Awarded to Women by Race and Ethnicity, 1999–2000 (e.g., of all law degrees awarded to non-Latino whites, 44.0% went to women). Note: White = Non-Latino White; Black = Non-Latino Black. *Source:* National Center for Education Statistics, 2002c (Table 22, p. 42).

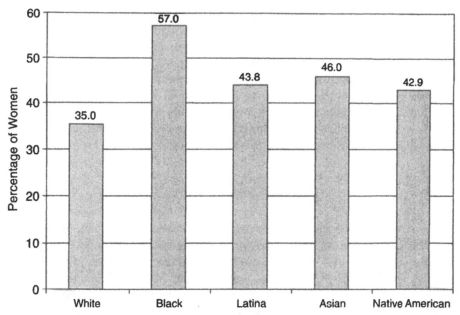

Figure 4.11. Percentage of Dentistry Degrees Awarded to Women by Race and Ethnicity, 1999–2000 (e.g., of all dentistry degrees awarded to non-Latino whites, 35.0% went to women). Note: White = Non-Latino White; Black = Non-Latino Black. *Source:* National Center for Education Statistics, 2002c (Table 22, p. 42).

Consequences of Differential Gender Socialization Among Social Classes for the Career Opportunities of Women

Given the inverse relationship between education and gender stereotyping, we would expect that women growing up in homes where parents were less educated would be less likely to pursue a college education. Pursuing and completing a college education is the single most important factor in determining an individual's eventual location in the social class system. Although it is diffi-

	Years of Education			
	Less Than 12	12	13–15	16
Disagree	64.1% (182)	83.9% (453)	88.5% (445)	93.3% (446)
Agree	35.9% (102)	16.1% (87)	11.5% (58)	6.7% (32)
Total	100% (284)	100% (540)	100% (503)	100% (478)

Figure 4.12. Relationship Between Educational Attainment and Agreeing or Disagreeing with the Statement: "Women should take care of running their homes and leave running the country up to men. *Source:* NORC (1998).

cult to tease out the effects of differential gender socialization per se compared to other factors associated with social class (e.g., having parents that do or do not possess enough income to significantly pay for a child's education; going to school in middle-class suburban setting where most high school seniors make the decision to go on to college versus going to an inner-city school where many of one's friends don't even complete high school), Figure 4.13 clearly shows that high school graduates having parents with no post–high school education are three times less likely to enroll in a four-year college than their counterparts who have a parent that graduated from college.

Summary

It is not biologic determinism but the socialization of individuals—which occurs within the contexts of the family, the educational system, the peer group, and the popular media—that ultimately has dramatic influences on gender inequality and the fates of working women. Although in recent years each of these contexts has become much more egalitarian, the framework for interpreting reality that is created and encouraged is one still moderately favoring many traditional stereotypes of desirable behavior for men and women. Such stereotypes reinforce traditional gender arrangements—arrangements that result in men being much more likely than women to become economically successful.

Parents are still more likely to give their sons toys that elicit more active and aggressive play and to their daughters toys that reinforce the gender stereotype of females having primary concern with home and family matters. Parental

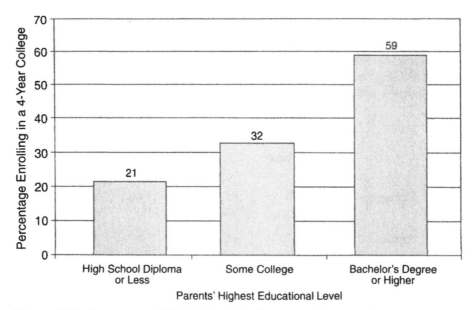

Figure 4.13. Percentage of High School Graduates Enrolling in a Four-Year College by Educational Attainment of Highest-Educated Parent, 1994. *Source:* National Center for Education Statistics (2002b, p. 77).

role models reinforce these stereotypes too; although most children see both mother and father in the workforce, they also see household chores still predominantly done by their mothers. Children are also likely to witness power imbalances in the interactions between their mother and father.

Schools are major arenas in which gender socialization occurs. Before 1970, virtually all aspects of the curriculum and extracurricular activities reinforced traditional gender roles. Since Title IX of the 1972 Education Amendments Act, dramatic changes in schools have taken place, with females gaining, though not yet attaining, much greater equality in both curricular and extracurricular activities. The most significant indicators of this equality are the narrowing between boys and girls in mathematical ability and in sports participation. These indicators are particularly important because success in mathematics is correlated with taking technical career tracks in college and entering traditionally male fields such as engineering and medicine, which pay considerably more than traditional female fields such as teaching and nursing. And team sports cultivate skills that are especially important for success in the workplace. Social scientists have long held that, in years gone by, girls were hurt in ways that eventually showed up economically by not participating in team sports. Despite greater gender egalitarianism in education philosophy and programs, the modern school still lacks full gender equity. In coeducational classrooms, boys are more likely to receive attention and encouragement to be assertive. Girls' sports participation is only three-fourths that of boys. And girls' SAT mathematics scores still fall 35 points shy of boys' scores. The overall impact is that boys are less likely to say they are "not good enough" or "not smart enough" to achieve their career goals. These problems are minimized for the small percentage of girls attending single-sex schools, where girls end up having greater cognitive development, higher occupational aspirations, and magnified self-confidence and self-esteem.

Child and adolescent peer groups are powerful agents of socialization, and they tend to encourage same-sex groups and gender-appropriate behavior. Youth culture encourages boys to be athletic and not overly expressive, while girls are encouraged to be beauty oriented and demure. For both sexes, to be "cool" is to be physically attractive and heterosexually popular. The youth culture reinforces the idea that males achieve status through accomplishment, while females achieve status by appearance and beauty.

Although the media act as a mirror to reflect the relationships and behavior of males and females in the dominant society, they also influence our expectations and perceptions of gender roles. More often than not, the media reinforce traditional gender stereotypes—men are aggressive, active, problem solvers, while women are passive and more interested in relationships than in work, politics, and power. Most non-news magazines oriented toward women often present female achievement in the work world as being dependent on physical attractiveness. Women in television are much more likely than men to be portrayed as submissive and unsuccessful. And when they are successful economically, television more often than not depicts an accompanying risk of being a failure in family life or with men.

Even though females have higher graduation rates from both high school and college, they are more likely than males to take educational tracks preparing them for lower-paying jobs. In high school, non-college-oriented boys are much more likely to take vocational courses that will lead them into higher-paying blue-collar trades (plumbing, carpentry, electrician work), while girls are much more likely to take vocational courses that prepare them for lower-paying office work (file clerk, bookkeeper, bank teller). The situation is similar at the college level: Women are more likely than men to major in subjects (e.g., elementary education, English, home economics, paralegal training, library science, the performing arts) that lead to lower-paying jobs than the majors in which men predominate (e.g., business, computer science, engineering, the physical sciences). The situation remains the same even at the level of graduate school, with women more likely to enroll in programs that will put them in careers that pay less (doctorates in education, English, and foreign languages and literature earn substantially less than doctorates in business, engineering, computer science, mathematics, and the physical sciences).

Because many women of color are less likely to be exposed to strong gender stereotypes, they are also more likely than their white counterparts to pursue undergraduate degrees in technical fields, as well as to pursue professional degrees in fields like law, medicine, and dentistry. On the other hand, except for Asian women, because they are more likely to come from less prosperous backgrounds they are less likely to pursue a college education to begin with, in part, because there is an inverse relationship between social class and gender role stereotyping.

Trend lines of higher-education data over the past three decades bode well for the future of gender equality: Women are increasingly likely to pursue higher levels of education, and when they do, they are increasingly likely to take up studies in technical fields and the professions. As we will find in the next two chapters, whether a woman graduates from college or not has a profound effect on the experiences and opportunities that working in the modern industrial world brings.

World Wide Web Resources

For voluminous census and survey data on working women, go to the Bureau of Labor Statistics Web site http://www.bls.gov/.

Media Reports to Women keeps up-to-date findings on the place of women in television, movies, and magazines; see http://www.mediareporttowomen.com/statistics.htm.

Education data on girls and women are available from large number of documents downloadable from the National Center for Education Statistics: http://nces.ed.gov/.

A number of items relating to gender socialization are a regular part of the biennial National Opinion Research Center's General Social Survey; data from this survey are available and can be readily analyzed online at: http://www.icpsr.umich.edu:8080/GSS/homepage.htm.

5 Women in Everyday Jobs: Clerical, Sales, Service, and Blue-Collar Work

While the professional woman and the woman who is on welfare are both increasingly visible in popular culture, the reality is that the majority of working women do not fall into either of these categories, but rather into the category of the "everyday" woman at work. This category encompasses a broad range of female workers, doing a variety of blue-collar or low-level white-collar jobs. These are the women who file folders for the professors at a university or for business executives. They sell apparel at department stores or, more invisibly, they stitch the apparel in the factory. They are the women who drive the bus or who ride the bus because they cannot afford a car. These women provide cheap domestic labor so that other women and men can fill the role of professional. Most of these women have only a high school degree (or less) with little or no college education. Most go to work either out of sheer economic necessity or to supplement the family income, although of course many also value the sense of challenge and accomplishment that comes with successfully completing a job.

In a society that places the greatest emphasis on those who have high-prestige or high-paying occupations, women employed in everyday jobs are often "invisible"—though essential—entities in the workplace. It is often only implicitly recognized that without a secretary the business person would not be able to function; without a domestic service worker in the home, many would not be able to devote as much time to their careers; without a salesperson to assist, many would return home from the store empty-handed. Although jobs discussed in this chapter are often dismissed as "everyday," they are vital not only in connection with our daily activities but also in the functioning of our very economic system, for low-skill laborers maintain capitalism by providing the necessary "back work." It is essential, if we are to understand the lives of people in the workplace, that these women not be dismissed as invisible or be marginalized in research (or in discussions such as ours) as they are in society.

Women in Clerical Occupations

Clerical work employs the largest percentage of these women, with approximately one in four women (22.9 percent) so employed (23.4 percent of all employed white women, 21.6 percent of employed African American women,

16.2 percent of employed Asian women, and 20.8 percent of working Latinas, and 24.9 percent of working Native American women; see Bureau of Labor Statistics 2003g; note: Native American data are for 1990, see Amott and Matthaei, 1996; allover percentages are for 2003). These women are the stenographers, word processors (typists), secretaries, clerks, data entry specialists, and bookkeepers.

The Feminization of Clerical Work: A Historical Examination

While women now dominate the clerical workforce, clerical occupations were once considered "men's work." In the nineteenth century, clerks were almost exclusively male. The 1870 census reported that of 76,639 office workers in the United States, only 1,860 (3.5 percent) were women (Davies, 1975).

Working as a clerk at the turn of the century was often the first step on the occupational ladder for men. Some men used clerkship as an "apprenticeship" and worked very closely with their bosses; often they moved up into the managerial ranks after "learning the ropes" as a clerk. A son of the owner might eventually take over the entire business. Even if the clerk were not using the clerkship as an apprenticeship, he still tended to develop highly personal relationships with his bosses over the forty or fifty years he worked in the office. Most clerks remained loyal to the company, hoping that their loyalty would be rewarded with promotions and raises, if not a stake in the company (Davies, 1975; McNally, 1979).

Despite their numbers and the demand for their services, nineteenth-century clerks were not organized as an occupational group. They did not join unions as a way to improve their working conditions or increase their economic benefits. Trade unions were considered a working-class phenomenon, and many clerks wanted to distance themselves from the industrial proletariat (working class). The position of the clerk had an aura of respectability, and it provided a means of obtaining the external trappings of the gentleman.

Though once the province of men, clerical occupations at the end of the nineteenth century rapidly became feminized. Corporations were experiencing a rapid expansion through the technological innovations of the telephone and the typewriter. There was an ever-increasing demand for clerical workers to keep pace with this expansion. This need extended clerical work opportunities to both genders.

The expansion of the corporate economy was not solely responsible for the integration of white women into the clerical workforce. The Remington Company, the first to make typewriters available to the public, used "type girls" to show how this new technological machine functioned (Davies, 1982). Linking women with typewriting helped to create a new space in the economy for women workers. Typewriting soon became identified as a "feminine specialty," allowing women to enter into the clerical workforce without being seen as pilfering jobs that "belonged" to men.

Women eventually moved beyond the "woman's work" of typing and telephoning into the traditionally male-dominated, more skilled clerical duties.

Secretary at office machine, circa 1920.

While they would never completely escape the association with typing, women were becoming more educated and better able to perform these other duties. More women were graduating from high school and searching for work, producing a larger labor pool from which employers could draw. The women seeking clerical work in this time period tended to be single, supporting themselves until they were able to get married. Other women worked to help their families avoid poverty. Typing and eventually clerical and secretarial work were a way for women to help themselves or their families without having to work in the abject conditions of much blue-collar employment. The only other opportunity for educated women desiring work at the time was teaching, but it was believed that clerical work paid better.

The women who were providing this new pool of clerical workers did not include women of color. Significant numbers of African American women were not employed in clerical work until the 1960s (see Table 5.1), and even then they continued to face discrimination in the workplace. Before the 1960s, they were almost completely excluded from clerical occupations. While this discrimination did not necessarily manifest itself visibly, it was quite apparent that black women were not welcome as clerical workers. "No signs appeared over the employment offices . . . reading 'Negroes need not apply.' But for all practical purposes that sign was out for clerical applicants to read" (Noland and Bakke, 1949, as cited in King, 1993, p. 1105).

Table 5.1.
PERCENTAGE OF EMPLOYED WOMEN IN CLERICAL WORK BY RACIAL
AND ETHNIC ORIGINS, 1900–2003

			Asian			Latina		
	White	Afr. Amer.	Chinese	Japanese	Filipina	Chicana	Puerto Rican	Nat. Amer.
1900	6.9	0.1	0.5	0.1	n/a	n/a	n/a	0.1
1930	25.3	0.6	11.7	3.7	1.6	2.8	n/a	3.3
1960	34.5	8.0	32.1	30.5	24.6	21.8	13.9	14.2
1970	36.8	20.7	30.8	34.7	30.0	25.9	29.7	25.9
1980	32.3	25.8	24.7	31.6	28.2	26.2	31.9	27.4
1990	28.2	25.8	20.7	28.0	28.0	24.7	31.0	24.9
2003	23.4	21.6		16.2*			20.8**	n/a

*Combined: all Asians (Chinese, Japanese, Filipina, Other).
**Combined: all Latinas (Chicana, Puerto Rican, Other)
Sources: Amott and Matthaei (1996); Bureau of Labor Statistics (1980, 2003g).

The number of clerical positions more than doubled between 1940 and 1960 (from 4.4 to 9.8 million) and almost doubled again between 1960 and 2003 (to 19.4 million), as the U.S. economy shifted from manufacturing to distribution, finance, and service and as the number of large and complex information-processing business and governmental organizations increased (Bureau of Labor Statistics, 2003g; Gutek, 1988). It was during this latter period that minority women made inroads into the clerical field. Finally, African American, Asian, Latina, and Native American women broke open the doors to—and solidified their presence in—occupations that had previously been the domain of white women; their movement into clerical positions is the most significant example of the integration of the workplace (King, 1993). Although clerical work is not considered a prime occupation because of low wages, little autonomy, and limited opportunity for advancement, for minority women it signaled an upward move in the occupational hierarchy, away from domestic service, farm work, and low-level manufacturing jobs. An increasing need for clerical workers opened the doors for minority women, but the doors were still most welcoming to white women. Traditionally, many minority women were confined to the lowest-paying clerical occupations and were denied opportunities to advance even when their credentials were as good as or better than those of their white counterparts (Malveaux, 1985; Power and Rosenberg, 1993). Current wage data reveal that this tradition is fading: In 2001 the median weekly wage of non-Latina white women employed full time in administrative support/clerical work was $469, while it was $461 for African American women, and $424 for Latinas (Bureau of Labor Statistics, 2003d). Recent in-depth, systematic interviews with hundreds of employers in four major U.S. cities (Atlanta, Boston, Detroit, and Los Angeles) reveal that employers are more likely to hire and promote whites and Asians over African Americans and Latinas because of average skill differences among the groups—which is actually a hopeful finding for the future, as increases the schooling and training will reduce discrimination. On the

other hand, these interviews also reveal that many managers still "hold negative stereotypes of blacks and, to a lesser extent, Latinos, and act on these stereotypes by discriminating in hiring" (Moss and Tilly, 2001, pp. 3–4). Interviews
with 9,000 employees in these same four cities cohere with the employer interviews: 31.8 percent of blacks and 18.4 percent of Latinos versus 7.8 percent
of Asians and 9.5 percent of whites reported that within the past year that they
had personally experienced workplace discrimination (for example, being passed
over for raises or promotions; see Moss and Tilly, 2001, pp. 7–8).

In sum, from the early 1900s to the early 2000s, clerical work changed from
a male-dominated occupation to one in which women comprised 80 percent of
all file clerks; 92 percent of bookkeepers; 95 percent of stenographers, typists,
and data entry keyers; 98 percent of receptionists; and 99 percent of secretaries
(Bureau of Labor Statistics, 2003e). Clerical jobs also underwent a transition
from being a means to climb the ladder of occupational prestige to being dead-
end work with little hope of advancement. The old paternal relationship between the boss and his clerical worker disappeared; instead such workers became information handlers in the large organization.

Besides the feminization of typing, another reason why women came to
dominate clerical occupations is that they were not seen as a challenge to male
authority. While women may have been resisted in the workplace at first, they
were eventually seen as beneficial to business operation, as "compliant, cheerful, and non-competitive for male positions" (Wichroski, 1994). With the perception that the "feminine" traits of clerical workers were thus beneficial, the
association of clerical work and femininity became ingrained. Women who were
interested in clerical work had to fill more than the necessary requirements of
a high school education and general literacy; they were now required to have a
pleasant personality, with good interpersonal skills and good manners (Gottfried
and Fasenfest, 1984; Gutek, 1988).

Clerical Work as "Female" Labor

With the large number of women now employed as clerical workers, "it seems
to be one of the jobs that managers regard as 'natural' for women workers, as
common and normal as homemaking" (Gwartney-Gibbs and Lach, 1994,
p. 618). Along with the sex-typing of clerical work has come the expectation
that women doing it behave in ways appropriate for traditional gender roles.
They are expected to have a traditionally "feminine" demeanor and to be "nice."
They are supposed to be clean, neat, and attractive in their workspace. And they
are supposed to remain very loyal to their bosses. Clerical work places an emphasis on being nurturant, supportive, and loyal to the employer. It also neces-
sitates a willingness to stand in the background and support the work of those
higher up in the company (Gutek, 1988; Kanter, 1977).

This perception has produced a system in which much of the work that a
secretary performs is "invisible." These women perform the obvious labor of
word processing (or typing) and answering the telephone, but they also perform
a large amount of work that does not get noticed. These tasks are never stated

in the job description, but are implicitly demanded by the sex-typing of the occupation. Hochschild (1983) calls this "emotional work." It is part of the role of the secretary, for example, to keep the office functioning well at an emotional level; this work often requires that the secretary manipulate her own feelings and the feelings of others to keep the office running smoothly (Wichroski, 1994). This "emotional labor" most often remains unrecognized.

The sex-typing of office work has imposed on women working as secretaries other, more concrete tasks that are outside the job description. Some women do these tasks ungrudgingly because of their positive relationship with their boss. "I've done personal Christmas shopping, personal banking, and personal letters . . . lots of these. . . . One guy asked me to register his car for him. I guess that's a bit much, but I like the guy so I did it" (Wichroski, 1994, p. 38). Other women refuse to do labor that is not within the bounds of their job description. However, it can hurt them if they do not comply with their bosses' requests. "I wasn't hired to be a maid. I used to wash his desk . . . only once a week maybe. That's why I didn't get merit raises. Even today I get coffee. I don't drink coffee but I do it . . . begrudgingly. I've been expected to make coffee, wash tables, mop up spills, etc. . . . A secretary should not be expected to do housekeeping" (Wichroski, 1994, p. 38). Such requests are viewed as legitimate by the bosses because of the notions of gender that pervade our society. These men are higher up in the occupational and gender hierarchy, so asking a woman to do the menial labor that they don't have the time or the desire to do is not anything they perceive as inappropriate. Some male bosses make requests that require their secretaries to act as if they were a surrogate wife: "I've been asked to make travel arrangements for my boss's wife, and to type and edit his children's term papers" (Wichroski, 1994, p. 38).

In the early part of the twentieth century, women gained acceptance as secretaries, in part, because their work roles were subservient to male authority.

Women Bosses: A New Reality for Clerical Workers

In 2003, there were nearly 8.5 million women managers in the United States compared to just over 10 million men doing such work (Bureau of Labor Statistics, 2003g). With women nearing parity with men in lower and middle management, there is now nearly a one in two chance that a secretary will find herself working for a female boss. How do women managers and their secretaries, stenographers, and typists (98 percent of whom are women, Bureau of Labor Statistics, 2003d) relate to one another on the job?

Some research depicts this relationship as filled with conflict. The model for the relationship is the mother-daughter dyad, which is often filled with strife and competition. Harriman (1996, p. 109) suggests that many secretaries view a female boss as a negative role model; more specifically, "clerical women may feel that the woman manager's position or behavior is sex-role deviant or inappropriate. She may perceive the woman as neglecting or abandoning her role as wife or mother, in effect denigrating these roles."

Indeed, the first empirical research done in this area found that women preferred not to work for other women (Ferber, Huber, and Spitze, 1979). Women in clerical positions were found to be drawn to those whom they perceived as holding power in the organization, and their woman bosses were not viewed in that light. Secretaries therefore felt that they did not need to provide their female bosses with the support and assistance needed to function within the managerial position. Nevertheless, there was a silver lining in this research. The authors concluded that the preference for a female boss was dependent on the extent to which an individual was actually exposed to one. It was expected that as more women managers entered the managerial ranks and clerical staff had more experience working with women in a variety of managerial capacities, there would be more opportunity to assess their strengths and capabilities and less reliance on hearsay and stereotypical attitudes and values concerning women managers.

Later research actually found that women managers developed closer-knit relationships with their secretaries, due, in part, to women's greater socialization to invest in interpersonal relationships (see Caldwell and Peplau, 1982; and Statham, 1988, p. 226). For example, Statham (1987, 1988, 1996) intensively interviewed twenty-two female and eighteen male managers. The men and women were similar in age, education, years with the corporation, and number of hours worked per week. She found women managers both "people" and "task" oriented. They often talked about themselves as "teachers" and "mothers," and their secretaries perceived them as concerned and thoughtful of others. One secretary expressed the following regarding female bosses:

> I think women are much more respectful of their secretaries, more sensitive to them, appreciate more the things they do. Just simple things like saying thank you for tasks that are completed. So many men just say good morning and good night to their secretaries and that's about it. I've watched a lot of these men interacting with their secretaries and thought "I don't think I could ever work for him!" (Statham, 1987, p. 417)

At the same time, Statham (1987) found that women managers were task oriented. They were highly focused on getting their work done and emphasized the many tasks they needed to accomplish on the job. Their secretaries felt that the woman managers "made more effective use of their services" (p. 418). One secretary noted: "She trusts me. . . . She doesn't question what I do. She has confidence . . . that makes you feel good. I worked for the man that sat in here prior . . . and that was just a bad experience. . . . He never let you do anything; he only told you what he wanted you to know. . . . I enjoy doing (these things) because she gives you credit" (p. 418).

Female managers often look toward advancing a secretary's career. Statham (1987, p. 419) notes that male managers give their secretaries tasks they themselves often did not want to do such as "detail work, organizing, following up on subordinates' tasks." They also look to their secretaries to do more traditionally "female" tasks, often bordering on that of a traditional wife. One male manager observed: "I really need a good secretary to take care of me. They take the air of responsibility off your mind, organizing yourself" (Statham, 1987, p. 419).

If women managers are more engaged in a "person" orientation, the men are more invested in how crucial their work is for "the organization and for society" (Statham, 1987, p. 419). It is important for male managers to see their jobs as pivotal to the functioning of the company. Men's styles are more "autonomy invested" (Statham, 1987, p. 420). While both women and men are task oriented in their jobs, male managers' delegation style differs from female managers in that men expect their secretaries to do their jobs independently with little input from management. Their philosophy is one of picking the right individual to do the job and expecting that the job is completed unless a problem arises: "The more you interfere, the less gets done. . . . People are more motivated if they feel they have a stake in it" (Statham, 1987, p. 421). Women managers who are task oriented delegators have a more "person-invested," delegation style—one that secretaries appreciate. One secretary notes her boss "follows up without making you feel she's checking up on you" (Statham, 1987, p. 420). This is seen to be an important "person-investment" style. On the other hand, female secretaries often see their male bosses' style as negative and do not always appreciate the autonomy they provide them and often see it as "neglect": "He . . . set me in an office across the street . . . gave me a stack of files, and said this is your job. Do it. I was totally frustrated; I had no guidance" (Statham, 1987, p. 423).

Thus, women managers tend to have a more personal investment style, while their male counterparts tend to use a more autonomous-based management style. Female managers are more likely to nurture secretaries—to guide and work *with* them—and are more concerned with their career aspirations. Male managers tend to be concerned about their place or image within the overall organization and how they contribute to organizational goals. They are more likely to see themselves as delegating responsibilities to their secretaries to enable them to see themselves as autonomous individuals. Sometimes, however, secretaries interpret this autonomy as a lack of supervision and neglect on the part of the male manager.

In sum, more recent research questions the relationship of managers to their secretaries as primarily one of strife and competition. Researchers such Statham suggest, instead, that there is mutual support and respect between secretaries and their female managers—as well as recognition on the part of managers of the career aspirations of their secretaries. Thus, a task-oriented management style is not mutually exclusive with one that is also person oriented—this combination, apparently more characteristic of women managers, may, in the long run, yield more job satisfaction for clerical workers.

Male Clerical Workers

What about the relatively few men that are left in clerical occupations? Henson and Rogers (2001) conducted in-depth interviews and participant observation research with several samples of male clerical temporary office workers in Chicago and Los Angeles and found that the strategies these men used to address the gendered nature of their work served to reinforce traditional masculine ideals and the subordination of women. For example, those men who entered this sex-atypical occupation tended to "rename or reframe" their work tasks. They refused to label their duties "secretarial" and instead described them in more masculine terms by emphasizing the "technical" nature and skills required to perform the clerical tasks in their job descriptions. Consider the account given by a twenty-three-year-old white male describing his secretarial position: "That was mostly work with IBM. You know, 'cause IBM is incredibly popular. So I used my WordPerfect a lot. And then when they didn't have any WordPerfect, they sent me out on proofreading assignments. To proofread these books that no one would ever, ever read. Basically, it's been a lot of word processing" (Henson and Rogers, 2001, p. 231).

The researchers also found the men gave "cover stories" for why they were employed in female-dominated occupations—stories that served to boost their masculine identity. For example, one man related to the researchers how he told his coworkers and boss he was really an actor "waiting to get a real job" (Henson and Rogers, 2001, p. 232). Henson and Rogers found that employers and coworkers drew out cover stories from men, but rarely inquired about the women in similar occupations. Thus, it is evident that the attitude that pervades the office is one emphasizing traditional gender roles. Employers and employees alike seemed to believe that men were "not" supposed to occupy these subordinate positions, while women, in contrast, simply "belonged" in them. Many of the men also refused to engage in what the researchers termed "deferential services," such as " smiling, waiting, taking orders, and tolerating the bad moods of their supervisors"; such noncompliant behaviors often placed many clerical men "at risk" for losing their jobs (Henson and Rogers, 2001, pp. 233, 235).

Sexual Harassment and Clerical Work

Sexual harassment has become a problem in every field of the workforce. It involves everything from creating a "hostile environment" via sexual innuendo or blatant vulgarities, to unwelcome touching, unwanted and persistent advances, promising promotions for engaging in sexual activity, and, occasionally, to attempted rape. Since 1986, U.S. laws have recognized two basic forms of harassment: *quid pro quo* (sleep with me or else you won't get the promotion) and *hostile-environment* (a work environment in which sexually tinted intimidation, ridicule, and insult are present). Both kinds of harassment are mainly perpetrated by men against women—indeed, of the 14,396 formal complaints lodged in 2002 with the U.S. Equal Employment Opportunity Commission (2003), 85 percent came from women. Almost half of all working women report that they have suffered from harassment over the course of their careers (NORC, 1996). In any one year, nearly 20 percent of working women report that they have been the victims of harassment (Galinsky and Bond, 1996, p. 91). And almost 10 percent of working women have quit a job because of sexual harassment (Gutek, 1988). While women have been successful in some cases at fighting back, most sexual harassment goes on in subtler ways that can be difficult to prove or to prosecute.

Women clerical workers are often faced with sexual harassment that stems from their sex-typed work role. As we have noted, women in clerical positions are often required to be attractive and to perform tasks that put them in the position of an "office wife." Nieva and Gutek (1981) call these traditional gender-role expectations that pervade the workplace of the clerical worker "sex-role spillover," which they argue contributes to sexual harassment of clerical workers. In an occupation that requires women to behave in a manner appropriate to traditional sex-typed roles, many men feel it is their prerogative to sexually harass women. Such men do not see their behavior as harassment, but instead as part of the playing out of sex roles.

Sexual harassment can, as a rule, be differentiated from the innocent flirtations that fill the workplace because harassment persists even when the woman declines the advance. Not only is this bothersome for the woman who has to face the man each day she goes to work, but it can also be disabling:

> I was a typist, and one of the men I worked for is always caressing my hair, or rubbing my back, or trying to hug me when he comes into the office. I pull away and tell him to stop, but he never seems to get the message. He acts hurt and says he's only being friendly. It's really upsetting, and I can't work when he is around. Having to face him every day ties my stomach into knots. I need to work—I got two kids; but you can't work like that, you just can't. (Working Women United Institute, 1980, p. 1)

Indeed, the documented effects of sexual harassment are manifold and serious. A special government task force in New York conducted a massive study of the problem and found that victims of sexual harassment often suffer significant psychological and physical consequences, including "depression, helplessness, decreased work or academic performance, withdrawal, devastating impacts on family, insomnia, chronic fatigue, nausea and other physiological complaints" (Avner, 1993, p. 21).

The sexual harassment that occurs within the confines of a white-collar office space most often remains subtle, though office clerical workers at the bottom of the occupational hierarchy often have to face much more blatant affronts—such as crude, suggestive remarks and physical assaults—than do their managerial or professional counterparts. In turn, clerical workers are not as likely to be faced with the more subtle sexual harassment of offers for after-work drinks, expensive lunches, and business trips—with the implicit message that sexual favors are expected (Backhouse and Cohen, 1981, p. 33).

Clerical work, because of its sex-typed roles, encourages the presumption of heterosexuality among women as well as men, but sexual harassment in the workplace is also an issue affecting the lives of lesbian women. Because they are not interested in developing a romantic relationship with their male coworkers, remarks that might be considered innocent and welcome by a heterosexual woman can produce a great amount of discomfort for lesbians (Moses, 1978). This discomfort is one of the reasons lesbians report sexual harassment in the workplace as frequently as heterosexual women of a similar race and age (Schneider, 1984). Many lesbians hide their sexual orientation in the workplace to avoid the repercussions of disclosure. Lesbians who come out in the workplace are often marginalized or face direct discrimination (Schneider, 1988). With the presumption of heterosexuality—in effect, a "compulsory heterosexuality" (Rich, 1980)—pervading the workplace, lesbian women who do not make a point of disclosing their sexual orientation are rendered "invisible."

There are many obstacles to reporting sexual harassment in the workplace. Sexually harassed women often are embarrassed or otherwise reluctant to report an incident. Many women fear what will happen to them if they report it—especially threats to their livelihood or the "fear that they will be ridiculed or made to feel guilty that they in some way were responsible by encouraging the harasser" (Backhouse and Cohen, 1981, p. 35). For a lesbian woman, reporting sexual harassment might require disclosure of her sexual orientation, which she may not want. Clerical workers, at the lowest rungs of white-collar occupational hierarchy, often do not have the power to report a superior or other male coworker. Too often, unless the offense cannot be ignored because of its seriousness, women reporting an incident are made out to be the ones acting wrongfully:

> I've talked to workers who've told me "My supervisor's driving me nuts because they're doing this and doing that." It's really hard to prove any of that stuff. They tell me lots of times that they come across as being the terrible person. If it's really an out-and-out illegal thing that the supervisor is doing, then you can get 'em for it. But if it just subtle little things, it's really hard. (Gwarmey-Gibbs and Lach, 1994)

Moreover, as the New York task force concluded, the "filing of a sexual harassment complaint often is a form of career suicide" (Avner, 1993, p. 21). Many of the women interviewed who had filed complaints found themselves the objects of retaliation. A sixty-two-year-old financial writer provided this description of what happened after she filed a "hostile environment" sexual harassment complaint:

> I was downgraded and told I was to receive a zero-percent salary increase. (I was the only one in the division who did not receive a 5 percent raise.) That was the beginning of a humiliating year-long constructive discharge, which included a change in title, loss of my window office, reduction of my responsibilities and other painful acts of retaliation that continued right up to my firing. For the last two months, I was assigned a menial job in a cold, isolated storage room that was not protected by the company's security system. This room had been burglarized during lunchtime at the Christmas holidays. (Avner, 1993, p. 42)

After this woman left, she, like many others in her shoes, had a difficult time trying to find another job. As another interviewee in the same situation complained, "I went out to look for another job [but when] I went in to fill out an application, I could not write the name of [my former] company as a reference" (Avner, 1993, p. 42). Lacking the power to report the incident without personal repercussions, women are often left to feel uncomfortable or upset while they are working with a man who will not respect their personal space or their refusals. In short, while state and federal Equal Employment Opportunity Commissions provide the institutionalized means for women to report harassment, it still remains a difficult and stigmatizing chore for most women.

The Clerical Worker and Technological Advancement

Clerical work has been revolutionized by the technological advances in recent decades. With computers becoming a staple in the workplace, almost no task is performed in the same manner it was twenty years ago. These technological changes have led to the hiring of a greater number of women clerical workers. They have also led to changes in the clerical worker's quality of life. Exactly how has technology helped or hindered the quality of life of the clerical worker?

Many claimed that the introduction of new computer technology into the office—especially those microprocessor-based systems such as the word processor—would free the secretary-clerk from dull and routine tasks, permit a shorter work week, and allow time for more responsible and challenging administrative tasks. Automated office equipment does reduce some of the old, dull, routine tasks associated with many jobs, but operating the equipment can be just as dull and routine, and just as dehumanizing—although perhaps in a different way. And it is just as likely that male employees will take on the more responsible and challenging administrative tasks. Indeed, some feared that word processors and other automated office equipment would further widen the gap between men's and women's work by de-skilling the female clerical employee, lowering the conceptual content of her tasks, and increasing managerial control of clerical workers (Morgall, 1981; Vallas, 1987; West, 1982). This prediction, fortunately, has not come to pass: Sophisticated systems such as Microsoft Office now dominate the office environment and clerical workers who master the likes of Word, Excel, and Power Point have both deepened and broadened their value to the organization.

That said, clerical workers are sometimes not given sufficient training to use a computer to do the work that needs to be done:

> My supervisor got a brand-new computer when all the departments were getting them. She gave me her old one, and said, "I bent over backwards to get you a computer," as if to make me feel grateful, but I knew she hadn't done anything special. I hadn't done anything on a computer before, so it was just sitting there. I was supposed to be typing onto disk, but I didn't have any training. She showed me how to type a letter, but not how to do the tabs. She gave me her notes from her word-processing class, and I went to an "Introduction to Microcomputers" class, where they show you how to turn it on and off and how to use the mouse. But it wasn't enough; it didn't have anything to do with word-processing. She expected me to figure out everything for myself, like she said she had learned. But that wasn't true; her husband came in after work and on weekends and trained her. But she still didn't even know how to put tabs in a letter. (Gwarmey-Gibbs and Lach, 1994, p. 621)

Even with training on how to operate the computers, workers often do not really understand the work they are doing. The operator of a check-sorting machine in a large bank describes her experience thus:

> In our area we have about sixty or seventy people working. . . . A lot of checks are not supposed to go through—like certain checks that should go to another bank or forged ones or some that the number isn't quite clear on. Unfortunately, once in a while some of them slip through. Then you have to ring the buzzer, and they have to come over and rebatch everything. And they know that sorter such-and-such let them go through. Now they have error sheets, so every time you make an error it gets marked down. People are making more errors now because they're so nervous about not making them. It's for performance reviews. They want statistics when it comes time for raises or promotions. They started marking down errors in January, but they didn't let us know until almost the end of the month. All of a sudden they hand you an error sheet. We didn't think it was fair not to let you know. It's almost like Big Brother. . . . These performance reviews . . . people are very upset about them. You're working faster because "times per hour" is going to be part of the statistics in your review. . . . Most of the people agree with me that they don't give you enough training on what happens to the check. They'll say, "You're running D.D.A today." Fine, I know that D.D.A. means you're running the main type of work with the orange separator card, but I don't know what "D.D.A" means . . . or "D.V." or "S.D.A." or "G.G.E.". . . . It would be nice if you knew what they were or where the checks come from or where they're going. It's just a feeling of not knowing. It's like the machine running you. You're a computer. "We'll run D.D.A. today." (Tepperman, 1976, pp. 26–27)

This is an instance of the de-skilling and alienating nature of computers in the workplace. In many big offices, such as the large financial and insurance headquarters, clerical activities are arranged as small, standardized tasks, usually with automated office machines to speed the work process. Pools of workers (the secretarial office pool) or individual workers specialize in one set of small tasks, performing these limited activities over and over again (Glenn and Feldberg,

1977). This specialization can create a factory-like atmosphere in the office. In certain cases, "when a word processor enters the office, an automated time and motion man may come along with it. In order to capitalize on their investment, management may decide to increase shiftwork and speed up the work process. A piece rate system may be introduced" (Morgall, 1981, pp. 94–95). Some observers believe that the growth of office mechanization, coupled with the division of office tasks into smaller and smaller routine operations, has blurred the distinction between manual and nonmanual work, making white- and blue-collar jobs more similar. In this view, the clerk can be considered a "helper's attendant" in a highly mechanized, high-speed process (Braverman, 1974).

Clerical work was already often done in the back rooms or was otherwise "invisible" in the workplace. The creation of "back-room" labor pools to use computers adversely affected the quality of work of the clerical staff; clerical workers lost flexibility, autonomy, and a relationship with a particular boss. Bosses were also affected by this reorganization of the office; they lost the convenience and the prestige of having a personal secretary (Wichroski, 1994). As a result of this mutual loss, many organizations have chosen not to set up such labor pools. While the implementation of computers in the workplace has often meant that one secretary now works for a number of bosses, the importance of retaining some autonomy in the clerical workforce has been recognized as beneficial to the productivity of the workplace and the quality of life of the clerical worker.

Because of their lower occupational status within the clerical workforce, minority workers tend to be the first to be displaced by office automation. While "back-room" pools of workers may sometimes have provided spaces for more minority women to enter clerical work, as greater computerization occurs their participation in the clerical workforce is likely to be reduced. Minority women might have progressed much farther if they had not been relegated to these "back-office staffs" (King, 1993).

Though technological advancement has sometimes had an alienating effect on the clerical workforce, one should not conclude that clerical workers derive no satisfaction from their work. Glenn and Feldberg's (1984, p. 329) in-depth study of women clerical workers revealed that, in addition to the income, the "opportunities to form and maintain social connections" were important. Work was also reported to give "direction and purpose to their lives by structuring their time and getting them involved in 'useful' activity" (1984, p. 329). For married women, work also provided "an identity separate from their family roles" (1984, p. 329). It must also be kept in mind that clerical work offers better employment opportunities, in terms of wages, working conditions, and job security, than do domestic service, agricultural work, and most service occupations. Indeed, the overwhelming majority of clerical workers express a good degree of job satisfaction. For example, eight out of ten women clerical workers, according the General Social Survey (NORC, 1998–2000) responded to the following question that they are either "very satisfied" (42.2 percent) or "moderately satisfied" (39.5 percent): "On the whole, how satisfied are you with the work you do?"

Organization of Clerical Workers

With its modest wages, little autonomy, and limited opportunities for advancement, clerical work would appear to be one of the occupations in which unionization would be most prevalent. Though more working women are engaged in clerical work than in any other occupation, they are still only minimally unionized (14.0 percent). In the past two decades, however, women have made substantial numeric (though not proportionate) inroads into unionization as clerks working in offices in both the public (42.0 percent of government workers are unionized) and private (9.3 percent unionized) sectors. In 2002, 6.63 million women (13 percent of employed women) were members of unions, up from 5.80 million in 1984 (12.5 percent). Although there has been only a tiny increase in the percentage, this must be viewed in light of the substantial decrease that occurred for employed men, whose unionized percentage dropped from 23.0 to 16.0 percent. With increasing numbers of women joining unions and decreasing numbers of men belonging to them, women's share of union employment rose from 34.0 to 42.0 percent during this period (see Bureau of Labor Statistics, 1997g; Herz and Wootton, 1996; and U.S. Department of Labor. 2002b, 2002c, 2002d). Clerical workers are significantly more likely than most other female workers to be unionized, with a rate of 14.0 percent (compared to 4.0 percent for sales workers and 9.5 percent for service workers other than those in the protective services—which have a relatively high rate of unionization at 39.5 percent). African American women (17.7 percent of whom are unionized) are significantly more likely than their Latina (11.1 percent) and white (12.3 percent) counterparts to belong to unions (U.S. Department of Labor, 2002b, 2002d).

Those women clerical workers spurred to activism in a union are attempting to combat what they see as workplace inequalities and injustice. Many clerical workers want to join because they feel underappreciated in their work role:

> When I first joined, I was having job problems. It was the typical thing with secretaries. I didn't think my work was appreciated. I wasn't respected and I didn't have any promotional opportunities. The boss was in charge and the secretary was supposed to do whatever he asked of her. And everyone . . . thought that was the way it should be. This bothered me and I thought that an organization like BWW (Baltimore Working Women) could help me. At least I could learn how I might make my own situation better. (Buxton, 1997, p. 340)

Not surprisingly, women clerical workers find it much easier to join unions if they have a supportive boss who encourages their participation, and if they have job security. The most active union members tend to have both (Buxton, 1997). Less active members may also have supportive bosses and job security, but they may have been asked by their superiors to be discreet about their union participation and to participate on their own time. Women who lack either a supportive boss or job security, those who are most in need of union membership, are least likely to be in a union or other working women's association. "Of all members, *inactives* were the most in need of any assistance BWW could offer, but, lacking the protection offered by a supportive boss or by long-term visibility as an activist, they rightfully feared reprisal if they took action to remedy their situations" (Buxton, 1997, p. 341).

One of the benefits of joining clerical work unions is a decrease in the hostility and animosity among coworkers. Sometimes superiors attempt to pit one clerical worker against another:

> On several occasions one of the professors showed me a paper another secretary had typed and complained that periods were left out or were in the wrong place. At first I thought it was terrible that she was so sloppy. And I was angry that she had the same position I did, but didn't work as carefully or as hard. Then I happened to be looking at one of the journals and found that she was just following a correct journal format. When I mentioned this to him, he said, "I doubt it, not her." (Buxton, 1997, p. 340)

Women involved in unions or other work organizations are more apt to recognize the ways in which superiors try to pit one worker against another, and less likely to go along. Active members of unions or other working women's organizations are less likely to "describe co-workers in negative terms, such as petty, bitchy, hostile, jealous, or overly competitive" (Buxton, 1997, p. 338).

In general, for all occupations, the earnings benefits of union membership are significant for both minority and white women. As was presented in Chapter 2 (Table 2.2), unionized African American, Latina, and white women all earn at least 30 percent more than their nonunionized counterparts. Moreover, unionized women are less likely to suffer gender inequality—more specifically, the ratio of women's to men's earnings for union members (85.5 percent) is greater than it is for nonunionized workers (78.2 percent; see U.S. Department of Labor, 2002a). This relationship holds for both whites and blacks, but not for Latinos. Nonunionized Latinos, both male and female, are much more likely than their nonunionized white and black counterparts (both male and female) to be working in low-skill laboring jobs (household, farm, and nonfarm), where gender inequality is significantly lower than in the executive, administrative, managerial, and professional jobs that are more likely to be held by whites and blacks.

Sales and Service Occupations

With the transition in the United States from a manufacturing to a service-based economy, it is not surprising that the next largest percentage of women (after clerical employees) work in service and sales occupations. These categories differ in that the latter jobs do not necessarily involve the exchange of a product. Service work (excluding private household work) comprises a range of jobs that include food preparation and service (e.g., waiters, waitresses, cooks), health service (e.g., dental assistants, nurses aids, orderlies), cleaning and building services (e.g., maids, janitors, elevator operators), personal services (e.g., barbers, hairdressers, childcare workers), as well as protective service (police officers, firefighters, security guards). Sales occupations include sales supervisors and proprietors; sales representatives in finance and business; and sales workers in retail and personal services businesses. From the mid-1930s to the early 2000s, the percentage of women working in the sales and service sector more than doubled. In 2003, 20.0 percent of employed women were in service occupations and 11.9 percent were in sales occupations, concentrated primarily in retail sales (Bureau of Labor Statistics, 2003g).

One of the most important factors behind the transition to a service-based economy has been the growing urbanization of society. Another reason for the decline in the industrial sector has been global restructuring. This refers to a process whereby assembly-line work is fanned out to less developed nations—where wages are lower—such as those in Southeast Asia and Latin America, while the research and management ends of production are based in the developed economies (like the United States). The Bureau of Labor Statistics (2003h) estimates that of the ten major occupational groups that comprise the U.S. labor market (e.g., service jobs, sales jobs, production jobs), service occupations will grow faster than all but those in the professions between 2000 and 2010.

The dramatic increase during the twentieth century in sales and service work for both white and minority women (except for Chinese women, many of whom worked in restaurants and laundry services before World War II) is evident in Table 5.2. We can also note here certain differences by racial and ethnic group. In 2003, Latina (31.0 percent) and African American (26.4 percent) women are more likely to hold a service job compared with white (18.9 percent) and Asian women (20.9 percent). On the other hand, white (12.1 percent), African American (11.1 percent), Asian (10.3 percent), and Latina (11.9 percent) women all have very similar probabilities of holding a sales job.

The service economy has created two types of jobs: a large number of low-skill, low-paying jobs and a small number of high-skill, high-paying jobs primarily in the protective services occupations (firefighters, police, detectives). While women presently make up a majority of service workers (56.8 percent) and about half of all sales workers (48.0 percent; see Bureau of Labor Statistics, 2003g), they are overrepresented in traditionally feminized jobs. Looking at full-time workers, women comprise 97.8 percent of family childcare providers, 96.0 percent of private household workers, 77.8 percent of cashiers, and 71.0 percent of wait staff (Bureau of Labor Statistics, 2003e). They also remain highly concentrated in lower-paying health service occupations (e.g., dental assistants, nursing aides), comprising 87.8 percent of all workers in this area. With a disproportionately large number of women working in these low-prestige, low-paying jobs, there is a considerable income differential between men and women in sales and service occupations. In 2001, women constituted only 17.7 percent of police and detective occupations (the most lucrative of the service occupations). Moreover, of those service workers earning $750 or more per week ($39,000 a year), only 21.8 percent were women (Bureau of Labor Statistics, 2003e). The situation is even more bleak for Latina and African American women. For example, even though they constitute 9.2 percent of all service workers, Latina women comprise only 1.9 percent of those in the protective services and only 2.3 percent of those earning $750 or more per week. Similarly, even though African American women constitute 12.4 of all service workers, they are only 4.9 percent of all those in the protective services, and only 4.0 percent of those earning $750 or more per week.

Table 5.2
PERCENTAGE OF EMPLOYED WOMEN IN SALES AND SERVICE (OTHER THAN PRIVATE HOUSEHOLD) WORK BY RACIAL AND ETHNIC ORIGINS, 1900–2003

	White		Afr. American		Asian						Latina				Nat. American	
					Chinese		Japanese		Filipina		Chicana		Puerto Rican			
	Sales	Service	Sales	Service	Sales	Service	Sales	Service	Sales	Service	Sales	Service	Sales	Service	Sales	Service
1900	4.1	3.8	0.1	7.9	1.0	8.7	0.2	3.8	n/a	n/a	n/a	n/a	n/a	n/a	0.2	12.1
1930	9.3	8.1	0.6	7.5	12.0	8.8	7.6	10.1	2.3	4.1	3.8	7.7	n/a	n/a	2.9	1.7
1960	9.2	13.2	1.6	23.0	8.3	9.2	6.7	12.9	5.7	16.7	16.5	8.1	2.8	7.3	25.8	3.6
1970	8.0	31.3	2.6	25.5	4.7	13.0	6.8	17.5	3.5	17.1	20.6	5.7	3.9	13.5	25.9	4.3
1980	12.1	15.3	6.1	24.2	9.7	13.0	11.3	15.8	6.6	15.8	20.4	9.5	8.0	14.4	23.9	8.0
1990	13.0	14.5	9.2	22.9	11.1	13.0	11.4	13.1	13.1	11.4	21.1	11.5	10.8	16.7	22.4	11.3
2003	12.1	18.9	11.1	26.4	10.3 (sales)*		20.9 (service)*				11.9 (sales)**		31.0 (service)**		n/a	n/a

*Combined: all Asians (Chinese, Japanese, Filipina, Other).
**Combined: all Latinas (Chicana, Puerto Rican, Other).
Sources: Amott and Matthaei (1996); Bureau of Labor Statistics (1980, 2003g).

Table 5.3
SERVICE OCCUPATIONS BY SEX AND PERCENTAGE EARNING $750 OR MORE PER WEEK FOR WHITE, AFRICAN AMERICAN, AND LATINO FULL-TIME WORKERS, 2001

	All					White					African American					Latino				
	N	% Men	% Men ≥$750	% Women	% Wom ≥$750	N	% Men	% Men ≥$750	% Women	% Wom ≥$750	N	% Men	% Men ≥$750	% Women	% Wom ≥$750	N	% Men	% Men ≥$750	% Women	% Wom ≥$750
Private household	354,000	4.2	13.3	95.8	1.2	279,000	4.4	16.7	95.7	3.7	47,000	6.4	0.0	93.6	0.0	154,000	3.9	16.7	96.1	0.0
Protective	2,166,000	82.3	63.8	17.7	37.6	1,660,000	84.3	68.0	15.7	40.5	437,000	75.5	46.1	28.3	16.5	218,000	80.7	57.4	42.9	19.0
Food	3,285,000	50.2	7.2	49.8	2.7	2,500,000	49.3	7.2	50.7	2.8	538,000	51.9	11.1	48.1	4.6	831,000	65.8	3.5	34.2	0.4
Health	1,867,000	12.2	11.9	87.8	7.1	1,149,000	12.4	9.8	87.6	7.9	619,000	12.0	10.8	88.0	5.0	217,000	13.8	10.0	86.2	8.6
Cleaning and building service	2,228,000	61.9	10.9	38.1	1.7	1,593,000	62.1	12.9	37.9	1.8	511,000	53.6	5.8	46.4	1.3	591,000	56.7	6.3	43.3	2.0
Personal	1,242,000	25.4	21.7	74.6	10.6	860,000	24.7	24.5	75.3	11.9	260,000	25.4	15.2	74.6	6.2	150,000	26.0	20.5	74.0	3.6
All Service Occupations	11,142,000	47.8	28.2	52.2	7.2	8,041,000	49.6	31.1	50.4	7.7	2,412,000	42.5	19.8	57.5	5.6	2,161,000	52.4	13.5	47.6	4.3

Source: Bureau of Labor Statistics (2003d).

As detailed in Table 5.3 and Figure 5.1, women workers in virtually all of the major service occupations are significantly less likely than their male counterparts to be "high-income" earners (≥$750 per week). Overall, men are four times more likely than women to earn a "high income" in the service occupations (28.2 percent versus 7.2 percent). Most dramatically, white men (31.1 percent of whom are high-income earners) are between five-and-one-half and seven times more likely to be high-income earners than their compeer service workers who are African American (5.6 percent) or Latina (4.3 percent) women.

In sales, too, women are far less likely to hold the most lucrative jobs. In 2001, women constituted 48.0 percent of all sales workers (Bureau of Labor Statistics, 2003g), yet looking at full-time workers, they were only 25.7 percent of all those earned $750 or more per week (and only 21.0 percent of all those earned $1,500 or more per week; see Bureau of Labor Statistics, 2003e). This is because women in sales occupations are segregated into the less lucrative fields of retail and personal services (comprising 56.7 percent of all such workers), while men are more likely to be found as sales representatives in the more lucrative fields of finance and business services (constituting 56.1 percent of all such workers, and 67.5 percent of those selling securities and financial services; Bureau of Labor Statistics, 2003d, 2003e).

Minority women fare even less well. For example, even though Latina women constitute 4.4 percent of all full-time sales workers, they comprise only 2.8 percent of the sales reps in finance and business services; and only 1.0 percent of those earning $750 or more per week. Though they fare somewhat better, African American women still fall short; for example, they constitute 5.7 percent of all full-time sales workers, yet are only 4.9 percent of the sales representatives in finance, commodities, and business services; and are only 1.7 per-

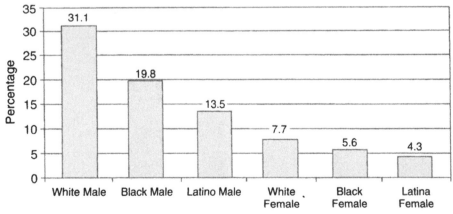

Figure 5.1. Percentage of Full-Time Workers Earning $750 or More per Week in a Service Occupation for White, African American, and Latino Men and Women, 2001. *Source:* Bureau of Labor Statistics (2003d).

In recent years, African American women have greatly narrowed the once wide gap between themselves and white women in being hired as sales workers.

cent of those earning $750 or more per week. Figure 5.2 summarizes the glaring differences between white men, on the one hand, and white and minority women on the other, in their probability of being high-income earners: white men (80.1 percent of whom are high-income earners) are nearly five times more likely to be high-income earners than their compeer sales workers who are African American women (17.0 percent) and six-and-a-half times more likely than their compeers who are Latina women (12.4 percent).

The wage gap between men and women in sales and service occupations can also be expressed in the differences between their median weekly earnings. Women working full time in sales make, on the average, $429 a week, compared with $692 for men. The ratio of women's to men's earnings in 2001 in sales occupations was thus 62.0 percent. The gap was even more extreme for minority women: African American women make only 48.3 percent and Latina women only 45.1 percent of what their white men counterparts do (while white women made 62.8 percent of white men's median weekly earnings).

The gender gap in wages in service occupations is a bit narrower, with the 2001 median weekly earnings for full-time workers being $438 for men and $335 for women, thus yielding a ratio of women's to men's earnings of 76.5 percent. But again, the situation was bleaker for women of color: African American women made only 71.5 percent and Latina women only 65.6 percent of

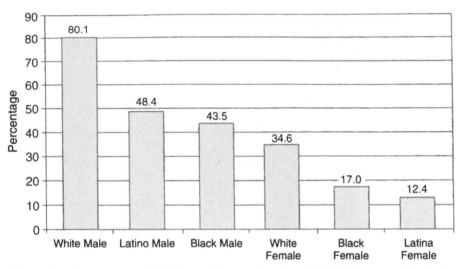

Figure 5.2. Percentage of Full-Time Workers Earning $750 or More per Week in a Sales Occupation for White, African American, and Latino Men and Women, 2001. *Source:* Bureau of Labor Statistics (2003d).

what their white male counterparts did (while white women made 73.7 percent of men's earnings).

The service sector is divided not only in terms of pay and skill level, but also by full-time or part-time work. Employers seek part-time workers because they rarely receive benefits and are generally the lowest on the pay scale. Women, youths, and minorities fill a disproportionate number of these part-time or contingent spaces. While the service sector overall is highly feminized, women and minorities remain overrepresented at the bottom levels. "From 1950 to 1990, 60 percent of all new service sector employment and 74 percent of all new low-skill jobs were filled by women" (Macdonald and Sirianni, 1996, p. 14). Black women, in particular, hold a disproportionate share of the least desirable jobs. While white women historically saw service work as a step up from the drudgery of factory employment, service employment for black women was not a move up, but, as Woody (1989, p. 54) notes, a "move over" from domestic service to another low-skill, low-wage occupation. Discrimination and unfair hiring practices continue to keep black women and other women of color in the lower-paying, low-prestige service jobs.

In the next sections, we will briefly examine the occupational experience of women in waitressing and retail sales, two of the most female dominated of the service and sales occupations.

Women in Waitressing

Although now almost half of food service workers are women (49.8 percent, see Table 5.3), until the 1920s commercial food establishments employed mostly

More than seven in ten table servers are women.

men (Cobble, 1991). Most food servers after the Civil War were black men. With the subsequent hotel boom, women were given a chance to fill men's waitering jobs when they served as strikebreakers. Employers soon determined that women were actually preferable to men as employees, as they were less expensive and more "obedient" (Cobble, 1991).

In the following decades, "eating out" was increasingly indulged in not only by the rich but by all classes, creating a demand for more waiters and waitresses and furthering the feminization of this occupation. Currently, women comprise 71.0 percent of the more than half-million table servers in the United States (see Bureau of Labor Statistics, 2003e).

Even so, proportionately more men appear as waiters in high-priced, fancier dining establishments and proportionately more women are waitresses in the lower-status coffee shops and family-style restaurants. Even within the same establishment, men often have the more lucrative posts—waiting during dinner and attending to liquor service (Cobble, 1991, pp. 27–28). Restaurants are much less likely to promote females to the better-paying kitchen or management positions, which are often reserved for male waiters (Berheide, 1988, p. 252).

Chances for upward mobility for waitresses are limited, since the educational level for waitressing is minimal and these women receive limited training from their employer. As Seidman (1978, p. 96) observes: "Waitresses and waiters can usually improve their status only by making new contacts and moving into openings at higher-priced restaurants where tips are greater." Traditional gender-role expectations tend to be built into such service jobs:

> Waitresses . . . are often expected to be young and sexy, to dress in provocative clothing, and to treat even the most obnoxious customer with grace and charm. Sometimes sexist expectations for women service workers are very explicit, as in the requirements of some airlines, under challenge in court, that flight attendants not exceed certain weight standards . . . these expectations often shape women's opportunities in service occupations. (Andersen, 1997, p. 122)

And, like secretarial work, waitressing also demands a great deal of "emotional labor":

> By furnishing the waitress with the script, costume, and backdrop of a servant, the restaurant encourages her to become absorbed in her role or . . . to engage in deep acting. In so doing, the company may hope to enhance the authenticity of the performance and reduce the possibility that their server will break character and express emotions incongruous with the role she is expected to play. (Paules, 1996, p. 283)

Sexual harassment is an occupational hazard. Male bosses encourage their female staff to use their sexuality to attract customers and, sometimes, bosses pressure these women for sexual favors:

> After all, the boss, accustomed to looking upon his employees with the same attitude that he regards a coffee urn, does not see why he cannot use the waitress's body for other purposes than waiting on the table, one server explained. After many suggestive approaches, such as walking into the dressing room when she is donning her uniform, attempting caresses and so on, he states the issue bluntly, be "nice or else." Refusal of such "offers" was a "common reason that girls are unjustly discharged for" and "is well known to any female food worker who has been in the business any length of time," she insisted. (Cobble, 1991, p. 44)

Customers, too, make unwanted sexual advances. Waitresses have filed a substantial number of complaints regarding "pats and grabs," sexual comments, and leers. In the servant role of waitress, a woman is in a subordinate economic power position vis-à-vis the customer. It may be difficult for those waitresses who are propositioned by customers to lodge a complaint because they fear they may lose a much needed tip or even be fired from their job.

Waitresses are depersonalized not only by such sexist expectations and advances, but also because their customers frequently refuse to view them as genuine, worthy human beings. As one waitress expressed it,

> They look at me like, "Oh my God. They have parents?" It's sometimes like we're not human. It's like they become more friendly when my parents are there and I get better tips off of them. And I've never gotten stiffed when my parents have been sitting there. They see that outside of this place I am a person and I have relationships with other people. (quoted in Paules, 1991, p. 133)

Too often, degradation is part of the food service experience. Women are treated as if they are *merely* servants. Moreover, women of color are in "double jeopardy" because of both sexist and racist attitudes (Andersen, 1997). Occasionally, a waitress refuses to accept this depersonalization and strikes back at a customer who treats her as a mere servant:

> He jumps up, he pushed me out of the way, and he goes, "You just blew your tip!. . . . I'm going to have your *job*! That's what I'm going to have." And I turned around and looked at him. I said, "Excuse me? . . . *You're* going to have my job? . . . *You* don't even have a job, and you're going to have *my* job?" . . . Because I don't take that, I told him, I said, "If you think I'm some stupid bimbo, don't know how to do nothing but wait tables, you're a *fool*. So don't even talk to me like that." . . . I have to tell people off . . . if they got a problem. (quoted in Paules, 1996, pp. 280–281)

One waitress even suggested that those who "serve the evening trade should be issued a 38-caliber automatic as part of their uniforms," in order to take care of the "few boneheads who can't keep their hands to themselves" (Cobble, 1991, p. 45).

Waitresses have employed other, less drastic, measures to gain some "control" over their occupational situation. Coping strategies observed among waitresses in a small family-style restaurant in New Jersey included imagining oneself as a "soldier" confronting enemy forces, or acting as an independent businessperson (Paules, 1991, 1996). The waitress-as-soldier views her work area as a battleground, with the customer as "the enemy." Paules notes: "the waitress's capacity to sustain this self-image while donning the costume of a maid and complying with the interpersonal conventions of servitude, attests to her strength of will and power of resistance" (1996, p. 272). The waitress as "private entrepreneur" focuses on tips, from which she typically gets the majority of her income. It is only through her hard work and friendly manner, she realizes, that she will receive decent pay (the majority from tipping). She then reasons that her responsibility to the establishment is limited to her territory (waiting on her tables). The small salary she receives is considered her retainer. With her primary objective—gaining the tip—firmly in mind, she is often willing to put on an ingratiating performance.

Women in Retail Sales

Women were involved in retail trade even in the early colonial economy. They worked in small family-owned shops, especially those that sold "feminine" products such as millinery. Our current retail culture has its roots in the mid- to late 1800s, with the development and spread of the department store, the chain store, and the mail-order company. In 1865, there were twenty-five chain stores; by 1880 there were a hundred (Stigler, 1956). Department stores evolved to provide customers with convenient service, although they did not offer the same low prices that were available at the chain stores. With a growing communications infrastructure, the mail-order catalog business was begun in 1872 by Aaron Montgomery Ward (Stigler, 1956).

Other service industries focused on providing routine personal services. These non-product-based services grew as the domestic service field dwindled. In the early 1900s, services such as hairdressing and manicuring that were once performed exclusively in the home became available in the public sphere for a certain price. As the demand for these services grew, so too did the numbers of people employed in the service labor force (Stigler, 1956). As the service sector grew, "almost from the beginning [it] sought the relatively cheap and supposedly docile labor of women" (Benson, 1986, p. 178).

While the retail sales occupations were low wage, they did provide viable work for white women who wished to escape domestic service. Retail work was assumed to require certain qualifications and skills that domestic work did not. Women were reminded constantly that they were in a dignified position and that they would "work but they would not serve" (Benson, 1986, p. 231). Retail work also promised advancement in terms of pay. With a growing number of women entering retail trade, women soon made up the highest percentage of retail workers. By 1940, women in department stores made up one-half to nine-tenths of the employees (Benson, 1986, p. 192). Women of color, though, were largely excluded from retail sales. While immigrants from the British Isles, Scandinavia, and Germany were able to find jobs in retail work, women of African descent or other women with dark skin were drastically underrepresented. Department stores sought to embody the characteristics of their clien-

Department store, 1920s.

tele in their salespeople. This made employers particularly wary of hiring black women: "Virtually no department store . . . would knowingly hire a Black woman as a saleswoman, although they were sometimes employed as . . . elevator operators and behind the scenes personnel" (Benson, 1986, p. 209).

Women in retail sales tended to be placed in the lower-paying departments, whereas men were channeled into the high-priced departments where their commissions were guaranteed to be higher than their female counterparts:

> Men were generally confined to men's clothing, sporting goods, rug, and appliance departments, while women sold most other items; among the few departments in which men and women sold together were silks, shoes, and men's furnishings. . . . The departments staffed by men, particularly the "big ticket" ones, paid higher base rates and often added a hefty commission. Saleswomen's earnings ranged from 42 to 63 percent of salesmen's. (Benson, 1986, p. 180)

Although women in retail work were encouraged to think of their occupation as dignified, skilled work, the reality of the work did not often merit these sentiments. Many customers saw saleswomen as no better than servants. Customers felt they had the prerogative to treat saleswomen as they wished, often in a degrading manner. As one saleswomen complained, "They treat us like the dirt under their feet, and seem to think that we never had anything and never will have anything, and that they can do as they please with us" (Benson, 1986, p. 258). In general, women who work in the service industries are encouraged to treat the customer as their boss and to practice the age-old credo "the customer is always right." Nevertheless, they have long practiced some forms of resistance to the demands of their customers, like these used by saleswomen in the 1920s and 1930s:

> Some saleswomen simply decided that the customer was an out-and-out enemy and treated her as such. They gloated after closing a sale, as if delighting that they had put something over on the unsuspecting purchaser. Feeling themselves victimized by their employers, they themselves delighted in victimizing customers. They loudly commented on customers' manners, dress, and taste, often within earshot of other customers as if to warn them not to commit similar blunders. A particularly disagreeable customer would be left to stew in a fitting room until her saleswoman deigned to rescue her. (Benson, 1986)

The sex segregation of sales work often promoted a sense of solidarity among saleswomen that enabled them to subvert the authority and demands of the usually all-male management, especially unwanted sexual harassment. Analyzing conditions for saleswomen in American department stores from 1890 to1940, Benson (1986, p. 266) observes:

> Because maleness coincided with higher levels of authority in the department store, women simultaneously protected their turf as workers and their turf as women. At Filene's, saleswomen used the *Echo's* [an employee-produced newsletter] gossip columns to warn male employees to desist from behavior that we would today call sexual harassment and to chide men who used language insulting to women. An offender received this message from the women

of the Basement Balcony: "Mr. Smith, our deal floor-man, seems quite interested in some of our girls. We wish he wouldn't do us any favors."

While such informal modes of resistance have not been uncommon, more formal strategies, such as organizing a union, have been infrequent. Some women
in retail sales engaged in union activity in the mid-1930s, but such activity among
saleswomen has traditionally been low—in part because of the high turnover.
In addition, the splitting of the store into departments has often cut down on
the ability of saleswomen to gain storewide support to build a union. These factors, coupled with management efforts to thwart union organizing through spy
networks and firing of union sympathizers, have hindered the ability of women
in retail sales to organize (Benson, 1986, pp. 269–270).

Women in retail sales face some difficult occupational issues in the years
ahead. Problems include the growing de-skilling of retail sales work and an increased movement toward the hiring of part-time help, as well as a growing sur-
veillance of the retail sales force through the use of computers and other technological devices.

> [B]efore World War II, salesclerks were trained and acknowledged as persons
> skilled in selling and merchandising. They were not well paid, but management
> recognized their importance and value, providing benefits and working condi-
> tions designed to reward them. After the war, labor costs were substantially re-
> duced through such tactics as recruiting high school and college students as
> well as housewives so as to increase the number of part-time workers (who typ-
> ically receive no benefits) and shifting the concept of selling from service to
> self-service. Centralizing the merchandising and buying has removed these du-
> ties from the clerk on the sales floor. Fewer and fewer clerks are found on sales
> floors, and the ones who are there typically know little about their merchan-
> dise. Sales clerks have gone from being knowledgeable through buying and dis-
> playing of their merchandise to being stock-handlers and cashiers. (Kemp, 1994,
> pp. 231–232)

With competition from large discount stores, American retailers are on the de-
fensive to cut costs and increase productivity. The coming of the computer to
retailing, with its "point-of sale terminals," has enabled management to get more
control over the work of retail sales personnel. Through the use of computer
monitoring, management can control staffing needs and, when possible, shift
sales personnel to where there is high volume on the floor, minimizing an employee's idle moments (Benson, 1986, p. 293).

At the large discount retailing companies such as Wal-Mart, Target, and
Kmart, employees are trained for a minimum number of hours to occupy dead-
end, low-paying positions—positions for which there are an abundance of individuals to fill. In her participant observation study of Wal-Mart, Ehrenreich
(2001, p. 184) describes this phenomenon that has become so common to the
world of discount retail:

> They talk about having spirit . . . , but they don't give us any reason to have
> any spirit. . . . Wal-Mart would rather just keep hiring new people than treat
> the ones it has decently. You can see for yourself: there's a dozen new people

coming in for orientation every day—which is true. Wal-Mart's appetite for human flesh is insatiable; we've even been urged to recruit any Kmart employees we may happen to know. They don't care that they've trained you or anything . . . they can always get someone else if you complain.

Sales and Service Outlook

Service and sales occupations comprise together almost a third of the jobs women hold in the American economy. Currently, 48.0 percent of all sales workers are women, as are 56.8 percent of all those in service occupations (Bureau of Labor Statistics, 2003g). Yet gender and racial segregation, as well as wage inequality, continue in this sector, with women occupying the lower-status and lower-paying jobs. Turnover rates and unemployment are high among these workers, which also contribute to their depressed wages. There is little opportunity for women to advance within these occupations, and they are given little or no on-the-job training. The conditions of employment often cast women into the role of "servant." They are expected to expend "emotional labor" on the job, acting as "nurturers"—an extension of their caretaker role within the household. Sexual harassment and degradation are occupational hazards.

A number of strategies have been suggested to improve women's situation within these occupations. While sales and service work is often low wage and low status, it is not necessarily unskilled. A move toward comparable worth (Jacobs, Steinberg, and Filer, 1990)—that is, equal pay for work of comparable skill level—would go a long way toward re-evaluating the worth of women's work in this sector. Such a system would require employers to design evaluation systems to take into account the extent to which men's and women's jobs, while different, are similar in terms of skill level. Comparable worth, although not useful to women who are in highly unskilled work, would at least begin to narrow the earnings gap between men and women in more skilled sales and service occupations, because it is believed that between 5 and 30 percent of the wage gap between men and women is the result of comparable-worth inequities (Reskin and Padavic, 1994, p. 119).

Management must also provide women in unskilled sales and service jobs with more on-the-job training to upgrade their skills and must remove discriminatory barriers to upward mobility in the more lucrative male-dominated lines of work. There is also a renewed interest in union organizing among women within the service and sales sector, which holds the promise of reversing some of the poor working conditions in these occupations (Benson, 1986). Unions, however, must be more responsive to the needs of these women. It has been suggested that part of the reason women have been reluctant to join unions is the failure of unions to take into account "women's culture":

I argue that women's absence or limited place results in large part for the exclusion of "women's culture" from the unions.

By "women's culture" in the work place I mean the ways of getting things done that women value, their sense of honor, the obligations they acknowledge to coworkers and the connections they make between their work and their womanhood. I argue that unions have to be transformed to include and support "women's culture" in the work place if they are to be revitalized as institutions that truly represent the working people of the United States. (Feldberg, 1987, p. 300)

Unions must recognize the diversity of experiences of women workers by race and ethnicity as well as social class. They need to include women in their leadership structures and provide opportunities for leadership training. They must also reckon with the particular issues diverse women face in combining work and family lives. In addition, unions will need to deal with the movement in sales and service occupations toward the mass hiring of part-time, part-year, and temporary employees—which has been fueled by management's need to have "flexibility" in their workforce and to contain costs—and a lack of commitment to employees.

Domestic Service

Domestic service has undergone a transition almost as drastic as that in the clerical occupations. While clerical work went from male- to female-dominated, the composition of domestic service workers has changed not in gender, but in race. Domestic service workers have always been predominantly female because of the association of women with work in the private sphere of the home. For decades, domestic servants were primarily African American women, doing the kind of work that was not too different from what many had done while slaves. As these women and eventually also masses of new immigrants "entered domestic service in the North, class and racial tensions heightened and native-born women began to avoid the occupation at all costs" (Romero, 1992, p. 77). In 1940, 60 percent of working black women were in domestic service, along with 11 percent of working white women. But by 2001, only 0.7 percent of the 6.6 million wage-earning African American women and 0.8 percent of their 34.9 million white counterparts were employed as full-time domestic service workers (Bureau of Labor Statistics, 2003d; King, 1993). Although the official percentage is still small for Latinas (3.2 percent of the 4.6 million Latinas working full time are domestics), they are significantly more likely to do this kind of work. To make sense of these changing percentages, we must consider that Latina immigrants looking for work have created a new labor pool in the United States. While African American women have a long legacy of serving as domestic service workers, with the growth of the clerical occupation (as noted before), many were able to make a step up on the occupational hierarchy and out of domestic service. On the other hand, any traveler to a major U.S. city cannot help but be struck by the large percentage of hotel maids who are first-generation Latinas. The relative importance of this work for Latina women is undoubtedly understated, as many such immigrants employed as domestics do not show up in official labor-force statistics (Romero, 1992).

The domestic service workforce has remained a sphere in which minority women are overrepresented—indeed, the only category of domestic worker in which white women appear in numbers proportionate to their presence in the overall labor force is as "childcare worker." In the past three decades, the employment of immigrant women in the domestic sector has increased well beyond private households. Today immigrant women dominate the domestic labor force in hotels, office buildings, and hospitals. Seventy-five to ninety percent of the office cleaning crews in many large cities in the United States are Hispanic and Asian Pacific Islander women (Freedman, 2002, p. 138). Because of this "lock" that domestic service has on so many minority women, it has been described as an "occupational ghetto": "For some white women, domestic service was simply a stage of life or a bridge to better opportunities. For black and Asian women, for Mexican and immigrant women who were neither Anglo-Saxon nor English-speaking, domestic service was a trap—a situation of being dominated from which they could not rise and which they had to pass onto their daughters" (Romero, 1992, p. 75).

While the overall history of domestic service is well documented, the actual numbers of domestic service workers are difficult to ascertain. They often work under informal labor arrangements and are therefore underreported and undercounted, forming part of an underground economy (Romero, 1992). Either because they are not legal immigrants or because their employers do not want to pay taxes, domestic service workers are often employed without having the proper papers. Another reason why these women are not fully visible is a function of the private sphere they work within, "those private worlds of family and personal relationships where women predominate" as opposed to the public world, "which is dominated by men" (Daniels, 1987, p. 403).

Women have always provided the labor necessary for men to focus their attention away from the home. Dorothy Smith (1978, p. 289) argues that women have traditionally been relegated to a role of subservience in a patriarchal "bifurcation of consciousness," which anchors men in the "abstract mode of action" and women in the "concrete and particular." For men to function in the "abstract," they must not be concerned with the everyday activities of the household, which have been relegated to women. Women's work, therefore, has facilitated and reinforced the patriarchal structure of our society, serving to reproduce women's own subordination. There is a parallel between this bifurcation of consciousness and Marx's concept of alienation: "The simplest formulation of alienation posits a relation between the work an individual does and an external order which oppresses her, such that the harder she works the more she strengthens the order which oppresses her" (Smith, 1978, p. 290).

Domestic servants have served to aid wives in their household duties, further enabling men to concern themselves with the outside, public world. It would, of course, be wrong to place wives and the domestic servants on the same level in their household service, however. White women with domestic servants often demean them. They request work of the women of color that they themselves would not do. Housekeeper Anne Ryder describes her defiant reaction to one such request:

> The [employers] would tell me to get on my knees and scrub the floor and I didn't do it. I didn't mess up my knees. I told one lady, "My knees aren't for scrubbing. My knees are made to bend and walk on." I didn't have a lot of bumps and no black knees from scrubbing floors. I took care of myself. (as quoted in Romero, 1992, p. 104)

As another domestic, Maggie Holmes, said, "They [white women employers] don't get on their knees, but they don't think nothin' about askin' a black woman" (as quoted in Romero, 1992, p. 104). White women employers often take advantage of their domestic service workers, sometimes degrading them to their face:

> Some of them were really hateful. They thought, you know, you're just anybody there to clean their house, and they really would take advantage of you. And I didn't enjoy it. . . . I don't know if it was just 'cause they thought, you know, that you were Spanish and stuff; they would just sort of take advantage of me, and I didn't like it. (as quoted in Romero, 1992, p. 114)
>
> She [employer] would make me feel like I was nothing or like I was doing this [domestic service] because I was so poor or because I was Mexican. One day she said that Mexican people are all very poor. They weren't educated. And that did it! I dropped what I was doing. I left it there and I said, "here take this and shove it. I don't have to take this abuse from you or from anybody. I'm Mexican, yes, but I'm proud of what I am and I'm working." (Mrs. Duran, as quoted in Romero, 1992, p. 114)

It is important to note that a domestic laborer's citizenship status can greatly affect both her wage and working conditions. Not having legal citizenship coupled with little knowledge of the English language makes immigrants more vulnerable to manipulation and mistreatment:

> "They dictated to me everything that I should do," Rosalie Vista complained of her job caring for a family of eleven. "I could not stand the way they treated me. . . . They just shouted and insulted me." (as quoted in Freedman, 2002, p. 139)

With white women ordering their domestic servants around, acting as their "informal" bosses, a dual system of oppression was created within the household: the white woman herself being oppressed by her own ties to domestic labor and in turn subjugating her servant.

Nowadays domestic servants are hired not only to help women (especially middle- and upper-middle-class women) with their household duties, but in effect to replace them. Domestic service work has become a necessity for many in the movement of white women out of the home and into the public sphere of the economy: "The cheap domestic labor of women of color is one means by which white middle-class women escape oppressive aspects of their domestic roles" (Romero, 1992, p. 29). Too often, white career women exploit their service workers by requiring them to work long hours for little pay, with no benefits, no social security, and no official acknowledgment. Middle- and upper-class working women are therefore able to find "affordable" daycare by exploiting the labor of immigrant women, many of whom are undocumented workers.

Sociologist Arlie Hochschild (2000) talks about the presence of a "Nanny Chain" to describe a "global chain of caring" in which mothering has become a commodity that is bought and sold on the global marketplace. Very often third world women find that their own ability to mother has been "displaced" from caring for their own children to caring for a child living in relative wealth and security. Hochschild notes that while Karl Marx remarked on the importance of the "capitalist" (the owner of the means of production) extracting profit from the worker in the form of "surplus value" from their workers, the domestic worker, by giving her love and care to another's child, provides another form of "surplus value"—that of maternal love to first world countries. Hochschild (2000, p. 1) describes a typical chain as follows:

> An older daughter from a poor family in a third world country cares for her siblings (the first link in the chain) while her mother works as a nanny caring for the children of a nanny migrating to a first world country (the second link) who, in turn, cares for the child of a family in a rich country (the final link).

Domestic service workers are an almost completely "invisible" labor force. They are often not documented in census literature or IRS records. They are also often rendered "invisible" because the work they perform is often not recognized, along with most female house duties, as legitimate work. Thus, organization or unionization of domestic service workers has been nearly impossible. However, in comparison with clerical work and blue-collar occupations, domestic service workers have a higher degree of autonomy. This gives them more opportunity for individual action to improve working conditions and duties. Often they are able to talk directly to their bosses to correct what is amiss:

> I told a young lady something about leaving her underclothes thrown around, and she asked me what was I there for? I went straight in, called her mother and told her the situation. Her mother came home from work and let the young lady have it. She (the mother) was thoroughly upset. I was not there to be her (the daughter's) personal maid and she was told that in no uncertain terms. (Romero, 1992, p. 365)

While domestic service work does involve considerable oppression, there are some advantages. One is the flexibility in a domestic's work schedule. These women often are able to schedule their hours around their home schedules. As Mrs. Garcia, a domestic worker, explains, "You can change the dates if you can't go a certain day and if you have an appointment, you can go later, and work later, just as long as you get the work done. . . . I try to be there at the same time, but if I don't get there for some reason or another; I don't have to think I am going to lose my job or something" (as quoted in Romero, 1992, p. 148). Domestic service work also typically provides enough income for these women to help their families avoid poverty, while allowing them to continue their rather traditional roles within those families.

Women in the Military

Military campaigns like the war with Iraq in the spring of 2003 have brought the issue of women's direct involvement in the military, especially the issue of women engaging in combat, to the forefront of American consciousness. The enormous publicity generated by the capture and subsequent rescue of Private First Class Jessica Lynch allowed many Americans to observe that women are, in fact, engaged in combat on the front lines. The overwhelming majority of these women—like their male counterparts—have poor or blue-collar/working-class roots; they join the all-volunteer military to gain "a free education or a marketable skill" (Halbfinger and Holmes, 2003, p. A1).

Women are currently permitted to fly in combat missions, yet they are not allowed to serve in direct combat battalions. However, since 1994 the U.S. military has endorsed "gender-diverse" support systems—like PFC Lynch's 507th Maintenance Company that was attacked in Iraq (Sailer, 2003). A 2001 Gallup Poll found that there is large-scale public support for allowing women to engage in combat, with 70 percent of the public agreeing that women should be allowed to fly combat aircraft and work on submarines; 63 percent favoring women's participation in special forces, and 52 percent in favor of women being a part of ground troops (Sailer, 2003). Prior to the 1900s, women were active in the military primarily in gender-specific roles such as nurses, cooks, and clerical support staff (Enloe, 1983). While they were not granted official military status, Congress did establish an Army Nurses Corps in 1901 and the Navy Nurses Corps in 1908. However, "these nurses were given an officer's title and uniform but not full military status in terms of equal pay, benefits, or a commission" (Hancock, 1991, p. 209).

It is important to note that, even though women have been restricted to noncombat roles within the military, they have always been exposed to combat experiences as nurses on the front lines—caring for the wounded, some even dying in this role (Hancock, 1991, p. 211). Moreover, some women so strongly desired to serve in combat that they disguised themselves as men in order to do so (Binkin and Bach, 1977, p. 5). The term "passing women" came to be given to women who passed successfully as males. As historian Julie Matthaei (1982, pp. 192–193) observes:

> Numbers of them fought in the Civil War. Indeed, we know of some of them only because their illness or death brought a medical examination during which their physical sex was inadvertently discovered. The shock of such a revelation was often great enough as to bring newspaper headlines, from which historians have gathered most of these accounts.

During World Wars I and II, personnel shortages caused the military to establish women's auxiliaries such as the Navy WAVES (Women Accepted for Volunteer Emergency Service) and the WAACs (Women's Auxiliary Army Corps). While these organizations were only meant to be temporary emergency

Although women are not allowed to serve in direct combat battalions in the U.S. military, the majority of Americans agree they should be allowed to do so. Pictured here is PFC Jessica Lynch, who was seriously wounded in ground combat and taken prisoner in the U.S.-led war with Iraq in March of 2003.

measures, they were "a turning point in the history of women's participation in the military" (Binkin and Bach, 1977, p. 77). They demonstrated to the military and to the wider society that women were capable of doing outstanding jobs in a variety of male-dominated occupations—despite the fact that women's entrance into the military was met with opposition in many circles. Titunik (2000, p. 241) offers an example of how this opposition crumbled in the thinking of many individuals with the following reflection by Dwight Eisenhower during World War II:

> Until my experience in London. . . . I had been opposed to the use of women in uniform. But in Great Britain I had seen them perform so magnificently in various positions including service in active anti-aircraft batteries, that I had been converted.

During World War II approximately 350,000 women participated in auxiliary services doing traditional jobs such as clerical and health care work, while others were gaining new skills and self-confidence from their work in nontraditional jobs like that of "airplane mechanic, parachute riggers, gunnery instructors, air traffic controllers, naval air navigators" (Binkin and Bach, 1977, p. 7). Of special interest were the women who piloted aircraft to and from enemy territory to deliver new planes. They also had the dangerous job of test-piloting new model aircraft. This group of eight hundred women was part of a special service known as the Women's Air Force Service Pilots (WASPs) (Dean,

1997, p. 8). However, groups like the WASPs were never granted any official military standing during the war. The WASPs were never militarized and were decommissioned in December 1944 (Dean, 1997, p. 8). It took many years of lobbying efforts well into the 1970s before the WASPs were finally granted military standing and given military benefits (Binkin and Bach, 1977, p. 5; Dean, 1997, p. 9).

A woman who joined the military—especially in a nontraditional capacity—found herself the target of sexual innuendo. Women serving in World War II went against tradition. Their male peers often felt threatened by their presence, especially with women in positions of authority. An especially vicious set of rumors grew up around the WAACs. These women had to contend with rumors concerning their loose morals and promiscuous life style. As it turned out, the rumors were started by the Army itself (Titunik, 2000, p. 242):

> Large numbers of WAACs were rumored to have become pregnant and returned home on that account, and one source claimed that the War Department intended to furnish WAACs with "[c]ontraceptives and prophylactic equipment." . . . But an Army Intelligence investigation, assisted by the FBI, concluded that the "rumors originated with 'Army Personnel.'"

Helen Clifford Gunter was a Navy WAVE. She was commissioned as a lieutenant "junior grade" officer. She held a PhD and was assigned to make training films for the Navy. She notes her experience upon arrival at her base:

> I found the same dissatisfaction and frustration at PSL that had existed when I left for Florida. As I look back, I feel this was due to the fact that the OIC [officer in charge] was an unpredictable alcoholic whose behavior and violent temper explosions kept lower echelons of personnel in constant apprehension. (Dean, 1997, p. 10)

Lieutenant Gunter further noted how she was often not given credit for her accomplishments, while those males above her often took the credit for the films she made (Dean, 1997, p. 10). As a military officer, her femininity and sexuality were also subjected to negative comments from her male peers as well as from women outside the military:

> Some of the macho males suggested that all Waves [sic] volunteered to snag husbands. On a train home on leave I remember a woman who said most of the WACs, WAVES, SPARS and LADY MARINES were "camp followers" with a knowing look that implied that they were prostitutes. (Dean, 1997, p. 11)

Women's participation in the military during World War II began the long climb for women's recognition and eventual integration into the military that would occur slowly over the next several decades. With the Women's Armed Services Integration Act of 1948, women were granted full military status, with a few exceptions. The first required that women only comprise 2 percent of the total military population; they hit a glass ceiling in not being allowed to occupy the position of general or admiral; and they could be dismissed if they became pregnant. Women could also not engage in combat (Beckett and Chien, 2002, p. 5; Titunik, 2000, p. 243).

The postwar years saw a rapid demobilization of women in the military. From 1945 to 1948, the number of females in the military decreased from 266,000 to just over 14,000, a mere 1 percent of all military personnel. The percentage of women in the military remained at a low 2 percent into the 1970s (Binkin and Bach, 1977, p. 10). The 1970s was a decade of change for women in the military, which also saw the restrictions of the Integration Act of 1948 gradually lifted. The emergence of the women's movement and the demands for equal treatment for all women, including in male-dominated occupations, placed some pressure on the military to re-examine its treatment of women with regard to enlistment policies and overall job advancement. At the same time, the military ended the draft and moved to an all-volunteer military; this had the effect of opening space for women in the military occupational structure, as there was a shortage of qualified male applicants (Hancock, 1991, p. 210). In the mid-1970s, women were given the opportunity for officer training at the major military academies at West Point, Annapolis, and Colorado Springs, as well as through the Reserve Officers Training Corp (ROTC) and Officer Candidate School (Hancock, 1991, p. 210).

More recently women have been making advances into many previously male-dominated military positions. During the 1990s, the Clinton administration changed policy to the point where the only positions women could not hold were those requiring front-line ground combat (Morris, 1996, p. 735). While military women remain in predominately female-dominated administrative and personnel positions, they are now expanding their reach into male-dominated occupations—including flying combat aircraft and commanding artillery (Hancock, 1991, p. 211; Titunik, 2000, p. 244).

Military Culture

To gain a sense of the conditions under which women in the military work, it is necessary to have a basic understanding of military culture. Katzenstein and Reppy (1999) identify two distinct characteristics of this culture: *masculinity* and *uniformity*. With regard to the first, military cultural norms are associated with "aggression, independence, risk-taking, and [hetero] sexual bravado"(Katzenstein and Reppy, 1999, p. 6). The second characteristic, uniformity, allows the military to predict, control, and govern its operations more efficiently. In the past, difference was dealt with through segregation—minorities and women were placed in different units. Given this historical context, "it is not surprising that the stereotype of the soldier as a heterosexual white male has shaped military culture in its own image"(Katzenstein and Reppy, 1999, p. 7). It is this traditional stereotype that has been a key factor in promoting sexual discrimination in the U.S. military. Those opposed to a fully integrated military contend that the acceptance of women and homosexuals presents a challenge to the "masculine warrior spirit critical to turning boys into effective soldiers" (Kier, 1999, p. 37). Ricks (1995) argues that such integration can act to destroy group solidarity based upon male superiority. It is for this reason that such anti-integration chants as the marines' famous "three-zero-five-six/We don't need no stinkin' chicks!" remain very popular (see Ricks, 1995, p. 37).

As a result of the persistence of such "anti-integration attitudes," it is no surprise that sexual harassment and rape have been pervasive problems in all branches of the U.S. armed forces, as well as in the elite military academies. Despite over fifteen years of efforts by the Department of Defense, sexual harassment and abuse remain at high, unacceptable rates within all branches of the military (Guenter-Schlesinger, 1999, p. 195). Yet, ironically, the military has been one of the most proactive organizations in fighting issues of discrimination of all kinds. For example, starting in 1971, the Defense Equal Opportunity Management Institute (DEOMI) provided training in race relations. Then, in the 1980s, the DEOMI initiated training to prevent of sexual harassment; this built upon programs that each branch itself had established in its leadership schools (Guenter-Schlesinger, 1999, p. 195).

Despite the Department of Defense's "zero-tolerance" attitude toward sexual harassment, a 1995 survey by the Defense Manpower Data Center showed that 78 percent of women questioned reported experiencing "behaviors that can be defined as sexual harassment" (Guenter-Schlesinger, 1999, p. 199). These behaviors include being "hit on," lewd sexual comments, and physical trauma. Here is a common example of such harassment provided by a female enlisted soldier:

> [While] on temporary duty in Belgium, the Lieutenant Colonel that I worked with and considered a friend (he was married and his wife was pregnant at the time) forced his way into my hotel room, grabbed me, and forced me onto the bed, kissing me, and groping me. I [pushed] him away and told him to leave. The next morning when we met to run, I told him that I never wanted him to do that again (I remember I was shaking like a leaf!). After that our relationship was very strained and when I left he never gave me an appraisal. He was since promoted to Colonel. (as quoted in Guenter-Schlesinger, 1999, p. 200)

This quote also points to the fact that, in addition to the emotional damage, women who experience sexual harassment and resist it can end up hurting their career advancement. It is "the necessity to escape sexual harassment [that] discourages women from remaining at one job long enough to acquire seniority and experience, to their detriment in employment" (MacKinnon, 1979, p. 210; as quoted in Guenter-Schlesinger, 1999, p. 201).

There is a form of nonsexual harassment that is also growing in the military—what Guenter-Schlesinger (1999, pp. 201–202) calls "second generation" harassment. It is a more "subtle" form. As women have begun to move up the military hierarchy, they find that there is "male culture" operating to exclude them from critical decision-making positions, thus excluding them from job opportunities and the critical information they need to compete on the job.

While the military has done much to implement training programs to prevent sexual harassment, programs alone do not appear capable of stemming the tide of sexual harassment within the military. To have an integrated military, there must be the perception on the part of everyone that rules against sexual harassment will be *enforced* and perpetrators will be prosecuted. Strong enforcement is needed to overcome the continued, strong existence of traditional military culture. Strong leadership at the top is also needed to ensure that all cases of sexual harassment are followed up and that harassers are held accountable for their actions. Women should not, and must not, feel intimidated or threatened in bringing a charge of sexual harassment before a review board (Morris, 1999, pp. 205–207).

Women in Blue-Collar Work

As we saw in Chapter 2, the employment of women in blue-collar work can be traced to the beginning of the industrial revolution, with the recruitment of young, single women into the textile industries that were springing up in New England in the 1830s and 1840s. By the beginning of the twentieth century, there were few industrial occupations in which women were not represented in at least some capacity. Yet most women were not allowed to enter the skilled trades; most were excluded from company trade-union apprenticeship programs and from the vocational training programs in some public schools. Hiring women became an economic necessity because of the numbers of jobs that opened in the industrial sector, but they were paid less than a living wage, which kept them dependent on their husbands or fathers. While the employment of women in the industries could have served to give women more independence in society, in actuality it reinforced their dependence on men and the roles prescribed to them by a patriarchal society (O'Farrell, 1992; Tentler, 1979).

Many women in the blue-collar workforce are still confined to low-skilled, low-wage occupations. The best-paying jobs in this sector—production work in heavy industry and the skilled crafts—have traditionally been dominated by men; and, despite the many gains working women have made over the past three decades, they still are. Although special-interest stories in newspapers sometimes highlight women doing traditionally male-dominated blue-collar craft work, statistically speaking women's representation in these fields is negligible; for example, 98 percent of construction workers and 95 percent of mechanics are men. Women have tended to be assigned to production (assembly-line/machine operator) jobs in light industry such as textiles, apparel manufacturing, and electronics. As societal constraints on gender work roles have lessened, women have marginally increased—by a few percentage points, from less than 1 percent in the early 1970s to the low single digits in the early 2000s—their presence in some of the better-paying fields in the blue-collar work world (e.g., carpentry, mechanical repair, metal-working). Nevertheless, as revealed in Table 5.4, women's presence in the skilled blue-collar world is miniscule; this stands in stark contrast to the progress detailed in Chapters 3 and 4 that women have made in the professions and the business world.

An example of how hard it is increase the numbers of women working in high-paying construction jobs is presented by an April 1978 Department of Labor program. It set ambitious goals to increase the number of females employed on federally financed construction projects. Hiring was set up so that over a three-year period women were to comprise up to 6.9 percent of the labor force on these projects. In addition, women's share of apprenticeship positions was to increase to between a fifth and a fourth of each group (Eisenberg, 1998, p. 3). Yet the implementation of this plan was disappointing, instead of the expected 25 percent of the federal construction workforce becoming female, women's overall presence has hovered at 2 percent.

Women employed as operatives in factories work mainly out of necessity. These jobs do not require much education, training, experience, or skill in English. Twenty-seven percent of such women lack a high school diploma, and most of the rest have only a high school education (U.S. Bureau of the Census, 2002a, Table 595, p. 384). While these jobs were once held primarily by white immigrant women, since the late 1970s more and more women of color have been so employed.

As revealed in Table 5.4, Latinas and Asians are more likely than African American women, who are in turn more likely than white women, to be working in blue-collar occupations—especially in production (factory) work. This reflects, in part, disparities in education (as we saw in Chapter 2, 24.1 percent of white women are college educated, versus 15.2 percent of African American and only 10.7 percent of Latina women), as well as the heavy immigration of Latina women into the United States during the 1980s and 1990s (immigrants typically begin their work careers in less prestigious fields). Asian women, as a group, are highly educated (with 40.4 percent having college degrees), but, as noted in Chapter 2, are bifurcated into two groups, one highly educated and the other poorly educated and speaking little English.

Although factory working conditions have improved dramatically in recent decades, they are still poor. For the most part, the work remains underpaid, dull, routine, and repetitive, often requiring little more than being able to put something in and out of a machine over and over again. One woman describes her experience working as a punch press operator thus:

> The set-up man has the machine all ready. It is a bench press. Not very big. . . . You can fit it right on the table. I sit and I take these little tweezers, I have two kinds of tweezers, and I take these little pieces [discs about the size of a dime] and put them on the press. . . . And there are two round tools that you put on them; I hit two buttons on either side, which is an excellent safety device, and the die comes down and punches it. . . . See that little notch, the die cut that. You just sit there and sit there and sit there and punch and punch. . . . I did 3,200 last night. (O'Farrell, 1988, p. 261)

Women in Everyday Jobs

Table 5.4
PERCENTAGE OF EMPLOYED WHITE, BLACK, LATINA, AND ASIAN WOMEN IN SELECTED OCCUPATIONS AND OCCUPATIONAL GROUPS IN THE EARLY 2000S

Occupation	% Held by Women	Number of Women	% of White Working Women in Occ	% of Black Working Women in Occ	% of Latina Working Women in Occ	% of Asian Working Women in Occ
All Occupations	46.8	64,436,000	100.0	100.0	100.0	100.0
Selected Blue-Collar Occupations*						
Carpenters	1.5	16,000				
Mechanics and Repairers	4.8	201,000				
Electricians	1.9	14,000				
Motor Vehicle Operators	1.7	8,000				
Construction Workers	2.1	94,000				
Broad Occupational Groups**						
Construction and Extraction	2.4	193,000	0.4	<.1	0.5	<.1
Installation, Maintenance, and Repair	3.9	193,000	0.3	0.4	0.8	<.1
Farming, Forestry, Fishing	20.1	193,000	0.4	0.1	1.3	0.3
Production	31.4	3,028,000	4.2	6.3	9.3	9.8
Transportation Workers	14.8	1,224,000	1.8	2.7	3.3	1.1

*Selected occupations are for full-time workers in 2001.
**Broad occupational groups are for all wage-earners (both full and part time) in 2003.
Source: Bureau of Labor Statistics (2003e, 2003g).

Although ballyhooed in the media, women in con-struction and the building trades are still a rarity.

Jean Tepperman (1970, pp. 116–117), who worked in a Chicago factory, vividly describes the alienation experienced by the contemporary factory woman:

> The woman who worked next to me on the line at Nadir was named Pat. She had two children and two grandchildren, and she would talk to me about them, about getting her hair done, and about cooking. Every morning, just before the bell rang to start work, she would give me a little "Well, here we go" look. One morning she said, "Every day you think you can't possibly hate it any more, and then the next day you hate it more." Then the bell rang and it was like going underwater and holding your breath for two hours (until the break). I worked on an assembly line of about forty women. I put little things on wires into something else, with wire-cutters. After a while, I found out what the little things were, but I never found out what they were used for. . . . Most of the jobs in the plant were like mine, a series of the same ten or so motions all day. All the men who were factory workers admitted that the women had the worst jobs, and that they (the men) would go crazy if they had to do that stuff.

As of the early 2000s, women continue to be paid less for their labor than their male counterparts (Bureau of Labor Statistics, 2003e). For example, women in craft occupations have weekly earnings that are only 74 percent of their male counterparts' ($479 versus $648); similarly, female machine operators earn just 71 percent of what male operators do ($360 versus $509). Of all the Census Bureau's major job classifications for blue-collar work, pay for "handlers, equip-

Women dominate production floors in the textile and apparel industries, staffing, for example, 73 percent of the sewing jobs.

ment cleaners, helpers, and laborers" is most nearly comparable, but even here women earn only 85 percent of what men do ($342 versus $401).

Many blue-collar service occupations—such as prison guard, police officer, fire fighter, and rapid transit operator—are traditionally male dominated. Women wanting to work in these fields have to deal with both institutionalized and individualized discrimination. While women have begun to fill these roles in increasing numbers, there is still much doubt in men's minds as to whether they can adequately do the jobs for which they have been hired. Many of the ways in which women fulfill their responsibilities differ from the male standard and therefore tend to be dismissed as inadequate.

Women working in blue-collar service occupations often have to face discrimination from male coworkers who are hostile to the invasion of their workspace by women. There are multifarious reinforcements of the message that they are not welcome. Women often fail to receive adequate training and socialization on the job; men may actively undermine women's work or confidence; and women often have to deal with persistent sexual innuendoes and harassment (Zimmer, 1997). They frequently must contend with their male supervisors and coworkers stereotyping their performance potential based on their gender. Some men over-explain even the most routine of operations:

> We went out of service and Train Operator F felt he had to explain to me how to discharge a train. I took it patiently. I think he doesn't like women on the job. I can't win and there's no sense taking it personally. (Swerdlow, 1997, p. 262)

Another way that men give women a hard time on the job is through constant criticism:

> Yesterday, Assistant Train Dispatcher F said to me, "You were on the wrong train yesterday. You and your motorman were so busy talking." . . . At first I was bewildered. Then I began to ask some questions and it dawned on me that if we were on the wrong train, it was his fault, and as I began to imply that, he quickly got out of the conversation. (Swerdlow, 1997, p. 262)

Even an occasional compliment can carry or be accompanied by a sexual innuendo:

> My motorman was saying "She's a fantastic conductor." Motorman L said, "Yeah, I know, I had her Saturday." My motorman went on, "She's got the greatest timing. . . . " "Well, of course," broke in Motorman B, "women have it, that's how they get pregnant." (Swerdlow, 1997, p. 262)

Men have created in these traditionally male-dominated occupations a male environment, a "sexualized workplace" (Enarson, 1984), with pinups, for instance, and with a culture of dirty jokes and other sexually explicit entertainment. This can produce uncomfortable situations for women:

> About six guys I didn't know were in the crewroom, watching a rape scene in a *Death Wish* movie. I was so beside myself that I just walked over and changed the channel. One changed it back and someone said, "That's the best part we're missing." . . . I went towards the television again, and someone, it may have been the same guy, physically pushed me away from the television. I left my food, I couldn't keep eating. I started crying and walked out of the crewroom. (Swerdlow, 1997, p. 264)

Of course, not all men within these occupations attempt to undermine or to marginalize women in the workplace. There are some who support women and attempt to make their work lives easier, offering reassurances like these: "You'll be okay, just don't look for trouble;" "It's not that bad, everyone talks about it, but . . . ;" "I did it for years. It wasn't anything" (Swerdlow, 1997, p. 267). Praise along with reassurance is not infrequent: "I worked with Motorman D, and after our first trip was over, he said, 'You do good work.' I thanked him and said, 'But I still don't do very well in emergencies.' 'That will come in time,' he said" (Swerdlow, 1997, p. 267).

While women are entering nontraditional fields in greater numbers than ever before, they are still marginalized. For women to be accepted within these fields, it is important that there be an understanding as to how their work differs from that of men. Often, the ways that women carry out their duties do not conform to the patterns of male behavior in the workplace. Women working as prison guards, for instance, cannot use the brute intimidation that many male guards do against inmates, so they have to develop innovative strategies based on the knowledge of the gender-specific ways that men respond to them. They have to learn how to manipulate the prison population without using force. "The data indicate that [female] workers, even in highly regulated environments like prisons, can develop innovative and successful ways to perform the job when they find established work roles inadequate or find they are blocked from achieving success using predetermined definitions of appropriate work behavior" (Zimmer, 1997, p. 289). While women are often dismissed by men as incompetent, sometimes they are just using different means to achieve the same end.

Sweatshops: Not in the United States?

Though we may tend to think that the existence of sweatshops is a faraway, third world problem, the reality is that such conditions are common even in the United States. Sweatshops are specific types of factories or homework businesses where "subcontractors" hire workers who try to outbid each other for contracts with manufacturers. Offering a competitive bid usually implies that workers will be paid very low wages for long hours of service in often uncomfortable conditions (Bonacich and Appelbaum, 2000, p. 3). Sweatshops are becoming a growing problem in the inner cities of several metropolitan areas, especially New York and Los Angeles. In New York State "manufacturers and contractors in the apparel industry continue to operate in violation of multiple, laws, codes and regulations" (New York State Dept. of Labor, 2002, p. 8). A recent task force for the apparel industry in New York State found that "33% of the firms visited were in violation of regislation requirements, 39% of the firms visited were found to have violated wagement or minimum wage requirements and 64% of the firms visited were found to be in violation of record-keeping requirements of the labor law" (N.Y. State Dept. of Labor, 2002, p. 8). Of the approximate 7,000 apparel firms that operate in Manhattan, about 4,500 can be classified as sweatshops, employing more than 50,000 workers. Such shops typically pay workers between $2.00 and $2.50 an hour for a twelve-hour work day. The workers are forced to toil in overcrowded conditions— having poor ventilation, unsanitary bathrooms, and stairwells in need of repair. In Los Angeles, a U.S. Department of Labor survey found 61 percent of the garment firms in violation of wage and hour regulations. "Workers were underpaid by an estimated $873 million dollars per year" (Bonacich and Appelbaum, 2000, p. 3).

The rise of the sweatshop industry in America is linked to the globalization of the apparel industry as a whole. The U.S. apparel industry moved its operations to less-developed countries in the 1980s and 1990s, where labor laws were lax. However, moving abroad requires longer waiting times, thereby increasing the risk of losing out on time-sensitive garments. Thus, there is a strong market force to keep apparel that is "in fashion" domestically produced (Bonacich and Appelbaum, 2000, p. 11).

What allowed the industry to take hold was the growing immigrant population. Los Angeles, for example, has been a major site for immigration from Mexico, Asia, and Central America. "Immigrants . . . provide the workforce and the entrepreneurship to run the contracting shops. Many of the immigrant workers are undocumented, which means that they often lack the political where-withal to resist exploitation." Moreover, Los Angles has a tradition of being an "antiunion" town (Bonacich and Appelbaum, 2000, p. 19).

In New York City, Chinese and Asian immigrants make up the majority of the apparel workers and have replaced Europeans and African Americans (Louie, 2001, p. 28). Their plight is captured in the commentary of Jenny Chen, who went to work in a sweatshop upon her marriage to a "gold mountain man" (Louie, 2001, p. 29):

> Aiyah. I regret coming here. When I was in China, after graduation from high school I worked in restaurants. I learned a lot of different things about how to run a restaurant. It was better work, more interesting. Now, I'm behind a ma-chine all day, sewing away. Sometimes when you pay you then hold back a por-tion of your pay. For the younger women like me, we often wish that we could go to school and get some different kind of work. Lots of times, you're not even getting paid, but you have to go into work on Sundays. Then you've got to look at the boss's face. Yuuhhh (laughs). You just wish you could do some-thing else. And you don't have any time to spend with you kids. I heard from my friends in San Francisco that the price is not as good as here. You go to work earlier and get out earlier, right? Here work varies a lot and you still see lights on in the shops at night. My daughter's friend's mother works in the day, comes home to feed her kids, then goes back to work at night. She's always tired.

In recent years, the Chinese Staff and Worker's Association (CSWA) has provided a haven for Chinese workers to gather and talk about their experiences as workers, and even organize for more rights and wages. The women's com-mittees of the CSWA have helped women break the silence of their exploita-tion and, on occasion, recoup wages that were never paid. In 1992, CSWA started a back-wage campaign to force companies to pay back wages, most hav-ing owed at least a month's paycheck per worker (Louie, 2001, p. 40).

CSWA also helped in the much-publicized fight against DKNY for cor-porate responsibility in June 2000. Overtime pay was being withheld and long worker hours were being mandated:

> [DKNY] felt like being in a prison. If we were two minutes late, we were docked one half-hour of our pay. We had to keep out heads down all the time once we started working. No looking up. No talking to anyone. Can you imagine? A big room with rows and rows of machines and all of us looking down. Three surveillance cameras watched everything we did. They checked our purses be-fore we left at the end of the day. No going through to the bathroom—it was often padlocked. No water, with the big drinking fountain broken. No making or receiving phone calls, even for emergencies. (Louie, 2001, p. 44)

While many women fear the repercussions of organizing against their bosses, over the past decade they have come together to fight the injustice. With sup-port networks like the CSWA, DKNY was hit with a class action lawsuit for failure to pay overtime wages for a seventy-five-hour workweek. Bilingual, bicultural organizations such as CSWA have been instrumental in creating a bridge between the Chinese community and the outside society; they provide the necessary support that these women need to fight injustices.

What can be done to deal with the conditions of sweatshops? Foremost, it is necessary to enforce existing laws against minimum wage violations and against child labor. This was goal of the Clinton administration during the 1990s—a goal that was largely unachieved. For example, in 1996, the U.S. Department of Labor issued violations against many sweatshop sewing manufactories, but many others were passed over. At the state level, in August 1998 in New York passed the Unpaid Wages Prohibition Act, making a manufacturer of apparel goods responsible for sweatshop factory conditions (Bonacich and Appelbaum, 2000, p. 245). The effect of this law, however, has yet to measured.

Another possible solution is for the workers themselves to organize. Like the Chinese immigrant workers, Mexican women immigrants are forced into low-wage, low-skill factory work when they come across the border to the United States. And, like the Chinese, many of these women have banded together to fight against unjust bosses. Maria del Carmen Dominguez, for instance, led the organization of her fellow workers at the CMT factory to receive holiday wages that her manager refused to pay:

> I was the organizer in my area, and we had ten women, and I controlled it (laughs). Yes, *ellas* (they) would say "I love you." And I would say, "I love you too." We were all partners. Yeah, I love to help the people. And I would fight, fight, fight in CMT, every day (laughs). Yes, that's a long time to fight! (as reported in Louie, 2001, p. 82)

Unionization within the garment industry, however, is difficult because subcontractors are vulnerable to losing their business and their employees are vulnerable to losing their jobs should a manufacturer find out that workers are attempting to unionize. More often than not, manufacturers drop a contractor whose employees are threatening to unionize. Workers know this and don't want to threaten their job security. Coupled with this threat is the fact that many of these workers are undocumented, making the possibility of unionizing much weaker (Bonacich and Appelbaum 2000, p. 166).

One important key to solving the problem of sweatshops is understanding the relationship between the role of producers and consumers of sweatshop commodities. Each of us has a choice whether to purchase a consumer item made under sweatshop conditions. One option available to each of us is to boycott this kind of item. Indeed, some individuals have taken this choice a step further and joined together in boycotting particular products: One of the more successful organized boycotts was the campaign against Jessica McClintock by the Asian Immigrant Women's Advocates (AIWA). This kind of effort has also succeeded at colleges and universities, where clothing and other items at campus bookstores have been assessed and approved if not from sweatshop manufacturers (Bonacich and Appelbaum, 2000, pp. 301–303).

Globalization of Factory Work

While a small percentage of American women toil away at oppressive low-skilled blue-collar manufacturing jobs, female factory laborers in other areas of the world face conditions far worse than those in the United States. Many women working in factories owned by U.S. corporations, such as the *maquilas* in Mexico (2,000 American-owned factories on the Mexican side of the U.S.–Mexico border), slave away to earn $4.50 a day, and return home to no running water or toilets, to homes that at best are constructed out of concrete or adobe, at worst, out of discarded lumber and tar paper. Many live in shacks in neighborhoods without showers or electricity. The U.S. corporations have moved into Mexican cities for the low wages and the lack of regulations, as Mexico has very few safety and environmental regulations in comparison to the United States, and no laws for protection of workers' health and safety.

The workforce that fills these *maquilas* is two-thirds female, working because they have to in order to sustain even a subsistence level of poverty. The dire, even dangerous conditions result in a high turnover rate, however (LaBotz, 1994). These women are disposable workers, and they are treated as such. The plant supervisors are virtually all men, and they commonly mistreat the women and girls under their management:

> In this situation—where most of the women have no labor unions and the government does not protect workers' rights—sexual harassment is endemic. . . . Sexual harassment and rape often go unreported . . . because women fear reprisals in the form of firing and because a lack of resources to deal with rape and harassment leads to a climate of shame and humiliation for the victims of these crimes. (LaBotz, 1994, p. 405)

There is no hope of unionization or organization because unions simply do not exist.

It is because there is less concern among consumers over how or where products are made than desire that they be durable and cheap that women and girls in Mexico's *maquilas* are forced into working in abject conditions for minimal wages. The U.S. companies argue that if they keep their factories in the States, they will have to pay higher wages and thus substantially raise product cost. In order to enable women in America to fill their houses with inexpensive products to make their lives easier and more pleasurable, women across the globe are being exploited, working in slave-like conditions to manufacture these products. While it is sometimes argued that this is good because it gives women in Mexico jobs they otherwise would not have, closer consideration cannot but lead to dismay and even horror at the enslavement and exploitation of these women in developing nations.

Where Do We Go from Here?

Women gain some autonomy when they become income earners, in any occupation. However, the future of "everyday" women workers appears less than

Circuit board assembly.

rosy. They are confined to low-skill, low-wage jobs with little opportunity for advancement. Many appear to be running harder simply to stay in place. They often have to deal with sexual harassment or demeaning treatment based on traditional sex-typed roles. They still have not joined unions or working women's organizations in large enough numbers to make significant changes. The problems of "everyday" women workers are magnified for women of color, who still face individualized and institutionalized discrimination.

Some working women (5.7 percent, up from 2.2 percent in 1970) have sought to supplement their incomes by taking on a second or even a third job. One in every six multiple job-holders in 1970 was a woman; by the early 2000s, almost one in every two was (47.5 percent; see U.S. Bureau of the Census, 2002a, Table 586, p. 377). Due to lack of education or low socioeconomic status, these women supplement one poor job with another equally poor job. This makes it increasingly difficult for them to move out of their occupational rut. Unfortunately, a second or even a third job is becoming a necessity of life, not a means of increasing the standard of living.

While many women workers are individually taking steps to deal with their occupational situations, they are not doing so in a collective manner. Some female workers are involved in unions or other working women's organizations, but their numbers (13 percent of all working women) are not substantial enough to make significant changes. By taking on a second or third job instead of challenging the institutional blocks that are influencing their economic status, these women are in effect condemning themselves to their role. They are not forcing the institutions that create the low-paying, low-skilled, sex-typed occupations to improve working conditions. Collective action must be predicated on an individual desire for change and a realization that change is possible and worth fighting for. There must be support from coworkers and also from those higher up in the company. The support must come in the form of job security.

Unfortunately, for most of these women, job security is nonexistent. Companies realize that if one worker is discontent, they can always find someone else, for there is a substantial pool of workers from which to draw to fill these jobs.

While unionization or other organization might reduce some of the more undesirable working conditions, especially the deplorable conditions existing within sweatshops, it alone cannot provide the total answer. In nontraditional blue-collar occupations, for instance, women constitute only a small percentage of the total number of workers, and thus, even if they mobilized, affecting change in their occupational positioning and conditions would be extremely difficult. Women who act out individually to change their working environment often face reprisals, if not outright hostility. For different reasons, as discussed earlier, unionization of other "everyday" women workers has not yet involved more than a minority.

"Everyday" women workers have been denied autonomy in their job status, but this does not preclude some independent action. At the individual level, workers need to combat actively the roles and positions to which they have been confined. This means that clerical workers must assert themselves and refuse to do certain activities that they deem inappropriate to their job description. Such women must deny their role as the "office wife." They ought not be penalized for such action, individually or collectively. Perhaps an organized refusal of sex-typed roles in the office would promote the message that even requesting such tasks is inappropriate and offensive.

While individual actions can create change at the personal level, for substantial changes to have permanence, they must permeate the institutional level. The very structure of certain occupations must change. With the increase in technology, much clerical work has become even more depersonalized and alienating, and these women are even more likely to be viewed as objects to be ordered around or otherwise demeaned. If, at the institutional level, such workers were allowed more autonomy and more chance for advancement, with a greater valuation of the clerical work role, clerical occupations would be greatly improved. In blue-collar work, and within the military, an important change would be the enforcement of sexual harassment laws and a restructuring of the workplace to preclude what was earlier referred to as the "sexualization of the workplace." This could involve an increased consciousness of the degrading effects of this "sexualization" on women workers. There must also be thoroughgoing training and equal socialization for women. A change that would significantly assist working mothers in all occupations would be on-site childcare. With an increasing institutional focus on making money at any cost, the worker is increasingly becoming a mere pawn, a tool. Even so, while most of these jobs are low-skill, low-paying, and offer little chance for advancement, there is still the potential for improvement through agitation at the individual level and changes at the institutional level.

World Wide Web Resources

For voluminous census and survey data on working women, go to the Bureau of Labor Statistics Web site: http://www.bls.gov/.

For current and historical data on sexual discrimination complaints, see the U.S. Equal Employment Opportunity Commission Web site at: http://www.eeoc.gov/. A good supplement to this site is the Sexual Harassment Resources page at: www.feminist.org/911/harass.html.

For information on women in blue-collar and nontraditional trades, see www.tradeswomen.org/.

6 Professional and Managerial Women

Professional and managerial occupations command a great deal of respect, authority, and prestige. People working in these occupations can expect a high degree of economic reward and recognition for their work.

Occupations considered "professional," such as law, are characterized by the practice of a systematic body of theoretical knowledge, with its own language and symbols. This knowledge is acquired through a high degree of education and training. A profession generally has a service orientation, and its members are bound by a strict occupational code of ethics. Usually they belong to a professional association, which involves a network of formal and informal relationships. In their practice, professionals often have a great deal of autonomy, power, and authority—as is recognized by their clientele and by the community at large. The profession as a whole has the ability to select and train new members, as well as to watch over and discipline them (Stromberg, 1988, p. 206).

Law and medicine are the professions that come closest to this "ideal type." However, even these professions "have never achieved the complete power over clients or the freedom from government regulation that we often imagine and . . . such professions can experience loss of power and deprofessionalization" (Stromberg, 1988, p. 207). While the professions are generally occupations with a high degree of autonomy and control, this is not always reflected in reality. Women in the professions, even those who work in law or medicine, are sometimes denied autonomy due to their gender. To understand how this gender bias functions, and how women have become locked into less autonomous work roles, it is important to understand the history of the professions and the semiprofessions.

The older, "core" professions, such as medicine and law, began as medieval guilds. Over the centuries, through professional associations and informal networks, there developed a set of occupational practices to control the internal workings of the professions, including routes of entry and access to the skills, knowledge, and credentials necessary to practice in a given field. This created a structure that tended to exclude groups such as women and minorities.

Of course, societal expectations concerning women's roles as wives and mothers have also dictated the type of work that women, especially highly educated women, should pursue outside the home sphere. Given these expectations, and with limited access to the "core" professional fields, women in the nineteenth and early twentieth centuries forged a new set of female-dominated professions, which eventually came to be termed the "semiprofessions":

secondary-school teaching, nursing, social work, and library work. Women's work has characteristically been in service to the needs of others, and these occupations followed in the same vein. Indeed, in some cases (social work in particular) they developed from volunteer activity women were doing for charitable organizations. These occupations were logical extensions of the role of wife and mother, and (mostly) young, educated, single white women were permitted and even encouraged to engage in them.

Semiprofessions require less training; "their status is less legitimated, their right to privileged communication less established, there is less of a specialized body of knowledge, and they have less autonomy from supervision or societal control than 'the professions'" (Etzioni, 1969, p. v). Whereas there has been considerable emphasis in the professions on further developing their knowledge base, the semiprofessions remain primarily concerned with the application—rather than the development—of knowledge. Increased specialized knowledge has tended to render the professions even more autonomous, while those in the semiprofessions tend to be subordinated to these professionals or to other hierarchical authorities. Typically, men in professional occupations have sought to control the semiprofessions with which they were closely aligned. The females in these occupations thus became "handmaidens" to the male professionals (Sokoloff, 1992, p. 8). Nursing is a prime example of this. There is a difference also in the ways in which men in the professions practiced: While they, too, served the public, they tended to create a more hierarchical relationship with their clients.

With the development of semiprofessions and the funneling of women into these positions, the traditional gender roles in society were maintained, even though women were working as professionals. Women did not have the autonomy or the prestige that the male professionals had. They existed in a hierarchical structure that placed them in a subordinate role to their white male "professional" counterparts.

The development of the semiprofessions can best be understood by examining the occupations that historically had disproportionately large percentages of women working in them.

A Brief History of the Feminization of Selected Semiprofessions: Teaching, Nursing, and Social Work

In the nineteenth and early twentieth centuries, teaching and nursing at the primary and secondary levels drew the largest percentage of white, professional women, closely followed by social work and librarianship.

Teaching

Historically, teaching had been mainly a "man's field." During the colonial era, "single women taught the younger children during the summer months [while] men taught older children during the rest of the year" (Matthaei, 1982, p. 207).

However, a movement to separate students into grades by age served to stratify the teaching profession, and eventually encouraged women to become teachers. Indeed, by the end of the nineteenth century, teaching had become female dominated (Matthaei, 1982, p. 207). Primary education levels were especially so, due to the restratification of the educational system, whereby those with more experience were teaching at the higher levels and those with less experience at the lower levels. In this way, those without much experience could be relegated to teaching the younger children at lower wages. This resulted in women being "hired often at half or a third of the wages of men"; in elementary or common schools, "men were employed at higher wages as superintendents, administrators, and teachers of older children" Stromberg (1988, p. 214). Women were grateful to have attained employment that was removed from the drudgery of the factories and were willing to work for lesser wages than their male counterparts.

Increasing urbanization, industrialization, and immigration contributed to the feminization of the teaching profession. The supply of men who could fill teaching positions declined as they took jobs within the more lucrative and prestigious managerial and professional fields and as many migrated westward to seek their fortunes. Women were a "logical" choice to fill these lower-level, lower-paid teaching slots. Remaining male teachers were most prevalent in the higher grades, including college teaching and in administration—where "women were virtually excluded except in certain subjects or institutions, such as women's colleges" (Matthaei, 1982, p. 208). Women were thus relegated to positions of low prestige and authority even in an occupation they dominated in number.

Nursing

Lack of prestige and authority was the reality for women in nursing as well. Originally, nursing and midwifery were viewed as unskilled, domestic occupations and, as late as 1900, were listed in the census under the category "Domestic and Personal Service." Before the Civil War, nurses earned such low wages that they supplemented their nursing income with sewing or other domestic work. These women worked autonomously and were not bound to hospitals or professionalized medicine. The nurses who did work within the walls of hospitals were lacking any form of instruction, and many occupied the lowest positions within society. "In the 1840s, hospitals on both sides of the Atlantic were gloomy, overcrowded, incredibly dirty places. . . . In these pestholes, the women who nursed were rarely better than their patients. Most of them were also dirty and drunken. Many had prison records or vices that should have made them candidates for jail" (Dodge, 1954, p. 19). Many of the first hospitals provided not only for patients but also for paupers and prisoners, and female prisoners were often given the role of nurse and caregiver within the hospital. Nursing as a profession lacked so much precision and training that physicians sent elderly inmates, many between seventy and eighty years of age, to serve as nurses in the wards because they could receive better food there (Dolan, Fitzpatrick, and Herrmann, 1983, p. 137).

The professionalization of nursing began with the work of Florence Nightingale, who introduced the nursing profession to middle- and upper-class women who could obtain the training required for the revolutionized nurse, comprising "educated, trained and refined women" (Dock and Stewart, 1938, p. 127). Nightingale's revision of the health care system and the standard of nursing was first hindered by her social position as a member of upper-class society, for "the place was still a hospital, and a young gentlewoman could only bring shame and disgrace upon her family by going to work in it" (Dodge, 1954, p. 20). However, with the arrival of the Crimean War and the Civil War, the demand for greater sanitation and medical care increased, and Nightingale's newly trained nurses proved to the medical community the need for a new generation of trained and educated nurses.

Although nurses gained more training and respectability, they remained subordinate to doctors in the male-dominated profession. After the Civil War, nursing "developed as an ancillary occupation in support of physicians who, along with hospital administrators, delegated functions but remained in charge. . . . [N]ursing emerged as an organization-based occupation rather than as an independent and entrepreneurial profession like medicine and law. Nurses, in fact, must respond to a dual chain of command—the hospital administrators and the physicians" (Stromberg, 1988, p. 208–209). One nurse testifying before the Society of the New York Academy of Medicine in 1984 noted: "One simply cannot 'sell' a role in which one profession is subjugated to the service of another profession" (Group and Roberts, 2001, p. 289).

Today, the nursing profession is in trouble. Berliner and Ginzberg (2002, p. 2742) argue that nurses "love" their work but "hate" their jobs. There is a nursing shortage in the United States, and the current situation "has turned into a full blown crisis" (Dworkin, 2002, p. 23). While nursing shortages are not new and have occurred throughout many decades (McKibbin, 1990), the current crisis has been unprecedented in its duration. While earlier shortages most often dealt with low wages, poor benefits, and overly long work hours, the present crisis has more to do with the scarcity of women who want to become nurses and the difficulty of getting those currently in the field to stay in hospital settings. The situation is compounded by the steady stream of nurses leaving their jobs because they are at the end of their career (Berliner and Ginzberg, 2002, p. 2742). The additive effect of these three factors comprise "the crux of the current and future shortage" (Berliner and Ginzberg, 2002, p. 2742). It should also be noted that profit-driven hospitals and HMOs are cutting "expensive" nurses and replacing them with cheaper "unlicensed assistive personnel" (UAPs), especially in nursing homes and other settings where patients are older (Group and Roberts, 2001, p. xliv). In 1995, for example, the American Nurses Association conducted a national survey of 200,000 registered nurses and found that 68.4 percent of the respondents had seen the number of RNs in their facilities drop, while 44.7 percent reported the increased use of UAPs (Group and Roberts 2001, p. 449).

One cause of the nursing shortage is the wider range of professional fields available to today's women than the traditional occupations of nursing and teach-

Two nurses, circa 1920. Even though there are more male nurses today than ever before, women still dominate the field: 91 percent of all full-time registered nurses are female.

ing. On top of·this, nurses report high levels of job dissatisfaction. A recent study reported that 40 percent of the nursing staff in hospital settings were dissatisfied with their work, compared to only 10 to 15 percent of workers in other professions (Aiken et al., 2001). This dissatisfaction has a number of sources. An important one is—in an effort to economize their operations—hospitals and medical centers sometimes rely on nurses to perform tasks not associated with their job level, from scrubbing floors to preparing patients for operations (Dworkin, 2002). Another source of dissatisfaction is the fact that the nursing job setting requires many workers to often shift their hours and days to accommodate holidays, vacations, and weekends. For women with young children, this frequent juggling of shifts can be especially difficult. As an alternative, some nurses have signed up with agencies to gain a degree of flexibility over their working hours. However, many of these agencies do not provide benefits such as health insurance (Dworkin, 2002, pp. 31–32).

With the increase in the number of UAPs and the downsizing of their jobs by hospital administrators, nurses feel their care is compromised: They find they must "speed up" their work to take care of a growing number of patients. As a result, high levels of "burnout" are common among many nursing staffs—not surprising given the long hours on the job, the lack of resources to do their work, and the frustration of not being able to properly take care of their patients. Group and Roberts (2001, p. 449) note the following account given to government investigators studying the decrease in the number of nurses in the state of New York:

> At one hospital, a woman visited her father after heart bypass surgery, only to find him lying in a pool of blood. She contacted the nurse, who had forty patients to care for and who said the father could not be a priority when compared to other patients. In another facility, many RNs were on duty three hours beyond their eight-hour days, and one RN, with only one medical technician and one aide, was caring for thirty-five patients. The nurses were refusing to sign non-RN notes. Such anecdotal evidence was supported by statistics: RNs, who once provided 90 percent of hospital care, now constituted only 65 percent to 75 percent of patient-care staff.

The American Association of Colleges of Nursing (2002) has come out with a policy statement on how we might put a halt to the nursing shortage. The association suggests a two-pronged approach to address both the educational and work environments. Regarding education, nurses must move through their graduate programs more quickly; and they need to be provided with upward mobility opportunities beyond entry-level work; for example, in teaching and staff development positions. Regarding the work environment, it is imperative to keep experienced nurses working directly with patients. To this aim, more flexibility needs be built into the overall job setting; moreover, there needs to be adequate staffing and increased control and autonomy on the job. The mentor-mentee relationship between older and younger nurses must be nourished and rewarded. Nursing salaries and benefits must remain competitive. Finally, the clash in values between the profit-making motives of "managed care" and the principles embedded in the nursing profession must be addressed. As one nurse has observed: "It is not clear to me who the managed care nurse is serving: is it the company, the patient or both? How does the managed care nurse ethically integrate the professional standard of patient advocacy with the employers goal of cost containment?" (Thompson, 1996, p. 5, as cited in Group and Roberts, 2001, p. 459). One resolution has been movement toward community-based care programs supported by federal grants and private foundation monies; such programs can fill in the gaps that the managed care system of health care has created in offering health care to poor communities. Nurse practitioners often direct and staff these programs and feel they play a vital role in the care and delivery of health services within these communities (Group and Roberts, 2001, p. 471).

Social Work

Female professionals in nursing and teaching share the experience of being subordinated in the male professional hierarchy and of filling an occupation that conforms to traditional gender expectations. Women who became professionals through careers in social work have endured a similar experience. At the origin of the field of social work, however, such was not the case. "In both teaching and nursing women were moving into a situation where men were already established. . . . In both teaching and nursing women were mainly engaged at a level which was inferior to that of men, in teaching younger children and giving medical care and attention under the direction of a doctor. In social work there was no such pre-set pattern" (Walton, 1975, p. 14). With social work there was not one recognizable task that could define the occupation. While men initiated many of the branches of social work that we recognize today, three branches owe their inception solely to women: moral welfare work, housing management, and social work with delinquents. Women's place in social work grew out of white middle- and upper-class women's nurturing role within their families and, by extension, the larger community. "Charitable work with poor families was deemed a perfect fit with women's 'natural talents' for nurturance and self-sacrifice" (Leighninger, 1996, p. 114). Social work seemed to be a natural fit for women, as it seemed not an occupation, but a means to further broaden the reach of their innate ability to nurture and aid those surrounding them. As Carry Nation, a nineteenth-century social reformer wrote: "We hear 'A woman's place is at the home.' That is true but what and where is home? Not the walls of a house. . . . If my son is in a drinking place, my place is there. If my daughter, or the daughter of anyone else, my family or any other family, is in trouble, my place is there. [A woman would be either selfish or cowardly if she] would refuse to leave her home to relieve suffering or trouble" (as quoted in Amott and Matthaei, 1996, p. 121).

Women took the call to a variety of issues, treating the world as an extended family, deserving their love and saving. A variety of organizations were formed to combat the ills in society, including such groups as the American Women's Education Association, the Sanitary Commission, the Women's Christian Temperance Union, and Female Reform Societies. The women in social work were largely limited to one sector of society, white middle- and upper-class women. The money needed to initiate an organization or movement limited those who could participate. Octavia Hill (1838–1912) created a "ragged" school and later a working women's college, "yet in recognizing this there is no lessening of Octavia Hill's contribution to social work, but the acceptance that it would have been extremely difficult for a woman without financial means to have made a significant innovation in the development of social work" (Walton, 1975, p. 22). Another factor that limited the social class background of those drawn to social work was the creation of schools to produce educated future social workers, such as the Girls' Grammar School, which opened in 1875. The girls attending were "for the most part daughters or wives of small businessmen or men in the professions, comfortably off with a modest household" (Amott and Matthaei, 1996, p. 122). In terms of race, "social home-making campaigns focused more directly on the needs of the less fortunate, and brought upper- and middle-class, U.S.-born white women into direct contact and sometimes alliance with poor, immigrant, and enslaved women" (Amott and Matthaei, 1996, p. 122). While these facts create the image of white women helping to raise all races of women to a higher standard of living, in fact "the privileged white women in these movements were usually condescending and exclusionary of the women they were trying to help" (Amott and Matthaei, 1996,

p. 124). And, while many of the women involved shared the sentiments of Johanna Chandler, honorary secretary to a ladies' hospital committee, who stated, "but of this I am sure, helping others is the sweetest of all pleasures" (Walton, 1975, p. 27), women also discovered the employment potential that social work provided:

> Before 1890 women had been mostly patrons or volunteers in charitable en-
> terprise, and for a long time they liked to compare the volunteer, who gave
> willingly of herself, with the more perfunctory effort and vested interest of the
> paid agent. But as female paid agents increased in number and authority, the
> prospect of a new professional dignity caught the imagination. Women grew
> interested not just because the social problems so often included their poorest
> sisters but because the fact of employment seemed promising. It is significant
> that the predecessor of the professional association of social workers was the
> Inter-collegiate Bureau of Occupations, set up in 1911 in New York City to
> help graduates of elite women's colleges find work. (Leiby, 1978, p. 119)

These women had found a profession that still had open doors for females, at a time when work was almost an impossibility for women in a male-dominated world.

In sum, nursing, teaching, and social work remained largely the province of young, educated, white, single women. They worked under the control of male administrators who were also white. All three professions represented an extension of the "traditional" female role, and therefore white women were allowed—and even encouraged—to pursue them. Women who attempted to defy these traditional gender expectations and move into positions of power faced definite obstacles in their ascent.

A Short History of Women in Management

Management refers to executive, administrative, and managerial work in both the private and public sectors of the economy. Women made few significant in-roads into such occupations before the 1960s.

Middle- and upper-middle-class women in the nineteenth century were caught in a "functionalism paradigm" concerning a woman's role. As discussed in Chapter 2, the nineteenth-century concept of a lady was of a fragile, ideal, pure creature—submissive and subservient to her husband and to domestic needs. Managerial occupations, in strong contrast, were from the earliest days identified with the masculine domain: "Managers were stereotyped as strong, assertive, and rational—traits ascribed to men. For a woman to hold a managerial position—especially one that involved supervising men—violated the belief that male dominance was both natural and desirable" (Reskin and Phipps, 1988, p. 200).

Earlier, within the preindustrial economy of the American colonial period, women worked outside the home in a range of occupations (as we saw in Chapter 2) many of which we would consider managerial, even though that term was not used. In addition to managing plantations, farms, and even colleges (Kwolek-Folland, 1999, p. 212), women worked as innkeepers, merchants, and shopkeepers as well. Having been an apprentice in a Boston establishment that sold crockery and dry goods, Ann Brent (1768–1857), at twenty-one, successfully established her own shop in Boston importing goods from England (Alpern, 1993, pp. 23–24). A certain "Mrs. Ramage" managed a cotton mill on James Island near Charleston, South Carolina, in the late eighteenth century (Alpern, 1993, p. 23). Many who worked outside their homes were widows with dependent children, and most of these women took their husbands' places in family enterprises.

Despite the "cult of true womanhood," entrepreneurial spirit was also present in some middle-class women in the nineteenth century. These women gained important managerial skills through starting businesses that catered to female clients. One example (and also an important role model for women of color) was Sarah Breedlove McWilliams Walker (1867–1919):

> Better known as Madam C. J. Walker, she became a millionaire by marketing a hair straightening formula for black hair. A widow living in St. Louis, Missouri, she supported herself and her daughter for 18 years as a washerwoman. In 1905, she had a dream about hair and then created her successful formula and her "Walker method" of door-to-door demonstrations. President of the Madam C. J. Walker Manufacturing Company, which produced a complete line of cosmetics, she employed some 3,000 people, principally women. A philanthropist, she gave generously to her friend Mary McLeod Bethune's education projects for black women and black youth. (Alpern, 1993, p. 28)

Women also gained managerial experience through their participation in social reform, volunteer activities, and the suffrage movement (Alpern, 1993, p. 30). With greater access to education during the late nineteenth and early twentieth centuries, white middle- and upper-middle-class women were able to gain the necessary skills and confidence to move beyond stagnation in only the lowest levels of professionalized service. Women began to look beyond what society had deemed appropriate for them based on their traditional gender roles.

Within corporations, though, women tended to be segregated in the increasingly feminized occupation of clerical work, with few moving into managerial-level positions. The expansion of the corporation at the end of the nineteenth century saw the development of an even more complex corporate hierarchy, one in which jobs increasingly became subdivided into a series of low-level, dead-end positions. Concomitantly, there was a steady rise in the number of low- and middle-management positions. A "managerial revolution" was taking place (Burnham, 1941). These managerial positions required lengthy training and broad qualifications. Women were usually excluded from consideration and were concentrated instead in the lower levels of the office hierarchy. The job of clerk, once a typically male job that served as an apprenticeship for the young man to "learn the ropes" before moving up to a managerial position, had now become a low-level, dead-end job, increasingly defined as "women's work."

Beginning in the 1890s and early 1900s, the role of women in business began to change dramatically. Developments in technology coupled with demographic and economic transitions were redefining the role of women both within and outside their homes. Women started to become a significant part of the growing numbers of clerical and sales workers. Women's wages were crucial to the survival of the growing consumer economy. Debates arose over women's traditional role and whether or not, for example, married women had rights to property or to obtain credit in their own name (Kwolek-Folland, 1998, pp. 212–213). This period was "a time of intense scrutiny, sometimes extravagant claims, mushrooming organizational formation, and national debate over women's role in business" (Kwolek-Folland, 1998, p. 213).

As this development was taking place, however, debates over protective labor legislation and married women's work arose. What resulted were exclusionary practices—promoted by protective legislation laws enacted in the early twentieth century that regulated women's hours and working—often had the effect of placing unnecessary constraints on women (e.g., they could not work overtime). These constraints most affected women who sought a better and larger role in the labor force, especially those women who wanted to move up into managerial positions (see Alpern, 1993, pp. 30–31; Berch, 1982, pp. 46–51).

The World Wars I and II offered limited employment to women in managerial occupations, but only as a reserve army of laborers who were often withdrawn from these positions after the war. World War II provided only a temporary breakthrough in middle management for women: "women made up 11.7 percent of the managerial occupation in 1940. At the end of the war, in 1945, women in the managerial category had increased to 17.4 percent, but just two years later, their number had decreased to 13.5 percent" (Alpern, 1993, p. 38). The two world wars, however, did serve to change many traditional attitudes. By participating in the workforce and bringing home a paycheck, women gained a new sense of pride in themselves and forged a new sense of their own identities beyond that of traditional homemakers. Many men even desired to keep women as "reserves" for the labor force in case another war began, and some even went as far as encouraging women to become a part of the "national economy" (Kwolek-Folland, 1998, p. 154). The governor of New York established a new women's council as part of the commerce department, which was specifically designed to help women who had lost their jobs at the end of the war (Kwolek-Folland, 1998, p. 154). Nevertheless, it was not until the 1970s that women began to make nontransient, significant inroads into management, when representation increased sharply "from 16.6 percent in 1970 to 26.1 percent in 1980" (Reskin and Phipps, 1988, p. 200).

Contemporary Status of Women in Professions and Management

Women's presence in professional, managerial, and administrative occupations has risen steadily since the end of World War II. Today, more than one in every three working women holds such a job (37.7 percent in 2003, see Bureau of Labor Statistics, 2003g). As shown in Figure 6.1, the percentages vary widely by race and ethnic origin, with Asian women in managerial and professional occupations (41.3 percent of all employed Asian women) leading the way. Nearly as large a percentage of working white women (38.6 percent) fill these kinds of jobs; while African American (31.4 percent), and especially Latina (13.6 percent) women fall considerably behind.

At first wash, it appears that American women have reached—and in many cases even exceeded—parity with men in acquiring the most prestigious jobs in the occupational hierarchy. There have been many improvements in opportunity for women, especially in professions that have traditionally been male dominated. Among the more prominent examples are medicine, in which the percentage of female physicians rose from 15.8 in 1983 to 32.6 in 2001; dentistry, in which during the same period the percentage of female dentists rose from 6.7 to 31.8; law, in which the percentage of female lawyers rose from 15.3 to 34.1; and various managerial specialties in business, in which the percentage of women financial managers went from 38.6 to 51.6; personnel managers, from 43.9 percent female to 67.5 percent female; purchasing managers, from 26.6 percent female to 43.7 percent female, and marketing/public relations managers, from 21.8 percent to 38.0 percent female (Bureau of Labor Statistics, 2003e; U.S. Bureau of the Census, 1996a, p. 405). These examples demonstrate the vast increase in the numbers of women in the professions in recent years and aptly illustrate why women are assumed to have reached equality in the workplace (for the most sanguine interpretation of these data, see Furchtgott-Roth and Stolba, 1996).

Job Segregation

These optimistic figures, however, mask the persistent problems of lack of advancement and depressed wages women within management and the profes-

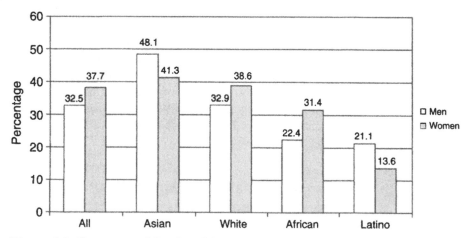

Figure 6.1. Percentage of Employed Persons in Managerial and Professional Occupations by Sex, Race, and Ethnicity, 2003. *Source:* U.S. Bureau of Labor Statistics (2003g).

sions continue to face. These statistics do not reveal that men hold the best-paying and most influential managerial and professional jobs. For example, as we noted in Chapter 3, women hold only 16 percent of the top executive positions in the nation's largest corporations (the Fortune 500). Similarly women comprise only 12 percent of the boards of directors of these companies. In the "core" professions, women comprise only 9.7 percent of engineers, 32.6 percent of physicians, 31.8 percent of dentists, and 34.1 percent of lawyers. They comprise only 15 percent of the partners in major U.S. law firms. On the other hand, women continue to be overrepresented in traditionally female professions. For example, 98.4 percent of prekindergarten and kindergarten teachers are female; 91.0 percent of registered nurses are female; 83.0 percent of librarians are female; 81.5 percent of elementary school teachers are female; and 70.3 percent of social workers are female (Bureau of Labor Statistics, 2003e). While women have entered the professions in numbers unprecedented historically, they are still far from being equal with men.

Further, for all managerial and professional specialties, the median weekly earnings of full-time working women are only 70.5 percent of full-time working men's—a percentage that has actually been falling in recent years (2.7 percent between 1996 and 2001; see Hesse-Biber and Carter, 2000, p. 159; also see Robertson, Carter, and Hesse-Biber, 2004). The discrepancies between men and women hold, for the most part, across almost all fields and all racial and ethnic backgrounds (see Table 6.1).

Interestingly, we find that Latinas and African American women suffer less gender income inequality than their white counterparts. Indeed, in health assessment and treating occupations, African American women do considerably better than African American men. However, compared with white men, minority women earn considerably less in all managerial and professional specialties. And there are proportionately fewer of them. While the number of women working in managerial, executive, administrative, and professional positions has been increasing since the 1970s and today exceeds that of men (50.5 percent of these positions are held by women; see Bureau of Labor Statistics, 2003g), the situation for minority women is different, especially for Latinas. In 2003, African American women constituted 12.5 percent of all working women, but only 10.4 percent of those women worked in the managerial and professional specialties. If life were equally good for all female groups, then they would find themselves proportionately represented in high-prestige jobs; that is, proportionate to their representation in the total female work force. Here, we find African American women not doing badly—with African American women slightly underrepresented in high-prestige work (they are 12.4 percent of all working women and 10.4 percent of the women in high-prestige jobs). More egregiously, Latinas comprised 10.7 percent of all working women, but only 5.9 percent of those were in the managerial and professional specialties. In contrast, white women constituted 81.2 percent of all working women but 83.1 percent of all women working in management and the professions, while Asian women represented 4.1 percent of all working women and 4.5 percent of all those women in managerial and professional occupations (Bureau of Labor Statistics, 2003g).

Table 6.1.
MEDIAN WEEKLY EARNINGS OF MEN AND WOMEN IN MANAGERIAL, ADMINISTRATIVE, AND PROFESSIONAL OCCUPATIONS BY RACIAL AND ETHNIC ORIGINS, 2001 (FULL-TIME WORKERS ONLY)

	All			White			Afr. Am.			Latino		
	Men	Women	(WM %)	Men	Women	(WM %)	Men	Women	(WM %)	Men	Women	(WM %)
All Managerial and Professional Specialty	1,038	732	70.5	1,055	736	69.8	773	658	85.1	826	649	78.6
Executive, administrative, and managerial	1,060	706	66.6	1,094	711	65.0	786	630	80.2	795	636	80.0
Officials and administrators, public administrative	1,037	738	71.2	1,054	737	69.9	844	750	88.9	1,090	667	61.2
Other executive, administrative, and managerial	1,120	728	65.0	1,138	734	64.5	769	637	82.8	770	624	81.0
Management-related occupations	942	670	71.1	961	673	70.0	808	608	75.2	793	637	80.3
Professional Specialty	1,021	749	73.4	1,025	754	73.6	768	679	88.4	864	670	77.5
Engineers	1,149	1,022	88.9	1,150	1,029	89.5	1,051	837	79.6	1,177	875	74.3
Mathematical and computer scientists	1,159	898	77.5	1,159	893	77.0	1,023	818	80.0	940	891	94.8
Natural scientists	996	758	76.1	998	760	76.2	767	700	91.3	794	730	91.9
Health diagnosing occupations	1,372	883	64.4	1,378	901	65.4	1,126	841	74.7	1,238	771	62.3
Health assessment and treating occupations	983	811	82.5	1,007	815	80.9	543	712	131.1	772	709	91.8
Teachers, college and university	1,126	844	75.0	1,122	877	78.2	1,148	760	66.2	1,159	788	68.0
Teachers, except college and university	780	707	90.6	797	720	90.3	705	632	89.6	720	638	88.6
Lawyers and judges	1,535	1,062	69.2	1,536	1,112	72.4	2,020	948	46.9	1,328	1,125	84.7
Other professional specialty	816	670	82.1	835	677	81.1	669	630	94.2	708	611	86.3

Source: Bureau of Labor Statistics, 2003d.

Today 31.4 percent of all African American working women are in management, administrative, or professional occupations.

Gender inequality in the managerial and professional specialties occurs, in part, because women tend to be newcomers in many fields and thus lack the rank and the pay that comes with seniority. It occurs because of the different educational tracks men and women take (see Chapter 4), and because of the lack of comparable-worth policies in an occupational structure that is still highly segregated by sex (see Chapter 3). But it also occurs because of the resegregation of women into lower-paying positions. Resegregation occurs when men leave certain positions and women become the statistical majority within that job category (Reskin and Roos, 1990). It results in women being concentrated in the lower-prestige and lower-paying jobs within a given profession. For example, females in medicine are much more concentrated in the specialties of family practice (three males to one female) or pediatrics (one to one), which average $130,00 and $126,000 per year, respectively, while males are much more likely to become surgeons (ten to one), who on average earn $240,000 per year (Bureau of Labor Statistic, 2003f). Women in management are much more likely to be in personnel, in which two out of three personnel managers are female, than in marketing (two out of three marketing managers are male), the former averaging a salary of $48,048 per year and the latter $56,940. One of the causes of this income gap is the segregation of the sexes that limits women to occupational positions that inherently do not pay as well as their male counterparts: "Segregation also reduces women's fringe benefits and their access to medical insurance, pensions, and Social Security income. By disproportionately relegating women to jobs with short or absent career ladders, segregation lowers a woman's chance of promotion as well. Both task and rank segregation restrict women's likelihood of exercising authority at work" (Reskin 1997, p. 69).

Sex segregation occurs when women and men are crowded into dissimilar occupations across a range of industries and jobs at multiple levels within the economy. Women perform different responsibilities or roles from their male counterparts, or may carry out the same job or role under another job description (Reskin, 1997, p. 69). Job segregation may be based on race, ethnicity, social class, gender, or sexual preference. The practice of placing workers based on these different characteristics is "one of the most enduring features of work in industrialized societies and a mainstay in preserving larger systems of inequality" (Reskin, 1997, p. 69).

Resegregation has taken place in several previously male-dominated fields. For example, in the 1980s the retail pharmacy field became resegregated (Sokoloff, 1992). The pharmacy profession began undergoing a structural trans-

Half of all medical school students today are female, though women are much less likely to enter high-paying specialties such as surgery.

formation in the years following World War II; this transformation led to drug manufacturers taking over compounding drugs and pharmacists becoming merely dispensers of drugs and record-keepers (Reskin and Phipps, 1988, p. 199). Technical skills became less important. This de-skilling of pharmacy— along with the decline of small, independently owned pharmacies and the growth of drugstore chain stores—made the occupation less attractive to those males seeking higher-paying and more prestigious work. Partly as a result, pharmacy schools stepped up their efforts to increase the enrollment of women students, and women have thus made significant inroads into this traditionally "male" profession (one in four pharmacists was female in 1983, but this rate had almost doubled by the early 2000s). Women have, however, been overwhelmingly concentrated in the retail sector, in which pharmacy has indeed become little more than pill dispensing and record-keeping. On the other hand, male pharmacists work disproportionately in the more prestigious and higher-paying research and management sectors of the profession (Phipps, 1990).

This same phenomenon—women finding themselves in the less prestigious/ lower-paying positions *within* a particular field—exists throughout the occupational structure. Even within the semiprofessions, which have been traditionally female dominated, the resegregation of women into the lower-paying jobs occurs with frequency. For example, in the teaching profession, the higher the position, the fewer the women: Women comprise 98 percent of preschool teachers, 82 percent of elementary teachers, 56 percent of high school teachers, 37 percent of college professors, and 17 percent of college presidents (American Council on Education, 2002; Bureau of Labor Statistics, 2003e).

The "Glass Ceiling" for Women in Management?

A recent federal government study on the status of women in management found a downward trend in gender equality in earnings, with women falling behind their male colleagues in pay and job mobility between 1995 and 2000 (Dingell and Maloney, 2002; also see Robertson et al., 2004). The study found that women managers' salaries decreased in seven out of the ten industries that employ three-fourths of all women managers. For example, in 1995, "a full-time female manager in the communications industry earned $0.86 for every $1.00 earned by a full-time male manager. Five years later, a full-time female manager in the same industry earned $0.73 for every $1.00 earned by a full-time male manager" (Dingell and Maloney, 2002, p. 7). Salary differentials were wider in private sector industries compared to public sector industries such as education and public administration. Women tend to be found in particular types of industries and occupations that often pay less, but allow them to combine their work and family life, such as "personnel and human relations" areas, while men were found in job such as "purchasing, marketing, and advertising" that often pay considerably more money (Dingell and Maloney, 2002, p. 9). Women are also found within areas of the corporation that are often less centralized and less powerful to a company's operations, requiring fewer years of education and typically dead-end jobs with fewer opportunities for upward mobility, even though they are labeled as "managerial" positions.

Women are further hampered in their efforts toward upward mobility by combining their work and family life, with some women limiting their careers in order to raise their families or deciding not to have children in order to have a career. The study found that "nearly 60 percent of male managers in these ten industries have children in the home, compared to little more than 40 percent of female managers (working full or part time)" (Dingell and Maloney, 2002, p.11). This statistical discrepancy suggests "difficulties in combining family and work are a significant constraint on women's attack on the glass ceiling" (Dingell and Maloney, 2002, p. 11). Women managers with young families who opt to work part time may also find themselves cut off from critical networking opportunities as well finding that they are placed in "nonstrategic" jobs with few or no benefits.

Structural Barriers to Women in the Professions and Management

There is a range of factors we need to consider in understanding why women have failed to attain the top jobs within managerial and professional occupations and why persistent wage differences by gender and race remain. One reason can be found in the specific individual-level characteristics women bring to the bargaining table: their level of human capital investment in such things as education and job training, as well as their attitudes, values, and expectations about the role of women vis-à-vis work and family issues. An "individualist" argument might readily assume, for example, that women's lack of representation in the professions and management can be attributed to women's lack of ambition or success (Horner, 1972). Current research reveals otherwise. For example, studies of women and men managers reveal that they "have similar values, traits, motivations, leadership styles, and skills and that women perform better than or equal to men" (Fagenson and Jackson, 1994, p. 395). Others point out that women's inability to obtain employment in the executive occupations partially stems from the fact that they have only recently made significant gains into middle management. More time is required for women to gain enough experience to move into executive positions. As we saw in Chapter 3, however, the "human capital theory" approach does not explain away the existing inequality in women's earnings and the sex segregation that women experience within and among occupations. Individual qualifications apart, society still holds on to many of the gender assumptions that place women at the bottom of the professional hierarchy.

As noted in Chapter 3, the blocking of women's opportunities in the professions and management has come to be known as the "glass ceiling" phenomenon. Elsie Vartanian, director of the Women's Bureau at the Department of Labor, described it thus: While women can see the next level, the "glass ceiling keeps you from grasping it. Working hard, sacrificing, and paying your dues will get you but so far. That real, yet invisible barrier can keep you from realizing that goal. It prevents you from turning your dream into a reality" (U.S. Congress, 1991, p. 5).

While white women confront a glass ceiling that may break once in a while, minority women, who face issues of racism as well as sexism, confront something more like a "concrete ceiling" (Ray, 1988). Historically, African American professionals were able to gain employment only in occupations that whites repudiated. "Thus black professionals were allowed to work in the small and often poor private sector in the black community or in a segregated public sector" (Sokoloff, 1992, p. 6). This racist segregation kept African American women in the least desirable jobs and kept their numbers in the professions and in management disproportionately small. Racial as well as gender discrimination continues to set up barriers for African American women in the professions and management. Sheryl George relates her experience as an import production manager overseeing $15 million worth of merchandise at a New York City firm, in which the management was evidently not comfortable with the notion of having an African American woman represent it overseas:

> I realized that unless I traveled abroad, following up on production and placing merchandise, I would never be more than a glorified clerk, but my superiors said that I wasn't ready. Yet, I got excellent performance reviews and most buyers and merchandise managers relied on me to resolve their problems. . . . I was not going to allow them to set me up for failure. I sat down with the president of the company and I told him straight out: "It appears that you've stacked the deck against me. Now, if part of the criteria for me to do my job is to be white, then I can't do my job, because I'm not going to be white today, tomorrow or any other day." (as quoted in Ray, 1988, p. 36)

Along with barriers to advancement, the status quo engenders special psychological difficulties for minority women, even among those who succeed. The sense of isolation and discrimination experienced by an African American woman economist is revealed in the following personal account:

> Another trap is the illusion of belonging. Although apprehensive at first, one often lets the guard down with time and becomes, at least superficially, "one of the crowd." That's until there is a need to remind you that you are, indeed, Black, female, and last. In one job situation, I felt especially close to others after a demanding report was produced on time, and then we had a cocktail party to celebrate. But the warmth and closeness were shattered when I overheard a "nigger" joke. . . . When my effort was needed, I was one of the crowd, but when the crunch was off, I was, again, just a Black woman. (Malveaux, 1979, pp. 53–54)

At a Conference on Minority Women Lawyers (Minority Women Lawyers Regional Seminar, 1979), African American women expressed concern that their very identities were threatened by becoming professional and managerial woman because the model for success was "to dress, think, talk and act as close to masculine and white as possible" (Collins, 1979, p. 11). In the minority community, there is often the sentiment that if a woman succeeds, she has somehow sold out (Flowers, 1979, p. 48; see also Benjamin, 1982).

The public sector and education have been havens for African American male and female professional and managerial workers:

> [R]igid racial barriers that limit black people's employment options in the private sector, in both male- and female-dominated occupations, keep their numbers in the private sector low. Therefore more black women, even those trained in traditionally male fields, find jobs in the public sector because there is less discrimination in hiring in this segment of the labor market. . . . Thus their professional training keeps them dependent upon the public sector for employment as teachers, social workers, nurses, and librarians. (Higginbotham, 1997, p. 243)

Public administration and education contain the highest proportion of African Americans at the management level compared to all other areas of managerial employment. While women in the male-dominated hierarchies often face strong barriers in their attempts to ascend to positions of authority or prestige, men in female-dominated occupations do not. There men are moved quickly into positions in administration. Williams has termed this phenomenon "the glass escalator," because men in the female-dominated occupations actually have to struggle to stay where they are: "Often, despite their intentions, they face invisible pressures to move up in their professions" (1992, p. 256). Thus, for example, although men comprise only 21 percent of all administrative support/ clerical workers, they constitute 34 percent of the supervisors; and, moreover, 50 percent of the administrative support/clerical workers earning more than $1,500 per week. In contrast, African American women make up 10 percent of the administrative support/clerical workforce and 11 percent of the supervisors (a significant improvement over the past decade), but only 6 percent of those earning more than $1,500 per week; similarly, Latinas comprise 7 percent of all administrative support/clerical workers, but only 4 percent of the supervisors and only 2 percent of those earning more than $1,500 per week (Bureau of Labor Statistics, 2003b, 2003e).

The glass escalator is understandable when we consider the pervasiveness of gender roles and gender stereotypes within the workplace. Men have traditionally been cast into the role of "breadwinner." Women have historically been subordinated to man's breadwinner role and have not had the autonomy to escape completely this subjugation. While the structure of the traditional family and of the workplace is shifting, the glass ceiling and the glass escalator are ways in which these traditional roles are reinforced in society. Women who enter into male-dominated occupations are already defying their "traditional" gender roles, and if they ascend up the organizational ladder they will be filling a position of power over men. While this is occurring in greater numbers than ever before, there is still a hesitance to promote women into these altogether unconventional roles. For men in the female-dominated occupations, however, the roles function in the opposite manner: "Several men reported that their female colleagues often cast them into leadership roles. Although not all savored this distinction, it did enhance their authority and control in the workplace. In subtle (and not-too-subtle) ways, then, differential treatment contributes to the 'glass escalator' men experience in nontraditional professions" (Williams, 1992, p. 261). Also operative is the fact that men who enter traditionally "female" occupations are viewed by the greater society as somehow "deviant," "feminine," or "wimpy." For them to stay within these occupations at a level below administration, they have to face potential ridicule for not having entered a traditionally "masculine" profession.

Organizational Culture, Policies, and Practices

The policies and practices of an organization often encourage sex segregation and depress wages. These "structural" factors are part of an organization's cultural climate and are important to our understanding of women's lack of success in reaching the top of professional and managerial occupations.

Organizational Culture. How individuals in an organization act, what assumptions govern their actions, and what loyalties hold the organization together are, in large part, determined by organizational culture. Certain elements of organizational culture discriminate against women. Organizational theorist Edward Schein (1990, p. 60) envisions this culture as operating at various levels of visibility. The least visible is the "preconscious" level. It constitutes the basic assumptions held by an organization concerning its relationship to the environment, the nature of social reality and the concept of truth, and the condition of human relationships. These are often things an organization "takes for granted." They are its "mental model" or deeply ingrained values and assumptions. This "preconscious level" of culture can be compared to a paradigm, or a way of thinking. A paradigm provides a conceptual window through which individual members of an organization can understand their social reality. We saw in Chapter 1 that a "functionalist paradigm," defining women's place at home and men's place at work, has been the dominant model for understanding the situation of women and men in society. While these assumptions often lie at the "preconscious" level of an organization's culture, they are powerful in structuring the day-to-day operations of the organization. Deeply ingrained traditional assumptions about the role of men and women are gender stereotypes that can serve to influence employers' behavior in a variety of ways—from hiring and evaluation to promotion practices and policies. Research has demonstrated the presence of stereotypes regarding managers within organizational environments. More specifically, "both men and women [perceive] successful managers to possess more characteristics typically associated with males than characteristics typically associated with females. . . . [W]omen managers are perceived as less aggressive and independent than their male counterparts, though typically possessing better interpersonal skills" (Northcraft and Gutek, 1993, p. 220–221).

A second and more perceptible level of organizational culture comprises the values espoused by the organization—as reflected in its mission statement, official documents, policies, and procedures. A third, most visible level, is that of artifacts—the technology and artistic and social creations of the organization (e.g., organizational symbols, designs, and ceremonies) (Schein, 1990, p. 61). At these more visible organizational levels women are also often downplayed or excluded:

> Examples of male-associated signs include dominant use of the male pronoun and other male references (such as chairman) throughout official documents, memos, and other communications. The use of motivational and other organizational metaphors that draw upon male-associated sports and military references; the use of demeaning and derogatory terms for women [in association with] . . . little or no use made of positive . . . images of women in presentations of corporate image; male control of the communications system (that is, male chair persons); formal and informal dress codes that stress traditional male notions of femininity (such as pressure on women to wear dresses rather than slacks). (Mills, 1996, p. 322)

The impact of organizational culture on women's advancement is a product of all these levels. Some organizations realize that their cultures have deleterious impacts on women, but make only cosmetic changes at the more visible levels. Unfortunately, this type of change is often of the "add women and stir" variety. What is needed is an examination of these deep-rooted and subconscious assumptions, those that seem so "natural" on the surface, as well as how they are reflected in an organization's structure, policies, and leadership.

Political scientist and lawyer Mona Harrington (1995) interviewed over a hundred women lawyers working in a variety of occupational settings. One woman partner in a prestigious law firm noted how difficult it was to be part of the male-centered culture there, for deep-rooted assumptions about a woman's traditional role were pervasive. Continually confronting these assumptions and behaviors was frustrating and discouraging:

> What I find very frustrating is, now I've paid my dues, I've climbed up the ladder, I've made partner, but I find there is still resistance to giving women a real voice of authority and really listening to what they say. . . . Even women who bring in business, who are very bright, women with very strong personalities, they're just not members of the club. . . . It's very hard to pin down. . . . The wall that you beat your head against is getting the respect, having people listen to you on an administrative matter, on promotion things, just sort of the running of the firm, and that I think women still have to a much lesser degree than men. . . . And the younger men I see coming up in the firm are no different. They're still very macho, male oriented, into male, hierarchical games. You would expect that generation to be different, but they aren't. They're still into that masculine, tough-it-out, we're-going-to-beat-the-shit-out-of-you-so-you-can-prove-to-us-that-you're-a-real-man kind of thing. It's very frustrating. (as quoted in Harrington, 1995, p. 24)

Professional women often defy stereotyped traditional gender expectations by their performance in the workplace. However, like this lawyer, they often still find themselves outside the "male culture" there. Like this lawyer, they may not be interested in playing the same "hierarchical games" that men often do. This may sometimes be perceived by male colleagues as lack of motivation or a personal flaw of the female professional, when in truth women many times do not view these as necessary or desirable on-the-job behaviors.

The Clockwork of Male Careers.   Professional and managerial occupations appear wedded to a particular view of success based on a traditional male life cycle. This "sprint" model assumes early and intense devotion to career, with employees expected to devote countless hours pursuing it. Men have been able to devote this time because they have wives at home who take care of family demands. The sprint model of career success is a deeply rooted part of most organizational cultures. The academic career, for instance,

> is founded on some peculiar assumption about the relation between doing work and competing with others, competing with others and getting credit for work, getting credit and building a reputation, building a reputation and doing it while you're young, doing it while you're young and hoarding scarce time, hoarding scarce time and minimizing family life, minimizing family life and leaving it to your wife—the choir of experiences that seems to anchor the traditional academic. Even if the meritocracy worked perfectly, even if women did not cool themselves out, I suspect there would remain in a system that defines careers this way only a handful of women at the top. (Hochschild, 1976, p. 252)

Women in these occupations find that if, as they encounter the heavy demands of both work and family, their career path veers off a "sprint" model, they—not the organizational culture—are the target of blame; it is concluded that women are less motivated, less committed to their jobs. Such "individualistic" explanations regarding women's presumed "insufficient commitment" are used by some to account for women's lack of upward mobility.

Networking ("The Old-Boys Network").   Among organizational policies and practices that tend to block women's achievement or stifle their desire to work is the existence of "old-boys networks," important informal networks of communication that have grown up in and around the male-dominated workplace. These informal networks are vital communication links for exchanging information and conducting business deals that are necessary for overall advancement within organizations (Ragins and Sundstrom, 1989; Tharenou and Conroy, 1994). A long line of research demonstrates that women are excluded from these networks (Fagenson and Jackson, 1994; Kanter, 1977). They thereby miss out on important client referrals and the like. A woman physician in her thirties who was starting a practice at a new community hospital, for example, found great difficulty in gaining physician's referrals because she was not part of tile "old-boys" network:

> I'm out of the mainstream there. I come to make rounds and I go back up here. There's a club there. A club of members, where you would have coffee together, and you would be out there politicking, bullshitting, and talking, and wasting a lot of time, and getting the referrals. I don't do any of that there, so I don't get any consults there. (Lorber, 1984, p. 58)

Similarly, a woman attorney described a related experience with this gender barrier in her profession:

> It comes down to the old boys' network—men feeling more comfortable with men—and if you're a woman you always have that as a barrier. In terms of career advancement, particularly nowadays in the private bar, the private world, people are hungry; they want people who are going to go out there and get clients, and getting those clients generally means courting or schmoozing up to people in high places. Those people in [high] places tend to be males who tend to be more comfortable with other males. So it affects your advancement, because you don't have the client contact, you don't have the exposure, and you're not bringing in as much business, which affects your advancement. (Brockman, 2001, p. 98)

Women also miss out on important ways of learning how to behave and conduct themselves. These networks are not formally recognized by the organization, so there is no way to officially mandate the inclusion of women. In many ways it is impossible to integrate women, since women are not permitted entrance into some of the places where these connections are made, such as men's locker rooms.

Mentors.   In most organizations, positions are arranged in the shape of a pyramid: the higher up one goes, the fewer the number of positions and the greater the authority, prestige, and salary. How fast an employee rises up the pyramid is partly dependent on the degree to which he or she is "groomed" for success and the degree to which he or she "networks" with influential people both within and outside the organization.

Being groomed for success means that an employee receives competent instruction on the ins and outs of doing well—not only in the technical aspects of the actual work involved, but also in the "politics" (who has influence) and "culture" (the unwritten rules of social interaction, the values that underlie these rules) of the company. This training often involves one or more "mentors"; that is, seasoned colleagues, supervisors, or bosses who take special interest in the employee and give him or her the guidance needed for success. Moreover, mentors often provide the employee with opportunities to demonstrate his or her abilities. They may "cover" his or her mistakes to minimize negative repercussions. They typically nominate the employee for promotions. Mentors are motivated to play this role because they expect their protégés to work hard and thereby make the department look good. Mentors also expect loyalty, for the protégé has become a member of the mentor's team. Many companies give recognition to mentors for helping to nurture young talent (indeed, Dow Jones, Colgate-Palmolive, NYNEX, and selected other large corporations have even formalized the mentor relationship).

The impacts of mentoring on career success are real and well documented (for a review of this research, see Greenberg and Baron, 1997, pp. 216–219; Nelson and Quick, 1997, pp. 517–520). Unfortunately, women in many organizations find themselves on the outside of this system, with no recourse to combat their outsider status. Of great interest to students of gender inequality is the fact that—compared to men—women report stronger barriers to finding a mentor (Ragins and Cotton, 1991) *and* are less willing to serve as mentors (Labrich, 1995). A fundamental principle of sociology is that likes are attracted to likes: Individuals of the same social backgrounds who have had similar experiences are more likely to form and sustain relationships than individuals from differing social backgrounds with differing experiences. Thus, males—who predominate in senior management—are more likely to feel comfortable around males. Moreover, and not surprisingly, Pierce (1995) found that many men are reluctant to mentor female employees because they fear that the close relationship built during the mentoring process will be misperceived as romance. On the other hand, women in management report a greater reluctance than their male counterparts to become mentors because they have a greater fear of failure; that is, they fear that the protégé might fail and make both herself and the mentor look bad. In sum, women are less likely than men to find mentors, which in part accounts for the glass ceiling many women hit in the corporate world.

Women denied mentorship are unprepared for many aspects of their working environment. A female lawyer just out of law school describes how she suffered from having no mentor to guide her through the details of her new job:

> The first job I'd had in my life, and it hit me between the eyes. I had no clue how to function. I got no help from the women above me. There were a few. I'm not sure what I expected them to do. . . . The men there . . . had the code down. They knew what to wear. The women entering the firm would come in print dresses. Some carried backpacks. Not to thumb their noses, they just didn't know. But the males understood that you need a Cross pen and a London Harness briefcase. The men entering conducted themselves better. They wouldn't be emotive. They wouldn't express fear, ramble on when they didn't understand something, and expose their ignorance. . . . I went on a very severe diet. . . . I didn't need to lose weight. I think that was a response of wanting to get away. I would shrink my body so I didn't have to walk into the hall. (quoted in Harrington, 1995, p. 84)

The picture for professional women and women managers is changing, and there are signs that women are developing and expanding mentor relationships. The number of formal professional and management women support organizations has grown steadily since the early 1980s, and in one 1990s survey "78 percent of senior female executive respondents reported that they were 'actively grooming' women below them for top management positions" (Northcraft and Gutek, 1993, p. 224). Nevertheless, the lack of mentorship and the denial of access to a network of important connections has historically left many female professionals in a bind. While men had networks of their counterparts to whom they could turn with questions or use for important connections, women more commonly have lacked this support. Since there were so few women in the ranks of professional workers, they were often left to fend for themselves.

Tokenism.   Until recently, and still in many organizations, women often have been only a token presence and they have had to deal with difficulties due to their lack of numbers and lack of acceptance. Because of their lack of numbers, these women stand out and are therefore watched closely; any "mistakes" they make tend to be attributed to their gender (being female) rather than to their individual personalities (e.g., "Didn't I say that a woman was too weak for this job?"). In short, female executives often feel as if they are performing within a "glass house." They are concerned that if they make an error, not only will their own advancement be limited, but it will also restrict the opportunities of women who follow them. As one woman executive described this pressure to *always* succeed: "I feel that if I fail, it will be a long time before they hire another woman for the job" (Morrison, White, and Van Velsor, 1992, p. 17).

Moreover, in an attempt to interpret the gender changes in their work environment, men often begin exaggerating differences between themselves and female workers. They test these presumed differences with sexual innuendoes and other forms of teasing, to see how the women will respond. The close scrutiny and the frequent teasing make these pioneering women feel very self-conscious and add stress and misery to their jobs (Kanter, 1977, p. 209ff.). Token women try to cope with performance pressures in a variety of ways. Some "overachieve" in comparison to their peers. This may work for those women who are exceptional in their fields, but it is unlikely to work for those without extraordinary skills. Still other women will try to use tokenism to their advantage by stressing their difference. This strategy, however, may alienate the dominant group (e.g., "For a woman, she did a great job securing that contract, she must have received help from her boss"). Others may try to make themselves "invisible"; they may go out of their way to avoid recognition for their accomplishments at work.

There are other, more successful strategies for coping. Token women sometimes establish a particular area of competence and make themselves invaluable to their organizations because of their expert knowledge (Fairhurst and Snavely, 1983). The attention they receive is focused on their "area of expertise," their competence and knowledge, and not their "gender." This is perhaps the best way to escape the negative labeling that comes with tokenism.

Rosenberg, Perlstadt, and Phillips (1997, p. 255) interviewed a sample of 220 women lawyers working in government jobs and smaller firms in a medium-sized midwestern metropolitan area. Among their most important findings was that women working in token settings (i.e., those settings in which men comprise 80 percent or more of the legal staff) reported more negative work experiences than those who were not token women. Moreover, token women were "roughly twice as likely to report differential treatment with regard to salary (51.8 to 28.9 percent), promotion (42.5 to 22.3 percent), and office facilities (34.6 to 15.3 percent). They also report[ed] significantly more discrimination in legal assignments (41.9 to 29.1 percent) and pretrial work (36.6 to 17.8 percent)—probably reflecting their typically low status and concentration in less remunerative specialties." Finally, "tokens were more likely to state they experience unwanted sexual advances (34.6 to 20.5 percent)."

Women entering corporations as tokens face a subtle sense of not belonging. A company with a few well-placed women can deflect accusations of sex discrimination, touting the notion of gender equity. However, one or a few women is not equivalent to having a number proportionate to their overall presence in the particular occupational category. These token women are left with a sense of alienation. They do not have access to some of the important facets of organizational culture and therefore are at a distinct disadvantage in comparison to their male counterparts. These women often feel as if their jobs are at a dead-end, given the way "positionality" operates within the company.

Positionality.   Even in companies with more than token representation, *where* a woman is structurally placed in the hierarchy of an organization or profession has profound consequences for her present and future performance and her promotion possibilities. For example, a woman placed in a structurally powerless job will take on attributes associated with her position. Over time, her level of motivation will decrease, she will become less aggressive, avoid taking risks, and so on (Kanter, 1977). Women who are placed in positions with few resources to distribute are locked into powerless roles. They often find their work less central to their organization. They have little contact with senior-level officials (Kanter, 1983). More often than not, women *are* in positions of low power within organizations (Kanter, 1977, 1983), as, for example, these women internists:

> The problem with women internists is that there are many of them who do "menial" jobs, who work in the general medical clinics, and do things that are not visible intramurally or extramurally. Many of them must be excellent, and they could do fantastic jobs if they were given the opportunity on a professional level and department chairman level. They probably don't know themselves how much of the potential they have because they weren't given the opportunity. They are hidden. (Lorber, 1984, p. 4)

Women may have less power in organizations even as "managers," due to the fact that they are more likely to work in departments that do not have as much power as the male-dominated occupations: "A woman who is offered the highest-ranking position in the lowest-ranking department is not likely to be on her way to the top of the company" (Lips, 1991, p. 167; also see Ragins and Sundstrom, 1989). Women are often placed in career positions with a low possibility for power. This is a central reason for why they do not move up within their respective organizations. For example, women are often placed in "nonstrategic" areas of the organization such as human resources. Wirth (2001) found that there has been an increase in the number of women in such positions. In the United States, the number of women managers in the area of "personnel and labor relations" increased from 21 percent in 1970 to 58 percent in 1991; as noted earlier, this figure now stands at 68 percent. Women find it difficult to move into the more male-dominated spheres of management such as research and development and finance. These positions are strategic in that they provide for upward mobility and higher salaries. They are the "central pathways to key executive positions in the pyramidal structure that is characteristic of large organizations" (Wirth, 2001, p. 47).

Because the majority of women occupy less powerful positions within the modern organization, it has been assumed that their lack of advancement must be due to their traditional gender-role attributes (e.g., wanting to devote more time to family over work, fear of success, wanting to work fewer hours). However, behavior is a function of position. If you placed men in a structurally powerless position, they too would exhibit the same traits thought to belong to women as a category (Fagenson and Horowitz, 1985; Kanter, 1977; and Riger and Galligan, 1980).

To more fully understand these phenomena, Fagenson (1990, pp. 270–271) argues that we need to look beyond position to the whole "organizational context, a broader concept than structure. . . . The organizational context includes such factors as the corporation's culture, history, ideology, policies . . . as well as its structure." Organizations are embedded in the wider society, with "particular cultural values, histories, societal and institutional practices, ideologies, expectations, and stereotypes regarding appropriate roles and behaviors for men and women." As this wider society can also affect the ways women are viewed and treated within an organization, with this approach, more variables in women's ascension up the corporate ladder are accounted for and a more accurate picture is drawn. For example, affirmative action laws and maternity leave policies can directly affect women's chances for advancement and how women are viewed within their organization.

Summary

While the numbers of women working in the "professions" and "management" have grown substantially in recent years, the aggregate data are deceiving. The jobs and subspecialties in which women work and the treatment that they face continue to reflect a "gendering" of work based on traditional stereotypes of men's and women's roles.

Women in the professions and management often face "job resegregation" that places them in positions having the least amount of money, job prestige, and security. In addition, women may find they are hired only as tokens without mentors. Women in professional and managerial occupations may be subject to gender-based discrimination from their male colleagues. They may experience a "glass ceiling," and lack the power or resources with which to move up the organizational ladder.

Minority women, blocked by racial discrimination as well as gender, often face a "concrete ceiling." Although the barriers to white women are slowly being broken down, those that exist to impede minorities remain extremely prevalent in the private sector.

These organizational barriers are quite tangible, though they are often dismissed as unreal. This dismissal has the effect of removing the focus of analysis of the problem from the institution onto the individual. Women who do not advance are pronounced unable, unwilling, or insufficiently motivated. An "individualistic" explanation of women's lack of advancement permits organizations to continue to simply "add women and stir," without addressing the deeply ingrained traditional gender-role assumptions that affect women's employment opportunities. Masculine organizational culture permeates many business and professional institutions and often creates barriers to the career advancement of women. A female executive who has a different managerial style and attitude toward her job may be considered "deviant" by dominant masculine organizational culture. Her actions may be interpreted as "wrong" or "ineffective," and she may be considered unqualified to hold an upper-level position. Challenging these gendered assumptions is the first step to gaining any true advances for women beyond tokenism. Change, however, must take place at the structural level of the corporation and profession. The glass and concrete ceilings that block women's advancement must be shattered. Females in the professions and management need to be given equal resources and on-the-job training. They must have access to mentors and the informal routes of communication within the organization, both of which are essential to upward mobility within and among organizations.

In addition, women professionals and managers need to come together to create a system of mutual support. This is not to suggest the creation of an "old-girls network" that might further divide the workplace between women and men. A women's support system could, however, create a way in which women who have been left out of a mentorship system could "learn the ropes." It could be an important step toward the dissolution of the old-boys network and the creation of a sense of community in the workplace instead of a divided workforce.

These changes will not occur in a vacuum. Stereotypes in the wider society must change as well. As long as society views women in terms of their traditional gender roles, they will not be able to escape this labeling within the institution. The assumption that women are to bear the most responsibility for housework and childcare burdens women in society and within the workplace. Placing these responsibilities almost entirely on women oppresses female professional and managerial women, as well as others, with the double duty of work and domestic labor.

There must also be a commitment by corporations to enforce the statutes that mandate equal treatment for women and a workspace free from sexual harassment. Corporations can no longer be permitted to "get by" with token female representation or a lax policy toward sexual harassment. Corporations that go out of their way to be "family friendly" should also receive societal recognition for their efforts to help families combine work and family obligations. Corporations that only put up a facade of equal employment and opportunity, without genuinely following through on these commitments, need to face public reprisal, perhaps even being branded as "dead-beat corporations."

All of this will come about only if there is a commitment by society in tandem with corporations to challenge traditional gender stereotypes and an effort by the individuals within and around the corporations to force this change.

World Wide Web Resources

A 1998 article from *The Magazine of the International Labor Organization* concludes that "while substantial progress has been made in closing the gender gap in managerial and professional jobs, for women in management it's still lonely at the top." See: http://www.ilo.org/public/english/bureau/inf/magazine/23/glass.htm.

The National Organization of Women has a "Women-Friendly Work Place Campaign" link that speaks to many of the issues brought up in this chapter (e.g., tokenism; the old boys' network); see: http://www.now.org/issues/wfw/index.html.

Since 1996, The Glass Ceiling Web site has provided valuable articles and other resources on this topic; see: www.theglassceiling.com.

7　Working Women and Their Families

[H]ere, you see, it takes all the running you can do to keep in the same place. If you want to get somewhere else, you must run at least twice as fast as that.
　　　　　　　　　　　　　　　　　—Lewis Carroll (*Through the Looking Glass*)

The family has long been thought of as a private space separated from the public world and the economy. Only in the last three and a half decades, with the emergence of the women's movement, have families been addressed as part of the public sphere. For, indeed, there is a dynamic interaction between work and families. The ways in which the economy and workplace are organized affect family life. Conversely, the ways families are arranged, and specifically the opportunities offered and the constraints placed on women within them, affect women's experience in the workplace.

The idea that families are separated from the rest of society is a vestige of an ideology that arose to rationalize and justify the rapid changes taking place as a result of industrialization. As we have seen in Chapter 2, the development of industrialization produced a spatial and temporal separation between work and activities that took place at home. As part of society's adjusting to these rapid changes, a new ideology separated women from men, placing the former in the private, family sphere and the latter in the public, work sphere. However, this ideology was highly problematic to many: Not only did some upper- and middle-class women find it restrictive, but most African American and working-class women could not live up to it. Today, with 60 percent of women in the labor force, this separation has become even more a myth.

Even though this ideology has not matched reality for many, it has unfortunately had an enormous power in shaping the ways social scientists and policy makers have confronted work/family issues. The functionalist paradigm (see Chapter 1), so prevalent in this century, is based on these ideas:

> If any one statement can be said to define the most prevalent sociological position on work and family, it is the myth of separate worlds. The myth goes like this: In a modern industrial society, work life and family life constitute two separate and non-overlapping worlds, with their own functions, territories, and behavioral rules. Each operates by its own laws and can be studied independently. . . . A corollary of the myth is the assumed separation of men's and women's domains, with the family, woman's place. (Kanter, 1977, pp. 16, 20)

The "myth of separate worlds" has resulted in distorted interpretations of women's and men's lives. Only recently, with the dramatic economic and demographic changes of the past few decades, which have affected the work and fam-

ily lives of so many white, middle-class women, have researchers been prompted
to challenge this myth and expose the interconnectedness of work and family.

Despite this new conceptualization in research, similar changes in public
policy have not occurred. Cultural and social policies continue to adhere to a
"separate worlds" model, and corporations continue to be geared toward the
traditional family model. This cultural and institutional lag is creating a growing dissonance between family and work. Our outmoded values and institutions
are resulting in stresses and problems, in conflicts and overloads for women and
men in their work and family roles, as well as in their relationship with each
other. Many modern American families are living a "quasi-schizophrenic existence" in which traditional family roles are increasingly impossible to maintain
in light of the demands of the workplace (Googins, 1991).

It is women who most feel the tensions of this quasi-schizophrenic existence.
They are the ones who are most caught up in the dilemmas involved with both
having a family and being a worker. Massive increase in women's employment
and occupational attainment in the labor market during the twentieth century
has been seen as revolutionary. However, there has not been an equivalent revolution in the household. Women have not been relieved of the primary responsibility for childcare and domestic tasks. This has been a missed or "stalled
revolution" (Hochschild and Machung, 1989). Consequently, America's working women are tired. In the U.S. Department of Labor Women's Bureau (1994)
survey "Working Women Count!," American women put "too much stress" at
the top of their list of workplace problems. And in the fall of 2002, the Gallup
Organization found that 65 percent of working mothers, compared to 55 percent of working fathers, reported that they have "little time to relax" (which also
points out that the modern world of work is stressful on working fathers as well
as on working mothers, even though survey data reveal that combining work and
family roles takes greater toll on women than on men; see Jones, 2002).

But are stress, fatigue, and unfairness for millions of women all that is at
stake? No, for as we will see, there is a direct relationship between women's unequal position in the household and women's unequal position in the economy
and society. Each reproduces and perpetuates the other; each becomes an outcome of and a rationale for the other.

Inequality in the labor force is closely linked to women's double day. Because women's second shift at home is extremely costly in time and energy,
men's employment, hindered less by responsibilities at home, becomes propor-
tionally more important and rewarded. The wage gap thus obtained then encourages men's commitment to work and discourages women's. Because men
will earn on the average more than women will, a family's prospects will be improved when the man devotes his time and energy to paid employment. Therefore, the division of labor in the home is in part structured by the workplace.
Labor-force segregation, the wage gap, and employer expectations and policies
promote the notion that housework and family are mainly women's responsibilities, and that men are—at best—to give a helping hand. Once this is established, children grow up expecting this pattern to be repeated for them. This
further recreates a gendered division of labor in the home and perpetuates
women's economic dependence on men.

Employed mothers are much more likely than employed fathers to be responsible for cooking, cleaning, shopping, and childcare.

The situation for single mothers, and sometimes for women who earn more than their male partners, is somewhat different. These women cover the roles of both primary provider and caretaker—and consequently (especially for single mothers) may be subject to even more stress and fatigue. The move toward single motherhood has been especially pronounced among African Americans, Latinos, and Native Americans (see Figures 7.1 and 7.2). For example, in 1999, two-thirds (68.9 percent) of all African American births were to unmarried women, and nearly half (44.0 percent) of all African American families were headed by females (U.S. Bureau of the Census 2001d; 2002a, p. 59).

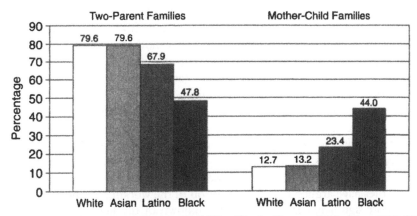

Figure 7.1. Two-Parent and Mother-Child Families by Race and Ethnicity, 2000. Note that Latino rates for mother-child families vary considerably among national origins, with Cubans having the lowest rate (18.3%) and Puerto Ricans having the highest rate (35.8%); Mexicans (21.1%) and Central and South Americans (24.6%) fall in between. *Sources:* U.S. Bureau of the Census (2001c, 2001d, 2001e).

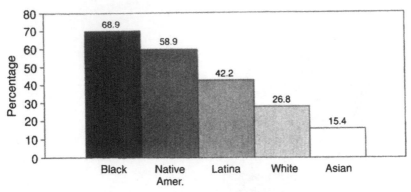

Figure 7.2. Percentage of Births to Unmarried Mothers by Race and Ethnicity, 1999. Note that Latino rates vary considerably among national origins, with Cubans having the lowest rate (26.4%) and Puerto Ricans having the highest rate (59.6%); Mexicans (40.1%) and Central and South Americans (43.7%) fall in between. Also note that the Asian rates vary considerably by national background, with Chinese having the lowest rate (6.9%) and Hawaiians having the highest rate (50.4%); Japanese (9.9%) and Filipinos (21.1%) have rates that fall in between. *Source:* U.S. Bureau of the Census (2002a).

A wide variety of survey data gathered over the past decade supports the notion that women suffer both materially and emotionally when they try to combine their traditional caregiver status with their new status of being in the paid workforce. For example, a third of U.S. working parents agree with the statement that "at my place of employment, employees have to choose between advancing in their jobs or devoting attention to their family or personal lives"; about the same percentage agree that "there is an unwritten rule that you can't take care of family needs on company time"; and nearly 40 percent agree that "employees who put their personal or family needs ahead of their jobs are not looked on favorably" (Galinsky and Bond, 1996). Well over a third (38 percent) of U.S. adults disagree with the statement that "a working mother can establish just as warm and secure a relationship with her children as a mother who does not work," even a more (47 percent) agree with the pronouncement that "a preschool child is likely to suffer if his or her mother works" (NORC, 2000). In short, given the traditional and still existing cultural standard that women are to be the primary caregivers to children (and aging parents, too), such workplace norms and wider societal beliefs take a heavier toll on women than they do men, and cannot help but contribute to gender inequality.

Despite the enormous amount of psychological and emotional stress placed on working mothers today, it remains very important to discuss the positive effects that this movement of women out of the domestic sphere has had on both children and the society at large. Those with more traditional attitudes toward gender roles have argued that the evolution of the working mother has been the single most significant factor in the breakdown of the family structure in the United States. Nearly fifty years of research on this issue has, however, demonstrated otherwise. These studies have shown that maternal employment itself has not been a fundamental factor in determining the well-being and achievement levels in children. Rather, issues such as the marital status of the mother, the sex of the child, and most critically the family's socioeconomic position tend to be the deciding factors (Hoffman and Youngblade, 1999, p. 1). According to Hoffman and Youngblade (1999, p. 281), a mother's employment *does* have a substantial impact on her children, *however,* this impact has been shown to be distinctly positive. Such beneficial effects of dual-earner families include "a less gender-stereotyped division of roles" as well as a "higher motivation for achievement, and more academic competence for girls." Indeed, the majority of stable families accommodate a mother's employment without too much difficulty. Fathers simply tend to assume more housework and childcare responsibilities, thus providing a very healthy environment for children to grow and mature (Hoffman and Youngblade, 1999, p. 280); and, in fact, "although employed married women spend more time on chores than employed married men do on both workdays and days off work . . . this gap has narrowed quite substantially over the past twenty years" (Bond et al., 1997). Other researchers have shown that children can benefit from having a working mother and that family ties can be strengthened by maternal employment. For example, in a dual-earner family the children will be compelled to interact more with their fathers due to the simple fact that their mothers will absent from the home for hours at a time. When questioned about the impact their employment had on father-child relationships, 58 percent of young mothers in a sample of middle-class white Americans responded that the effect was "unequivocally positive." An even higher percentage of men in the sample agreed (Eastbrooks and Goldberg, 1988, as cited in Crosby, 1991, p. 140). There tends also to be a greater amount of valuable interaction between children and grandparents when both the mother and father are employed, many times for childcare reasons. And, as a function of the growing need for quality childcare comes the benefit of interpersonal contact among children of different dual-earner families. Children attending high-quality childcare centers "show benefits in their intellectual and emotional development as a result of contact with other children and adults outside of the family" (Crosby, 1991, p. 141). Finally, and of the utmost importance to the breakdown of traditional sex-role assumptions, is the effect that dual-earning families has on children's social development in understanding gender. A significant number of studies on the sex-role attitudes of children of housewives versus those of employed mothers reveal "rather compellingly that children lose some of the rigidity of their sex-role stereotyping when they have mothers who play the provider role as well as the nurturer role" (Crosby, 1991, p. 141). This serves to create a much more egalitarian perception of gender in the children of working mothers compared to those of housewives.

In sum, in addition to benefitting from a much needed second income for American families, the children of dual-earner parents can benefit in various ways from not spending all day and night with mom. They are forced to strengthen relationships with their fathers, their extended family, and even can excel in their social development as a result of contact with other children in childcare facilities. Thus, the argument that working mothers are disrupting family harmony does not comport with the research on the dynamics of dual-earning households. Rather, under the proper conditions—such as good childcare and the availability of time by other relatives to spend time with the children—the family structure can be strengthened when the mother is employed (Crosby, 1991, p. 144).

Because women's responsibilities in the home are so central to understanding women's position in the economy, we next examine housework as women's work and as women's double burden.

Impact of Industrialization and Capitalism on Housework

Housework is the shared experience of most women. Few American women today are full-time homemakers. According to the General Social Survey (NORC, 2000), only one in five (19 percent) of them are. Nevertheless, housework is still women's responsibility (whether they do it themselves or, sometimes, arrange for it to be done by others); it is women's work. Both working mothers and working fathers readily agree that women take on the lion's share of family and homemaking responsibilities, including the cooking, cleaning, shopping, bill-paying, and care of children (see Tables 7.1 and 7.2). Notwithstand-

Table 7.1
EMPLOYED PARENTS' DIVISION OF FAMILY WORK BY SEX

Family Work Area	Mothers	Fathers	Overall
Cooking Responsibility:	(n = 180)	(n = 212)	(n = 392)
Respondent	82.5	11.3	44.0
50–50 split	3.9	12.5	8.6
Spouse	13.5	76.2	47.4
Other	0.0	0.0	0.0
Cleaning Responsibility:	(n = 180)	(n = 212)	(n = 392)
Respondent	81.4	5.8	40.5
50–50 split	10.0	24.4	17.8
Spouse	8.5	69.9	41.7
Other	0.0	0.0	0.0
Shopping Responsibility:	(n = 180)	(n = 212)	(n = 392)
Respondent	89.2	11.3	47.1
50–50 split	7.5	27.1	18.1
Spouse	3.3	61.5	34.8
Other	0.0	0.1	0.0
Bill-Paying Responsibility:	(n = 180)	(n = 212)	(n = 392)
Respondent	66.6	32.5	48.1
50–50 split	14.6	17.1	15.9
Spouse	17.1	49.5	34.6
Other	1.7	1.0	1.3
Childcare Responsibility:	(n = 165)	(n = 192)	(n = 357)
Respondent	67.6	5.4	34.1
50–50 split	20.1	33.2	27.2
Spouse	12.3	61.4	38.7
Other	0.0	0.0	0.0

Source: Families and Work Institute (1992).

Table 7.2
AVERAGE NUMBER OF HOURS SPENT PER WEEK ON
HOUSEHOLD-RELATED WORK ACTIVITES BY SEX

Activity	Women	Men
Meals	7.8	2.5
Dishes	4.9	2.0
Cleaning	6.1	1.9
Shopping	2.5	1.4
Laundry	4.0	0.8
Outdoor and Maintenance	1.5	5.0
Auto Repair	0.2	1.7
Bills	1.5	1.3
Driving Others	1.5	1.1
Total	30.0	17.7

Note: all respondents married.
Source: Adapted from Hersch and Stratton (2000).

ing the dramatic changes that have taken place in the last century, womanhood and housework are still linked, much as they were in the nineteenth century. Our lives today are still shaped by aspects of nineteenth-century ideologies. The organization of household labor has not kept up with women's massive entry into the labor force. It is thus anything but surprising that the cry and plea of many working women is "I need a wife too."

In our culture, unpaid work means invisible work. As we saw in Chapter 1, housework is invisible to economists: It is not included in GNP estimates. It has also been invisible to social scientists for a long time: It was not until the emergence of the women's movement in the 1970s that studies of housework from women's perspectives were begun (Oakley, 1974). Still today, it is largely ignored by policy makers, who view housework and childcare as a private concern. Furthermore, housework is not only invisible, it is often not even considered "work." That is, many still view it not as labor but as a matter-of-course feminine activity.

A division of labor by gender existed in previous historical periods, as we have seen. However, although men and women performed different tasks, their labor was equally valuable to family survival. What then caused this diminishment in the value of housework? What has led people to say, "She doesn't work, she's only a housewife"?

Industrialization and capitalism have played a major role in establishing women's subordinate position in the household and in the economy. Capitalism has exacerbated preexisting gender inequality. Together, industrialization and capitalism have been major causes of housework's invisibility and consequent devaluation.

Housework was changed by industrialization both materially and ideologically. Industrialization diminished the economic value of women's work at home and rendered it invisible. Two factors have contributed to this diminishment: family dependence on men's wages and technological advances easing the physical burden of housework. With the advent of industrialization, the production of goods was taken outside the home and the importance of men's wages increased. Although industrialization had a greater initial effect on the household labor of men (taking them away from the home to the factory and office), with time women's domestic labor was also affected. Appliances and manufactured products for household consumption became available and affordable, and women's responsibilities shifted from household production to consumption and childcare management. Although technological advances made housework lighter, they also contributed to making women's household labor less visible and less valued.

The material changes brought about by industrialization were underscored at the ideological level through the cult of domesticity and the ideology of separate spheres. These reinforced the public/private split and the separation between work and family. Magazines and advertisements portrayed housework as women's responsibility. Women were shown as naturally suited for housework and men for employment. Today, we can witness vestiges of this ideology in some men's comments about the "natural talent" of their wives or companions for doing laundry or washing the dishes. Furthermore, because housework today includes a variety of tasks, ranging from physical to emotional, and because of the intangibility of some tasks (such as giving support, sustaining a conversation, caring for young and old family members), housework has come to be equated with what women are, not what they do. Housework is gendered. Housework is by definition women's work.

Women's Double Day

With 60 percent of women in the labor force, increasing numbers of women combine paid and domestic work. The "double day" refers to the combination of paid and unpaid work done by these women (Hochschild and Machung, 1989). Unpaid work—women's "second shift"—includes cleaning, shopping, cooking, childcare, care for the elderly, and emotional labor. The greatest difficulty for women with a double day is finding the time for both types of work. These women report being constantly pressed for time, and feel that their quality of life is greatly diminished by their attempts to shoulder work and family demands. Women in the double day sleep less. They talk about sleep the way a hungry person talks about food (Hochschild and Machung, 1989, p. 9). One major study on how parents balance work and family found that working mothers "are more stressed, coping less satisfactorily in their lives, more burned out by their jobs, less satisfied with their marital relations, and less satisfied with themselves as parents" (Galinsky and Bond, 1996, p. 80).

Time-budget studies vary as to the specific number of hours of housework done by women and their partners. Nevertheless, what most studies seem to confirm is that the division of labor in the household is far from equitable: Housework is still for the most part women's responsibility. Summarizing six famous studies on the division of household labor, Coverman (1989) came to the following conclusions: (1) wives spend two to four times as much time in domestic labor as husbands, even when they are employed; (2) wives perform three to four times as many tasks as husbands do; (3) wives do about 75 percent of all domestic tasks; (4) employed wives spend less time on housework than nonemployed wives; (5) full-time housewives spend over fifty hours per week on housework and childcare; and (6) employed wives average twenty-six to thirty-three hours per week doing housework. These conclusions are generally consistent with current data—as presented in Tables 7.1 and 7.2—even though these data show a narrowing of the gender gap in housework.

Hochschild and Machung (1989) also averaged estimates from the major time-budgeting studies for married couples and found that women work fifteen hours a week more than men do (note that this is slightly more than—but still consistent with—more current data, as, for example, the numbers presented in Table 7.2). This additional work adds up to an extra month of twenty-four-hour days a year. Since most of the time-budgeting estimates on the household division of labor have been calculated based on white married couples, the actual hours women work in the double day are probably higher (Andersen, 1997, p. 136). Inclusion of African Americans, Latinos, and Asians would raise the hours, since women in these families are more likely to work outside the home and to hold more than one job. Having a husband in and of itself tends to increase the amount of housework, for married women spend more time in domestic labor than single heads of households (Hartmann, 1981). Husbands generate more dishes and laundry than they clean up. The term "husband care" refers to the difference between housework generated and housework done by husbands.

It is not surprising that there is a "leisure gap" between men and women at home: Married women tend to have less discretionary time than their spouses do (Hochschild and Machung, 1989). As a consequence, women are consistently more time stressed than men are. They sleep less and are more likely to suffer from physical and emotional strain. There are fewer men who say they are severely pressed for time, and the life stage of starting a family and raising children does not seem to affect men's levels of stress. All this is an indication of the uneven burden placed on women.

Not only is there a discrepancy in the number of hours of work done by men and women, there is also a qualitative difference in the kinds of domestic tasks they perform. Even within housework, there is such a thing as "women's work" and "men's work." Women are most likely to cook, wash dishes, do laundry, clean the house, and take care of children. On the other hand, men do most maintenance and repair work (see Table 7.2). Hochschild and Machung (1989) have outlined three major differences between "his" and "her" work. First, women's work comprises mostly daily jobs and time-bound jobs. Men's jobs are time-flexible. Children must be fed every day at a certain time, whereas oil changes can be scheduled at the most convenient time. Thus, men have more discretion in the allocation and distribution of their time. Second, women often do more tasks at once. They prepare dinner while keeping an eye on a toddler, whereas men perform solitary tasks like changing the oil in the car or mowing the lawn. Third, women seem to carry the primary responsibility for the temporal coordination of family activities. Women are the "time-and-motion experts." They juggle the schedules of all family members, try to get everyone out the door to school and work every morning, and arrange for pick-ups and drop-offs throughout the year.

Generally, American men are doing more housework than they used to, and American women less. Over the past two decades, married mothers' hours of housework have declined from about thirty to about twenty hours per week; however, "married fathers picked up only part of the slack, increasing their household work from about five hours a week to about ten hours" (Spain and Bianchi, 1996, p. 169). The presence of a young child at home may increase men's domestic contributions (Shelton, 1992; Thompson and Walker, 1991). Younger and better-educated men with less traditional gender-role beliefs are more likely to participate in housework (Ross, 1987; Waite and Goldscheider, 1992). Some research reveals that African American and Hispanic men do slightly more work than other men do (Hossain and Roopnarine, 1993; Shelton and John, 1993; Taylor et al., 1991; Willie, 1985), but other research shows they do less (Stohs, 1995, 2000). The historically greater likelihood of African American mothers being in the labor force has not encouraged a degree of egalitarianism within African American families that one might have otherwise expected. There is little doubt, however, that stereotypes of men of color being uninvolved with household work or childcare are not supported by social science research. Moreover, in the case of African American fathers, it appears that that the degree of involvement with their families tends to depend little upon social class. For example, Kelley's (1997) study of low-income African American couples with children found results similar to Hossain and Roopnarine's (1993) study of African American dual-earner families of moderate means. Men report performing less childcare than their spouses or partners, but poor African American fathers "appear at least as involved as majority (white) fathers in caregiving activities" (Kelley, 1997, p. 97). African American males in low-income families also report involvement in household chores, primarily engaging in traditionally "male work" such as car repairs and outdoor jobs (Kelley, 1997, p. 97). These data challenge traditional stereotypes of African American males as unstable fathers lacking commitment to their families. In short, while like fathers of all races, they do not equally share in childcare and household chores, their level of involvement with their families is substantial (Hossain and Roopnarine, 1993, p. 581; Kelley, 1997, p. 98).

Within Latino families, some research suggests there is less support for equitable sharing of the division of labor within the household and a stronger belief that men should serve as the "breadwinners" of their families (John, Shelton, and Luschen, 1995). This said, however, other research reveals that Latino families are more egalitarian than the ideal of machismo and prevailing stereotypes suggest (Baca Zinn, 1976; Mirandé, 1979; Ybarra, 1977). Similarly, there is greater egalitarianism in Chicano couples in which both partners work (Ybarra, 1982).

Stohs (2000) conducted a study of 400 multicultural women (of African, Asian, Hispanic, and Middle Eastern origins). The women completed a questionnaire on the household division of labor and perceived conflicts over this division, including the type and frequency of conflicts. The amount of arguing in multicultural marriages was significantly more than that found within white marriages, with 73 percent of multicultural women reporting an argument that week versus 58 percent of white women reporting the same. From the Stohs's study, it is also evident that, in general, multicultural women are doing more household labor. They report spending sixteen hours on housework compared with twelve hours reported for the white sample. Nevertheless, their satisfaction the household division of labor is higher compared to their white counterparts (Stohs, 2000, p. 258).

As for nontraditional households, lesbian couples tend to be more egalitarian and flexible in their work arrangements than gay and heterosexual cohabiting couples (Blumstein and Schwartz, 1983; Kurdek, 1993; Reilly and Lynch, 1990). Compared to their heterosexual counterparts, lesbian couples with children are more likely to share tasks equitably and less likely to find themselves with a lopsided workload falling on the shoulders of one partner (Sullivan, 1996). It is important to note, however, that in families that adopt traditional roles of one partner working and one raising the family, the partner staying at home loses status—just like mothers in heterosexual relationships. This demonstrates that the distorted image of the stay-at-home mom does not change with same-sex families (Sullivan, 1996, p. 764). The fact remains, however, that lesbian nuclear families tend to share household and childcare labor more equally (Patterson, 1995a, 1995b; Sullivan, 1996).

Wives in households with an egalitarian division of housework report greater satisfaction than those who do all of the housework. Women who receive help with housework from their husbands are usually more satisfied with their jobs than those who do not (Krause and Markides, 1985). Employed women whose husbands cooperate by doing their share of household tasks and childcare indicate a higher degree of well-being—fewer depressive symptoms, less anxiety, greater life satisfaction (Stripling and Bird, 1990). This is true of husbands as well. Men who share more of the family work are less distressed than those who do not. Men who are the most distressed are those who remain traditional in their gender-role attitudes and behavior and try hardest to resist change (Pleck, 1985).

It is usually up to women to persuade men to help with the chores. Indeed, women have the extra job of soliciting "help." They must negotiate for more sharing from husbands and male partners. This usually involves changing their own mindset and standards about how meals should be prepared, groceries bought, clothes washed, and diapers changed to better fit with husbands' ways of doing things. Husbands typically resist by "disaffiliating themselves." This involves exaggerating their inexperience and incompetence by performing tasks in a clumsy and distracted way—"a male version of playing dumb" (Hochschild and Machung, 1989, p. 201). Disaffiliating oneself also includes delaying chores or "dragging one's feet" and out-waiting one's wife. Waiting for women's request for a help is a very successful strategy of resistance. Because asking for help can be a veritable extra chore in an already stressful day, some women find that often it is just not worth the effort. Moreover, some husbands respond to requests for help by becoming disagreeable and irritated. Sometimes men resist by downplaying the need for certain tasks, substituting offerings, or selectively encouraging their wives (Hochschild and Machung, 1989). For example, they might argue that there is no need for a home-cooked meal or no need for clothes to be ironed. According to some men, women have an innate talent for housework, enjoy it more, or have a greater need for clean clothes, household order, and balanced meals. Other men might alleviate the tension caused by their lack of contribution to housework by giving emotional support to their wives. Husbands may praise their wives' efficiency and organization to get out of certain tasks ("darlin' no one can do dishes like you can").

What About the Children?

As noted earlier in this chapter, a significant portion of Americans believe that working mothers end up hurting their children emotionally. Hoffman and Youngblade (1999) studied the impact of working mothers on children's well-being by interviewing the mothers, fathers, and children in 369 families with elementary school children. The sample drew from a broad spectrum of income levels and from several race/ethnic backgrounds (including African American, Latino, and white). The sample also represented working and nonworking mothers in both intact, two-parent families as well as in nonintact, single-mother families. Finally, evaluations and reports by teachers were gathered; for example, teachers were asked to rate a child according to his or her "likeability" by classroom peers. Most of the findings of this study can only be characterized as showing benefits for children. For example, when a mother goes to work, there is a corresponding increase of the father's involvement with children and housework. Children, especially girls, exhibit cognitive advantages when they spend more time with their fathers. One reason for this is that fathers tend to have different areas of interest—such as mathematics, mechanics, fixing, and repairing. Moreover, a father's involvement in childcare has a positive outcome on a child's academic performance (Hoffman and Youngblade, 1999, p. 282). "This finding held true across ethnic groups . . . and for the subgroup of children living in poverty." Moreover, among children with married mothers, teachers rated children with employed mothers as having fewer learning problems than children with nonemployeed mothers (Hoffman and Youngblade, 1999, p. 168). Finally, the Hoffman and Youngblade study found that the children of working mothers are less likely to manifest traditional attitudes concerning gender roles. For example, they are less likely to stereotype activities such as childcare, cooking, and cleaning as "women's work."

This same kind of positive developmental outcome for children also tends to occur when the children of working parents are given over to daycare. More specifically, daycare centers can provide children with "interpersonal resourcefulness and resilience" (Crosby, 1991, pp. 140–141). These benefits are most evident when families have the economic resources to afford "high-quality" daycare.

Perhaps the greatest benefit to children with a working mother is their exposure early on to a world where they have more options concerning their work and family roles. In short, these children are less likely to manifest rigid sex-role stereotyping. A mother's working opens up the possibility for transmitting new values and ideals about women's gender roles to the next generation, especially when children also see this accompanied by changes in the division of labor within their own households (Hoffman and Youngblade, 1999, p. 281).

Unfortunately, as we shall see, these benefits to children are sometimes at the expense of working mothers' emotional and psychological well-being. At the end of the day, the pressure of work in combination with the stresses of home (the "second shift") can be extremely demanding

Men's Resistance to Housework

Why do men resist housework? Why do women perceive the status quo to be fair (if they do)? Why is it that housework is divided unequally? Several theories and explanations have been advanced to answer these questions. Evidence shows that the more work a woman does for pay, the greater her bargaining power within the marriage and the less housework she will do (Blau and Ferber, 1992). Indeed, the likelihood of sharing household responsibilities rises with a wife's income. The smaller the discrepancy between what a woman earns and what her husband makes, the more equal the marital power structure and the more egalitarian the family decision making (Bird and Bird, 1984). However, the higher the husband's income, the greater the likelihood that the wife will do all of the housework. These data support what is known as rational economic theory, in which the rules governing the division of housework are tied to relations of economic support and dependency. According to this view, wives continue to perform most domestic work because they earn less than their husbands. Thus, the wage gap in the workplace reinforces the traditional division of labor, since wives' time spent in the paid labor force is worth less than men's.

A competing view is that, the more wives work outside the home, the more traditional the division of labor within the home, because men and women will struggle to define appropriate gender roles within the family. Housework is thus a "symbolic enactment of gender relations" (South and Spitze, 1994) and households are "gender factories" (Berk, 1985). The gendered division of labor provides a constant way in which people can reaffirm who they are and how they relate to others (West and Zimmerman, 1987). Men who feel that their gender role as provider is threatened can reaffirm their masculinity by refusing to perform certain tasks traditionally assigned to women. For example, they may refuse to wash the dishes. Indeed, men who are out of work or in low-income households do less work the more they depend on their wives for income (Brines, 1994). On the other hand, women may reaffirm their femininity by washing dishes. A wife's employment may paradoxically reinforce the traditional division of labor when housework is the primary way in which gender is defined by a couple, for instance, when a wife earns more than her husband (Brines, 1994). The division of labor in the home thus reaffirms women's subordination to men (Berk, 1985). Housework is one of the means by which gender is strengthened, perpetuated, and created in our society.

The unequal division of labor in the home can also be explained with socialization theory. As discussed in Chapter 4, gender socialization is the process by which children acquire their gender identity and learn appropriate gender behavior. Boys and girls learn how to behave as boys and girls. They learn what is expected of them when they become adult men and women. One way children are socialized is through adult models. Because children are more likely to see women performing housework, children will grow up associating housework with womanhood. Furthermore, parents assign household tasks differentially to their sons and daughters. After the age of five, girls on the average do more housework than their brothers, and the gap widens as children grow older (White and Brinkerhoff, 1987). This division has important implications for future families: If boys are not required to learn how to perform certain tasks and to be responsible for housework, it is less likely that as men they will increase their domestic contributions. Finally, the gendering of toys and games can also encourage boys and girls to learn or not to learn domestic skills. Boys usually play with athletic equipment, military toys, and building equipment. Girls' toys are usually miniature housework tools such as toy stoves, dishes, dollhouses, cooking sets, vacuum cleaners, and the equipment necessary for baby care (Shapiro, 1990). Boys play football and war games; girls play house. These artifacts and activities teach girls the mechanical skills and the attitudes and sentiments associated with housework and domesticity. In part, therefore, the unequal division of labor is reproduced through socialization.

Men may resist the increasing social and marital pressures to share housework because they receive mixed cultural messages about their family involvement (Pleck, 1985). There is a general societal belief that men's primary responsibility is bread-winning and that family involvement is positive only as long as it does not interfere with a man's primary obligation as provider. Bergen's (1991) research has shown that as a result of these societal forces, men's devotion of time to employed and domestic labor tends to remain constant, even when faced with variations in economic need. Women are thus obliged to pick up the financial shortfall by increasing their workload. When children enter into the situation, a mother's division of both paid and domestic labor becomes hard to manage. She often cuts back her involvement in the labor force while the need for home work increases by a factor that is more than the time freed by the out-of-home work reduction. Unfortunately, many workplace policies in the United States do not make effective accommodations for such work and family issues (Bergen, 1991, p. 141). Furthermore, men in particular receive little support from their coworkers and supervisors for being involved with their families. Family-oriented men are seen as less committed to their jobs. Some research suggests that fathers who spend more time with their families may be given mixed signals on the job from both coworkers and their boss. While some at work may consider it admirable for a male colleague to want to spend more time with his family, especially to show his more "nurturing" side, others may tend to view this as a lack of commitment to the organization or even a sign that he has become "emasculated." It has been suggested that "the personal adjustment of the more active father, and by extension the adjustment of the dual-earner family, is determined in part by how well he can withstand the view of others about his family role" (Kerpelman and Pittman, 1993, p. 99). Thus, men who share housework and participate in family roles do so at some cost to their egos, in addition to their careers. This is especially risky for men in blue-collar occupations who are responsible for their family's economic survival. It is clear that work practices and policies and societal attitudes must change to accommodate the need for men to be more involved with their families.

According to Hochschild and Machung (1989), three fears are at the root of men's resistance to housework: the fear of losing decision-making power in the family, the fear of losing face with family members and friends, and the fear of losing control in the marital relationship. Men whose work life is not satisfactory resist work at home as a way of "balancing scales" with their spouses. Men who make less than their wives resist housework as a way of regaining power in the relationship. Lastly, men do not want to give up the privilege of having a homemaker wife. They report not being brought up to believe in an egalitarian division of labor, or they say that their work lives are too draining to take on added responsibilities.

Women's Coping Strategies/Individualistic Resolutions

There are a number of coping strategies available to women. These are individualistic strategies in that they are adopted in the attempt to solve the work/family dilemma at the micro level. Although these are strategies women choose to adopt, we should not forget that individuals make their choices within the limits of the society in which they live. Furthermore, although these strategies are attempts made by individuals to cope with certain problems, they also have major repercussions at the societal or structural level. In other words, we should not forget that there is a continuum between individual and society and between families and the workplace.

We can divide these strategies into three categories: demographic, occupational, and situational. Demographic strategies focus on the family and include women's decisions and plans concerning marriage and fertility. Occupational strategies focus on the workplace and involve women's work arrangements and career choices and aspirations. Lastly, situational strategies are aimed at coping with and improving the situation at hand. These involve such solutions as hiring out and efficient time management. Very often, a combination of these strategies is adopted. However, as we will see, each of these strategies is problematic.

Hiring household help is a common situational strategy, although not accessible to everyone. Two-career couples with high-paying jobs can afford it, but most working couples cannot pay for this luxury. Women hiring help find that babysitting and housekeeping are expensive services, especially in comparison with their own paycheck. In turn, the relatively poor pay received by babysitters and housekeepers reinforces the low prestige of these occupations and further exploits women who are in them. In fact, although hiring a maid may eliminate the inequality in housework between a man and a woman, it may reinforce the problem of inequity across class and race, between employer and maid—for currently, as historically, most domestic workers are minority women of the working class. Since domestic work as it is structured nowadays is especially devalued, low paid, and oppressive, hiring help may not necessarily be a good "solution" to the problem of gender inequality in the division of labor (Ehrenreich and Hochschild, 2003; Rollins, 1985; Romero, 1992).

Other situational strategies include limiting the number of obligations, learning to say no at home and on the job, delegating certain responsibilities, and managing and planning for events and changes in one's life (Bliss, 1976; Fensterheim and Baer, 1975; Hall and Hall, 1979; Lakein, 1974). Writers on time management stress the use of a daily "to do" list, which specifies and orders the tasks one may realistically hope to accomplish on a given day. Next to each task, one ranks it in importance, as A, B, or C. One then starts to work with the A-1 task and continues with it until completion. If interrupted, one needs to weigh the interruption against the importance of the task, by asking "Can I afford to take time out?" Although time-management strategies can help dual-earner couples, the schemes are often mechanistic in their approach. Many of the techniques were originally devised for business organizations to increase the efficiency of their employees. Treating the dual-earner couple like a business organization can promote the "superman" and "superwoman" notion that one can "have it all" if only time is managed more effectively and efficiently.

Delaying marriage and children and/or having fewer children are some of the demographic strategies women adopt. Women are spending fewer years married. The realization that they will likely do most of the housework may contribute to their reluctance to marry or remarry (Spain and Bianchi, 1996). Women may try to marry men who will share the housework. This may involve "marrying down" (Mahony, 1996) or marrying men with egalitarian gender ideologies. Women are also limiting their fertility and postponing childbearing. Many women in professional jobs either postpone children until they are established in their careers or have fewer children than they might otherwise. An increasing number of employed women are opting not to have children. Among officers and directors of Fortune 500 companies, for instance, few men but 40 percent of women are childless (University of California at Los Angeles/Korn-Ferry, 1993). The crossnational data tell a similar story. For example, "a survey among managers in Germany in 1997 found that 43 percent of women managers were unmarried compared to only 4 percent of men managers. A similar survey in the United Kingdom found that 88 percent of men managers were married, compared to 60 percent of women in the same position" (United Nations, 2000). Throughout the world, highly educated women and women in the labor force have the lowest birth expectations and the highest expectations for childlessness (Spain and Bianchi, 1996).

One of the most common occupational strategies women adopt is to choose jobs that accommodate family obligations, making employment and parenthood easier to reconcile (Feiner and Roberts, 1990). Secretarial and clerical jobs are typical occupations that permit easy entry and reentry, with minimal skill and wage loss after a period of unemployment. Here we can see how this individualistic adaptive strategy has consequences at the macroscopic level: Occupational segregation is in part perpetuated by women's attempts to combine work and family (Polachek, 1981). Employed women also try to work closer to home than men; indeed, despite great changes in women's career goals and their actual entering into the paid labor force en masse over the past several decades, nearly one in two women report that they would prefer to have a stay-at-home job so that they could take care of the house and family—a rate that is twice as high as it is for men, and a rate that has changed little over the two-and-a-half decades (see Table 7.3). Convenience may be a factor in accepting a job (Rutherford and Werkerle, 1988). The assignment of priority to proximity and their status as secondary wage earners limits women's job choices, and their information network on jobs is typically based more locally than men's. These factors often result in the reproduction of occupational segregation (Spain and Bianchi, 1996).

Part-time jobs and flextime schedules are other occupational strategies used by women in their attempt to balance work and family. Women often choose part-time jobs because of their compatibility with child rearing. However, this decision comes with great economic costs in terms of wage-rate erosion, loss of seniority, and often loss of benefits and job security. Flextime refers to flexible work schedules that allow workers to balance the demands of work and family life. Although flextime would seem to address the problems parents are facing, it is not an ideal solution. First, it is flexible for both employees and employers. Employees may be asked to work a different schedule every week, which interferes with their ability to plan other activities. Second, flextime may entail that the number of hours worked as well as the schedule be flexible. This can mean that employees must always be on call in case their employer needs them, or that sometimes they do not get enough work. Third, if the number of hours varies, pay also varies. Employees on flextime may earn less than they need, first because they are working fewer total hours, but also because they may earn less

Table 7.3
PERCENTAGE OF WOMEN VERSUS MEN PREFERRING TO
WORK OUT OF THE HOME, BY SEX (1983, 1994, 2001)

Year	Women	Men
1983	47	21
1994	47	15
2001	45	24

Gallup Organization survey question: "If you were free to do either, would you prefer to have a job outside the home, or would you prefer to stay at home and take care of the house and family?"
Source: Gallup Organization (2003).

per hour. Although flextime has been shown to reduce tardiness and absenteeism and has increased productivity (Sullivan, 1984), it is not—in the way it is currently structured—a solution to work/family problems. Flextime needs to be accompanied by reliable and sufficient wages and benefits, and the decision to reduce hours needs to be made voluntarily by the employee (Hartmann, 1991; Negrey, 1990).

Another occupational solution was put forth by Felice Schwartz, President of Catalyst, an organization interested in improving women's access to high-level jobs. Schwartz (1989) proposed that employers distinguish between women who are "career primary" and those who are "career and family." Women who are "career primary" will not interrupt their careers for children and can therefore remain on the fast (male) track. On the other hand, women who are "career and family" will be placed on a career path with less demanding work schedules and slower promotions: the mommy track. Mommy trackers could be allowed to stay in middle management and avoid the pressure of excelling and competing for promotions. Although, at first, this may seem an ideal solution to the work/family dilemma, there are several problems with it. First, the mommy track may help women balance their work and family lives, but it diminishes them in the workplace by reducing their pay and prestige. Second, whereas the track might be chosen by some women, others might be pushed into it by their employers. Thus, the mommy track might legitimate discrimination against women. Third, it has been noted that higher-level jobs, compared with middle- and lower-level jobs, actually give employees more flexibility and authority to create solutions to work/family problems (Glass and Camarigg, 1992). Finally, the mommy track rests on the assumption that family is women's work. It leaves unaltered and indeed reinforces the traditional, unequal division of labor in the home, while perpetuating sex differences in promotions, prestige, and authority in the workplace.

Structural Solutions

We have examined how women with families are individually coping with workplace problems. There are also structural solutions—solutions that have been put forth by the state and by employers regarding ways in which the workplace is adjusting to family demands. Some of these solutions, such as flextime, part-time work, and the mommy track, have already been discussed. Indeed, these solutions represent both strategies adopted by the individual and solutions or options made possible by the workplace. In this section, we will focus on two other important ways in which the workplace is attempting to accommodate the family obligations of employees: the Family and Medical Leave Act and childcare. In both cases, we will see that current arrangements are problematic and inadequate and that further efforts are needed at the public-policy level.

While most industrialized countries offer paid parental leaves to their citizens, until 1993, when the Family and Medical Leave Act was signed, the United

States did not mandate job protection for pregnancy and childbirth. Family sociologist Phyllis Moen notes that the explanation for this lack of family-based legislation can be attributed to some deep-seated ideologies within American political culture. Until 1993, the federal government had always been unwilling to pass any legislation that bridged the divide between home and workplace. Since the nation's origin, the people of the United States have maintained what has come to be known as the "doctrine of two spheres," which regards the home as a distinctively private realm, a place where children are instilled with values and belief systems, and a place primarily the province of wives and mothers. As such, any intervention by the state into the domestic realm, regardless of the potential benefits of the legislation, had been minimal (Moen, 1992, p. 6). The promotion of traditional values like free enterprise and individualism has resulted in keeping family initiatives out of the political forefront. Such laissez-faire principles in American society have most often served to grant economic interests precedence over anything else, including the welfare of the family. This was made clear in 1990 when former republican president George H. W. Bush vetoed the first attempt to pass the Family and Medical Leave Act because of the threat it posed to the business world (Moen, 1992, p. 6).

However, with the eventual signing of the Family and Medical Leave Act in 1993 by democratic president William Clinton, all public sector employers, as well as those private sector companies with fifty employees or more, are now required to grant their workers up to twelve weeks of unpaid leave after childbirth or adoption—given that the employee involved has worked for the public agency or private company at least one year (1,250 hours in the preceding twelve months). Leave is also available for personal illness or to care for a seriously ill family member. An employee taking leave is guaranteed the same job or a comparable position upon return and is entitled to receive health care benefits while on leave. Although this bill is important because it guarantees that people will not lose their jobs as a result of their personal and family obligations, it has several significant drawbacks. First, about a third of the workforce is not eligible because the private sector businesses involved are too small (fewer than fifty employees); another significant proportion does not meet the length of service requirement; the result is that four in ten employees are ineligible for family leave (U.S. Department of Labor, 2003). Second, there is the problem of economic access: Because the leave is unpaid, it is not accessible to everyone. Many workers cannot survive without their paychecks. Third, the act's definition of family is problematic in that it leaves out same-sex domestic partners. Last, the leave may reinforce the existing sexual division of labor. On account of the earnings gap, the leave is economically more advantageous for women than for men. A survey of the 1,000 largest U.S. companies found that, although 31 percent offered paternity leave, only about 1 percent of employees took advantage of it (Robert Half International, 1990). Because of these drawbacks, the act has been seen as having a placebo effect on addressing the problems of working families (O'Brien and Fassinger, 1993). A recent U.S. Department of Labor study revealed that "significant minority of employees . . . have expressed a need for leave that as yet remains unmet. Among employees who need but do not take leave, fully 63.9 percent cannot afford the accompanying loss of wages, underscoring the importance of wage replacement. Hourly workers, African Americans, and employees with some college education are most likely to be among those employees who need, but do not take leave" (U.S. Department of Labor, 2003, p. 5). In short, for family leave to be a real solution to the work/family problems facing many women (and men), it must be paid and it must be made available to employees of all companies.

Childcare is one of the most difficult and stressful problems working parents must face. Since more and more mothers of preschoolers are in the workforce today—many of whom need to be there for economic survival—this problem is even more critical than ever. Presently, difficulty in obtaining reliable and affordable childcare is one of the major reasons women give for their inability to enter the labor force. Due to their limited resources, poor families have fewer childcare options than affluent families. Poor mothers with low education are the ones who suffer most. Lack of marketable skills makes poor women less likely to get jobs that pay enough for affordable childcare. This, then, becomes a vicious circle: Without work, poor women cannot afford childcare and, without childcare, poor women are unable to work. Therefore, the image of the welfare mother as lazy is cruel and shortsighted. If policies were to provide affordable childcare to low-income women, their labor-force participation would increase and public assistance costs could be reduced (Mason and Kuhlthau, 1992). As it is, poor families typically rely on relatives and friends for childcare. Puerto Rican and African American single mothers who have relatives between the ages of sixteen and sixty-four and other young children at home are more likely to be employed than other single mothers who lack this support (Figueroa and Melendez, 1993). However, these women are more likely to be absent from work if these caretakers become unavailable (O'Connell and Bloom, 1987; Wilkie, 1988). Moreover, nondaytime and shift work (such as janitors, cashiers, truck drivers, cleaners) have been the fastest growing job sectors in the last decade, yet the majority of childcare centers continue to be available only weekdays from 8 a.m. to 6 p.m. Finally, at present, when low-income children are placed in a childcare center, as often as not the center is "inadequate or minimally adequate in meeting their developmental needs" (Coley, Chase-Lansdale, and Li-Grining, 2001, p. 6).

While some businesses are now offering on-site or near-site childcare and other related benefits, they remain a minority. Only about one in twenty-five of all employers (private and government) currently provide direct subsidies or on-site (or near-site) childcare (Bureau of Labor Statistics, 1997i, 2003f). A larger percentage provide a childcare benefit to be used at centers off-site. In total, about 14 percent of all workers receive either direct or indirect childcare assistance. It should be noted that such assistance is much more common in the public sector and in large companies than in smaller businesses: 17 percent of government workers, 15 percent of the employees in companies with a hundred or more employees, and 5 percent of workers in businesses with fewer than a hundred employees receive employer assistance for childcare (Bureau of Labor Statistics, 1995a, 1997i, 1997j, 2003f; King and Baker, 2001, p. 5). However, small companies—those with fewer than a hundred employees—employ 43 percent of workers in the private sector (Headd, 2000). Furthermore, companies favor skilled workers (managers and professionals) in their allocation of childcare benefits; for example, in businesses employing a hundred or more workers, 15 percent of the professional and technical staff receive childcare benefits, but the equivalent percentages for clerical and sales (7 percent) and blue-collar and low-level service (3 percent) employees lag far behind (Bureau of Labor Statistics, 1997j). In short, the better educated, higher-skilled workers are given more access to childcare. In the early 2000s, professionals were four-and-a-half times more likely than clerical and sales workers and six-and-a-half times more likely than blue-collar and low-level service workers to have access to childcare-related employment benefits (Bureau of Labor Statistics, 2003f; for earlier, but similar, data related to educational attainment, see Kleinman, 1993).

Because of its structural repercussions, it has become increasingly clear that childcare is not a private concern but a public issue. It is evident that a policy at the national level is needed. Affordable childcare is the most important issue for families with employed mothers (U.S. Department of Labor Women's Bureau, 1994), yet the United States is the only industrialized nation that does not have comprehensive and integrated childcare policies (Kamerman and Kahn, 1991). Instead there is a patchwork of laws that leave many working parents, especially those from the lower middle-class, under constant financial and emotional stress to provide adequate care for their children. Mothers who qualify for TANF (Temporary Assistance to Needy Families, the new federal welfare program that replaced AFDC/Aid to Families with Dependent Children in 1997) are now guaranteed subsidized childcare; however, TANF benefits are federally mandated for a maximum of only five years, which has been reduced to just two years in several states (see the next section for further discussion of TANF). Federal tax laws provide for a dependent-care tax credit; however, the credit generally covers only a small portion of total childcare expenses, and only three in ten parents use it (Galinsky and Bond, 1996, p. 95). The tax laws also allow employers to set up reimbursement accounts, which allow employees to set aside pretax funds to defray childcare expenses; however, such accounts are generally available only in the public sector and in businesses with over a hundred employees—and all told, only 30 percent of workers have access to them (Bureau of Labor Statistics, 1997i). The upshot is that 96 percent of working parents pay for childcare entirely out of their own pockets; at $60 to $70 per week during the mid-to-late 1990s, these expenses represent about 9 percent of annual household income for middle-class families, but 27 percent for poor families (Galinsky and Bond, 1996, p. 95; Peters, 1997, pp. 280–281). Although data are not available by race and ethnicity, given our documentation in earlier chapters of the inequalities suffered by African American and Latino workers, it can be assumed that for them childcare expenses are even more burdensome.

The Impact of Welfare Reform

As the twentieth century ended, one of the most crucial social issues under heated debate was welfare reform. Voters were demanding a revamping of welfare, and they applied increased pressure on politicians to change the welfare system. It is important to note that much of this pressure was a result of the media and its constant portrayal of the welfare mother as too dependent on the current welfare system and overall as a drain on society. As a result, in 1996 the Personal Responsibility and Work Opportunity Reconciliation Act (PRWORA) was signed by President Clinton, thus ending sixty-one years of federal welfare benefits to poverty-stricken families (Hays, 2003, p. 5). Welfare reform, Congress announced, would "end the dependence of needy parents on government benefits by promoting job preparation, work, and marriage" (U.S. Congress, 1996, PL104-193). What this legislation did was provide welfare programs at the state level with federal funding in amounts that matched those years having the maximum national caseloads (1992 to 1995). This included a 10 percent average budget increase, as well as a considerable amount of federal funding for more and better-quality childcare facilities and welfare-to-work programs. As a result of this legislation, welfare was renamed, as noted earlier, TANF (Temporary Assistance to Needy Families), and it emphasized the public demand that all able mothers receiving government benefits engage in the paid labor force or go to school. The legislation dictated that no one receiving assistance could use the lack of childcare for not going to work or finishing school; that is, it required states to make childcare provisions for TANF recipients (Hays, 2003, p. 4). However, as noted, TANF benefits cannot last more than five years according to federal law (with exceptions for hardship cases that, for example, involve abuse), but they can and have been reduced to only two years in Arkansas, Idaho, and Indiana—and to just twenty-one months in Connecticut.

In the five years following PRWORA, welfare rolls declined by over half, from 12.2 million recipients to 5.3 million recipients by 2001. However, despite the apparent success suggested by these numbers, many believe that the new policy has been overly harmful to poor women and their children. Advocates for the poor are concerned about taking away the one critical economic safety net for this population. Most specifically, children's advocates, feminists, and other observers point out "that welfare reform specifically target[s] women, children, and a disproportionate share of nonwhites, thus adding to the hardship of those who already face widespread discrimination" (Hays, 2003, p. 6). In addition, some have argued that the welfare policy itself arose out of a climate in which welfare itself had become "racialized":

> Politicians have blamed black mothers who must rely on welfare for nearly every social problem in the United States, including violent crime; the illegal drug epidemic; the decline of families, communities, and schools; the growth of rampant immorality; and even poverty itself. Black mothers receiving welfare have been cast not simply as prototypical villains, but as a collective internal enemy that threatens the very foundation of U.S. society. They are por-

trayed as dishonest and irresponsible individuals who purchase bottles of vodka with food stamps intended to help feed their children, or as immoral and promiscuous individuals who are said to breed children to rip off the welfare system for more benefits. (Neubeck and Cazanave, 2001, p. 3)

However, if one looks at the statistics of who in fact was on welfare the year PRWORA was passed, the percentage of African American families was nearly the same as that for white families: 37 percent compared to 36 percent (Neubeck and Cazenave, 2001, p. 5). Poll after poll of the American population reveals that it has a "racialized" view of welfare recipients, as well as stereotypical views of their behaviors on welfare. For example, in a poll conducted by the Anti-Defamation League, 35 percent of whites stated that "African Americans preferred welfare to work" (Nuebeck and Cazenave, 2001, p. 5). In another poll conducted by the National Opinion Research Center, three-quarters of the white sample stated that African American were less likely to want to be "self-supporting" than whites (Nuebeck and Cazenave, 2001, p. 5).

Has welfare reform achieved its goals? If one sees the primary goal of TANF to cut welfare rolls, it can be argued that it has been a great success. On the other hand, if one sees the goal of welfare reform to decrease poverty, the outcome has been much less than a great success, as well as more complicated to determine. For example, in the years immediately following the estabishment of TANF, the economy was booming and there were plenty of employment opportunities to allow welfare recipients to move off public aid. However, recent years have seen many families having to return to public assistance, as the economy has taken a downturn. Moreover, even though many women left welfare to take jobs, "their income often rose little because families must substitute earnings and other sources of income for welfare payments" (Hofferth, 2002, p. 45). Also, when many women were eliminated from state aid programs, they were required to pay for the entire amount of such necessities as housing, childcare, and health care, thus further decreasing their net earnings. Former recipients of public aid are required to earn much higher incomes to pay for these expenses, in large part because the jobs mothers are employed in are those that do not offer such benefits (Hofferth, 2002, p. 45).

The post-AFDC era has been marked by increasing criticism regarding the availability of quality childcare for low-income families. One major study has shown that low-income parents face much greater obstacles than wealthier families in acquiring good childcare. These roadblocks consist of unaffordable daycare, limited childcare options for nonstandard shift work during evenings and weekends, lack of transportation, and a higher chance of living in a low-income neighborhood that has few licensed, high-quality childcare facilities (Coley et al., 2001, p. 1). Similar results have come about with the advent of "family-friendly" policies that many companies have adopted since the inception of TANF. More often than not, low-income families do not have access to the benefits of such policies, despite the fact that they need them more than anyone else. Indeed, the Families and Work Institute has concluded that "workers who most need benefits such as child care and flexible hours are the least likely to get them" (Holcomb, 2000, p. 102). The Institute's research has demonstrated that low-wage mothers are "half as likely as managers and professionals to have flextime, less likely to have on-site child care, more likely to lose a day's pay when they must stay home to care for a sick child, [and] three times less likely to get company-sponsored tax breaks to help pay for their child care" (Holcomb, 2000, p. 102). Finally, women who enter the workforce at entry-level, low-paying jobs find it next to impossible to be granted paid maternity leave. Benefits such as these—in the rare times that they do exist—seem to be reserved only for higher-status and managerial employment positions. The Family and Work Institute's research coheres with the findings of the federal government's most recent National Compensation Survey, which shows, for example (as noted earlier), that professional workers are six-and-a-half times more likely to have employer-assisted childcare than blue-collar and service workers, and twelve times more likely to be offered flextime (Bureau of Labor Statistics, 2003g).

In sum, the legacy of TANF remains unclear. Welfare rolls have been cut in half, and many former recipients have successfully entered the workforce. However, poverty rates in the early 2000s have been rising (see, for example, Proctor and Dalaker, 2002), and, many, if not most, of those poverty-stricken women who have left welfare continue to struggle financially: Living-wage jobs with benefits remain difficult to find (Cancian and Meyer, 2000; Waller, 2003). As the discussion here reveals, many of the conditions of the post-welfare vision, such as quality childcare and tax breaks to companies with family-friendly policies, have tended not to benefit those who need them most. Low-income families have the greatest need for such benefits, yet evidence shows that this has not been the case thus far. What has occurred since the reform of the welfare system is that many poor families have remained just that, poor.

Where Do We Go from Here?

We have seen in this chapter that the growing tensions and challenges posed by work and family are met only in part by individualistic strategies. We have also seen that the existing structural solutions are far from adequate. Where do we go from here? To solve the work/family dilemma, we as a nation need a coherent approach to corporate and public policy, as well as a radical shift in cultural values and attitudes. We must recognize that to live in a more humane society and to improve the quality of our lives, we need to alter our gender-role attitudes and behaviors, bringing them into balance with the reality of labor-force participation for both sexes. We need to adapt the institutions of work and family and our attitudes about them to the realities of modern life.

A necessary precondition for responding effectively to the work/family conflict is the recognition that work and family issues do not pertain only to women. On the contrary, work/family conflicts affect just about everyone. While wives are struggling to balance household and childcare responsibilities, husbands are facing new expectations and responsibilities in the home. Children are spending more time in the care of people other than their parents, and aging parents are also feeling the impact of these changes. The myth of separate spheres has resulted in an erroneous framing of the problem as a women's issue. A reflection of this can be seen in the comment of a management consultant when asked about the work/family issues at his company: "Work/family is not an issue because there are no women in this firm" (Bailyn, 1993, p. 8). A solution to these challenges will only be found when this issue is reframed as a universal one.

The recognition that more and more families are dependent on two incomes and that women are needed in the workplace must be counterbalanced by the acknowledgment that men have responsibilities for family work. Corporate and public policies that merely enable women to combine work and family leave men's roles unaltered. If policies are gendered in this way, they can hurt women by reinforcing their subordinate position in the labor market and in the home (Bergmann, 1986). We need social policies that recognize that men's family roles must be changed. Fatherhood in America must change. This involves overcoming the expectations of corporate America that job responsibilities, not family, always have top priority; men must be free to "father" without sanctions from the workplace. To accomplish this, corporate policies should create alternatives to the male career model (the continuous, full-time work that constrains men from full involvement in their families). This change will be achieved only if employers allow true flexibility in hours and places of work, as well as in long-term career pathways. The male model of work should be one of many genuine options from which to choose.

We also need to rethink how we can strengthen the status of poor women and their children. Current efforts to reform the welfare system have not fulfilled the promise of promoting economic independence for the majority of women on the welfare. Finding a job has not led to economic self-sufficiency and the number of children living in poverty has begun rise in recent years. The replacement of AFDC by TANF has removed the safety net women and their children once had, and it is not clear what, if anything, will take its place.

Another condition that would help create a balance between work and family is a greater valuing of women's work. Occupational segregation by gender as well as the persistent earnings gap create a situation in which women's heavier domestic responsibility is legitimized on account of their lack of economic and bargaining power. The unequal division of labor in the household could be altered if genuine attempts were made to remunerate men's and women's work equally. A redistribution of power in the household can be accomplished only within a general redistribution of power within society at large. This can be achieved by increasing the number of women in politics and other positions of power to guarantee that family needs are a priority on the public agenda.

In conclusion, solutions to issues of balance and equality in work and family will be found only when we rethink our basic gender-role assumptions and offer choices of life scripts open to both men and women. This change entails revising the assumption that housework and child rearing are women's responsibility. Insofar as women enter the labor force "with their house on their heads" (see: Matthaei, 1982), women will be at a disadvantage in the workplace and consequently in society. For women to achieve equality, effective structural resolutions must be adopted. These involve the creation of policies and services that change both the workplace and the family and make them equally the domains of both men and women. Housework would then not be seen as "women's work" and men would be free to "father" without sanctions from the workplace. We need to recognize that our family life must be protected and promoted, and that caregiving, one of the most basic human acts, must be cherished and equitably shared.

World Wide Web Resources

A large number of studies on the relationship between work and family can be found at Cornell University's Couples and Careers Study: http://www.blcc.cornell.edu/cci/current.html.

The Family and Work Institute sponsors research and a host of activities related to the balancing of work and family for both men and women: http://www.familiesandwork.org/.

The National Partnership for Women and Families promotes fairness in the workplace, access to quality affordable health care, and policies that help women and men meet the dual demands of work and family: http://www.nationalpartnership.org/index.cfm.

The Women's Rights Division of Human Rights Watch fights against the dehumanization and marginalization of women and promotes women's equal rights and human dignity: http://www.hrw.org/women/.

8 Changing the Lives of Working Women

Eleanor McMahon . . . started teaching at a junior high school in Pawtucket [Rhode Island] in 1950. Several years later she married and resigned for personal reasons. At the request of the superintendent, she returned to teaching in the fall of 1955, only this time she was assigned to a Pawtucket elementary school. Her pay was reduced from $3,600 to $2,400 a year, but not because she was teaching at a lower level. When she got married, she lost her status as a regular teacher and become a "permanent substitute"—a policy in the Pawtucket schools at the time. . . . "It seems like we lived in another century," McMahon said.

In the fall of 1964, a month after she started teaching at a Warwick [Rhode Island] elementary school, Marsha Berger and her husband found out that she was pregnant. She promptly told her principal, who notified the district's administrators. They asked her to resign when she started to "show." Seeing no alternative, Berger agreed. "There was no such thing as maternity leave," Berger recalled.

"Teaching was seen as women's work" [before 1970, according to Professor D. Scott Moloy of the University of Rhode Island]. "We didn't pay women anything to run the households. Why should we pay them anything to run the schools?"

In those days, teachers, most of whom were women, had few rights and worked at the mercy of their employers.

—Elliot Krieger and Elizabeth Rau (1998)

The Women's Movement

Of all the social movements of the 1960s and following decades (e.g., black civil rights, Latino rights, gay rights, anti-war), the feminist crusade has probably had the most far-reaching historical impact (Burns, 1990, p. 168). The various political women's groups, most powerfully represented by the National Organization of Women (founded in 1966), pushed for and won dozens of important national-level legislative acts, court decisions, and executive orders that have led to growing equality between the sexes. Today, in consequence, the above-described treatment of women employees like Marsha Berger and Eleanor McMahon seems incredible and outrageous. As documented in Chapter 5, equal rights victories of the women's movement have gone hand-in-hand with a lessening of inequalities in wages and occupational prestige.

The women's movement has perhaps had its most dramatic impacts on the attitudes and behaviors of young women since the mid-1980s. Their reality is fundamentally different from that of their mothers. More specifically,

> few young women expect to spend their lives as full-time housewives; few accept discrimination against women as justified and inevitable; few consider battering and sexual assault something women want or deserve. Most are aware

that opportunities for women in politics and the professions have increased substantially over the past decade; most expect their husbands to share housework and child care. . . . The sense of changeless repression, of constant pressure for women to become kitchen-bound domestic servants that animated young feminists in the late 1960s, is not reflected in the experience of younger women today. (Ferree and Hess, 1985, pp. 181–182)

The movement has also had a significant impact on young men, especially in their roles as fathers. Although it does not negate the findings we presented in Chapter 7 on women's "second shift," one large-scale study of dual-career families revealed that men are now sharing in household chores and childcare at unprecedented levels (sponsored in the spring of 1998 by the Families and Work Institute; see Lewin, 1998). In the mid-1970s, men spent 30 percent as much time as women on workday chores; by 1998, this percentage rose to 75. In 1977, working mothers spent an average of 3.3 workday hours caring for and doing things with their children—and they spent about the same in 1998. However, working fathers increased their average workday hours spent with children from 2.0 to 2.3 hours. In the words of Ellen Galinsky, president of the Families and Work Institute (the survey's sponsoring organization), "you look through all these numbers and you begin to hear a theme song about men and women. There are real changes in what men and women are doing" (as quoted in Lewin, 1998, p. A-4). The findings of the Families and Work Institute are buttressed by those of the Cornell Couples and Careers Study; for example, this study of 1,062 dual-career couples found that men are just as likely as women, even women with young children, to take advantage of company programs intended to help employees balance their work and family responsibilities, including taking advantage of on- or near-site childcare, personal/dependent-care leave, parental leave with pay, flextime, telecommuting, and time off for volunteering (see Still and Strang, 2003).

In sum, the women's movement and feminism have realized much success over the past three-and-a-half decades, gaining greater gender equality in virtually all of society's major social institutions. But there is new turf on which to strive for further change. Although within the movement there are diverse strands (from liberal feminism wanting to achieve equal opportunities for men and women within existing social institutions, to radical feminism wanting to create new institutions specifically for women), it is united in wanting to redefine the nature of modern work organizations. As we have seen, the American workplace is still based, in large part, on the notion of the traditional family— that there will be one family member (usually the husband) devoted to the workplace and another family member (usually the wife) devoted to the home. Individuals with childcare or elder-care responsibilities are at a disadvantage. Some women have tried to adapt by working part time, but most have found that their workplaces "are intolerant of part-time employees, who often function without benefits and without reasonable career paths" (Christensen and Gomory, 2003, p. viii). Other women—mainly professionals and others from the middle or upper-middle classes—have adapted by shifting much of their caregiving responsibilities to poorer women (Ehrenreich and Hochschild, 2003). But those women staying behind to render caregiving personally, as well as those women paid to do so, "are shortchanged in pay, pensions, insurance, and other benefits" (Ferree and Hess, 1994, p. 207). Thus, the women's movement is now seeking ways to give caregivers more economic, social, and psychological rewards.

Because race and ethnicity correlate with social class so strongly in the United States, the women's movement is also seeking to become more inclusive, reaching out from its traditional white, middle-upper-middle class base to African American, Latina, Asian, and other minority group women. As the movement matured and won so many of its early battles, many feminists began to realize the irony of affluent and mostly white women propelling themselves forward economically by way of the meager wages and benefits they were giving to the poor (mostly minority) women they hired to act as housekeepers and caregivers.

Judith Rollins (1985) was one of the first to document not only that domestic workers received low wages, no paid vacations, no sick-leave, and no Social Security (even though, by law, the employers of domestics are supposed to pay Social Security taxes), but that their affluent employers (mostly white professional women) were generally indifferent to these working conditions. Moreover, Rollins (1985, p. 130) found that immigrants were preferred because "they had come from hell" (as one employer put it) and were consequently more vulnerable, more subservient, more obsequious—all highly desirable qualities from the employers' perspective. Indeed, the "essence of the employer-domestic relationship [is] that employers appreciate some forms of deference and outward signs of subservience" (p. 147). Qualities considered undesirable include being too educated, too intelligent, too materially well off, or too attractive. Research like Rollins's has forced the women's movement to begin emphasizing the transformation of women's ideas concerning one another, and thereby attempting to eradicate the psychological exploitation that is part and parcel of the economic exploitation of women; such eradication implies breaking down barriers between and among women across the lines of social class, race, religion, ethnicity, and sexual preference.

The strategies the women's movement will use are partly dictated by what has and has not worked well in the past and what women learn from one another when they embrace their diversity, as well as looking at what is reducing gender inequality in other societies. Thus, for example, efforts at promoting comparable-worth policies have waned in recent years due to the resistance (discussed in Chapter 3) of both private industry and government (even though 45 states and 1,700 local and county governments adopted some form of pay equity policy during the 1980s); many feminists are themselves against the idea because they see it as reinforcing gender stereotyping of occupations rather than breaking down gender barriers in the workplace (see Blum, 1991). On the other hand, the notion of making benefits universal has become particularly attractive in recent years because it would do away with backlashes from groups being denied benefits, and, additionally, help eradicate the condescending attitudes (paternalism/maternalism) that programs directed only at women, the poor, or racial/ethnic minorities encourage. Thus, for example, making government-assisted childcare universal promotes the interests of all social classes and all minorities, as well as the interests of both mothers and fathers. So would making family leave time available to both working mothers and working fathers, as was partly accomplished by the 1993 Family and Medical Leave Act, which requires employers of more than fifty persons to grant unpaid leaves of up to twelve weeks a year to any employee to meet family obligations.

The controversies surrounding the issues of flextime and "job sharing" exemplify the kinds of internal struggles the women's movement must sort through. Flextime allows workers to work longer than normal hours on some days, some weeks, and shorter than normal hours on other days, other weeks; job sharing (two individuals sharing one job) cannot only give a working woman a degree of material benefit, but also allow her to keep her foot in the water, so to speak, so that she can keep up with the ever-changing character of many technical occupations and professions. The notion of having great flexibility in structuring one's workweek is appealing to most working women with heavy childcare and related family responsibilities, and it is especially appealing to middle-class and professional women. However, the labor unions representing working-class and low-level service job-holding women are opposed to flextime and job sharing because they "would dilute the legal sanctity of the forty-hour work week by enabling employers to rig work schedules to avoid paying time-and-a-half for overtime" (Hess, 1997, p. E1), a much greater concern for workers who punch time clocks.

Despite the wide varieties of "feminism" and the conflicts they have produced within the women's movement, the movement has always promoted the *idea* of gender equality both institutionally (in the media and in education) and for the individual, and it has always actively resisted those ideas that might encourage gender inequality. Moreover, the movement has always promoted women gaining more power within the institutions that control their lives. As already documented in this book, women have made enormous strides not only in the occupational world, especially at the middle levels of occupational prestige, but also in political, health care, and legal institutions. This is not to deny that great inequality still exists, nor that minority women—at every level of the social class system—tend to suffer even more. But it would be wrongheaded and overly pessimistic not to pause from time to time to savor the triumphs that women of all backgrounds have made over the past forty years.

Backlash

The huge interest in gender inequality in the last four decades has been motivated by the observation that women seem outlandishly unequal to men with regard to society's big rewards; namely, power, privilege, prestige, wealth, and income. However, there has been a backlash, which has waxed and waned since the early 1970s. The backlash has three major strands of thought running through it, and the proponents of each do not necessarily agree with one another (similar to the way the women's movement itself is splintered). First, many individuals, both men and women, see no inherent problem in gender inequality. They believe that it represents the natural order of the world and the most efficient division of labor for society in general and within the family in particular: Men should work, provide for their families, and keep matters outside of the home running smoothly, while women should keep matters within the home running smoothly. Second, many feel that while the post-1960 women's movement had value in its early phase in working toward gaining women equal opportunities, in its later phases it has gotten out of hand; in particular, men are being hurt by affirmative-action programs, as well as by laws concerning sexual harassment, divorce, child custody, and spouse abuse. Third, some of those studying gender inequality point out that on various measures of well-being, the gap between men and women is now negligible (e.g., single women under thirty-five earn 98 percent of what their male counterparts earn) and that on other measures men fall far short of women—the most striking being life expectancy, with men tending to die much younger than women (seven years younger for whites, eight years for blacks).

The first strand of thought is too value-laden to be resolved by social science data, even though some conservatives like to point to the correlation between the advancement of women's economic rights and their rising presence in the paid labor force, on the one hand, and rising rates of divorce, out-of-wedlock births, and juvenile delinquency on the other hand. However, the second and third strands were assessed here, in earlier chapters, in light of the relevant data—and the arguments were found to be wanting. In short, the data reveal no systematic pattern of men being hurt by sexual harassment laws and affirmative-action programs; but the data do reveal that significant gender wage gaps persist throughout the occupational structure.

Via existing academic, religious, political, business, and other types of organizations, as well as by way of the Internet, the varieties of the backlash against the women's movement have culminated in a burgeoning men's movement. What the groups involved in this movement have in common is their belief that in the struggle for gender equality men are not—and should not be considered—the "enemies"; that current social arrangements are not optimal for either gender, for both men and women suffer indignities; and, finally, that men too need—and should receive—social support and encouragement in their quest to maximize both society's and their own well-being.

We have no quarrel with these general beliefs. We recognize that both sexes are in the midst of a struggle to balance work and family in a society whose institutions have not been fully retooled so as to allow everyone to attain this goal without undue tribulation. Indeed, a late 1990s Time/CNN poll revealed that the overwhelming majority of adults in the United States agree that both men and women have a great deal of difficulty balancing work and family (Bellafante, 1998, p. 59). The General Social Survey also offers strong evidence that men are feeling about the same level of discomfort as women in balancing work and family. As revealed in Table 8.1, only about a third of both men and women are truly satisfied with this balance in their own lives. Moreover, both sexes are nearly equal in their reports of having to cut back on working hours because of

Table 8.1.
HOW SUCCESSFUL DO YOU FEEL AT BALANCING YOUR PAID WORK AND YOUR FAMILY LIFE?

	Percentage Reporting		
Response	All	Men	Women
Not at all	2.3	1.7	2.9
Not very	11.5	12.6	10.4
Somewhat	49.2	51.3	47.1
Very	31.9	28.8	34.9
Completely	5.1	5.6	4.7

Source: NORC (1996).

family responsibilities and, conversely, of having their family responsibilities being hurt by their jobs (Table 8.2).

Certainly, the workplace needs to be not only mother-friendly, but father-friendly too; we see no benefit for men in developing their version of "split dreams": of feeling the constant pressure to balance their work and family dreams, of feeling torn in many different directions. Accomplishing this will be one of the major challenges for businesses and corporations in the twenty-first century. That many men also suffer from current cultural, social, and economic arrangements reminds us of the central thesis of this book: that the causes of gender inequality are deeply rooted in the basic institutions of society and, consequently, the most successful strategies for achieving equality must involve changing these institutions. We believe that making benefits (governmental and corporate) universal is the best path for encouraging such change, as it obviates

Table 8.2
SELECTED GENERAL SOCIAL SURVEY QUESTIONS INDICATING THAT BOTH MEN AND WOMEN HAVE DIFFICULTIES IN BALANCING WORK AND FAMILY

	Percentage Reporting "Yes"		
Item	All	Men	Women
In your present/most recent job, have you ever done/did you ever do any of the following because of your responsibilities to members of your family:			
Refuse to work overtime or extra hours?	22.5	20.3	24.3
Cut back on your work?	23.1	22.0	24.0
In your present/most recent job, have you ever done/did you ever do any of the following because of your responsibilities to the job:			
Miss a family occasion or holiday?	49.8	58.8	42.3
Been unable to care for a sick child or relative?	17.2	15.7	18.6

Source: NORC (1996).

the backlashes from those being denied benefits and eliminates the condescending attitudes that are encouraged by programs directed only at women (or any other disadvantaged group).

In general, the women's movement is fearful of the men's movement—afraid that it might ultimately cause the dismantling of affirmative action and of women's post-1960 gains in the work world, health care, politics, and the legal system (see Faludi, 1991). But, in our view, this needn't be the case. Even if affirmative action were dismantled, the juggernaut of women's progress would not be easily sidetracked. Women's labor-force participation at all levels is far too great for the economy to thrive without it. Moreover, many of women's gains have become institutionalized in the practices of government and business, and now that less discriminatory policies are in place, bureaucratic inertia will resist their removal. Furthermore, most women are extremely well qualified for their new positions and, even in a period of backlash, employers would not want to lose them. "Under conditions of recession, when competition for scarce jobs intensifies, the tendency to prefer male applicants could undercut women's recent gains in nontraditional occupations. But women today are in a stronger legal and occupational position to challenge discriminatory hiring and promotion decisions" (Ferree and Hess, 1994, p. 205). Finally, women's aspirations—and the ramifications for career planning there-from—have changed dramatically over the past generation. In the 1960s, only 30 percent of women expected to be working at age thirty-five (National Longitudinal Surveys, 1997). Most women's educational and career choices were not geared toward lifelong employment nor toward filling our society's most prominent jobs. By the early 1990s, most women expected to work outside of the home, and their educational and career choices changed accordingly. In the past two decades, women have increased their share of MBAs, MDs, and JDs by more than 400 percent. Between the early 1970s and the early 2000s, the percentage of MBAs earned by women rose from three to forty, of MDs from eight to forty-three, and of JDs from five to forty-six. These changes are now—and will continue to be—reflected in women finding themselves in positions of power in the nation's major corporations. The prediction of Lynch and Post in 1996 that "women will be the CEOs, chief surgeons, and law partners of tomorrow" (p. 34) is coming to pass. This is a rosy prediction that reflects our own hopes for the future. However, we recognize that the social system is powerful and generally conservative; and that it has used gender, in conjunction with class, race, ethnicity, and sexual preference, as an organizing principle in the occupational hierarchy.

An analysis of American attitudes shows that we have come a long way, but that the picture is unclear as to whether the progress of working women will continue.

Attitudes Toward Working Women

Attitudes toward "women working" are complex and changing. Without doubt, Americans became increasingly comfortable with the idea of women, whether

Table 8.3
SELECTED GENERAL SOCIAL SURVEY QUESTIONS INDICATING THAT
AMERICAN ATTITUDES TOWARD GENDER ROLES HAVE BECOME
GENERALLY MORE EGALITARIAN

Item	Years	Percentage Agreeing		
		All	Men	Women
Women should take care of running their	1974–76	35.6	35.7	35.5
homes and leave running the country	1985–86	25.3	23.3	26.8
up to men.	1994–96	14.9	15.4	14.6
Do you approve or disapprove of a married	1974–76	70.1	67.6	72.3
woman earning money in business or	1985–86	82.2	83.4	81.3
industry if she has a husband capable of	1994–96	82.2	82.7	81.9
supporting her?				
A working mother can establish just as warm	1974–76*	49.0	41.6	55.1
and secure a relationship with her children	1985–86	61.6	54.3	67.3
as a mother who does not work.	1994–96	67.9	58.5	74.9
	2000–02	61.0	53.8	66.5
[Do you] prefer:	1994–96			
a. A relationship where the man has the man		29.7	31.7	28.1
responsibility for providing the household				
income and the woman has the main				
responsibility for taking care of the home				
and family?				
or				
b. A relationship where the man and woman	1994–96			
equally share responsibility for providing		70.3	68.3	71.9
the household income and taking care of				
the home and family?				

*Includes 1977 GSS.
Sources: NORC (1974–1976, 1984–1986, 1994–1996, 2000–2002 Cumulative GSS Data Files).

married or single, being in the paid labor force between the mid-1970 and the mid-1990s. Indeed, as revealed in Table 8.3, by the mid-1970s most people were already comfortable with this idea, and they became steadily more so by the mid-1990s. For example, whereas about one in three (35.6 percent) of Americans believed in the mid-1970s that women should take care of running their homes and leave running the country up to men, only about one in seven (14.9 percent) believed this by the mid-1990s, with men and women differing little on this issue in each decade

Similar changes can be seen in the General Social Survey (GSS) question concerning whether one approves or disapproves of a married women earning money in business or industry if she has a husband capable of supporting her. A little under a third (29.9 percent) disapproved in the mid-1970s, but only about a sixth (17.8 percent) did so by the mid-1990s. Moreover, when asked whether they would prefer a traditional family or one in which the man and woman equally share responsibility for providing the household income and taking care of the home and family, two-thirds of both men (68.3 percent) and women (71.9 percent) say they would prefer an equal-sharing family. Finally, although there is a significant divergence in the attitudes of men and women, with women much more likely to agree, by the mid-1990s more than half of Americans (one in two men; two in three women) came to agree with the proposition that a working mother can establish just as warm and secure a relationship with her children as a mother who does not work. However, the data for this item indicate that the trend in more egalitarian attitudes toward gender roles may have begun slow down, if not outright decline. More specifically, in the early 2000s, for the first time since the GSS was begun in 1972, the percentages of men and women agreeing with this item fell. As we will note shortly, this drop fits with other GSS data revealing a lingering traditionalism in American attitudes toward gender roles.

Americans are also strongly in favor of gender equality in the workplace, even though they recognize that this often is not the case because of discriminatory treatment of women as such and of all those with greater responsibilities for caregiving (who are overwhelmingly likely to be women). For example, when asked why they think women who are employed full-time earn less than men earn, more than four-fifths of the population (80.6 percent) agrees with the proposition that it is because employers tend to give men better paying jobs than they give women. Two-thirds (69.5 percent) attribute earnings inequality also to women's family responsibilities keeping them from putting as much time and effort into their jobs as men do (see Table 8.4).

In sum, the evidence presented in Tables 8.3 and 8.4 indicates that the functionalist paradigm ("men should work, women should stay at home") we discussed in Chapter 1 has waned greatly in the general American psyche and reached an all-time low in the mid-1990s.

On the other hand, when the issue turns to mothers working, we find that this paradigm is still far from dead. As we see in Table 8.3 (item three), a third

Table 8.4
SELECTED GENERAL SOCIAL SURVEY QUESTIONS INDICATING THAT AMERICANS BELIEVE THAT WOMEN SUFFER ECONOMICALLY FROM DISCRIMINATION IN THE WORKPLACE

	Percentage Agreeing		
Item	All	Men	Women
On average, women who are employed full-time earn less than men earn . . . this might be so [because]:			
Employers tend to give men better paying jobs than they give women	80.6	78.8	81.8
Women's family responsibilities keep them from putting as much time and effort into their jobs as men do.	69.5	72.8	67.1
Men work harder on the job than women do.	35.4	40.9	31.3

Source: NORC (1996).

of American women and almost half of American men presently disagree with the notion that working mothers can be as close to their children as nonworking mothers. Indeed, most Americans (82.1 percent) still believe that women are biologically better-suited to care for children (Table 8.5), and when asked if everyone benefits if women take the main responsibility for the care of the home and children, while men take the main responsibility for supporting the family financially, two-thirds of the adult population was in agreement (67.8 percent). Finally, near half of adults (45.5 percent) believe that preschool-age children suffer when their mothers work, with men (53.7 percent) significantly more likely than women (39.3 percent) to express this belief. (This fits the general trend found in the GSS items dealing with gender roles, where we find women more likely to express "liberal" attitudes.)

The traditional attitudes expressed in the GSS harken back to those that produced so much punishment for Eleanor McMahon and Marsha Berger, and for millions of their contemporaries in the pre-1970s era—an era in which both public and corporate policy stigmatized working mothers and routinely allowed for different pay scales for men and women performing exactly the same job. Of course, if couples freely *choose* to divide responsibilities in this traditional way, that is their option—but surely it needs to *be* an individual choice, rather than a societal expectation or prescription. We strongly believe that the lives of working women will only be enhanced as long as they too are given the choice to pursue their careers to the same extent as men.

The persistence of such traditional attitudes indicates that the equality women have gained over the past thirty years needs to be guarded carefully and that future reductions in gender inequality will not happen "automatically." Unfortunately, few women today are strongly concerned about the issue of gender equality and equal rights (according to a 2000 Gallup Poll, only one in every twenty-five adult women expresses concern over this issue; see Newport, 2000). We regard this as unfortunate because we believe that a strong women's move-

Table 8.5

SELECTED GENERAL SOCIAL SURVEY QUESTIONS INDICATING THAT ATTITUDES TOWARD GENDER ROLES ARE STILL TRADITIONAL

Item	Percentage Agreeing		
	All	Men	Women
Women are biologically better-suited to care for children.*	82.1	87.0	78.1
In many married couples, women take the main responsibility for the care of the home and children, while men take the main responsibility for supporting the family financially. Does everyone benefit from this?*	67.8	71.3	65.0
A preschool child is likely to suffer if his or her mother works.**	45.5	53.7	39.3

Sources: *NORC (1994–1996); **NORC(2000–2002).

ment is the key to countering the risk of retrogressing—of losing the gains in gender equality—as well as to the continuing pursuit of greater gender equality than our society has thus far realized. Moreover, we believe that the goals of the movement will ultimately benefit both men and women, eventually allowing everyone's dreams of fulfillment in both work and family life *not* to be "split" but rather to be satisfactorily integrated in day-to-day reality.

World Wide Web Resources

The National Partnership for Women and Families promotes fairness in the workplace, access to quality affordable health care, and policies that help women and men meet the dual demands of work and family: http://www.nationalpartnership.org/index.cfm.

The Women's Rights Division of Human Rights Watch fights against the dehumanization and marginalization of women, and promotes women's equal rights and human dignity: http://www.hrw.org/women/

References

Abbot, Edith. 1910. *Women in Industry*. New York: Appleton.

Abbott, Pamela, and Clair Wallace. 1997. *An Introduction to Sociology: Feminist Perspectives*. New York: Routledge.

Acker, Joan. 1978. "Issues in the Sociological Study of Women's Work." Pp. 134–161 in Ann H. Stromberg and Shirley Harkness (eds.), *Women Working: Theories and Facts in Perspective*. Palo Alto, CA: Mayfield.

———. 1988. "Class, Gender, and the Relations of Production." *Signs* 13(3):473–497.

Aguiar, Neuma. 1986. "Research Guidelines: How to Study Work in Latin America." Pp. 22–33 In June Nash and Helen I. Safa (eds.), *Women and Change in Latin America*. South Hadley, MA: Bergin and Garvey.

Aiken, Linda H., Sean P. Clarke, Douglas M. Sloane, and Julia A. Sochalski. 2001. "Nurses' Reports on Hospital Care in Five Countries." *Health Affairs* 20:43–53.

Albert, Alexa A., and Judith R. Porter. 1988. "Children's Gender-Role Stereotypes: A Sociological Investigation of Psychological Models." *Sociological Forum* 3(2):184–210.

Aldridge, Delores. 1975. "Black Women in the Economic Marketplace: A Battle Unfinished." *Journal of Social and Behavioral Sciences* 21(Winter):48–62.

Allen, Laura S., and Roger A. Gorski. 1992. "Sexual Orientation and the Sizes of the Anterior Commissure in the Human Brain." *Proceedings of the National Academy of Sciences* 89:7199–7202.

Almquist, Elizabeth M. 1979. *Minorities, Gender and Work*. Lexington, MA: Heath.

Alpern, Sara. 1993. "In the Beginning: A History of Women in Management." Pp. 19–51 in Ellen A. Fagenson (ed.), *Women in Management: Trends, Issues, and Challenges in Managerial Diversity*. Newbury Park, CA: Sage.

Ambrogi, Robert J. 1992. "Comparable Work Must Get Equal Pay, Jude Decides— Ruling Puts Spotlight on Rarely Used State Law." *Massachusetts Lawyers Weekly* (August 24):2.

American Association of Colleges of Nursing. 2002. "Strategies to Reverse the New Nursing Shortage: A policy statement from Tri-Council Members. 2001." Retrieved from http://www.aacn.nche.edu/Publications/positions/tricshortage.htm.

American Association of University Women (AAUW). 1994. *Shortchanging Girls, Shortchanging America: Executive Summary*. Washington, DC: AAUW.

———. 1998. *Gender Gaps, Where Schools Still Fail Our Children: Executive Summary*. Washington, DC: AAUW.

American Council on Education. 1997. P. 365 in John J. Macionis, *Sociology*. 6th ed. Upper Saddle River, NJ: Prentice-Hall.

———. 2002. *The American College President, 2002 Edition*. Washington, DC: American Council on Education.

Amott, Teresa L. and Julie A. Matthaei. 1996. *Race, Gender, and Work: A Multicultural Economic History of Women in the United States*. Rev. ed. Boston: South End Press.

Amsden, Alice. 1980. *The Economics of Women and Work*. New York: St. Martin's Press.

Andersen, Margaret L. 1996. *Thinking About Women: Sociological Perspectives on Sex and Gender*. 4th ed. Boston: Allyn and Bacon.

———. 2003. *Thinking about Women: Sociological Perspectives on Sex and Gender*. 6th ed. Boston, MA.: Allyn and Bacon.

Anderson, Elaine A., and Jane W. Spruill. 1993. "The Dual Career Commuter Family: A Lifestyle on the Move." *Marriage and Family Review* 19(1–2):131–147.

Anderson, Karen. 1981. *Wartime Women: Sex Roles, Family Relations, and the Status of Women During World War II*. Westport, CT: Greenwood Press.

———. 1996. *Changing Woman: A History of Racial Ethnic Women in Modern America*. New York: Oxford University Press.

Anthony, Susan B. 1943. *Out of the Kitchen—Into the War*. New York: Daye.

Apter, T. E. 1993. *Working Women Don't Have Wives: Professional Success in the 1990s*. New York: St. Martin's Press.

Audits and Surveys. 1991. *The Study of Magazine Buying Patterns*. Port Washington, NY: Publishers Clearinghouse.

Avner, Judith I. (Chairperson). 1993. *Sexual Harassment: Building a Consensus for Change. The Governor's Task Force on Sexual Harassment*. Albany: New York State Division for Women.

Baca Zinn, Maxine. 1976. "Chicanas: Power and Control in the Domestic Sphere." *De Colores* 2:19–31.

Backhouse, Constance, and Leah Cohen. 1981. *Sexual Harassment on the Job*. Englewood Cliffs, NJ: Prentice-Hall.

Baer, Judith A. 1978. *The Chains of Protection: The Judicial Response to Women's Labor Legislation*. Westport, CT: Greenwood Press.

Bailyn, Lotte. 1970. "Career and Family Orientations of Husbands and Wives in Relation to Marital Happiness." *Human Relations* 23:97–113.

———. 1993. *Breaking the Mold: Women, Men, and Time in the New Corporate World*. New York: Macmillian.

Baker, Elizabeth F. 1964. *Technology and Women's Work*. New York: Columbia University Press.

Bardwell, J. R, S. W. Coebran, and S. Walker. 1986. "Relationship of Parental Education, Race, and Gender to Sex Role Stereotyping in Five-Year-Old Kindergartners." *Sex Roles* 15:275–281.

Barnett, Rosaline, and Grace Baruch. 1979. "Career Competence and the Well-Being of Adult Women." Pp. 95–102 in Barbara A. Gutek (ed.), *New Directions for Education, Work and Careers: Enhancing Women's Career Development*. San Francisco: Jossey-Bass.

Barrett, Nancy S. 1979. "Women in the Job Market: Unemployment and Work Schedules." Pp. 63–98 in Ralph E. Smith (ed.), *The Subtle Revolution: Women at Work*. Washington, DC: Urban Institute.

Barron, Richard David, and Geoffrey Michael Norris. 1976. "Sexual Divisions and the Dual Labor Market." Pp. 47–69 in Diana L. Barker and Sheila Allen (eds.), *Dependence and Exploitation in Work and Marriage*. London: Longman.

Baruch, Grace, Barnett Rosalind, and Caryl Rivers. 1983. *Lifeprints: New Patterns of Love and Work for Today's Women*. New York: McGraw-Hill.

Baxandall, Rosalyn, Linda Gordon, and Susan Reverby. 1976. *America's Working Women: A Documentary History—1600 to the Present*. New York: Vintage Books.

Becker, Gary S. 1957. *The Economics of Discrimination*. Washington, DC: Brookings Institute.

———. 1964. *The Economics of Discrimination*. Washington, DC: Brookings Institute.

———. 1975. *Human Capital: A Theoretical and Empirical Analysis, with Special Reference to Education*. New York: National Bureau of Economic Research.

Beckett, Megan, and Chiayung Sandy Chien. 2002. *The Status of Gender Integration in the Military: Supporting Appendices.* Santa Monica, CA: Rand.

Beechey, Veronica. 1977. "Female Wage Labour in Capitalist Production." *Capital and Class* 3:45–66.

Bell, Carolyn Shaw. 1978. "Women and Work: An Economic Appraisal." Pp. 10–28 in Ann H. Stromberg and Shirley Harkness (eds.), *Women Working: Theories and Facts in Perspective.* Palo Alto, CA: Mayfield.

Bellafante, Ginia. 1998. "Feminism: It's All about Me!" *Time* 151(June 29):54–60.

Beneria, Lourdes, and Marta Roldan. 1987. *The Crossroads of Class and Gender.* Chicago: University of Chicago Press.

Benjamin, Lois. 1982. "Black Women: An Isolated Elite." *Sociological Inquiry* 52(2): 141–151.

Benmayor, Rina. 1991. "Testimony, Action Research, and Empowerment: Puerto Rican Women and Popular Education." Pp. 159–174 in Sherna Berger Gluck and Daphne Patai (eds.), *Women's Words: The Feminist Practice of Oral History.* New York: Routledge.

Benokraitis, Nijole, and Joe R. Feagin. 1995. *Modern Sexism: Blatant, Subtle, and Covert Discrimination.* 2nd ed. Englewood Cliffs, NJ: Prentice-Hall.

Benson, Susan Porter. 1986. *Counter Cultures: Saleswomen, Managers, and Customers in American Department Stores, 1890–1940.* Urbana: University of Illinois Press.

Berch, Bettina. 1982. *The Endless Day: The Political Economy of Women and Work.* New York: Harcourt Brace Jovanovich.

Bergen, E. 1991. "The Economic Context of Labor Allocation: Implications for Gender Stratification." *Journal of Family Issues* 12(2):140–157.

Bergmann, Barbara. 1971. "The Effect on White Incomes of Discrimination in Employment." *Journal of Political Economy* 79 (March-April): 294–313.

———. 1986. *The Economic Emergence of Women.* New York: Basic Books.

Berheide, Catherine White. 1988. "Women in Sales and Service Occupations." Pp. 241–257 in Ann Helton Stromberg and Shirley Harkness (eds.), *Women Working: Theories and Facts in Perspective.* 2nd ed. Mountain View, CA: Mayfield.

———. 1992. "Women Still 'Stuck' in Low-Level Jobs." *Women in Public Services: A Bulletin for the Center for Women in Government* 3 (Fall). Albany: Center for Women in Government, State University of New York

Berk, Sarah Fenstermaker. 1985. *The Gender Factory: The Apportionment of Work in American Households.* New York: Plenum.

Berkin, Carol. 1996. *First Generations: Women in Colonial America.* New York: Hill and Wang.

Berliner, Howard S., and Eli Ginzberg. 2002. "Why This Hospital Nursing Shortage Is Different." *Journal of the American Medical Association* 288(6):2742–2744.

Bernard, Jessie. 1971. "The Paradox of the Happy Marriage." Pp. 85–98 in Vivian Gornick and Barbara K. Moran (eds.), *Woman in Sexist Society: Studies in Power and Powerlessness.* New York: Basic Books.

———. 1972. *The Future of Marriage.* New York: World Books.

———. 1974. *The Future of Motherhood.* New York: Free Press.

Bernstein, Nina. 1996. "Equal Opportunity Recedes for Most Female Lawyers." *New York Times* (January 8):A12

Binkin, Martin, and Shirley J. Bach. 1977. *Women in the Military.* Washington, DC: Brookings Institution.

Bird, Gloria, Gerald Bird, and Marguerite Scruggs. 1984. "Determinants of Family Task Sharing: A Study of Husbands and Wives." *Journal of Marriage and the Family* 46(2):345–355.

Blau, Francine. 1977. *Equal Pay in the Office*. Lexington, MA: Heath.

Blau, Francine, and Carol L. Jusensius. 1976. "Economists' Approaches to Sex Segregation in the Labor Market: An Appraisal." Pp. 181–199 in Martha Blaxall and Barbara Regan (eds.), *Labor and Trade Unionism*. New York: Wiley.

Blau, Francine, and Marianne Ferber. 1992. *The Economics of Women, Men, and Work*. 2nd ed. Englewood Cliffs, NJ: Prentice-Hall.

Bliss, Edwin. 1976. *Getting Things Done*. New York: Scribners.

Blum, Linda M. 1991. *Between Feminism and Labor*. Berkeley: University of California Press.

Blumrosen, Alfred W. 1995. "How the Courts Are Handling Reverse Discrimination Claims—Draft Report of Reverse Discrimination Commissioned by Labor Department." Reprinted in *Daily Labor Report* (March 23). Washington, DC: Bureau of National Affairs.

Blumstein, Philip, and Pepper Schwartz. 1983. *American Couples: Money, Work, Sex*. New York: William Morrow.

Bonacich, Edna. 1972. "A Theory of Ethnic Antagonism: The Split Labor Market." *American Sociological Review* 37(5):547–559.

Bonacich, Edna, and Richard P. Appelbaum. 2000. *Behind the Label: Inequality in the Los Angeles Apparel Industry*. Berkeley: University of California Press.

Bond, James T., Ellen Galinsky and Jennifer Swanberg. 1998. *National Study of the Changing Workforce, Executive Summary*. NY: Families and Work Institute.

Borch, Fred L. III. 2000. "Military Law and the Treatment of Women Soldiers: Sexual Harassment and Fraternization in the U.S. Army." Pp. 337–354 in Gerard J. DeGroot and Corinna Penniston-Bird (eds.), *A Soldier and a Woman: Sexual Integration in the Military*. Harlow, England: Pearson Education.

Bose, Christine. 1987. "Devaluing Women's Work: The Undercount of Women's Employment in 1900 and 1980." Pp. 95–115 in Christine Bose, Roslyn Feldberg, and Natalie Sokoloff (eds.), *Hidden Aspects of Women's Work*. New York: Praeger.

Bose, Christine, Roslyn Feldberg, and Natalie Sokoloff (eds.). *Hidden Aspects of Women's Work*. New York: Praeger.

Braverman, Harry. 1974. *Labor and Monopoly Capital*. New York: Monthly Labor Review Press.

Brettell, Caroline B., and Carolyn F. Sargent. 2001. "Colonialism, Development, and the Global Economy." Pp. 507–512 in Caroline B. Brettell and Carolyn F. Sargent (eds.), *Gender in Cross Cultural Perspective*. Upper Saddle River, NJ: Prentice Hall.

Brines, Julie. 1994. "Economic Dependency, Gender, and the Division of Labor at Home." *American Journal of Sociology* 100(3):652–688.

Brockman, Joan. 2001. *Gender in the Legal Profession: Fitting or Breaking the Mold*. Vancouver, BC: UBC Press.

Brooks, Nancy Rivera. 1993, June 30. "Gender Pay Gap Found at Highest Corporate Levels." *Los Angeles Times*, p. A1.

Brooks-Gunn, Jeanne. 1986. "The Relationship of Maternal Beliefs about Sex Typing to Maternal and Young Children's Behavior." *Sex Roles* 14(1/2):21–35.

Brown, Richard. 1976. "Women as Employees: Some Comments on Research in Industrial Sociology." Pp. 21–46 In Diana Backer and Sheila Allen (eds.), *Dependence and Exploitation in Work and Marriage*. London: Longman.

Brownlee, W. Eliott, and Mary M. Brownlee. 1976. *Women in the American Economy: A Documentary History, 1675–1929*, New Haven, CT: Yale University Press.

Bularzik, Mary. 1978. "Sexual Harassment in the Workplace: Historical Notes." *Radical America* 12(4):25–43.

Bureau of Labor Statistics. 1971. *Current Population Survey March 1971 Supplement.* Washington, DC: Bureau of the Census.

———. 1974. *Current Population Survey 1974 Annual Averages.* Washington, DC: Bureau of the Census.

———. 1975. *Current Population Survey March 1975 Supplement.* Washington, DC: Bureau of the Census.

———. 1979. *Women in the Labor Force: Some New Data Series.* Washington, DC: Bureau of the Census.

———. 1980. *Perspectives on Working Women: A Databook* (Bulletin 2080). Washington, DC: Bureau of the Census.

———. 1994a. *Current Population Survey 1948–1994 Annual Averages.* Washington, DC: Bureau of the Census.

———. 1994b. *Current Population Survey March 1994 Supplement.* Washington, DC: Bureau of the Census.

———. 1994c. *Comparative Labor Force Statistics: Ten Countries, 1959–1993.* Unpublished tabulations prepared by Constance Sorrentino. Washington, DC: Bureau of the Census; as cited in Daphne Spain and Suzanne M. Bianchi. *Balancing Action: Motherhood, Marriage, and Employment Among American Women.* New York: Russell Sage Foundation, 1996, p. 101.

———. 1995a. *BLS Reports on Employee Benefits in State and Local Governments 1994.* http://www.bls.gov/news.release/ebs2.toc.htm.

———. 1995b. *BLS Reports on Employee Benefits in Small Private Industry Establishments, 1994.* http://www.bls.gov/news.release/ebs.toc.htm.

———. 1996a. *Employment and Earnings* 43:7 (July). Washington, DC: U.S. Government Printing Office.

———. 1996b. *Annual Demographic Survey, March Supplement.* Washington DC: U.S. Government Printing Office.

———. 1996c. *Occupational Outlook Handbook, 1996–1997 Edition* (Bulletin 2470). Washington, DC: U.S. Government Printing Office.

———. 1997a. "Table A-19: Usual Weekly Earnings of Employed Full-Time Wage and Salary Workers by Occupation, Sex, Race, and Hispanic Origins." Unpublished table based on data taken from the *Current Population Survey 1996 Annual Averages.* Washington, DC: Bureau of the Census.

———. 1997b. "Labor Force Statistics from the *Current Population Survey.*" http://www.bls.gov/

———. 1997c. "Table 1: Employed and Experienced Unemployed Persons by Detailed Occupation, Sex, Race, and Hispanic Origins." Unpublished table based on data taken from the *Current Population Survey 1996 Annual Averages.* Washington, DC: Bureau of the Census.

———. 1997d. *Employment and Earnings* 44:5 (May). Washington, DC: U.S. Government Printing Office.

———. 1997e. *Historical Income Tables—Persons.* http://www.census.gov/ftp/pub/hhes/income/histinc/incperdet.html.

———. 1997f. *Employment and Earnings* 44:1 (January). Washington, DC: Bureau of the Census.

———. 1997g. *Union Members Summary.* Washington, DC: Bureau of the Census.

———. 1997h. *BLS Releases New 1996–2006 Employment Projections.* Washington, DC: Bureau of the Census.

———. 1997i. *Child-Care Benefit to Employee Emerging.* Washington, DC: Bureau of the Census.

————. 1997j. *BLS Reports on Employee Benefits in Medium and Large Private Industry Establishments, 1995*. Washington, DC: Bureau of the Census.

————. 2001a. "2001 National Occupational Employment and Wage Estimates: Healthcare Practitioners and Technical Occupations." Washington, DC: U.S. Department of Labor. http://www.bls.gov/oes/2001/oes_29He.htm.

————. 2003a. "Table 37. Median Weekly Earnings of Full-Time Wage and Salary Workers by Selected Characteristics." Unpublished table based on 2000 and 2001 data taken from the *Current Population Survey*. Washington, DC: U.S. Department of Labor. ftp://ftp.bls.gov/pub/special.requests/lf/aat37.txt.

————. 2003b. "Table 1. Employed and Experienced Unemployed Persons by Detailed Occupation, Sex, Race, and Hispanic Origin, Annual Averages 2001." Unpublished table based on 2001 data taken from the *Current Population Survey*. Washington, DC: U.S. Department of Labor.

————. 2003c. "Table A-17. Usual Weekly Earnings of Employed Full-Time Wage and Salary Workers by Educational Attainment, Age, Sex, Race, and Hispanic Origin, 2001 Annual Averages." Unpublished table based on 2001 data taken from the *Current Population Survey*. Washington, DC: U.S. Department of Labor.

————. 2003d. "Table A-19. Usual Weekly Earnings of Employed Full-Time Wage and Salary Workers by Occupation, Sex, Race, and Hispanic Origin, 2001 Annual Averages." Unpublished table based on 2001 data taken from the *Current Population Survey*. Washington, DC: U.S. Department of Labor.

————. 2003e. "Table A-26. Usual Weekly Earnings of Employed Full-Time Wage and Salary Workers by Detailed (3-Digit Census Code) Occupation and Sex, 2001 Annual Averages." Unpublished table based on 2001 data taken from the *Current Population Survey*. Washington, DC: U.S. Department of Labor.

————. 2003f. "Table 22. Percent of Workers with Access to Selected Benefits, by Work and Establishment Characteristics, Private Industry, National Compensation Survey, 2000." Unpublished table based on 2000 data taken from the *National Compensation Survey*. Washington, DC: U.S. Department of Labor. http://www.bls.gov/news.release/ebs2.t02.htm.

————. 2003g. "Table A-20. Employed Persons by Occupation, Race, Hispanic or Latino Ethnicity, and Sex." Unpublished table based on May 2002 and 2003 data taken from the *Current Population Survey*. Washington, DC: U.S. Department of Labor.

————. 2003h. "Table 2. Employment by Major Occupational Group, 2000 and Projected 2010." Washington, DC: U.S. Department of Labor. http://www.bls.gov/news.release/ecopro.t02.htm.

Burnham, James. 1941. *The Managerial Revolution*. New York: Day.

Burns, Alisa, and Ross Homel. 1989. "Gender Division of Tasks by Parents and Their Children." *Psychology of Women Quarterly* 13(1):113–125.

Burns, Stewart. 1990. *Social Movements of the 1960s: Searching for Democracy*. Boston: Twayne.

Burris, Val, and Amy Wharton. 1981. "Sex Segregation in the U.S. Labor Force, 1950–1979." Paper presented at the Annual Meeting of the Society for the Study of Social Problems, Toronto.

Buxton, Joan Keller. 1997. "Dilemmas of Organizing Women Office Workers." Pp. 335–344 in Dana Dunn (ed.), *Workplace/Women's Place: An Anthology*. Los Angeles: Roxbury.

Cahn, Ann Foote. 1977. *American Women Workers in a Full Employment Economy*. A compendium of papers submitted to the Subcommittee on Economic Growth and Stabilization of the Joint Economic Committee. U.S. Congress, Joint Economic Committee Hearing, September 16, 1977. Washington, DC: U.S. Government Printing Office.

Caldwell, Mayta, and Letitia Peplau. 1982. " Sex Differences in Same Sex Friendships." *Sex Roles* 8(7):721–732.

Callahan, David. 2002 "Private Sector, Public Doubts" *The New York Times* (January 15):21.

Cancian, Maria, and Daniel Meyer. 2000. "Work After Welfare: Women's Work Effort, Occupation and Economic Well-Being." *Social Work Research* 24(2):69–86.

Cantor, Milton, and Bruce Laurie. 1977. *Class, Sex, and the Woman Worker.* Westport, CT: Greenwood.

Cantor, Muriel G. 1987. "Popular Culture and the Portrayal of Women: Content and Control" Pp. 190–214 in Beth. B. Hess and Myra Marx Ferree (eds.), *Analyzing Gender.* Newbury Park, CA: Sage.

Catalyst. 2003a. *2001 Catalyst Census of Women Board Directors of the Fortune 1000.* http://www.catalystwomen.org/research/censuses.htm.

———. 2003b. "Catalyst Charts Growth of Women on America's Corporate Boards." Press Release. http://www.catalystwomen.org/press_room/press_releases/wbd2001.htm.

CAWP (Center for the American Woman and Politics). 1995. "CAWP Study Traces Impact of "Women in Congress." New Brunswick, NJ: Eagleton Institute of Politics, Rutgers University.

———. 1997a. "Women in Elective Office 1997." New Brunswick, NJ: Eagleton Institute of Politics, Rutgers University.

———. 1997b. "Women in State Legislatures 1997." New Brunswick, NJ: Eagleton Institute of Politics, Rutgers University.

———. 1997c. "Sex Differences in Voter Turnout." New Brunswick, NJ: Eagleton Institute of Politics, Rutgers University.

———. 1997d. "The Gender Gap: Voting Choices, Party Identification, and Presidential Performance Ratings." New Brunswick, NJ: Eagleton Institute of Politics, Rutgers University.

———. 1997e. "Women Make News as Voters, Edge Upward as Officeholders." New Brunswick, NJ: Eagleton Institute of Politics, Rutgers University.

———. 1997f. "Women's PACs and Donor Networks." New Brunswick, NJ: Eagleton Institute of Politics, Rutgers University.

———. 2001. "Women Appointed to Presidential Cabinets." New Brunswick, NJ: Eagleton Institute of Politics, Rutgers University.

———. 2002. "Sex Differences in Voter Turnout." New Brunswick, NJ: Eagleton Institute of Politics, Rutgers University.

———. 2003. "Women in Elective Office 2003." New Brunswick, NJ: Eagleton Institute of Politics, Rutgers University.

Chafe, William. 1972. *The American Woman: Her Changing Social, Economic, and Political Roles, 1920–1970.* New York: Oxford University Press.

———. 1977. *Women and Equality: Changing Patterns in American Culture.* New York: Oxford University Press.

Christensen, Kathleen, and Ralph Gomory. 2003. "Foreword." Pp. vii–viii in Phyllis Moen (ed.), *It's about Time: Couples and Careers.* Ithaca, New York: Cornell University Press.

Clegg, Jeremy. 1996. "The Development of Multinational Enterprises." Pp. 103–134 in P.W. Daniels and W.F. Lever (eds.), *The Global Economy in Transition.* Essex, England: Addision Welsey Longman.

Cobble, Dorothy Sue. 1991. *Dishing It Out: Waitresses and Their Unions in the Twentieth Century.* Urbana: University of Illinois Press.

Coffey, William J. 1996. "The 'Newer' International Division of Labour." Pp. 40–61 in P.W. Daniels and W.F. Lever (eds.), *The Global Economy in Transition.* Essex, England: Addison Wesley Longman.

Cohn, Samuel. 1996. "Human Capital Theory." Pp. 107–109 in Paul J. Dubeck and Kathryn Borman (eds.), *Women and Work: A Handbook.* New York: Garland.

Colapinto, John. 2000. *As Nature Made Aims.* New York: HarperCollins.

Coley, Rebekah Levine, P. Lindsey Chase-Lansdale, and Christine P. Li-Grining. 2001. *Child Care in the Era of Welfare Reform: Quality, Choices, and Preferences.* Policy Brief 01–04. Baltimore, MD: Johns Hopkins University.

Collins, Sharon. 1979. "Making Ourselves Visible: Evolution of Career Status and Self-Image of Minority Professional Women." Pp. 4–14 in Lucy Ann Geiselman (ed.), *The Minority Woman in America: Professionalism at What Cost?* Proceedings of the Program for Women in Health Science Conference at the University of California, San Francisco. San Francisco: University of California.

Committee of 200. 2002. "National Survey: Today's Teen Girls Avoid Business Careers." http://www.c200.org/external/press/102202.asp.

Comstock, George, and Haejung Paik. 1991. *Television and the American Child.* San Diego: Academic Press.

Conrad, Pamela J., and Robert B. Maddux. 1988. *Guide to Affirmative Action.* Menlo Park, CA: Crisp Publications.

Corcoran, Mary, and Gregory J. Duncan. 1979. "Work History, Labor Force Attachment, and Earnings Differences Between the Races and Sexes." *Journal of Human Resources* 14(Winter):3–20.

Coser, Rose Laub, and Gerald Rokoff. 1971. "Women in the Occupational World: Social Disruption and Conflict." *Social Problems* 18(4):535–554.

Costello, Cynthia, and Barbara Kivimae Krimgold (eds.). 1996. *The American Woman, 1996–97: Women and Work.* New York: W. W. Norton.

Cotter, David A., JoAnn DeFiore, Joan M. Hermsen, Brenda Marsteller Kowalewski, and Reeve Vanneman. 1997. "All Women Benefit: The Macro-Level Effect of Occupational Integration on Gender Earnings Equality." *American Sociological Review* 62(5):714–734.

Coverman, Shelley. 1989. "Women's Work Is Never Done: The Division of Domestic Labor." Pp. 356–370 in Jo Freeman (ed.), *Women: A Feminist Perspective.* Mountain View, CA: Mayfield.

Crosby, Faye J. 1991. *Juggling: The Unexpected Advantages of Balancing Career and Home for Women and Their Families.* New York: Free Press.

Daily Labor Report. 1995. "Proponents, Opponents of Affirmative Action Point to Statistics" (August 1). Washington, DC: Bureau of National Affairs.

Daniels, Arlene Kaplan. 1987. "Invisible Work." *Social Problems* 34(5):403–425.

Davies, Margery W. 1975. "Women's Place Is at the Typewriter. The Feminization of Clerical Labor Force." Pp. 279–296 in Richard C. Edwards, Michael Reich, and David M. Gordon (eds.), *Labor Market Segmentation.* Lexington, MA: DC Heath.

———. 1982. *Women's Place Is at the Typewriter: Office Work and Office Workers, 1870–1930.* Philadelphia: Temple University Press.

Dean, Donna M. 1997. *Warriors Without Weapons.* Pasadena: The MINERVA Center.

Deaux, Kay. 1992. "Sex Differences." Pp. 1749–1753 in Edgar F. Borgatta and Marie L. Borgatta (eds.), *Encyclopedia of Sociology.* Vol. 3. New York: Macmillan.

DeChick, J. 1988. "Most Mothers Want a Job, Too." *USA Today* (July 19):D1.

DeSlippe, Dennis A. 2000 *"Rights, Not Roses": Unions and the Rise of Working-Class Feminism, 1945–1980*. Urbana: University of Illinois Press.

Dexter, Elisabeth Williams. 1924. *Colonial Women of Affairs: Women in Business and the Profession in America Before 1776*. 2nd ed. Boston: Houghton Mifflin.

Dickens, William T., and Kevin Lang. 1985. "A Test of Dual Labor Market Theory." *American Economic Review* 75(September):792–805.

Dickinson, Torry. 1997. "Selective Globalization: The Relocation of Industrial Production and the Shaping of Women's Work." Pp. 109–129 in Randy Hodson (ed.), *Research in the Sociology of Work: The Globalization of Work*. Vol. 6. Greenwich, CT: JAI Press.

Dickinson, Torry and Robert K. Schaeffer. 2001. *Fast Forward: Work, Gender, and Protest in a Changing World*. Lanham, MD: Rowman and Littlefield, Publishers, Inc.

Dill, Bonnie Thorton, Lynn Weber Cannon, and Reeve Vanneman. 1987. "Race and Gender in Occupational Segregation." Pp. 7–70 in *Pay Equity: An Issue of Race, Ethnicity, and Sex*. Washington, DC: National Committee on Pay Equity.

Dingell, John D., and Carolyn B. Maloney. 2002. *A New Look Though the Glass Ceiling: Where Are the Women? The Status of Women in Management in Ten Selected Occupations. Executive Summary*. Washington, DC: U.S. General Accounting Office. http://www.equality2020.org/glass.pdf.

Dock, Lavina L., and Isabel M. Stewart. 1938. *A Short History of Nursing from Earliest Times to Present Day*. New York: G. P. Putnam's.

Dodge, Bertha S. 1954. *The Story of Nursing*. Boston: Little, Brown.

Dodson, Debra L., Susan J. Carroll, and Ruth B. Mandel. 1995. *Voices, Views, Votes: The Impact of Women in the 103rd Congress*. New Brunswick, NJ: Eagleton Institute of Politics, Rutgers University.

Doeringer, Peter B., and Michael Piore. 1971. *Internal Labor Markets and Manpower Analysis*. Lexington, MA: Heath.

Dolan, Josephine A., M. Louise Fitzpatrick, and Eleanor Krohn Herrmann. 1983. *Nursing in Society: A Historical Perspective*. Philadelphia: Saunders.

Doob, Christopher Bates. 1995. *Social Problems*. New York: Harcourt Brace.

Dublin, Thomas. 1979. *Women at Work: The Transformation of Work and Community in Lowell, Massachusetts, 1826–1860*. New York: Columbia University Press.

Dubnoff, Steven Jan, Joseph Veroff, and Richard A. Kulka. 1978. "Adjustment to Work: 1957–1976." Paper presented to the American Psychological Association, Toronto.

Dworkin, Ronald W. 2002. "Where Have All the Nurses Gone?" *Public Interest* 148: 23–36.

Easterbrooks, M. Ann, and Wendy A. Goldberg. 1988. "Effects of Early Maternal Employment on Toddlers, Mothers, and Fathers." *Developmental Psychology* 21:774–783.

Eastwood, Mary. 1978. "Legal Protection Against Sex Discrimination." Pp. 108–123 in Ann H. Stromberg and Shirley Harkess (eds.), *Women Working: Theories and Facts in Perspective*. Palo Alto, CA: Mayfield.

Edwards, Richard C. 1979. *Contested Terrain: The Transformation of the Workplace in America*. New York: Basic Books.

Edwards, Richard C., Michael Reich, and David Gordon (eds.). 1975. *Labor Market Segmentation*. Lexington, MA: Heath.

——. 2002. *EEOC Issues Fiscal 2001: Enforcement Data*. Washington, DC: U.S. Equal Employment Opportunity Commission. http://www.eeoc.gov/press/2-22-02.html.

Ehrenreich, Barbara. 2001. *Nickel and Dimed: On (Not) Getting by in America*. New York: Metropolitan Books.

Ehrenreich, Barbara, and Arlie Russell Hochschild. 2003. *Global Woman: Nannies, Maids, and Sex Workers in the New Economy*. New York: Metropolitan Books.

Eichler, Margrit. 1991. *Nonsexist Research Methods: A Practical Guide*. New York: Routledge.

Eisenberg, Susan. 1998. *We'll Call You: Experiences of Women Working Construction*. Ithaca, NY: Cornell University Press.

Eisenhart, Margaret A. 1996. "Contemporary College Women's Career Plans." Pp. 232–235 in Paula J. Dubeck and Kathryn Borman (eds.), *Women and Work: A Handbook*. New York: Garland.

Elson, Diane. 1992. "Male Bias in Structural Adjustment." Pp. 46–68 in Haleh Afshar and Carolyne Dennis (eds.), *Women and Adjustment Policies in the Third World*. New York: St. Martin's.

Elson, Diane, and Ruth Pearson. 1981. "Nimble Fingers Make Cheap Workers: An Analysis of Women's Employment in Third World Export Manufacturing." *Feminist Review* 7(Spring): 87–107.

Enarson, Elaine Pitt. 1984. *Woods-Working Women: Sexual Integration in the U.S. Forest Service*. Birmingham: University of Alabama.

England, Paula. 1982. "The Failure of Human Capital Theory to Explain Occupational Sex Segregation." *Journal of Human Resources* 17(3): 358–370.

Enloe, Cynthia. 1983. *Does Khaki Become You? The Militarization of Women's Lives*. London: South End Press.

———. 1995. "The Globetrotting Sneaker." *Ms* 5(March 5):10–15.

Espiritu, Yen Le. 1997. *Asian American Women and Men*. Thousand Oaks, CA: Sage.

Etaugh, C. 1974. "Effects of Maternal Employment on Children: A Review of Recent Research." *Merrill-Palmer Quarterly* 20(2):71–98.

Etzioni, Amitai (ed.). 1969. *The Semi-Professions and Their Organization*. New York: Free Press.

Evans, Sara M., and Barbara J. Nelson. 1989. "Comparable Worth: The Paradox of Technocratic Reform." *Feminist Studies* 15(10):171–190.

Fagenson, Ellen A. 1990. "At the Heart of Women in Management Research, Theoretical and Methodological Approaches and Their Biases." *Journal of Business Ethics* 9:267–274.

Fagenson, Ellen A., and Janice J. Jackson. 1994. "The Status of Women Managers in the United States." Pp. 388–401 in Nancy J. Adler and Dafna N. Izareli (eds.), *Competitive Frontiers: Women Managers in a Global Economy*. Cambridge, MA: Basil Blackwell.

Fagenson, Ellen A., and Sandra V. Horowitz. 1985. "On Moving Up: A Test of the Person-Centered, Organization-Centered and Interactionist, Perspectives." Pp. 345–349 in Richard B. Robinson, Jr., and John A. Pearce II (eds.), *Academy of Management Best Paper Proceedings*. San Diego, CA: Annual Meeting of the Academy of Management.

Fairhurst, Gail Theus, and B. K. Snavely. 1983. "Majority and Minority Group Relationships: Power Acquisition and Communication." *Academy of Management Review* 8(2):292–300.

Families and Work Institute. 1992. *National Study of the Changing Workforce*. NY: Families and Work Institute.

Federal Glass Ceiling Commission. 1995. *Good for Business: Making Full Use of the Nation's Human Capital*. Washington, DC: U.S. Government Print Office.

Feiner, Susan, and Bruce Roberts. 1990. "Hidden by the Invisible Hand: Neoclassical Economic Theory and the Textbook Treatment of Race and Gender." *Gender and Society* 4:159–181.

Feldberg, Roslyn L. and Evelyn Nakano Glenn. 1979. "Male and Female: Job Versus Gender Models in Sociology of Work." *Social Problems* 26:524–538.

Feldberg, Roslyn L. 1987. "Women and Trade Unions: Are We Asking the Right Questions?" Pp. 299–322 in Christine Base, Roslyn Feldberg, and Natalie Sokoloff (eds.), *Hidden Aspects of Women's Work*. NY: Praeger.

Fensterheim, Herbert and Jean Baer, 1975. *Don't Say Yes When You Want to Say No.* NY: McKay.

Ferber, Marianne, Joan Huber and Glenna Spitz. 1979. "Preference for Men as Bosses and Professionals." *Social Forces* 58(2):466–476.

Ferber, Marianne A., and Barbara Birnbaum. 1982. "The Impact of Mother's Work on the Family as an Economic System." Pp. 84–143 in Sheila B. Kamerman and Cheryl D. Hayes (eds.), *Families That Work: Children in a Changing World*. Washington, DC: National Academy Press.

Ferguson, Marjorie. 1983. *Forever Feminine: Women's Magazines and the Cult of Femininity*. London: Heinemann.

Fernandez-Kelly, Maria Patricia. 1983. *For We Are Sold, I and My People: Women and Industry in Mexico's Frontier*. Albany: SUNY Press.

Fernandez-Kelly, Maria Patricia, and Anna Garcia. 1988. "Economic Restructuring in the United States." Pp. 49–65 in Barbara Gutek, Ann Helton Stromberg, and Laurie Larwood (eds.), *Women and Work: An Annual Review*. Vol. 3. Beverly Hills, CA: Sage.

Ferree, Myra Marx. 1987. "The Struggles of Superwoman." Pp. 161–180 in Christine Bose, Roslyn Feldberg, and Natalie Sokoloff (eds.), *Hidden Aspects of Women's Work*. New York: Praeger.

Ferree, Myra Marx, and Beth B. Hess. 1985. *Controversy and Coalition: The New Feminist Movement*. Boston: G.K. Hall.

———. 1994. *Controversy and Coalition: The New Feminist Movement Across Three Decades of Change*. New York: G.K. Hall.

Ferree, Myra Marx, and Elaine J. Hall. 1990. "Visual Images of American Society: Gender and Race in Introductory Sociology Textbooks." *Gender and Society* 4(4):500–533.

Figueira-McDonough, Josefina. 1985. "Gender, Race, and Class: Differences in Levels of Feminist Orientation." *Journal of Applied Behavioral Science* 21(2):121–142.

Figueroa, Janis Barry, and Edwin Melendez. 1993. "The Importance of Family Members in Determining the Labor Supply of Puerto Rican, Black, and White Single Mothers." *Social Science Quarterly* 74(December):867–883.

Finch, Janet. 1983. *Married to the Job: Wives' Incorporation in Men's Work*. London: Allen and Unwin.

Fischer, Agneta H., and Annelies E. M. van Vianen. 2002. "Illuminating the Glass Ceiling: The Role of Organizational Culture Preferences" *Journal of Occupational and Organizational Psychology* 75:315–323.

Fishman, Pamela M. 1983. "Interaction: The Work Women Do." *Social Problems* 25(April):397–406.

Flexner, Eleanor. 1959. *Century of Struggle: The Women's Rights Movement in the United States*. Cambridge, MA: Belknap Press.

Flowers, Lorna K. 1979. "Being a Minority Professional Woman." Pp. 39–51 in Lucy Ann Geiselman (ed.), *The Minority Woman in America: Professionalism at What Cost?*

Proceedings of Program for Women in Health Sciences Conference at the University of California, San Francisco. San Francisco: University of California.

Foerstel, Karen, and Foley, Caroline. 1894. "The Employment of Women." *Economic Journal*. London: Royal Commission on Labour.

Foner, Philip S. 1978. *The Factory Girls*. Urbana: University of Illinois Press.

———. 1979. *Women and the American Labor Movement: From Colonial Times to the Eve of World War I*. New York: Free Press

Foo, Lora Jo. 2002. *Asian American Women: Issues, Concerns, and Responsive Human and Civil Rights Advocacy*. New York: Ford Foundation.

Fox, Mary Frank, and Sharlene Hesse-Biber. 1984. *Women at Work*. Palo Alto, CA: Mayfield.

Fox-Genovese, Elizabeth. 1988. *Within the Plantation Household: Black and White Women of the Old South*. Chapel Hill: University of North Carolina Press.

Foxworth, Jo. 1980. *Wising Up: The Mistakes Women Make in Business and How to Avoid Them*. New York: Dell.

Freedman, Estelle B. 2002. *No Turning Back: The History of Feminism and the Future of Women*. New York: Ballantine Books.

Freeman, Derek. 1983. *Margaret Mead and Samoa: The Making and Unmaking of Anthropological Myth*. Cambridge, MA: Harvard University Press.

Friedan, Betty. 1963. *The Feminine Mystique*. New York: W. W. Norton.

Friedman, Thomas. 1999. *The Lexus and the Olive Tree: Understanding Globalization*. New York: Farrar-Straus-Giroux.

Frisch, Hannah L. 1977. "Sex Stereotypes in Adult-Infant Play." *Child Development* 48(4):1671–1675.

Fuchs, Victor. 1971. "Differences in Hourly Earnings Between Men and Women." *Monthly Labor Review* 94(May):9–15.

Fuentes, Annette, and Barbara Ehrenreich. 1983. *Women in the Global Factory*. Boston: South End Press.

Fumento, Michael. 1996. "The Labor Department's Biased Report on Reverse Bias." http://www.fumento.com/bomiss.html.

Furchtgott-Roth, Diana, and Christine Stolba. 1996. *Women's Figures: The Economic Progress of Women in America*. Arlington, VA: Independent Women's Forum.

Gadio, Comba Mar, and Cathy A. Rakowski. 1998. "Women's Changing Roles and Status in Thieudeme, Senegal: The Impact of Local and Global Factors." Working Paper Series: *Women in Development*. East Lansing: Michigan State University.

Galbraith, John Kenneth. 1973. "The Economics of the American Housewife." *Atlantic Monthly* 232(2): 78–83, as cited in Barbara Rogers, 1980, *The Domestication of Women: Discrimination in Developing Societies*. London: Tavistock Publications, p. 61.

Galinsky, Ellen, and James T. Bond. 1996. "Work and Family: The Experience of Mothers and Fathers in the U.S. Labor Force." Pp. 79–103 in Cynthia Costello and Barbara Kivimae Krimgold (eds.), *The American Woman, 1996–97*. New York: W. W. Norton.

Gallup Organization. 1997. *The Gallup Poll Social Audit on Black/White Relations in the United States—Executive Summary, Final Revised Version*. Princeton, NJ: The Gallup Organization.

———. 2001, July 10. *Black-White Relations in the United States, 2001 Update*. Princeton, NJ: The Gallup Organization.

———. 2003. *Poll Topics and Trends: Work and Work Place*. Princeton, NJ: The Gallup Organization.

Gates, Margaret J. 1976. "Occupational Segregation and the Law." Pp. 61–74 in Martha Blaxall and Barbara Reagan (eds.), *Women and the Workplace: The Implications of Occupational Segregation*. Chicago: University of Chicago Press.

Geis, Florence L., V. Brown, J. Jennings Walstedt, and N. Porter. 1984. "TV Commercials as Achievement Scripts for Women." *Sex Roles* 11(9/10):513–525.

Gelb, Joyce. 1987. *Women and Public Policies*. 2nd ed. Princeton, NJ: Princeton University Press.

Gelb, Joyce, and Marian Lief Palley. 1982. *Women and Public Policies*. Princeton, NJ: Princeton University Press.

Gerbner, G. 1993. *Women and Minorities on Television: A Study in Casting and Fate—A Report to the Screen Actors Guild and the American Federation of Radio and Television Artists*. Philadelphia: Annenberg School of Communications, University of Pennsylvania.

Gershuny, Jonathan, and John P. Robinson. 1988. "Historical Changes in the Household Division of Labor." *Demography* 30(2):281–290.

Giele, Janet Z. 1988. "Gender and Sex Roles." Pp. 291–323 in Neil J. Smelser (ed.), *Handbook of Sociology*. Newbury Park, CA: Sage.

Ginsberg, Eli. 1966. *Life Styles of Educated Women*. New York: Columbia University Press.

Glass, Jennifer, and Valerie Camarigg. 1992. "Gender, Parenthood, and Job-Family Compatibility." *American Journal of Sociology* 98(1):131–151.

Glazer, Nathan. 1980. "Overworking the Working Woman: The Double Day in a Mass Magazine." *Women's Studies International Quarterly* 3:79–95.

Glazer, Sarah. 1994. "Women's Health Issues." *CQ Researcher* 4(May 14):410–431.

Glenn, Evelyn Nakano. 1987. "Racial Ethnic Women's Labor: The Intersection of Race, Gender, and Class Oppression." Pp. 46–73 in Christine Bose, Roslyn Feldberg, and Natalie Sokoloff (eds.), *Hidden Aspects of Women's Work*. New York: Praeger.

———. 1992. "From Servitude to Service Work: Historical Continuities in the Racial Division of Paid Reproductive Labor." *Signs* 18(1):1–43.

Glenn, Evelyn Nakano, and Roslyn Feldberg. 1977. "Degraded and Deskilled: The Proletarionization of Clerical Work." *Social Problems* 25(1):52–64.

———. 1984. "Clerical Work: The Female Occupation." Pp. 316–336 in Jo Freeman (ed.), *Women: A Feminist Perspective*. Palo Alto, CA: Mayfield.

Goldberg, Steven. 1974. *The Inevitability of Patriarchy*. New York: William Morrow.

Goldin, Claudia. 1977. "Female Labor Force Participation: The Origins of Black and White Differences, 1870 and 1880." *Journal of Economic History* 37(March):87–108.

Goldscheider, Frances, and Linda Waite. 1991. *New Families, No Families? The Transformation of the American Home*. Berkeley: University of California Press.

Googins, Bradley. 1991. *Work/Family Conflicts: Private Lives—Public Responses*. Westport, CT: Auburn House.

Gordon, Ann, Mari-Jo Buhle, and Nancy Schrom. 1971. "Women in American Society: A Historical Contribution." *Radical America* 5(4):3–66.

Gordon, David M. 1972. *Theories of Poverty and Underemployment*. Lexington, MA: Lexington Books.

Gorman, C. 1992. "Sizing Up the Sexes." *Time* (January 20):42–51.

Gottfried, Heidi, and David Fasenfest. 1984. "Gender and Class Formation: Female Clerical Workers." *Review of Radical Political Economics* 16(1):89–104.

Greenberg, Jerald, and Robert A. Baron. 1997. *Behavior in Organizations: Understanding and Managing the Human Side of Work*. 6th ed. Upper Saddle River, NJ: Prentice-Hall.

Greenwald, Maurine Weiner. 1980. *Women, War and Work: The Impact of World War I on Women Workers in the United States.* Westport, CT: Greenwood Press.

Greider, William. 1997. *One World, Ready or Not: The Manic Logic of Global Capitalism.* New York Simon & Schuster.

Groneman, Carol, and Mary Beth Norton (eds.). 1987. "Introduction." *To Toil the Livelong Day: America's Women at Work, 1790–1980.* Ithaca, New York: Cornell University Press.

Grossman, Allyson Sherman. 1975. "Women in the Labor Force: The Early Years." *Monthly Labor Review* 98(11):3–9.

Group, Thetis M., and Joan I. Roberts. 2001. *Nursing, Physician Control, and the Medical Monopoly: Historical Perspectives on Gendered Inequality in Roles, Rights, and Range of Practice.* Bloomington: Indiana University Press.

Guenter-Schlesinger, Sue. 1999. "Persistence of Sexual Harassment: The Impact of Military Culture on Policy Implementation." Pp. 195–211 in Mary Katzenstein and Judith Reppy (eds.), *Beyond Zero Tolerance: Discrimination in Military Culture.* Lanham, MD: Rowan and Littlefield.

Gutek, Barbara A. 1988. "Women in Clerical Work." Pp. 225–240 in Ann Helton Stromberg and Shirley Harkness (eds.), *Women Working: Theories and Facts in Perspective.* 2nd ed. Mountain View, CA: Mayfield.

Gutman, Herbert G. 1974. *The Black Family in Slavery and Freedom, 1750–1925.* New York: Pantheon.

Guzmán, Betsy. 2001. The Hispanic Population: Census 2000 Brief. C2KBR/01-3 (May). Washington, DC: U.S. Bureau of the Census.

Gwarmey-Gibbs, Patricia A., and Denise H. Lach. 1994. "Gender Differences in Clerical Workers' Disputes Over Tasks, Interpersonal Treatment, and Emotion." *Human Relations* 47(6):611–639.

Hacker, Sally L. 1987. "Feminist Perspectives on Computer Based Systems and Democracy at the Workplace." Pp. 177–190 In Gro Bjerkenes, Pelle Ehn, and Morton Kyng (eds.), *Computers and Democracy: A Scandinavian Challenge.* Aldershot: Avebory.

Halbfinger, David M., and Steven A. Holmes. 2003. "Military Mirrors a Working-Class America." *New York Times* (March 30): A1, B13.

Hale-Benson, Janice E. 1986. *Black Children: Their Roots, Culture, and Learning Styles.* Rev. ed. Provo, UT: Brigham Young University Press.

Hall, Francine, and Douglas Hall. 1979. *The Two-Career Couple.* Reading, MA: Addison-Wesley.

Hancock, C. R. 1991. *Women Officers at the United States Military Academy: A Study of Acceptance Patterns and Coping Mechanisms.* Unpublished doctoral dissertation, University of North Carolina, Chapel Hill.

Harrell, Margaret C., and Laura L. Miller. 1997. *New Opportunities for Military Women: Effects Upon Readiness, Cohesion and Morale.* Santa Monica, CA: Rand.

Harriman, Ann. 1996. *Women/Men/Management.* 2nd ed. Westport, CT: Praeger.

Harrington, Mona. 1995. *Women Lawyers: Rewriting the Rules.* New York: Penguin.

Harris, Richard L., and Melinda J. Seid. 2000. "Critical Perspectives on Globalization and Neoliberalism in the Developing Countries." Pp. 1–26 in Richard L. Harris and Melinda J. Seid (eds.), *Critical Perspectives on Globalization and Neoliberalism in the Developing Countries.* Brill: Leiden, The Netherlands.

Hartmann, Heidi. 1976. "Capitalism, Patriarchy, and Job Segregation by Sex." *Signs* 1(pt. 2):137–169.

———. 1981. "The Family as the Locus of Gender, Class and Political Struggle: The Example of Housework." *Signs* 6(3):366–394.

————. 1991. "Women's Work and Diversity and Employment Stability: Public Policy Responses to New Realities." *Testimony Before U.S. Senate Committee of Labor and Human Resources*. Washington, DC: Institute for Women's Policy Research.

Harvey, Elizabeth. 1999. "Short-Term and Long-Term Effects of Early Parental Employment on Children of the National Longitudinal Survey of Youth." *Developmental Psychology* 35(2):445–459.

Hays, Sharon. 2003. *Flat Broke with Children: Women in the Age of Welfare Reform*. Oxford: Oxford University Press.

Headd, Brian. 2000. *The Characteristics of Small-Business Employees*. Washington, DC: Bureau of Labor Statistics. http://www.bls.gov/opub/mlr/2000/04/art3full.pdf.

Headlee, Sue, and Margery Elfin. 1996. *The Cost of Being Female*. Westport, CT: Praeger.

Hennig, Margaret, and Anne Jardim. 1977. *The Managerial Woman*. New York: Pocket Books.

Henson, Kevin D., and Jackie Krasas Rogers. 2001. Why Marcia You've Changed! Male Clerical Temporary Workers Doing Masculinity in a Feminized Occupation." *Gender & Society* 15(2):218–238.

Hersch, Joni, and Leslie S. Stratton. 2000. *Housework and Wages*. Cambridge, MA: Harvard Law School. Discussion Paper No. 300. http://www.law.harvard.edu/programs/olin_center/.

Herz, Diane E., and Barbara J. Wootton. 1996. "Women in the Workforce: An Overview." Pp. 44–78 in Cynthia Costello and Barbara Kivimae Krimgold (eds.), *The American Woman, 1996–97*. New York: W. W. Norton.

Hess, David. 1997. "Flex-Time Furor Is Holding Up Popular 'Comp-Time' Legislation." *Providence Journal-Bulletin* (June 10):E1–E2.

Hesse-Biber, Sharlene, and Gregg Lee Carter. 2000. *Working Women in America: Split Dreams*. New York: Oxford University Press.

Hewlett, Sylvia Ann. 2002. *Creating a Life: Professional Women and the Quest for Children*. New York: Talk Miramax Books.

Higginbotham, Elizabeth. 1997. "Black Professional Women: Job Ceilings and Employment Sectors." Pp. 234–246 in Dana Dunn (ed.), *Workplace/Women's Place: An Anthology*. Los Angeles: Roxbury.

Hochschild, Arlie Russell. 1976. "Inside the Clockwork of Male Careers." Pp. 251–266 in Jerome H. Skolnick and Elliott Currie (eds.), *Crisis in American Institutions*. Boston: Little Brown.

————. 1983. *The Managed Heart: Commercialization of Human Feeling*. Berkeley: University of California Press.

————. 2000. "The Nanny Chain." *The American Prospect* 11(4):32–36.

Hochschild, Arlie Russell, and Anne Machung. 1989. *The Second Shift: Working Parents and the Revolution at Home*. New York: Viking.

Hodge, Robert, and Patricia Hodge. 1965. "Occupational Assimilation as a Competitive Process." *American Journal of Sociology* 71(November):249–264.

Hofferth, Sandra. 2002. "Did Welfare Reform Work? Implications for 2002 and Beyond." *Contexts: Understanding People in Their Social Worlds* 1(Spring): 45–51.

Hoffman, Lois Wladis. 1961. "Effects of Maternal Employment on the Child." *Child Development* 32(1):187–197.

————. 1974. "Effects of Maternal Employment on the Child—A Review of the Research." *Developmental Psychology* 10(2):204–228.

————. 1979. "Maternal Employment." *American Psychologist* 34:859–865.

Hoffman, Lois Wladis, and F. I. Nye. (eds.). 1974. *Working Mothers*. San Francisco: Jossey-Bass.

Hoffman, Lois Wladis, and Lise M. Youngblade. 1999. *Mothers at Work: Effects on Children's Well-Being*. New York: Cambridge University Press.

Holcomb, Betty. 2000. "Family Friendly Policies: Who Benefits?" *Ms.* 12(2):102–103.

Holmstrom, Lynda Lytle. 1972. *The Two Career Family*. Cambridge, MA: Schenkman.

Honey, Maureen. 1984. *Creating Rosie the Riveter: Class, Gender, and Propaganda During World War II*. Amherst: University of Massachusetts Press.

hooks, bell. 1984. *Feminist Theory: From Margin to Center*. Boston: South End Press.

Horner, Matina S. 1972. "Toward an Understanding of Achievement-Related Conflicts in Women." *Journal of Social Issues* 28(2):157–175.

Hossain, Ziarat, and Jaipul Roopnarine. 1993. "Division of Household Labor and Child Care in Dual-Earner African American Families with Infants." *Sex Roles* 29(9/10): 571–583.

Hossfeld, Karen J. 1990. "Their Logic Against Them: Contradictions in Sex, Race, and Class in Silicon Valley in Women Workers and Global Restructuring." Pp. 149–178 in Kathryn Ward (ed.), *Women Workers and Global Restructuring*. Ithaca, New York: ILR Press.

Huber, Joan. 1976. "Sociology." *Signs* 1(3, pt. 1):685–697.

Institute for Research in Social Sciences. 1991. *Harris/911105*. IRSS Study Number S911105. Chapel Hill, NC: Institute for Research in Social Science, University of North Carolina. http://www.irss.unc.edu.

Isaaks, L. 1980. *Sex Role Stereotyping as It Relates to Ethnicity, Age, and Sex in Young Children*. Unpublished dissertation, East Texas State University.

Jacklin, Carol Nagy. 1989. "Female and Male: Issues of Gender." *American Psychologist* 44(2):127–133.

Jacobs, Jerry A., Ronnie J. Steinberg, and Randall K. Filer. 1990. "Compensating Differentials and the Male-Female Wage Gap: Evidence from the New York State Comparable Worth Study." *Social Forces* 69(2):439–468.

Jacobsen, Joyce P., and Laurence M. Levin. 1992. "The Effects of Intermittent Labor Force Attachment on Female Earnings." Paper presented at the American Economic Association Meetings, New Orleans.

Japp, Phyllis M. 1991. "Gender and Work in the 1980s: Television's Working Women as Displaced Persons." *Women's Studies in Communication* 14:49–74.

John, Daphne, Beth Anne Shelton and Kristen Luschen. 1995. "Rare, Ethnicity, Gender and Perceptions of Fairness." *Journal of Family Issues* 16(3):357–379.

Jones, Jacqueline. 1985. *Labor of Love, Labor of Sorrow*. New York: Vintage.

Jones, Jeffrey M. 2002, November 8. *Parents of Young Children Are Most Stressed Americas: Working Moms Least Likely to Have Adequate Relaxation Time*. Princeton, NJ: The Gallup Organization.

Jones, Lisa. 2000. "David Reimer, Gender, and Biology." teachsoc@vawoc.irss.unc.edu, Feb. 17.

Jung, David, Cyrus Wadia, and Murray J. Haberman. 1996. *Affirmative Action and the Courts*. CRB-LIS-96-001. Sacramento: California Research Bureau, California State Library. http://home.psrynet.com/sprynet/kknutsen/aadoc.htm.

Kamerman, Sheila, and Alfred Kahn. 1991. *Child Care, Parental Leave, and the Under 3s: Policy Innovation in Europe*. Westport, CT: Auburn-House-Greenwood Group.

Kandiyoti, Deniz. 1988. "Bargaining with Patriarchy." *Gender and Society* 2(3):274–291.

Kanter, Rosabeth Moss. 1977. *Men and Women of the Corporation*. New York: Basic Books.

———. 1983. "Women Managers: Moving Up in a High Tech Society." Pp. 21–37 in Jennie Farley (ed.), *The Woman in Management: Career and Family Issues*. Ithaca, New York: ILR Press.

Katzenstein, Mary Fainsod, and Judith Reppy. 1999. "Rethinking Military Culture." Pp. 1–21 in Mary Katzenstein and Judith Reppy (eds.), *Beyond Zero Tolerance: Discrimination in Military Culture*. Lanham, MD: Rowan and Littlefield.

Kelley, Michelle L. 1997. "The Division of Family Work among Low-Income African Americans." *Journal of African American Men* 2(4):87–102.

Kelly, Rita Mae. 1991. *The Gendered Economy: Work, Careers, and Success*. Newbury Park, CA: Sage.

Kemp, Alice Abel. 1994. *Women's Work: Degraded and Devalued*. Englewood Cliffs, NJ: Prentice Hall.

Kerpelman, Jennifer L., and Joe F. Pittman. 1993. "Family Work of Husbands and Fathers in Dual-Earner Marriages." Pp. 89–112 in Judith Frankel (ed.), *The Employed Mother and the Family Context*. New York: Springer Company.

Kessler-Harris, Alice. 1975. "Stratifying by Sex: Understanding the History of Working Women." Pp. 217–242 in Richard C. Edwards, Michael Reich, and David Gordon (eds.), *Labor Market Segmentation*. Lexington, MA: Heath.

———. 1981. *Women Have Always Worked: A Historical Overview*. Old Westbury, New York: Feminist Press.

———. 1990. *A Woman's Wage: Historical Meanings and Social Consequences*. Louisville: University of Louisville Press.

Kier, Elizabeth. 1999. "Discrimination and Military Cohesion: An Organizational Perspective." Pp. 28–52 in Mary Katzenstein and Judith Reppy (eds.), *Beyond Zero Tolerance: Discrimination in Military Culture*. Lanham, MD: Rowan and Littlefield.

King, Mae C. 1975. "Oppression and Power: The Unique Status of the Black Woman in the American Political System." *Social Science Quarterly* 56 (June):116–128.

———. 1993. "Black Women's Breakthrough into Clerical Work: An Occupational Tipping Model." *Journal of Economic Issues* 27(4):1097–1125.

King, Jerome E. and Cathy A. Baker. 2001. "Childcare Benefits Continue to Evolve." *Compensation and Working Conditions*. Summer: 4–10.

Kirk, Gwyn, and Margo Okazawa-Rey (eds.). 2001. *Women's Lives: Multicultural Perspectives*. Mountain View, CA.: Mayfield Publishing.

Kleinman, Carol. 1993. "Study Shows Job Status Skews Family Benefits." *Chicago Tribune* (February 8):C3.

Komarovsky, Mirra. 1962. *Blue Collar Marriage*. New York: Random House.

Korzeniewicz, Roberto Patricio. 1997. In William C. Smith and Robert P. Korzeniewicz (eds.), *Politics, Social Change, and Economic Restructuring in Latin America*. Boulder, CO: Lynne Rienner.

Krause, Neal, and Kyriakos S. Markides. 1985. "Intergenerational Solidarity and Psychological Well-Being Among Older Mexican Americans: A Three–Generations Study." *Journal of Gerontology* 40(3):390–392.

Kreps, Juanita. 1971. *Sex in the Marketplace: American Women at Work*. Baltimore, MD: Johns Hopkins University Press.

Krieger, Elliot, and Elizabeth Rau. 1998. "Teachers Turned to Unions." *Providence Journal Bulletin* (May 6):A–1, A–14—A–15.

Kuhn, Thomas. 1962. *The Structure of Scientific Revolutions*. Chicago: University of Chicago Press.

Kurdek, Lawrence A. 1993. "The Allocation of Household Labor in Homosexual and Heterosexual Cohabiting Couples." *Journal of Social Issues* 49(3):127–139.

Kwolek–Folland, Angel. 1998. *Incorporating Women: A History of Women and Business in the United States*. New York: Twayne Publishers.

LaBotz, Daniel. 1994. "Manufacturing Poverty: The Maquiladorization of Mexico." *International Journal of Health Services* 24(3):403–408.

Labrich, Kenneth. 1995. "Kissing Off Corporate America." *Fortune* (February 20):44–47, 50, 52.

Lackey, Pat N. 1989. "Adults' Attitudes About Assignments of Household Chores to Male and Female Children." *Sex Roles* 20(5/6):271–281.

Lai, Tracy. 1998. "Asian American Women: Not for Sale." Pp. 209–216 in Margaret L. Andersen and Patricia Hill Collins (eds.), *Race, Class and Gender: An Anthology*. 3rd ed. Belmont, CA: Wadsworth.

Lakein, Alan. 1974. *How to Get Control of Your Time and Your Life*. New York: New American Library.

Lamb, Michael E. 1982. "Maternal Employment and Child Development: A Review." In Michael E. Lamb (ed.), *NonTraditional Families*. Hillsdale, NJ: L. Erlbaum.

Lauer, Robert H. 1992. *Social Problems and the Quality of Life*. 5th ed. Dubuque, IA: William C. Brown.

Laws, Judith Long. 1976. "Patriarchy as Paradigm: The Challenge from Feminist Scholarship." Paper presented at the Annual Meeting of the American Sociological Association, New York.

———. 1979. *The Second X: Sex Role and Social Role*. New York: Elsevier.

———. 1980. "Problems of Access and Problems of Success in Women's Career Advancement." Paper presented at N. I. E. Conference on Attitudinal and Behavioral Measurement in Sociological Processes/Women's Research, Washington, DC.

Lazier-Smith, Linda. 1989. "A New Generation of Images of Women." Pp. 247–260 in P. J. Creedon (ed.), *Women in Mass Communication*. Newbury Park, CA: Sage.

Lebsock, Suzanne. 1990. " 'No Obey': Indian, European, and African Women in Seventeenth-Century Virginia." Pp. 6–20 in Nancy Hewitt (ed.), *Women, Families, and Communities*. Vol. 1. Glenview, IL: Scott, Foresman, Little, Brown Higher Education.

Lee, Rex E. 1980. *A Lawyer Looks at the Equal Rights Amendment*. Provo, UT: Brigham Young University Press.

Lees, Sue. 1986. *Losing Out: Sexuality and Adolescent Girls*. London: Hutchinson.

Leggon, Cheryl Bernadette. 1980. "Black Female Professionals: Dilemmas and Contradictions of Status." Pp. 189–202 in La Frances Rodgers-Rose (ed.), *The Black Woman*. Beverly Hills, CA: Sage.

Leiby, James. 1978. *A History of Social Welfare and Social Work in the United States*. New York: Columbia University Press.

Leighninger, Leslie. 1996. "Social Work: The Status of Women in a 'Female Profession.' " Pp. 111–134 In Joyce Tang and Earl Smith (eds.), *Women and Minorities in American Professions*. Albany: State University of New York Press.

Leonard, Bill. 1996. "Concern about Case Backlog Leads to Boost in EEOC Budget." *HR Magazine* 41(September):7–8.

Leonard, Eugenie Andruss, Sophie Hutchinson Drinker, and Miriam Young Holden. 1962. *The American Woman in Colonial and Revolutionary Times, 1565–1800*. Philadelphia: University of Pennsylvania Press.

Lerner, Gerda. 1972. *Black Women in White America: A Documentary History*. New York: Vintage.

LeVay, Simon. 1993. *The Sexual Brain*. Cambridge, MA: MIT Press.

Lever, Janet. 1978. "Sex Differences in the Complexity of Children's Play and Games." *American Sociological Review* 42(August):471–483.

Lewenhak, Sheila. 1992. *The Revaluation of Women's Work*. London: Earthscan Publications.

Lewin, Tamar. 1998. "Men Today Are Playing Bigger Role in the Home." *Providence Journal Bulletin* (April 15):A-1, A-4.

Lim, Linda Y. C. 1983. "Capitalism, Imperialism, and Patriarchy: The Dilemma of Third-World Women Workers in Multinational Factories." Pp. 70–92 in June Nash and Maria Patricia Fernandez-Kelly (eds.), *Women, Men and the International Division of Labor*. Albany: SUNY Press.

Lips, Hilary. 1991. *Women, Men and Power*. Mountain View, CA: Mayfield.

Liu, Tessie. 1994. "Teaching the Differences Among. Women from a Historical Perspective: Rethinking Race and Gender as Social Categories." Pp. 571–583 in Ellen Carol DuBois and Vicki L. Ruiz (eds.), *Unequal Sisters: A Multicultural Reader in U.S. Women's History*. 2nd ed. New York: Routledge.

Lloyd, Cynthia B., and Beth T. Niemi. 1979. *The Economics of Sex Differentials*. New York: Colombia University Press.

Lockheed, M. E., and S. S. Klein. 1985. "Sex Equity in Classroom Organization and Climate." Pp. 189–217 in Susan S. Klein (ed.), *Handbook for Achieving Sex Equity Through Education*. Baltimore: Johns Hopkins University Press.

Lorber, Judith. 1984. *Women Physicians—Careers, Status and Power*. New York: Tavistock.

Lorenzana, Noemi. 1979. "La Chicana." Pp. 336–341 in Eloise C. Snyder (ed.), *The Study of Women: Enlarging Perspectives of Social Reality*. New York: Harper & Row.

Louie, Miriam Ching Yoon. 2001. *Sweatshop Warriors: Immigrant Women Workers Take on the Global Factory*. Cambridge, MA: South End Press.

Lynch, Michael, and Katherine Post. 1996. "What Glass Ceiling?" *Public Interest* 124(Summer):27–36.

Macdonald, Cameron Lynne, and Carmen Sirianni. 1996. *Working Women in the Service Society*. Philadelphia: Temple University Press.

MacKinnon, Catharine. 1979. *Sexual Harassment of Working Women: A Case of Sex Discrimination*. New Haven, CT: Yale University Press.

Mahony, Rhona. 1996. *Kidding Ourselves: Breadwinning, Babies, and Bargaining Power*. New York: Basic Books.

Malec, Michael A. 1997. "Gender Equity in Athletics." Pp. 209–218 in Gregg Lee Carter (ed.), *Perspectives on Current Social Problems*. Boston: Allyn and Bacon.

Malveaux, Julianne. 1979. "Three Views of Black Women: The Myths, the Statistics, and a Personal Statement." *Heresies* (Winter):50–55.

———. 1985. "The Economic Interests of Black and White Women: Are They Similar?" *Review of Black Political Economy* 14(Summer):5–27.

Marchand, Marianne H. 1994. "Latin American Voices of Resistance: Women's Movements and Development Debates." Pp. 127–143 in Stephen J. Roscow, Naeem Inayatullah, and Mark Rupert (eds.), *The Global Economy as Political Space*. Boulder, CO: Lynne Rienner.

Marini, Margaret Mooney, and Beth Anne Shelton. 1993. "Measuring Household Work: Recent Experience in the United States." *Social Science Research* 22(4):361–382.

Martin, Carol Lynn. 1989. "Children's Use of Gender-Related Information in Making Social Judgments." *Developmental Psychology* 25(1):80–88.

Mason, Karen Oppenheim, and Karen Kuhlthau. 1992. "The Perceived Impact of Child Care Costs on Women's Labor Supply and Fertility." *Demography* 29(4):523–543.

Matthaei, Julie A. 1982. *An Economic History of Women in America: Women's Work, the Sexual Division of Labor, and the Development of Capitalism*. New York: Schocken.

McCoy, N. L. 1985. "Innate Factors in Sex Differences. Pp. 74–86 in Alice G. Sargent (ed.), *Beyond Sex Roles*. 2nd ed. St. Paul, MN: West.

McCracken, Ellen. 1993. *Decoding Women's Magazines*. New York: St. Martin's Press.

McDowell, Nancy. 1984. *The Mundugumor*, as cited in Jane Howard, *Margaret Mead, A Life*. New York: Ballantine Books.

McKibbin, Richard C. 1990. *The Nursing Shortage and the 1990s: Realities and Remedies.* Kansas City: American Nurses Association.

McNally, Fiona. 1979. *Women for Hire: A Study of the Female Office Worker.* New York: St. Martin's Press.

Mead, Margaret. 1994. "Sex and Temperament in Three Primitive Societies." Pp. 467–471 in Gregg Lee Carter (ed.), *Empirical Approaches to Sociology.* New York: Macmillan.

Media Report to Women. 1992. "Report Traces Media's Polarizing Influence in Society, Politics." 4(Fall):8–9.

———. 1993a. "Newspaper Gender Gap Widening, Says Newspaper Association of American." 2(Spring):5.

———. 1993b. "Scoring the News Media: Underrepresentation of Women Continues." 2(Spring):2–3.

———. 1993c. "Briefs—The Associated Press in December." 7(Winter):5.

———. 2003. "Industry Statistics." http://www.mediareporttowomen.com/statistics.htm.

Messner, Michael. 1992. *Power at Play: Sports and the Problem of Masculinity.* Boston: Beacon.

Metzger, Gretchen. 1992. "T.V. Is a Blonde, Blonde World." *American Demographics* 5(November):51.

Michelson, William. 1985. *From Sun to Sun: Daily Obligations and Community Structure in the Lives of Employed Women and Their Families.* Totowa, NJ: Rowman and Allenheld.

Mies, Maria. 1986. *Patriarchy and Accumulation on a World Scale: Women in the International Division of Labour.* London: Zed.

Mies, Marla, and Veronika Bennholdt-Thomsen, and Claudia von Werlhof (eds.). 1988. *Women: The Last Colony.* London: Zed.

Milkman, Ruth. 1980. "Organizing the Sexual Division of Labor: Historical Perspectives in 'Women's Work' and the American Labor Movement." *Socialist Review* 10(1):95–105.

———(ed.). 1985. *Women, Work, and Protest: A Century of U.S. Women's Labor History.* Boston: Routledge and Kegan Paul.

———. 1993. "Organizing Immigrant Women in New York's Chinatown: An Interview with Katie Quan." Pp. 281–298 in Dorothy Sue Cobble (ed.), *Women and Unions: Forging a Partnership.* Ithaca, NY: ILR Press.

Mills, Albert J. 1996. "Organizational Culture." Pp. 321–322 in Paula J. Dubeck and Kathryn Berman (eds.), *Women and Work: A Handbook.* New York: Garland.

Mills, Janet Lee. 1985. "Body Language Speaks Louder than Words." *Horizons* (February):8–12.

Mincer, Jacob. 1962. "Labor Force Participation of Married Women: A Study of Labor Supply." Pp. 63–105 in H. Gregg Lewis (ed.), *Aspects of Labor Economics.* A Report of the National Bureau of Economic Research. Princeton, NJ: Princeton University Press.

Mincer, Jacob, and Solomon W. Polachek. 1974. "Family Investments in Human Capital: Earnings of Women." *Journal of Political Economy* 82(March–April, Pt 2):S76–S108.

Minority Women Lawyers Regional Seminar. 1979. "Surviving as a Minority Woman Lawyer: Developing Coping Skills." NAACP Legal Defense and Educational Fund, Inc. Stanford University, Stanford, CA.

Mintz, Sidney. 1971. "Men, Women, and Trade." *Comparative Studies in Society and History* 13(3):247–269.

Mirandé, Alfredo. 1979. "Machismo: A Reinterpretation of Male Dominance in the Chicano Family." *De Colores* 6(1&2):17–31.

Moen, Phyllis. 1992. *Women's Two Roles: A Contemporary Dilemma*. New York: Auburn House.

Money, John, and Anke A. Ehrhardt. 1994. *Man and Woman, Boy and Girl*. Northvale, NJ: Jason Aronson Publishers.

Morgall, Janine. 1981. "Typing Our Way to Freedom: Is It True That New Office Technology Can Liberate Women?" *Feminist Review* 9(October):87–101.

Morgan, Elaine. 1972. *The Descent of Women*. NY Stein and Day.

Morris, Madeline. 1996. "By Force of Arms: Rape, War and Military Culture." *Duke Law Journal* 45(4):651–781.

———. 1999. "In War and Peace: Incidence and Implications of Rape by Military Personnel." Pp. 163–194 in Mary Katzenstein and Judith Reppy (eds.), *Beyond Zero Tolerance: Discrimination in Military Culture*, Lanham, MD: Rowan and Littlefield.

Morrison, Ann M., Randall P. White, and Ellen Van Velsor. 1992. *Breaking the Glass Ceiling: Can Women Reach the Top of America's Largest Corporations?* Reading, MA: Addison-Wesley.

Moses, Alice E. 1978. *Identity Management in Lesbian Women*. New York: Praeger.

Moss, Philip, and Chris Tilly. 2001. *Stories Employers Tell: Race, Skill, and Hiring in America*. New York: Russell Sage Foundation.

National Center for Education Statistics. 1996a. *Digest of Education Statistics 1996*, NCES 96-133. Washington, DC: U.S. Government Printing Office.

———. 1996b. *Schools and Staffing Survey, 1993–94* (Public School Teacher Questionnaire). Washington, DC: US Department of Education.

———. 2000. *Trends in Educational Equity of Girls and Women*. NCES 2000-030. Washington, DC: U.S. Government Printing Office.

———. 2001. *The Condition of Education 2001*. NCES 2001-072. Washington, DC: U.S. Government Printing Office.

———. 2002a. *Digest of Education Statistics 2001*. NCES 2002-130. Washington, DC: U.S. Government Printing Office.

———. 2002b. *The Condition of Education 2002*. NCES 2002-25. Washington, DC: U.S. Government Printing Office.

———. 2002c. *Postsecondary Institutions in the United States: Fall 2000; and Degrees and Other Awards Conferred: 1999–2000*. NCES 2002-156. Washington, DC: U.S. Government Printing Office.

National Longitudinal Surveys. 1997. *National Longitudinal Surveys of Labor Market Experience Annotated Bibliography 1968–1996*. http://www.nlsbibliography.org/.

———. 1996b. *Schools and Staffing Survey, 1993–94* (public School Teacher Questionnaire). Washington, DC: U.S. Department of Education.

National Longitudinal Surveys. 1997. *National Longitudinal Surveys of Labor Market Experience Annotated Bibliography 1968–1996*. http://www.chrr.ohio-state.edu/nls-bib/bib-heim.htm.

National Science Foundation. 1982. *Science and Engineering Education: Data and Information*. Washington, DC: National Science Foundation.

Negrey, Cynthia. 1990. "Contingent Work and the Rhetoric of Autonomy." *Humanity and Society* 14 (1):16–33.

Nelson, Debra L., and James Campbell Quick. 1997. *Organizational Behavior: Foundations, Realities, and Challenges*. 2nd ed. NY West Publishing Co.

Neubeck, Kenneth J., and Noel A. Cazenave. 2001. *Welfare Racism: Playing the Race Card Against America's Poor*. New York: Routledge.

New York State Department of Labor. 2002. *Special Task Force for the Apparel Industry: Annual Report.* www.labor.stat.ny.us/agency/annual_reports.html.

New York State Nurses Association. 1995. Concern for Patients Spurs Nurses to Action. Report 25 (9, January/February): 7.

Newport, Frank. 2000, March 17. "Women's Most Pressing Concerns Today Are Money, Family, Health, and Stress." Princeton, NJ: The Gallup Organization.

Nichols, John. 2002. "Women Move Up." *The Nation* 275 (Oct. 7): 24.

Nieva, Veronica F., and Barbara A. Gutek. 1981. *Women and Work: A Psychological Perspective.* New York: Praeger.

Noland, E. William, and E. Wight Bakke. *Workers Wanted: A Study of Employers Hiring Policies, Preferences and Practices in New Haven and Charlotte.* New York: Harper & Brothers, 1949. As cited in Mary C. King, "Black Women's Breakthrough into Clerical Work: An Occupational Tipping Model" *Journal of Economic Issues* (27):1097–1118.

NORC (National Opinion Research Center). 1974–76. *Cumulated General Social Survey, 1974–1976.* Chicago: National Opinion Research Center, University of Chicago.

———. 1984–1986. *Cumulated General Social Survey, 1984–1986.* Chicago: National Opinion Research Center, University of Chicago.

———. 1991–1994. *Cumulated General Social Survey, 1991–1994.* Chicago: National Opinion Research Center, University of Chicago.

———. 1994. *General Social Survey, 1994.* Chicago: National Opinion Research Center, University of Chicago.

———. 1994–1996. *Cumulated General Social Survey, 1994–1996.* Chicago: National Opinion Research Center, University of Chicago.

———. 1996. *General Social Survey, 1996.* Chicago: National Opinion Research Center, University of Chicago.

———. 1997. *General Social Survey. 1997.* Chicago: National Opinion Research Center, University of Chicago.

———. 1998. *General Social Survey, 1998.* Chicago: National Opinion Research Center, University of Chicago.

———. 1998–2000. Cumulated General Social Survey, 1998–2000. Chicago: National Opinion Research Center, University of Chicago.

———. 2000. *General Social Survey, 2000.* Chicago: National Opinion Research Center, University of Chicago.

———. 2000–2002. Cumulated General Social Survey, 2000–2002. Chicago: National Opinion Research Center, University of Chicago.

Nordic Council of Ministers. 1994. *Women and Men in the Nordic Countries: Facts and Figures 1994.* Copenhagen: Nordic Council of Ministers.

Northcraft, Gregory, and Barbara A. Gutek. 1993. "Point-Counterpoint: Discrimination Against Women in Management—Going, Going, Gone or Going But Not Gone?" Pp. 219–245 in Ellen A. Fagenson (ed.), *Women in Management: Trends, Issues, and Challenges in Managerial Diversity.* Newbury Park, CA: Sage.

Norton, Mary Beth. 1980. *Liberty's Daughter: The Revolutionary Experience of American Women, 1750–1800.* Boston: Little Brown.

Oakley, Ann. 1974. *The Sociology of Housework.* New York: Pantheon.

———. 1982. *Subject Women.* London: Fontana.

O'Brien, Karen M., and Ruth E. Fassinger. 1993. "A Causal Model of the Career Orientation and Career Choice of Adolescent Women." *Journal of Counseling Psychology* 40(4):456–469.

O'Connell, Martin, and David E. Bloom. 1987. *Juggling Jobs and Babies: America's Child Care Challenge*. Population Trends and Public Policy, No. 12, Washington, DC: Population Reference Bureau.

O'Farrell, Brigid M. 1988. "Women in Blue-Collar Occupations: Traditional and Non-traditional." Pp. 258–272 in Ann Helton Stromberg and Shirley Harkness (eds.), *Women Working: Theories and Facts in Perspective*. 2nd ed. Mountain View, CA: Mayfield.

Ohlott, Patricia J. J. 1992. *We Pay Union Dues: Women, Unions, and Nontraditional Blue Collar Jobs*. Philadelphia: Temple University Press.

Oliver, William. 1984. "Black Males and the Tough Guy Image: The Dual Dilemma of Black Men." *Journal of Social Issues* 34(Winter):10–20.

Oppenheimer, Valerie Kincade. 1970. *The Female Labor Force in the United States*. Berkeley: University of California Press.

Orenstein, Peggy. 1997. "Shortchanging Girls: Gender Socialization in Schools." Pp. 43–52 in Dana Dunn (ed.), *Workplace/Women's Place: An Anthology*. Los Angeles: Roxbury.

Papanek, Hanna. 1973. "Men, Women, and Work: Reflections on the Two-Person Career." *American Journal of Sociology* 78(4):852–872.

Parcel, Toby L., and Elizabeth G. Menaghan. 1994. *Parents' Jobs and Children's Lives*. New York: Aldine de Gruyter.

Parsons, Talcott. 1942. "Age and Sex in the Social Structure of the United States." *American Sociological Review* 7(5):604–616.

Parsons, Talcott, Robert Bales, James Olds, Morris Zilditch, and Philip E. Slater. 1955. *Family, Socialization, and Interaction Process*. New York: Free Press.

Patterson, Charlotte J. 1995a. "Families of Lesbian Baby Boom: Parents' Division of Labor and Children's Adjustment." *Developmental Psychology* 31(1):115–123.

———. 1995b. "Lesbian Mothers, Gay Fathers, and Their Children." Pp. 262–290 in A. D'Augelli and C. Patterson (eds.), *Lesbian, Gay, and Bisexual Identities Over the Lifespan*. New York: Oxford University Press.

Paules, Greta Foff. 1991. *Dishing It Out: Power and Resistance Among Waitresses in a New Jersey Restaurant*. Philadelphia: Temple University Press.

———. 1996. "Resisting the Symbolism of Service Among Waitresses." Pp. 264–290 in Cameron Lynne MacDonald and Carmen Sirianni (eds.), *Working in the Service Society*. Philadelphia: Temple University Press.

Pearce, D. 1978. "The Feminization of Poverty: Women, Work, and Welfare." *Urban and Social Change Review* 11(1–2):28–36.

Peters, H. Elizabeth. 1997. "The Role of Child Care and Parental Leave Policies in Supporting Family Work Activities." Pp. 280–283 in Francine D. Blau and Ronald C. Ehrenberg (eds.), *Gender and Family Issues in the Workplace*. New York: Russell Sage Foundation.

Peterson, Sharyl Bender, and Mary Alyce Lach. 1990. "Gender Stereotypes in Children's Books: Their Prevalence and Influence on Cognitive and Affective Development." Gender and Education 2(2):185–197.

Peterson, Sharyl Bender, and Traci Kroner. 1992. "Gender Biases in Textbooks for Introductory Psychology and Human Development." *Psychology of Women Quarterly* 16(1):17–36.

Petras, James, and Henry Veltmeyer. 2001. *Globalization Unmasked: Imperialism in the Twenty-first Century*. London: Zed Books.

Phelps, Edmund S. 1972. "The Statistical Theory of Racism and Sexism." *American Economic Review* 62(September):659–661.

Phillips, F. B. 1978. "Magazine Heroines: Is Ms. Just Another Member of the Family Circle?" Pp. 115–24 in G. Tuchman, A. K. Daniels, and J. Benet (eds.), *Hearth and Home*. New York: Oxford University Press.

Phipps, Polly. 1990. "Industrial and Occupational Change in Pharmacy: Prescription for Feminization." Pp. 111–128 in Barbara F. Reskin and Patricia A. Roos (eds.), *Job Queues, Gender Queues: Explaining Women's Inroads into Male Occupations*. Philadelphia: Temple University Press.

Pierce, Charles A. 1995. *Attraction in the Workplace: An Examination of Antecedents and Consequences of Organizational Romance*. Albany: unpublished dissertation, State University of New York.

Pinchbeck, Ivy. 1930. *Women Workers and the Industrial Revolution (1750–1850)*. London: Virago Press.

———. 1969. *Women Workers and the Industrial Revolution (1750–1850)*. London: Virago Press.

Piore, Michael J. 1975. "Notes for a Theory of Labor Market Stratification." Pp. 125–150 in Richard C. Edwards, Michael Reich, and David Gordon (eds.), *Labor Market Segmentation*. Lexington, MA: Heath.

Pleck, Elizabeth H. 1979. "A Mother's Wages: Income Earning Among Married Italian and Black Women, 1896–1911." Pp. 367–392 in Nancy Cott and Elizabeth Pleck (eds.), *A Heritage of Her Own: Toward a New Social History of American Women*. New York: Simon & Schuster.

Pleck, Joseph. 1985. *Working Wives, Working Husbands*. Newbury Park, CA: Sage.

Polachek, Solomon. 1976. "Occupational Segregation: An Alternative Hypothesis." *Journal of Contemporary Business* 5(Winter):1–12.

———. 1978. "Sex Differences in Education: An Analysis of the Determinants of College Major." *Industrial and Labor Relations Review* 31(4):498–508.

———. 1979. "Occupational Segregation: Theory, Evidence, and a Prognosis." Pp. 137–157 in Cynthia B. Lloyd, Emily Andrews, and Curtis L. Gilroy (eds.), *Women and the Labor Market*. New York: Columbia University Press.

———. 1981. "Occupational Self-Selection: A Human Capital Approach to Sex Differences in Occupational Structure." *Review of Economics and Statistics* 63 (February):60–69.

Pomerleau, Andrée, Daniel Boduc, Gérard Malcuit, and Louise Cossette. 1990. "Pink or Blue: Environmental Gender Stereotypes in the First Two Years of Life." *Sex Roles* 22(5/6):359–367.

Power, Marilyn, and Sam Rosenberg. 1993. "Black Female Clerical Workers: Movement Toward Equality with White Women?" *Industrial Relations* 32(2):223–237.

Proctor, Bernadette D., and Joseph Dalaker. 2002. *Poverty in the United States: 2001*. Washington, DC: U.S. Bureau of the Census. (http://www.census.gov/prod/2002pubs/p60-219.pdf).

Purcell, Piper, and Lara Stewart. 1990. "Dick and Jane in 1989." *Sex Roles* 22(3/4): 177–185.

Ragins, Belle Rose, and Eric Sundstrom. 1989. "Gender and Power in Organizations: A Longitudinal Perspective." *Psychological Bulletin* 105(1):51–88.

Ragins, Belle Rose, and John L. Cotton. 1991. "Easier Said than Done: Gender Differences in Perceived Barriers to Gaining a Mentor." *Academy of Management Journal* 34(4):939–951.

Rakowski, Cathy A. 2000. "Obstacles and Opportunities to Women's Empowerment under Neoliberal Reform." Pp. 115–138 in Richard L. Harris and Melinda J. Seid (eds.), *Critical Perspectives on Globalization and Neoliberalism in the Developing Countries*. Leiden, the Netherlands: Brill.

Ray, Elaine. 1988. "Black Female Executives Speak Out on the Concrete Ceiling." *Executive Female* 11(6):34–38.

Reilly, Mary Ellen, and Jean M. Lynch. 1990. "Power-Sharing in Lesbian Partnerships." *Journal of Homosexuality* 19(3):1–30.

Renzetti, Claire M., and Daniel J. Curran. 1995. *Women, Men, and Society.* 3rd ed. Boston: Allyn and Bacon.

———. 2003. *Women, Men, and Society.* Boston, MA: Allyn and Bacon.

———. 1996. "Sex Segregation in the Workplace." Pp 94–98 in Paula Dubeck and Kathryn Borman (eds.), *Women and Work.* New York: Garland Publishing.

Reskin, Barbara F. 1997. "Sex Segregation in the Workplace." Pp. 69–73 in Dana Dunn (ed.). *Workplace/Women's Place.* Los Angeles, CA: Roxbury Publishing Co.

Reskin, Barbara F., and Irene Padavic. 1994. *Women and Men at Work.* Thousand Oaks, CA: Pine Forge Press.

Reskin, Barbara F., and Patricia A. Roos. 1990. *Job Queues, Gender Queues: Explaining Women's Inroads into Male Occupations.* Philadelphia: Temple University Press.

Reskin, Barbara F., and Polly Phipps. 1988. "Women in Male-Dominated Professional and Managerial Occupations." Pp. 190–205 in Ann Helton Stromberg and Shirley Harkness (eds.), *Women Working: Theories and Facts in Perspective.* 2nd ed. Mountain View, CA: Mayfield.

Rich, Adrienne. 1980. "Compulsory Heterosexuality and Lesbian Existence." *Signs* 5(4):631–660.

Ricks, Thomas E. 1995. "Separation Anxiety: 'New' Marines Illustrate Growing Gap Between Military and Society." *Wall Street Journal* 27(July):1.

Riger, S., and P. Galligan. 1980. "Women in Management: An Explanation of Competing Paradigms." *American Psychologist* 35:902–910.

Riordan, Cornelius. 1990. *Girls and Boys in School: Together or Separate?* New York: Teachers College Press.

———. 1997. "Minority Success and Single-Gender Schools." Pp. 175–193 in Gregg Lee Carter (ed.), *Perspectives on Current Social Problems.* Boston: Allyn and Bacon.

Ritzer, George. 1975. *Sociology: A Multiple Paradigm Science.* Boston: Allyn and Bacon.

Robert Half International. 1990. *Parent Track Survey.* Menlo Park, CA: Robert Half International.

Robertson, Robert E., Gregg Lee Carter, and Sharlene Hesse-Biber. 2004. "Gender Inequality in the Workplace: The Example of Women in Management." Pp. 489–497 in Gregg Lee Carter (ed.), *Empirical Approaches to Sociology.* 4th ed. Boston: Allyn and Bacon.

Robinson, John. 1988. "Who's Doing the Housework?" *American Demographics* 10:24–28.

Rollins, Judith B. 1985. *Between Women: Domestics and Their Employers.* Philadelphia: Temple University Press.

Romero, Mary. 1992. *Maid in the USA.* New York: Routledge, Chapman, and Hall.

Rosenberg, Janet, Harry Perlstadt, and William R. F. Phillips. 1997. " 'Now That We Are Here': Discrimination, Disparagement, and Harassment at Work and the Experience of Women Lawyers." Pp. 247–259 in Dana Dunn (ed.), *Workplace/ Women's Place: An Anthology.* Los Angeles: Roxbury.

Ross, Catherine. 1987. "The Division of Labor at Home." *Social Forces* 65(3):816–833.

Rossi, Alice. 1977. "A Biosocial Perspective on Parenting" *Daedalus* 106:1–31.

Rubin, Lillian, 1983. *Intimate Strangers.* New York. Harper and Row.

Rutherford, Brent, and Gerda Werkerle. 1988. "Captive Rider, Captive Labor: Spatial Constraints and Women's Employment." *Urban Geography* 9(2).

Ryan, William. 1971. *Blaming the Victim.* New York: Pantheon Books.

Ryscavage, Paul. 1979. "More Wives in the Labor Force Have Husbands with 'Above Average' Incomes." *Monthly Labor Review* 102(6):40–42.

Saad, Lydia. 2003. "Pondering Women's Issues,' Part II." Princeton, NJ: The Gallup Organization. February 18.

Sachs, Albie, and Joan Huff Wilson. 1978. *Sexism and the Law: A Study of Male Beliefs in Britain and the United States*. Oxford, England: Robertson.

Safa, Helen I. 1981. "Runaway Shops and Female Employment: The Search for Cheap Labor." *Signs* 7(2): 418–433.

Sailer, Steve. 2003. "Saving Private Lynch" *United Press International* (April 4):1–3.

Sakamoto, Arthur, and Meichu D. Chen. 1991. "Inequality and Attainment in a Dual Labor Market." *American Sociological Review* 56(June):295–308.

Scarpitti, Frank R., Margaret L. Andersen, and Laura L. O'Toole. 1997. *Social Problems*. 3rd ed. New York: Longman.

Scharf, Lois. 1980. *To Work and to Wed: Female Employment, Feminism, and the Great Depression*. Westport, CT: Greenwood Press.

Schein, Edward. 1990. "Organizational Culture: What It Is and How to Change It." In Paul Evans, Yves Doz, and Andre Laurent (eds.), *Human Resource Management in International Firms*. New York: St. Martin's.

Schneider, Beth E. 1984. "Peril and Promise: Lesbian Workplace Participation." In Trudy Darty and Sandee Potter (eds.), *Women-Identified Women*. Palo Alto, CA: Mayfield.

———. 1988. "Invisible and Independent: Lesbians Experiences in the Workplace." Pp. 273–286 in Ann Helton Stromberg and Shirley Harkness (eds.), *Women Working: Theories and Facts in Perspective*. 2nd ed. Mountain View, CA: Mayfield.

Schneider, Dorothy, and Carl J. Schneider. 1993. *Women in the Workplace*. Santa Barbara, CA: ABC-CLIO, Inc.

Schwartz, Felice N. 1989. "Management, Women and the New Facts of Life." *Harvard Business Review* 67 (January-February):65–76.

Seidman, Ann. 1978. *Working Women: A Study of Women in Paid Jobs*. Boulder, CO: Westview Press.

Shapiro, Laura. 1990. "Guns and Dolls." *Newsweek* 28(May):56–65.

Shelton, Beth Anne. 1992. *Women, Men, and Time: Gender Differences in Paid Work, Housework, and Leisure*. Westport, CT: Greenwood Press.

Shelton, Beth Anne, and John, Daphne. 1993. "Ethnicity, Race, and Difference: A Comparison of White, Black, and Hispanic Men's Household Labor Time." Pp. 131–150 in Jane Hood (ed.), *Men, Work, and Family*. Newbury Park, CA: Sage.

Siegal, Alberta Engvall, and Miriam Bushkoff Haas. 1963. "The Working Mother: A Review of Research." *Child Development* 34(3):513–542.

Silverstein, Brett, L. Perdue, B. Peterson, and E. Kelly. 1986. "The Role of the Mass Media in Promoting a Thin Standard of Bodily Attractiveness for Women." *Sex Roles* 14(9/10):519–532.

Simon, David R., and Joel H. Henderson. 1997. *Private Troubles and Public Issues: Social Problems in the Postmodern Era*. New York: Harcourt Brace.

Sivard, Ruth Leger. 1995. *Women: A World Survey*. Washington, DC: World Priorities.

Smith, Caroline, and Barbara Lloyd. 1978. "Maternal Behavior and Perceived Sex of Infant: Revisited." *Child Development* 49(4):1263–1266.

Smith, Dorothy. 1978. "A Peculiar Eclipsing: Women's Exclusion from Man's Culture." *Women's Studies International Quarterly* 1(4):281–296.

Smuts, Robert. 1971. *Women and Work in America*. New York: Schocken.

Sokoloff, Natalie. 1980. *Between Money and Love*. New York: Praeger.

————. 1992. *Black Women and White Women in the Professions: Occupational Segregation by Race and Gender, 1960–1980*. New York: Routledge.

Soroka, Michael P., and George J. Bryjak. 1994. *Social Problems: A World at Risk*. Boston: Allyn and Bacon.

South, Scott, and Glenna Spitze. 1994. "Housework in Marital and Nonmarital House-holds." *American Sociological Review* 59(June):327–347.

Spain, Daphne, and Suzanne M. Bianchi. 1996. *Balancing Action: Motherhood, Marriage, and Employment Among American Women*. New York: Russell Sage Foundation.

Spender, Dale (ed.). 1981. *Men's Studies Modified: The Impact of Feminism on the Academic Discipline*. New York: Pergamon Press.

Statham, Anne 1987. "The Gender Model Revisited: Differences in the Management Styles of Men and Women." *Sex Roles* 16(7/8):409–427.

————. 1988. "Women Working for Women: The Manager and Her Secretary." Pp. 225–243 in Anne Statham, Eleanor M. Miller, and Hans O. Mauksch (eds.), *The Worth of Women's Work: A Qualitative Synthesis*. Albany, New York: SUNY Press.

————. 1996. *The Rise of Marginal Voices: Gender Balance in the Workplace*. New York: University Press of America.

Stevenson, Brenda E. 1996. *Life in Black and White: Family and Community in the Slave South*. New York: Oxford University Press.

Stevenson, Mary. 1975. "Relative Wages and Sex Segregation by Occupation." Pp. 175–200 in Cynthia B. Lloyd (ed.), *Sex, Discrimination, and the Division of Labor*. New York: Columbia University Press.

Stichter, Sharon, and Jane L. Parpart (eds.). 1990. *Women, Employment, and the Family in the International Division of Labor*. Philadelphia: Temple University Press.

Stigler, George Joseph. 1956. *Trends in Employment in the Service Industries*. Princeton, NJ: Princeton University Press.

Still, Mary C., and David Strang. 2003. "Institutionalizing Family-Friendly Policies." Pp. 288–309 in Phyllis Moen (ed.), *It's about Time: Couples and Careers*. Ithaca, New York: ILR Press.

Stohs, Joanne Hoven. 1995. "Predictors of Conflict Over the Household Division of Labor Among Women Employed Full-Time." *Sex Rules* 32:257–275.

Stohs, Johanne Hoven. 2000. "Multicultural Women's Experience of Household Labor, Conflicts, and Equity." *Sex Roles: A Journal of Research* 42(5–6):339–361.

Stoker, Linda. 1991. *Having It All: A Guide for Women Who Are Going Back to Work*. London: Bloomsburg.

Strate, L. 1992. "Beer Commercials." Pp. 78–92 in S. Craig (ed.), *Men, Masculinity and Media*. Newbury Park, CA: Sage.

Stripling, M., and G. Bird. 1990. "Antecedents and Mediators of Well-Being Among Employed Women." Paper presented at the meeting of the National Council on Family Relations, Seattle, WA.

Strober, Myra. 1975. "Bringing Women into Management: Basic Strategies." Pp. 77–96 in Francine E. Gordon and Myra Stober (eds.), *Bringing Women into Management*. New York: McGraw-Hill.

Stromberg, Ann Helton. 1988. "Women in Female-Dominated Professions." Pp. 206–224 in Ann Helton Stromberg and Shirley Harkness (eds.), *Women Working: Theories and Facts in Perspective*. 2nd ed. Mountain View, CA: Mayfield.

Sullivan, Joyce. 1984. "Family Support Systems Paychecks Can't Buy." Pp. 310–319 in Patricia Voydanoff (ed.), *Work and Family: Changing Roles of Men and Women*. Palo Alto, CA: Mayfield.

Sullivan, Maureen. 1996. "Gender and Family Patterns in Lesbian Coparents." *Gender and Society* 10(6):747–767.

Sullivan, Thomas J. 1997. *Introduction to Social Problems.* 4th ed. Boston: Allyn and Bacon.

Suter, Larry, and Herman Miller. 1973. "Income Differences Between Men and Career Women." *American Journal of Sociology* 78(January): 962–974.

Swerdlow, Marian. 1997. "Men's Accommodations to Women Entering a Nontraditional Occupation: A Case of Rapid Transit Operatives." Pp. 260–270 in Dana Dunn (ed.), *Workplace/Women's Place: An Anthology.* Los Angeles: Roxbury.

Task Force on Working Women. 1975. *Exploitation from 9 to 5.* Report of the Twentieth-Century Fund Task Force on Women and Employment. Lexington, MA: Heath.

Tavris, Carol. 1992. *The Mismeasure of Woman.* New York: Simon and Schuster.

Tavris, Carol, and Carole Wade. 1984. *The Longest War: Sex Differences in Perspective.* 2nd ed. New York: Harcourt Brace Jovanovich.

Taylor, Robert, et al. 1991. "Developments in Research on Black Families: A Decade Review." *Journal of Marriage and the Family* 52(4):993–1014.

Tentler, Leslie W. 1979. *Wage-Earning Women: Industrial Work and Family Life in the United States, 1900–1930.* New York: Oxford University Press.

Tepperman, Jean. 1970. "Two Jobs: Women Who Work in Factories." Pp. 115–124 in Robin Mogan (ed.), *Sisterhood Is Powerful.* New York: Vintage.

———. 1976. *Not Servants, Not Machines: Office Workers Speak Out.* Boston: Beacon Press.

Terborg-Penn, Rosalyn. 1985. "Survival Strategies among African-American Women: A Continuing Process." Pp. 139–155 in Ruth Milkman (ed.), *Women, Work, and Protest: A Century of U.S. Women's Labor History.* Boston: Routledge and Kegan Paul.

Tharenou, P., and D. K. Conroy. 1994. "Men and Women Managers' Advancement." *Applied Psychology* 43:5–31.

Thompson, Linda, and Alexis Walker. 1991. "Gender in Families." Pp. 76–102 in Alan Booth (ed.), *Contemporary Families: Looking Forward, Looking Back.* Minneapolis: National Council on Family Relations.

Thompson, M.A. 1996. Letter to the Editor. *American Nurse* 28(7):5.

Thorne, Barrie, Cheris Kramarae, and Nancy Henley (eds.). 1983. *Language, Gender, and Society.* Rowley, MA: Newbury House.

Titunik, Regina. 2000. "The First Wave: Gender Integration and Military Culture." *Armed Forces and Society* 26(2, Winter): 229–257.

Tong, Benson. 1994. *Unsubmissive Women: Chinese Prostitutes in Nineteenth-Century San Francisco.* Norman: University of Oklahoma Press.

Treiman, Donald, and Heidi Hartmann. 1981. *Women, Work, and Wages: Equal Pay for Jobs of Equal Value.* Washington, DC: National Academy Press.

Trey, Joan Ellen. 1972. "Women in the War Economy—World War II." *Review of Radical Political Economics* 4(3):40–57.

Triece, Mary E. 2001. *Protest and Popular Culture: Women in the U.S. Labor Movement, 1897–1917.* Boulder, CO: Westview Press.

Ulrich, Laurel Thatcher. 1987. "Housewives and Gadder: Themes of Self-Sufficiency and Community in Eighteenth-Century New England." Pp. 21–34 in Carol Groneman and Mary Beth Norton (eds.), *To Toil the Livelong Day: America's Women at Work, 1790–1980.* Ithaca, New York: Cornell University Press.

United Nations. 1995a. *The World's Women, 1995.* New York: United Nations.

————. 1995b. *1994 Survey of the Role of Women in Development: Women in a Changing Global Economy*. New York: United Nations.

————. 1996a. *The Advancement of Women, 1945–1996*. New York: United Nations.

————. 2000. *The World's Women 2000: Trends and Statistics*. New York: United Nations.

U.S. Bureau of the Census. 1929. *Women in Gainful Occupations, 1870–1920*. Census Monograph No.9 (prepared by Joseph A. Hill). Washington, DC: U.S. Government Printing Office.

————. 1996a. *Statistical Abstract of the United States: 1996*. Washington, DC: U.S. Government Printing Office.

————. 1996b. *Percent of Persons 25 Years Old and Over Who Have Completed High School or College, by Race, Hispanic Origin, and Sex: Selected Years 1940 to 1995*. Washington, DC: U.S. Bureau of the Census.

————. 1996c. *Poverty 1995*. http://www.census.gov/hhes/poverty/pov95/povest1.html.

————. 1996d. "Money Income in the United States: 1995 (With Separate Data on Valuation of Noncash Benefits)." *Current Population Reports*, Series P60–193. Washington, DC: U.S. Government Printing Office.

————. 1997a. The Asian and Pacific Islander Population of the United States: March 1996. Washington, DC: U.S. Bureau of the Census.

————. 1997b. *Statistical Abstract of the United States: 1997*. Washington, DC: U.S. Government Printing Office.

————. 1997c. *Current Population Reports*, P20–495, *Household and Family Characteristics: March 1996 (Update)*. Washington, DC: U.S. Government Printing Office.

————. 2001a. "Table 11. Major Occupation Group of Employed Civilian Population 16 Years and Over by Sex, and Race and Hispanic Origin: March 2000." Washington, DC: U.S. Bureau of the Census.

————. 2001b. "HH-1. Households, by Type: 1940 to Present." June 29. Washington, DC: U.S. Bureau of the Census.

————. 2001c. "Table 4. Family and Nonfamily Household Type by Race and Hispanic Origin of Householder." *The Asian and Pacific Islander Population in the United States: March 2000 (Update) (PPL-146)*. June 28. Current Population Survey Washington, DC: U.S. Bureau of the Census. http://www.census.gov/population/socdemo/race/api/ppl-146/tab04.txt.

————. 2001d. "Table 4. Family and Nonfamily Household Type by Race and Hispanic Origin of Householder." *The Black Population in the United States: March 2000 (PPL-142)*. February 22. Current Population Survey Washington, DC: U.S. Bureau of the Census. http://www.census.gov/population/socdemo/race/black/ppl-142/tab04.txt.

————. 2001e. "Table 4.1. Family and Nonfamily Household Type by Race and Hispanic Origin of Householder." *The Hispanic Population in the United States: March 2000*. March 6. Current Population Survey Washington, DC: U.S. Bureau of the Census. http://www.census.gov/population/socdemo/hispanic/p20–535/tab04-1.txt.

————. 2002a. *Statistical Abstract of the United States: 2001* (121st ed.). Washington, DC: U.S. Government Printing Office.

————. 2002b. *United States Census 2000, Summary File 3*. http://www.census.gov/PressRelease/www/2002/sumfile3.html.

————. 2002c. "Table 4. Median Income of Families by Selected Characteristics, Race, and Hispanic Origin of Householder: 2001, 2000 1/, and 1999 2/." September 23. Washington, DC: U.S. Bureau of the Census. http://www.census.gov/hhes/income/income01/inctab4.html.

————. 2003a. "Full-Time Year-Round Workers by Median Earnings and Sex." *Historical Income Tables—People*. P-38 Table Series. http://www.census.gov/hhes/income/histinc/p38b.html; http://www.census.gov/hhes/income/histinc/p38c. html; http://www.census.gov/hhes/income/histinc/p38d.html; http://www.census.gov/hhes/income/histinc/p38e.html.

————. 2003b. "PINC-03. Educational Attainment—People 25 Years Old and Over, by Total Money Earnings in 2001, Working Experience in 2001, Age, Race, Hispanic Origin, and Sex: Male." Washington, DC: U.S. Bureau of the Census. http://ferret.bls.census.gov/macro/032002/perinc/new03_076.htm.

————. 2003c. "PINC-03. Educational Attainment—People 25 Years Old and Over, by Total Money Earnings in 2001, Working Experience in 2001, Age, Race, Hispanic Origin, and Sex: Female." Washington, DC: U.S. Bureau of the Census. http://ferret.bls.census.gov/macro/032002/perinc/new03_146.htm.

————. 2003d. "Table P-36. Full-Time, Year-Round Workes (All Races) by Median Income and Sex: 1955 to 2001." Washington, DC: U.S. Bureau of the Census. http://www.census.gov/hhes/income/histinc/p36.html.

————. 2003e. "Table A-2. Percent of People 25 Years Old and Over Who Have Completed High School or College, by Race, Hispanic Origin, and Sex: Selected Years 1940 to 2002 (Noninstitutional Population)." Washington, DC: U.S. Bureau of the Census. http://www.census.gov/population/socdemo/education/tabA-2.pdf.

U.S. Congress. 1996. *Personal Responsibility and Work Opportunity Reconciliation Act of 1996.* Public Law 104–193, H.R. 3734.

————. 1991. *Women and the Workplace: The Glass Ceiling: Hearing Before the Subcommittee on Employment and Productivity of the Committee on Labor and Human Resources.* Committee on Labor and Human Resources. Subcommittee on Employment and Productivity. United States Senate, One Hundred Second Congress, First Session, October 23. Washington, DC: U.S. Government Printing Office.

U.S. Department of Human Services. 1999. *Agenda for Research on Women's Health in the Twenty-first Century.* Bethesda, MD: National Institutes of Health. NIH Publication No. 99-4385.

U.S. Department of Labor. 2002a. "Table 2. Median Weekly Earnings of Full-Time Wage and Salary Workers by Union Affiliation and Selected Characteristics." Washington, DC: U.S. Department of Labor. http://www.bls.gov/news.release/union2.t02.htm.

————. 2002b. "Table 1. Union Affiliation of Employed Wage and Salary Workers by Selected Characteristics." Washington, DC: U.S. Department of Labor. http://www.bls.gov/news.release/union2.t01.htm.

————. 2002c. *Union Members in 2002.* Washington, DC: U.S. Department of Labor. http://www.bls.gov/news.release/union2.nr0.htm.

————. 2002d. "Table 3. Union Affiliation of Employed Wage and Salary Workers by Occupation and Industry." Washington, DC: U.S. Department of Labor. http://www.bls.gov/news.release/union2.t03.htm.

————. 2003. *Families and Employers in a Changing Economy.* Washington, DC: U.S. Department of Labor. http://www.dol.gov/esa/regs/compliance/whd/fmla/summary.htm.

U.S. Department of Labor Women's Bureau. 1980a. *Employment Goals of the World Plan of Action: Developments and Issues in the United States.* Washington, DC: U.S. Government Printing Office.

————. 1980b. *Perspectives on Working Women: A Databook.* Bulletin 2080. Washington, DC: U.S. Government Printing Office.

——. 1986. *Employment and Earnings*. Washington, DC: U.S. Government Printing Office.

——. 1994. *Working Women Count! A Report to the Nation*. Washington, DC: U.S. Government Printing Office.

——. 2000. *Women of Hispanic Origin in the Labor Force*. No. 00–04 (April). Washington, DC: U.S. Department of Labor. http://www.dol.gov/wb/wb_pubs/hispwom2.htm.

——. 2003. *20 Leading Occupations of Employed Women, 2001 Annual Averages*. Washington, DC: U.S. Department of Labor. http://www.dol.gov/wb/wb_pubs/20lead2001.htm.

U.S. Equal Employment Opportunity Commission. 2002. *Job Patterns for Minorities and Women in Private Industry, 2000*. Washington, DC: U.S. Department of Labor.

——. 2003. "Sexual Harassment Charges, EEOC & FEPASs Combined: FY1992–FY2002." Washington, DC: U.S. Equal Employment Opportunity Commission. http://www.eeoc.gov/stats/harass.html.

United States Information Agency. 1997. "Cabinet Profiles: Attorney General, Department of Justice, Janet Reno." http://usiahq.usis.usemb.se/usa/cabinet/na23.htm.

University of California at Los Angeles/Korn Ferry International. 1993. *Decade of the Executive Woman*. Los Angeles: University of California at Los Angeles.

Vallas, Steven P. 1987. "White-Collar Proletarians? The Structure of Clerical Work and Levels of Class Consciousness." *Sociological Quarterly* 28(4):523–540.

Villones, Rebecca. 1989. "Women in the Silicon Valley." Pp. 172–176 in Asian Women United of California (ed.), *Making Waves: An Anthology of Writings by and About Asian American Women*. Boston: Beacon.

Waite, Linda, and Frances Goldscheider. 1992. "Work in the Home: The Productive Context of Family Relationships." Pp. 267–299 in Scott South and Stewart Tolnay (eds.), *The Changing American Family*. Boulder, CO: Westview.

Waller, Margy. 2003. *Testimony of Margy Waller—Senate Committee on Finance, "Welfare Reform: Building on Success."* Washington, DC: Brookings Institution. http://www.brookings.edu/dybdocroot/views/testimony/waller/20030312.pdf.

Walsh, Mary R. 1977. *Doctors Wanted—No Women Need Apply: Sexual Barriers in the Medical Profession*. New Haven, CT: Yale University Press.

Walshok, Mary Lindenstein. 1981. *Blue-Collar Women: Pioneers on the Male Frontier*. New York: Anchor Books.

Walton, Ronald G. 1975. *Women in Social Work*. London: Routledge and Kegan Paul.

Ward, Kathryn. 1990. "Introduction and Overview." Pp. 1–22 in Kathryn Ward (ed.), *Women Workers and Global Restructuring*. Ithaca, New York: ILR Press.

Webster, Juliet. 1996. *Shaping Women's Work: Gender, Employment and Information Technology*. London: Longman.

Weissman, Myrna M., and Eugene S. Paykel. 1974. *The Depressed Woman: A Study of Social Relationships*. Chicago: University of Chicago Press.

Wertheimer, Barbara Mayer. 1977. *We Were There: The Story of Working Women in America*. New York: Pantheon.

West, Candace, and Don Zimmerman. 1987. "Doing Gender." *Gender and Society* 1:125–151.

West, Jackie. 1982. "New Technology and Women's Office Work." Pp. 61–79 In Jackie West (ed.), *Work, Women, and the Labour Market*. London: Routledge & Kegan Paul.

White, Lynn, and David Brinkerhoff. 1987. "Children's Work in Families: its Significance and Meaning." Pp. 204–219 in Naomi Gerstel and Harriet Engel Gross (eds.), *Families and Work*. Philadelphia: Temple University Press.

Whitehouse.gov. 2003. "President Bush's Cabinet." http://www.whitehouse.gov/government/cabinet.html.

Wichroski, Mary Anne. 1994. "The Secretary: Invisible Labor in the Workworld of Women." *Human Organization* 53(1):33–41.

Wichterich, Christa. 2000. *The Globalized Woman: Reports from a Future of Inequality.* New York: Zed Books.

Wilkie, J. R. 1988. "Marriage, Family Life, and Women's Employment." Pp. 149–166 in Ann Helton Stromberg and Shirley Harkness (eds.), *Women Working: Theories and Facts in Perspective.* 2nd ed. Mountain View, CA: Mayfield.

Williams, Christine. 1992. "The Glass Escalator: Hidden Advantages for Men in 'Female' Professions." *Social Problems* 39(3):253–267.

Williams, Joan. 2001. "Majority Rule?" *Legal Times* (November 13). http://www.law.com/special/supplement/legal_careers/story5_majority.html.

Willie, Charles V. 1985. *Black and White Families: A Study in Complementarity.* Bayside, New York: General Hall.

Wilson, Edward O. 1975. *Sociobiology: The New Synthesis.* Cambridge, MA: Harvard University Press.

Wirth, Linda. 2001. *Breaking the Glass Ceiling: Women in Management.* Geneva: ILO Publications.

Wise, Nancy B., and Christy Wise. 1994. *A Mouthful of Rivets: Women at Work in World War II.* San Francisco: Jossey-Bass.

Wolff, Alexander. 2002. "The High School Athlete." *Sports Illustrated Magazine (SI.Com).* November 13. http://sportsillustrated.cnn.com/si_online/news/2002/11/12/high_school/

Women Mayors of American Cities. 2003. "Women's Mayor Group." http://www.usmayors.org/uscm/about/affiliate_organizations/elected_affiliates/women_m.html.

Woo, Deborah. 1985. "The Socioeconomic Status of Asian American Women in the Labor Force: An Alternative View." *Sociological Perspectives* 28(July)3:307–338.

———. 1998. "The Gap Between Striving and Achieving." Pp. 247–256 in Margaret L. Andersen and Patricia Hill Collins (eds.), *Race, Class and Gender: An Anthology.* 3rd ed. Belmont, CA.: Wadsworth.

Woody, Bette. 1989. *Black Women in the New Services Economy: Help or Hindrance in Economic Self-Sufficiency?* Wellesley, MA: Wellesley College Center for Research on Women.

Working Women United Institute. 1980. *Project Statement: Sexual Harassment on the Job.* New York: Working Women United Institute.

Yamanaka, Keiko, and Kent McClelland. 1994. "Earning the Model-Minority Image: Diverse Strategies of Economic Adaptation by Asian-American Women." *Ethnic and Racial Studies* 17(1):79–114.

Ybarra, Lea. 1977. *Conjugal Race Relationships in the Chicano Family.* Unpublished dissertation, University of California, Berkeley.

———. 1982. "When Wives Work: The Impact on the Chicano Family." *Journal of Marriage and the Family* 44 (1):169–178.

Zavella, Patricia. 1987. *Women's Work and Chicano Families: Cannery Workers of the Santa Clara Valley.* Ithaca, New York: Cornell University Press.

Zimmer, Lynn. 1997. "How Women Reshape the Prison Guard Role." Pp. 288–299 in Dana Dunn (ed.), *Workplace/Women's Place: An Anthology.* Los Angeles: Roxbury.

Author Index

Subject Index

affirmative action, 100–103; legislation, 100; possible elimination, 253;proposition, 101, 260; public support of, 101; *Quirin vs. Pittsburgh*, 100; reverse discrimination, 100

African-American women: blue collar work, 170; concrete ceiling, 208–209; domestic service, 170–171; food service, 164; gender discrimination, 205–206; gender division of housework, 229–230; industrial period, 36–37; labor force participation, 24; overrepresentation in domestic service, 170–171; pre-industrial period, 24–27; racial discrimination, 168–169; retail, 166–168; single motherhood, 223; socialization, 131–132; wage gap in professional occupations, 202–207; WWI, 37

American Telephone and Telegraph Company (AT&T), 95

Asian-American women: assembly workers, 65–66clerical work, 66, definition of term, 63; Dragon Lady stereotype, 66; Lotus Blossom stereotype, 66; model minority, 66; preference of managers for Asian immigrant workers, 63–67, 202–203; race discrimination, 60–62; sex discrimination, 64; socialization, 131–132; working history, 63–66

backlash, 250–253
Bagley, Sarah, 93
Berger, Marsha, 247
blue collar work, 179–185; discrimination in male dominated fields, 184–185; globalization and factory work, 188; percentage of female blue collar workers by race and occupation, 180–181; sexual harassment, 183–184; wage gap, 182–183
Brent, Ann, 200
Brown, Murphy, 125

career, 10–11; career-family woman, 10–12; career-primary woman, 11; "fast-tracker," 11; monistic model, 10; sprint model, 213
Caucasian women, 21–24; labor force participation rates compared with women of color, 59–60; relationship with minority domestic workers, 283
Chicana women, 57–62; gender division of housework, 228–230; labor force participation rates, 43–44
childcare, 221–226; Family and Medical Leave Act, 238–239; lack of affordable care, 241; legislation, 188–189; minority women's

issues and childcare, 239–241; on-site care, 239–241; role of business in childcare issues, 238–241; Temporary Assistance to Needy Families (TAMF), 241; vicious cycle, 240

Chinese-Americans, 63–64
circle effect, 4
clerical workers, 141–156; benefits and drawbacks, 148–149; emotional work, 146; feminization of clerical work, 142–145; invisibility, 145; male temporary office workers, 149; sex-role spillover, 150; sexual harassment, 149–152; technological advancement, 152–154; unions, 155–156; women managing women, 147–149; Clinton Administration and military policy, 174–179

Clinton, William, 104–105
college, 78; differences in graduation rates by sex, 139–140; graduation rates for women, 77–78; undergraduate career aspirations, xiv–xv

colonial period, 20–30; legislation, 22
combining work and family, 221–246; experiences of African American families, 223–224, 230; experiences of Latino families, 230; experiences of Lesbian families, 231; father's impact on children's well-being, 232–233

comparable worth, 98–99
concrete ceiling, 209
conflict perspective, 69–70
coping strategies for working women, 235–238
"Cult of True Womanhood," 31

division of labor, 14, 228–232
Dole, Robert, 104
domestic service, 34, 43–44, 53, 170–174; overrepresentation of women of color, 170–171; unions, 179
double day 228–232
dual labor markets, 88–89; crowding effect, 88

earnings gap, 79–81; education, 118–121; changes due to feminist movement, 118–119; "Female Fields of Study," 125–126; gender bias within, 120; gender socialization, 118–122; increase in female teachers, 120; sex differences in academic preparation and achievement, 125–130; single-sex schools, 121; sports, 119–120

emotional work, 146
Equal Employment Opportunity Commission (EEOC), 102–103
Equal Pay Act, 97

295

About the Authors

Sharlene Nagy Hesse-Biber is Professor of Sociology at Boston College. She co-founded the Women's Studies Program at Boston College. She is founder and current director of the National Association for Women in Catholic Higher Education (NAWCHE). She is author of *Am I Thin Enough Yet? The Cult of Thinness and the Commercialization of Identity* (Oxford University Press, 1996). She is co-editor of *Feminist Approaches to Theory and Methodology: An Interdisciplinary Reader* (Oxford University Press, 1999), *Women in Catholic Higher Education: Border Work, Lived Experiences and Social Justice* (Lexington Books, 2003); *Feminist Perspectives on Social Research* (Oxford University Press, 2004); and *Approaches to Qualitative Research* (Oxford University Press, 2004). She is co-author of three upcoming new methods books from Sage Publications, *The Practice of Qualitative Research: A Primer* (2004), *Feminist Research Practice: A Primer* (2004), and *When Methods Meets Technology: Important Issues in Qualitative Software Evolution* (2005). She has published widely on the impact of sociocultural factors on women's body image and is co-developer of HyperRESEARCH, a qualitative data analysis software package. She is recipient of the 2002 New England Sociologist of the Year Award from the New England Sociological Association. She earned her PhD in sociology at the University of Michigan.

Gregg Lee Carter is Professor of Sociology at Bryant University in Smithfield, Rhode Island, where he is Chair of the Department of History & Social Sciences. He earned his MA, MPhil, and PhD degrees at Columbia University. He is a former president of the New England Sociological Association and has been an associate editor of *Teaching Sociology*. He is the author of *How to Manage Conflict in the Organization* (American Manage-ment Association, 1994), *Analyzing Contemporary Social Issues* (Allyn & Bacon, 1996, 2001), *The Gun Control Movement* (Prentice Hall International, 1997), *Doing Sociology with Student Chip: Data Happy!* (Allyn & Bacon, 1995, 1998, 2001, 2004), and *Learning Research Methods with SPSS* (Harcourt Brace, 2001). He is the editor of *Perspectives on Current Social Problems* (Allyn & Bacon, 1997), *Empirical Approaches to Sociology* (Allyn & Bacon, 1994, 1998, 2001, 2004), and *Guns in American Society: An Encyclopedia of History, Politics, Culture, and the Law* (ABC-CLIO, 2003). His writings on contemporary social issues have also appeared in more than a dozen academic journals. He is currently working on the second edition of *How to*

Manage Conflict in the Organization (American Management Association, 2005) and *Gun Control: A Reference Handbook* (ABC-CLIO, 2006). He is the recipient of the New England Sociological Association's Sociologist of the Year Award and the American Sociological Association's Outstanding Contributions to Instruction Award (Sociology and Computers Section).

CPSIA information can be obtained at www.ICGtesting.com
Printed in the USA
BVOW11s1258040914

365397BV00003B/8/P